TITHING

IN THE LIVES
OF ABRAHAM & JACOB

The Tithing Series:[a]

Book 1: Tithing in the Lives of Abraham & Jacob: How the New Covenant Removed the Need to Bargain with God

Book 2: Tithing in the Old Covenant: How the New Covenant Transformed the Jewish Ritual System

Book 3: Tithing in the Book of Malachi: How the New Covenant Broke the Curse of the Law and Opened the True Window of Heaven

Book 4: Tithing in the New Testament: How the New Covenant Changed the Priesthood & the Law of the Tithe

---

[a] For publication date of each book, see jttcm.com/books.

The Tithing Series
Book 1

TITHING

IN THE LIVES OF ABRAHAM & JACOB

How the New Covenant Removed the Need
to Bargain with God

DAVID G. MACKIN

Journey to Truth Christian Ministries, LLC
Marcellus, Michigan

Tithing in the Lives of Abraham & Jacob
How the New Covenant Removed the Need to Bargain with God

Journey to Truth Christian Ministries, LLC
jttcm.com

Copyright © 2018 by David G. Mackin. All Rights Reserved. No part of this book may be reproduced or distributed in any written, electronic, recording or photocopying form without written permission of the author except for brief quotations in reviews, articles or oral presentations.

ISBN 13: 978-0-9883101-0-0
ISBN 10: 0-9883101-0-4

Library of Congress Control Number: 2016909358

1. RELIGION / Biblical Studies / Old Testament
2. RELIGION / Christian Life / Stewardship & Giving

First Edition Printed in the United States of America

10 9 8 7 6 5 4 3 2 1

To obtain more copies of this book go to amazon.com.

ABOUT THIS BOOK

REBUTTAL FORMAT: This volume is organized using a claim/rebuttal format. Pro-tithing claims are presented and then respectfully rebutted.

FOOTNOTES & ENDNOTES ("NOTES"): Footnotes are alphabetized and found at the bottom of the page. Notes are numerical and found in the back of the book under the appropriate chapter. Sometimes both are combined as in c/12.

YHWH: To translate the name of the God of Israel, the Latin script "YHWH" is frequently used instead of "Yahweh" or "Lord."

DIACRITIC MARKS: Not all original language references and/or transliterations contain complete diacritic marks.

AUTHOR'S POSITION ON GIVING: Even though the author critiques many tithing claims, he believes in giving generously to the church, the poor and the kingdom of God. Also, he does not necessarily agree with everything published by his sources.

CONCLUSION: Since each chapter contains its own conclusion, the author did not write one for the book as a whole.

DISCLAIMER: Although precautions have been taken to verify the accuracy of the information contained herein, David G. Mackin and JTTCM, LLC assume no responsibility for any errors or omissions. Cited sources may contain their own proofing errors. Opinions, websites and/or web pages may have changed since the date of research and/or publication. No liability is assumed for damages that may result from the use of the information contained herein. The intention of this book is to encourage research, education and public discussion on the subject of tithing. Nothing written or implied is meant to defame a person's character, ministry, business or church.

Contents

Introduction

Overview & Approach 1
1 How to Interpret the Patriarchs' Tithes 5
2 Tithing Before the Law 19

Abraham's Tithe

3 A Motive Analysis 29
4 A Vow for a Safe Rescue 45
5 A Treaty Between Equals 59
6 A Gift Exchange 71
7 The Melchizedek Priesthood 79
8 The Lord's Table 85
9 The Abrahamic Covenant 93
10 The 'Covenant of Blessings' 113
11 Did Tithing Make Abraham Rich? 135
12 Did Tithing Make Isaac Rich? 145

Jacob's Tithe Bargain

13 A Tithe for a Safe Return 153

14 A Voluntary & Conditional Tithe 169

15 An Unpaid Tithe 181

16 A Deceptive Lifestyle 199

17 A Motive Analysis 207

18 Did Jacob's Tithe Vow Make Him Rich? 215

19 Tithing Vows & the New Covenant 223

A WORD FROM THE AUTHOR 231

NOTES 233

BIBLIOGRAPHY 289

ANNOTATED LIST OF CITED SOURCES 309

ABOUT THE AUTHOR 345

PREFACE

As I listened to a message by a church fund-raiser on the subject of tithing, I was surprised at how many verses he took out of context to validate his pro-tithing claims. I felt compelled to write on the subject and bring to light the original meaning of these verses. This book is a New covenant critique of tithing claims, which base themselves on Abraham's tithe to Melchizedek and Jacob's tithe vow at Bethel. It is the first of four volumes in *The Tithing Series*, which follows a claim/rebuttal format and is unique in that no other resource is as complete or supported by such a broad base of Old Testament and ancient Near Eastern scholarship. I will demonstrate how pro-tithers have no hermeneutical basis in the New covenant to apply the patriarchs' tithes to Christians.

Marcellus, Michigan   David G. Mackin
November, 2018

IN MEMORY OF

George & Barbara Mackin

ACKNOWLEDGEMENTS

Gary M. Schneider
for the seed, vision, and ongoing encouragement

&

Helen Mackin
for the consulting and great sacrifice

&

the many friends who helped along the way

Bible translations used in this book (in alphabetical order):

ESV: The Holy Bible, English Standard Version® (ESV®). Copyright © 2001 by Crossway of Good News Publishers. Used by permission. All rights reserved.

JSB: The Jewish Study Bible: TANAKH Translation. Jewish Publication Society. Copyright © 2004 by Oxford University Press.

MLB: The Modern Language Bible: The New Berkeley Version in Modern English, Copyright © 1923, 1945, 1969 by Zondervan, Grand Rapids, Michigan. All rights reserved.

NASB: New American Standard Bible,® Updated Edition. Copyright © 1960, 1962, 1963, 1968, 1971, 1972, 1973, 1975, 1977, 1995 by The Lockman Foundation. Used by permission. www.Lockman.org

NET: New English Translation (NET Bible® copyright ©1996-2006 by Biblical Studies Press, L.L.C. http://netbible.com).

NIV: The Holy Bible, New International Version®, NIV®. Copyright © 1973, 1978, 1984, 2011 by Biblica, Inc.™ Used by permission of Zondervan. All rights reserved worldwide.

NKJV: The Holy Bible, New King James Version®. Copyright © 1982 by Thomas Nelson, Inc. Used by permission. All rights reserved.

NLT: The Holy Bible, New Living Translation. Copyright © 1996, 2004, 2007 by Tyndale House Foundation. Tyndale House Publishers Inc. All rights reserved.

NRSV: New Revised Standard Version Bible. Copyright © 1989 by the Division of Christian Education of the National Council of Churches of Christ in the United States of America. Used by permission. All rights reserved.

Overview & Approach

Genesis contains two references to the tithe. First, Abraham gave a tithe (*ma'aser*) of war spoils to Melchizedek, the ruler of Salem,[a] and, second, Jacob promised to give a tithe (*asar*) to God at Bethel.[b] These two Hebrew words[c] appear over forty times in the Old Testament,[1] twenty-two times of which are in the Pentateuch.[d/2] Nine Old Testament books mention the tithe,[e] at least two of which describe it as *qodesh*, part of "the hallowed things,"[f] as well as *qadash dabar*, the "consecrated portion."[g] We also find the tithe in the civil and religious practices of Mesopotamia,[3] Sumer,[4] Ugarit,[5] Old Assyria,[6] Old Babylon[7] and Late Babylon.[8]

Does God require Christians to tithe because Abraham gave a tithe of plunder to Melchizedek and/or because Jacob promised a tithe as part of his vow to YHWH? Many Christian leaders claim he does, and only a few admit that both Abraham's tithe and Jacob's tithe vow were voluntary. Over time, the question of the mandatory tithe has proven to be serious; it has damaged friendships, split marriages, divided congregations, imprisoned believers, sparked wars and invited much distorted use of the Bible, including the book of Genesis.

---

[a] Genesis 14:18-20
[b] Genesis 28:20-22
[c] *ma'aser* (noun) = tenth part; *asar* (verb) = to take or give a tenth
[d] The Pentateuch consists of the books of Genesis, Exodus, Leviticus, Numbers and Deuteronomy.
[e] Genesis 14:20c; 28:22c; Leviticus 27:30-33; Numbers 18:21-24, 25-32; Deuteronomy 12:6, 11, 17; 14:22, 23, 24, 28; 26:12-15; I Samuel 8:15-17; 2 Chronicles 31:4-6, 11-12; Nehemiah 10:37-38; 12:44, 47; 13:5, 10, 12; Amos 4:4; Malachi 3:6-18
[f] Deuteronomy 26:13 (English) verse 14 (Hebrew)
[g] Nehemiah 12:47

From what we see in the New Testament, neither Jesus nor his apostles collected tithes.[a] After the time of the apostles, the early church fathers were divided on the issue.[9] Overall, church leaders did not collect tithes for the first four centuries of the church.[10] According to J. MacCulloch, even after the state church made tithing into law, the people paid their tithes "reluctantly and irregularly."[11] Contemporary sources indicate only 3-5% of adults tithe.[b/12] To increase such low numbers, some Christian leaders refer to Abraham's tithe to Melchizedek and Jacob's tithe vow at Bethel. The condemnation pro-tithers place on non-tithing believers has led many to wonder whether they are disobeying God. This question, along with many others, I will be addressing in *The Tithing Series*.

In Chapter 1, I examine the logic and hermeneutics[c] of many tithe claims that base themselves on the patriarchs. Chapter 2 addresses the claim that Christians should tithe because tithing began with the patriarchs centuries "before the Law." I will see if there is any connection between Genesis and the New Testament to justify such a conclusion. In chapters 3, 4, 5, 6 and 7, I present Abraham's tithe to Melchizedek in historical context. Because many tithe supporters remove Abraham's tithe from its original setting, I explore in Chapter 8 whether Melchizedek's gifts of bread and wine to Abraham hold any sacramental significance for Christians.

Some tithe advocates assert tithing was a part of the Abrahamic covenant, a covenant whose original oath was based upon a divine and unconditional promise. In Chapter 9, I address the relationship between the tithe, the Abrahamic covenant and the New covenant. In an effort to make tithing a part of the Abrahamic covenant, I demonstrate in Chapter 10 how one pro-tither so distorts God's promises to Abraham, he ends up inventing his own covenant.

---

[a] See Book 4 in *The Tithing Series*.
[b] It is difficult to say the exact percentage of believers who tithe because of the unknown number who may tithe anonymously and/or tithe to churches or ministries not surveyed.
[c] Hermeneutics is the art and science of Bible interpretation.

It is beyond question YHWH materially blessed the patriarchs from Abraham through Joseph. Nevertheless, it is another matter to assert the reason he blessed them was because they were faithful tithers. This is why I dedicate chapters 11, 12 and 18 to each of the major patriarchs asking whether tithing ever made any of them rich. In chapters 3 and 17, I also probe the motives behind the patriarchs' tithes; did Abraham tithe to get rich, and did Jacob promise YHWH a tithe to obtain the material blessings of the Abrahamic covenant?

Jacob's promise to give YHWH a tithe of the material blessings he would receive on his journey east, I address in chapters 13 and 14. Since both Abraham and Jacob made vows to God, I investigate in Chapter 19 whether the New Testament supports the claim that Christians should make tithe vows. Lastly, in chapters 15 and 16, I call attention to the fact that it was because of Jacob's deceptive lifestyle that he never fulfilled the tithe vow he made at Bethel.

In every book of *The Tithing Series*, I use the "Old by the New" method of Bible interpretation. With this approach, I view Old Testament references to the tithe in light of their meaning and significance, if any, in the New Testament. In covenantal terms, I interpret each covenant in the Old Testament in light of the New covenant and pay most attention to God's covenants with Abraham and Moses.

Even though the Old Testament holds great spiritual, moral and theological value for believers, the gospel obligates Christians, whenever they formulate church doctrine and practice, to interpret the Old Testament in light of the New. This includes their interpretations of the tithe narratives of Abraham and Jacob. Generally, most of the writers of the New Testament, in some way or another, took an "Old by the New" approach, as they gradually worked out the moral and spiritual implications of the gospel.[a] This same approach helps believers to avoid dangerous beliefs and behaviors. It also prevents legalisms, which

---

[a] Contrast Acts 15:19-21, 28-29 with Romans 14:14, 20. Compare Matthew 5:21-22, 27-28, 31-32, 33-34, 38-39, 43-44; Galatians 3:15-18; I Corinthians 14:21-22; 15:42-49, 54-56.

threaten New covenant freedoms.[a] In this book, I demonstrate how important it is for Christians to view Abraham's tithe to Melchizedek and Jacob's tithe vow to YHWH in historical, literary, theological and biblical context. I call into serious question both the logic and the hermeneutics of pro-tithers who ignore such contexts when they collect Christians' tithes.

---

[a] Compare Galatians 3:1-5; 5:1.

1

How to Interpret the Patriarchs' Tithes

The way to determine whether God expects Christians to follow the Old Testament tithe examples of Abraham and Jacob is to interpret the Scriptures properly. According to P. Verhoef, the issue is "primarily a hermeneutical question."[a]/[13] In this chapter, I draw heavily upon the material of D. Stuart, whose text on Old Testament exegesis is now in its fourth printing. Stuart writes, "...a passage cannot mean now what it could not originally have meant. That is, there is no valid modern application of a passage that was not also a potentially valid application of the passage for its original audience."[14] This means unless pro-tithers can demonstrate that tithing holds the same purpose and significance for Christians today as it did for the patriarchs, they have no hermeneutical basis to apply the patriarchs' tithes to believers.

To interpret any passage correctly, we must first understand what it meant in its original context. The process of doing this is called "exegesis," which comes from the Greek word *exêgeisthai*, equivalent to *ex* (out, from) + *hegeîsthai* (to guide). Thus, exegesis is the process by which we guide or bring out from the text what the original author(s) was conveying to his audience. On the other hand, "eisegesis" is the opposite of exegesis. It comes from the Greek word *eisêgesis*, equivalent to *eis* (into) + *hegeîsthai* (to lead) and means reading into the text one's own ideas, agendas or

---

[a] hermeneutics = the art and science of how to interpret the Bible (Ramm, Bernard, 1970., 1)

biases. Because tithe advocates use eisegesis instead of exegesis to form their tithing claims, they fall prey to various fallacies like: arguments from silence;[15] oversimplifications;[16] either-or misinterpretations;[17] all-or-nothing fallacies;[18] quantitative fallacies[19] and ancient history fallacies.[20] To avoid these and other eisegetical errors, Stuart suggests the following factors should be taken into consideration: (1) text; (2) translation; (3) historical context; (4) literary context; (5) form; (6) structure; (7) grammar; (8) lexical analysis; (9) biblical context; (10) theology; (11) secondary literature and (12) application.[21] If tithe advocates overlook any one of these steps when referring to the patriarchs' tithes, their claims become less credible, if credible at all.[22] Unfortunately, many skip steps 1-11 and, instead, focus on application (step 12). In so doing, they neglect 92% of what believers need to understand about these episodes.

Four Essential Contexts of the Patriarchs' Tithes

Context is critical to understanding the significance of the patriarchs' tithes, since words carry meanings specific to the frameworks in which they are used. The meaning and function of the Hebrew word translated "tithe" (*ma'aser*) differ according to the passage(s) in which we find it.[23] In the episode of Abraham's tithe to Melchizedek, for example, the context indicates the patriarch's tithe was a treaty gift;[a] the same word in Jacob's tithe promise, however, denotes a votive offering.[b] In Deuteronomy, one of the dominant functions of the tithe is charity for the landless poor.[c] In Malachi, the tithe is a temple salary for the priests and Levites.[d] In I Samuel, the word means a royal tax collected by the king to support his army and court.[e] Consequently, before tithe supporters can make any contemporary applications of the word "tithe," they must first understand the elements at play in each passage. From Stuart's

---

[a] See Chapter 6.
[b] See Chapter 14.
[c] Deuteronomy 12:10-14, 17-19; 14:27-29; 26:12-15
[d] Malachi 3:10a,b
[e] I Samuel 8:15-17

list, at the least, they must take into account the (1) historical; (2) literary; (3) theological and (4) biblical contexts, which I will now address.

Historical Context

Aside from a general reading of the texts, tithe supporters do not normally provide any historical background for Abraham's tithe to Melchizedek or Jacob's tithe vow at Bethel. To understand the patriarchs' tithes, we need to look at the political, economic, social, geographical and religious factors of the culture. This would provide us with an understanding of what the original audience(s) would have thought or known as they heard or read each passage.[24] In addition, we also have to discover (1) the content, (2) the recipient and (3) the frequency of the tithe episodes (only Abraham's since we have no evidence of Jacob ever tithing[a]). The content of Abraham's tithe consisted of enemy plunder, its recipient a Canaanite ruler and its frequency only once. If we are to use Abraham's tithe as an example to follow, the question then arises: how can pro-tithers expect Christians to tithe on their own income to YHWH every week?

Literary Context

When it comes to the literary context of the patriarchs' tithes, we need to understand how each tithe passage functions in its particular setting. We do this by noting what immediately precedes and follows each episode.[25] Tithe advocates rarely refer to the literary context; when they do, they often attempt to link Abraham's tithe in Genesis 14:20 with YHWH's covenant oath in 15:1-21.[b] I show in other chapters, however, that these two narratives are unrelated, and the type of tithe Abraham gave was different than the kind of tithe promoted today.[c] In Jacob's vow, the patriarch pledged a tithe only after YHWH promised he and his descendants would inherit the land of Canaan.[d] His vow was a

---

[a] Genesis 35:1-7. See chapters 15 and 16.
[b] See Chapter 9.
[c] See chapters 4, 5 and 6.
[d] Genesis 28:13-15; 21-22

bargain to ensure God would keep him safe until he returned to the land.[a] Thus, when pro-tithers claim Christians need to tithe because Jacob made a tithe vow, they ignore its literary context, which limits its purpose to one of personal safety relative to the land of Canaan.[b]

Theological Context

To begin to understand the theological context of the patriarchs' tithes, we need to identify which Bible covenant was in full and proper force at the time of each episode.[26] Even though it is clear Jacob made his tithe vow under the Abrahamic covenant,[c] we are not able to say the same for Abraham, since the covenant was not formalized with its oath and sign until Genesis chapters 15 and 17. Either way, the Abrahamic covenant was different from the Sinai covenant; it was not a conditional contract based on compliance to terms and conditions. Pro-tithers who assert that tithing was a part of the Abrahamic covenant attempt to add theological weight to their claim that Christians should tithe. In Chapter 9, I cover this in detail.

Biblical Context

To understand the biblical context of the patriarchs' tithe episodes, according to Stuart, we need to ask if they contain an "overall 'message.'"[27] If other parts of Scripture mention them, why and how are they referred to, and what issues or values, if any, do they address?[28] Outside of Genesis, the Old Testament never refers to the patriarchs' tithes, and the New Testament only mentions Abraham's.[d] This lack of attention is highly significant in terms of what ongoing message, if any, they held for later biblical writers and their audiences. When tithe advocates speak about Abraham's tithe to Melchizedek, they do not always mention its occurrence in Hebrews chapter 7, the only other place in the Bible recounting it. When they do, they usually read

---

[a] Compare Genesis 28:15,21; 30:25; 31:3,13; 32:9.
[b] See Genesis 35:1-7.
[c] Genesis 15:1-21; 17:1-14; 28:22
[d] Hebrews 7:1-10

only the first several verses. A full reading of the chapter, however, reveals how the New covenant abolished the tithe when it changed the priesthood.[a]

Consequences of Ignoring Context

We observed how some pro-tithers do not interpret or apply the patriarchs' tithes according to their historical, literary, theological or biblical contexts. In this section, I examine several consequences, which have occurred because of this neglect. They are: (1) adding to the word of God; (2) using multiple senses of Scripture; (3) limiting exegesis to a Bible concordance; (4) creating false theological links; (5) forming unfounded historical connections and (6) moralizing from narratives.

Adding to the Word of God

When tithe supporters fail to view the patriarchs' tithes in context, they read their own opinions into the word of God. As I examined many pro-tithing claims, I discovered a frightful progression of thought. Tithe advocates often begin with the plain statements of Scripture but end up with unbiblical notions, which cannot be found in the text. Abraham's tithe to Melchizedek is a good illustration. Even though Scripture records that Abraham tithed to the ruler of Salem only one time,[b] many tithe supporters imply or state he gave Melchizedek multiple tithes. Here are a couple of examples:

- "...Abraham...paid tithes."[29]
- "And since Abraham often was dwelling within a day's journey of Salem (that is, Jerusalem), we need not at all conclude that this was either the first or the last occasion on which Abraham paid a tenth of his increase to Melchizedek."[30]

---

[a] Hebrews 7:1-28, especially verses 5, 11-12; 18-19

[b] Genesis 14:20c, NASB

The first claim says Abraham "paid tithes" (plural). The second claim holds that since Abraham frequently lived relatively close to Salem, the patriarch must have tithed to its ruler more than once. It is true Abraham sojourned in Canaan.[a] It is also accurate to say "he stayed at some places for long periods."[31] Each of the places where Abraham spent much of his time was south of Salem: Beersheba (40 miles),[b/32] Mamre (30 miles),[c/33] Hebron (20 miles)[d/34] and Gerar, the capital of Philistia, (45 miles).[e/35] I assume Abraham traveled by camel,[36] and experts estimate camels travel between 20–100 miles per day. If these calculations are correct, this tithe proponent's observation that Abraham was frequently within a day's journey of Salem would be accurate. Geographical proximity, however, does not prove Abraham tithed more than once to Melchizedek. To make such a claim is not only pure speculation, it is an argument from silence. The pro-tither admits his assertion is only an "inference or supposition."[37] To have a tithe advocate concede his reliance on guesswork is a significant admission.

Once tithe supporters add to Scripture the idea Abraham tithed more than once, it is not difficult for them to depart even further from the text and claim, "Abraham was a tither."[38] Some even add the idea that Abraham grew up tithing. One asserts the patriarch "made a lifestyle...of tithing"[39] and another says "...he had learned to tithe when he was still young."[40] Abraham's father may have taught his son to tithe to the temples of Mesopotamia since his family was from Babylon, a place where tithing was known,[41] but this is hardly a solid basis for weekly Christian tithes.

Some pro-tithers make yet another addition to the text when they institutionalize the simple, historical statement of Genesis 14:20c. The following are some examples: "God instituted tithing through Abraham;"[42] Abraham's tithe was "the first biblical record of tithing"[43] and "...tithing, as established by Abraham..."[44]

---

[a] Genesis 12:8-9; 13:18
[b] Genesis 22:19
[c] Genesis 18:1
[d] Genesis 13:18; 23:2, 19
[e] Genesis 20:1,15

Using Multiple Senses of Scripture

During the Middle Ages, the state church used the Bible to collect tithes from its citizens.[45] For 1,000 years (approximately 600-1600 A.D.), Europe referred to Scripture as its basis for both church and state,[46] since there was little, if any, separation of powers. In this period, ecclesiastical authority legitimated four senses in its interpretation of Scripture: literal, allegorical, moral and mystical.[47] According to R. Pfeiffer, "By these four manners of interpretation the church could force the Old Testament to say whatever seemed desirable..."[48] Both popes and emperors applied the four senses of Scripture "as a precedent for expanding their authority..."[49] Along with other Old Testament verses, there is little doubt they used Abraham's tithe to Melchizedek, the king-priest of Salem, to validate their annual tithe demand.[50]

Even though the literal sense dominates pro-tithing literature,[51] and, at times, we observe an over-literalism,[52] some tithe supporters use the allegorical,[53] mystical[a]/[54] and moral[55] senses to justify their collection of Christian tithes. The following pro-tither, for example, ignores Stuart's four essential contexts for proper exegesis, and, instead, employs his own version of the moral sense when he refers to Abraham's tithe. Even though he begins his claim with the collective pronoun "we," he directs his question to non-tithing Christians. He asks:

- "Can we claim to be children of Abraham and claim the communion and the Priesthood of Jesus and still neglect to give tithes in this covenantal relationship?"[56]

This tithe advocate's question contains a biting judgment. When he says "...in this covenantal relationship,"[57] he uses the duty-laden term "covenant" to make non-tithing believers feel if they do not tithe, they are not living up to their New covenant

---

[a] As a part of the mystical interpretation of Scripture, I include those pro-tithers who claim the Lord has personally spoken to them about the ongoing and universal validity of tithes and their right to collect them.

responsibilities. Here he abuses the moral sense of Scripture, since Genesis 14:20 says nothing about Abraham's descendants, spiritual or otherwise, having a moral or covenantal duty to tithe. In essence, he questions whether believers can be genuine Christians if they do not tithe, an implication lacking New Testament support and one, which, little doubt, would have drawn sharp criticism from Paul in Galatians because it departs from the truth of the gospel.[a]

Limiting Exegesis to a Bible Concordance

One of the most popular study methods tithe advocates use to make their case for tithing is the Bible concordance method. A Bible concordance is a reference book, which gives readers a list of the location of different words in the Bible by book, chapter and verse. If one were to look up the English word "tithes," for example, in *Strong's Exhaustive Concordance of the Bible*,[58] one would see the first reference to the word is found in Genesis 14:20.

When using a concordance to prepare a message on tithing, a typical pro-tither will run his finger down a list of words like "tithe," "tithes," "tithing" or "tenth" without referring much to Bible lexicons, dictionaries or commentaries, which are essential to understanding what each verse meant to its original audience. One tithe supporter, for example, told me that after he read every reference to tithes and offerings in his concordance, he was convinced God wanted Christians both to tithe as well as give offerings over and above their tithes. Using this method exclusively, however, is one of the main reasons why tithe advocates take the patriarchs' tithes out of context; such a limited approach can give the false impression one has exhausted the subject and has no further need for study.

To conclude Christians are to tithe because the same word "tithe" appears in both old and new testaments is similar to concluding Christians are to observe Old Testament festivals like the "Sabbath,"

---

[a] Galatians 5:1

"Passover," "Pentecost," "Tabernacles" and "Dedication" because the names of these feasts appear in both places. The fact "Passover" appears in the New Testament, for example, does not mean believers are obligated to celebrate the feast as it was celebrated in the Old Testament. According to 1 Corinthians 5:7, Christ fulfilled and abolished Passover through his sacrifice on the cross. If we had only skimmed down a concordance list of "Passover" words, then we might have concluded falsely that Christians were required to celebrate the feast. O. Allis, in *Prophecy and the Church*,[59] warns against this type of hermeneutics when it comes to trying to establish the proper relationship between the old and new testaments. According to Verhoef, Allis "… expressly warned against the fallacy of a so-called 'horizontal' or 'dead level' method of interpreting Scripture and advocated a hermeneutical approach that would do justice both to the continuity and to the discontinuity between the old and new dispensations."[60]

To see how false the assumption is that every reference in a Bible concordance to the words "tithe" or "tithing" indicates believers should tithe, we need only refer to Abraham's tithe to Melchizedek. Abraham gave Melchizedek a tithe of plunder from the Elamite coalition, which he and his men won in battle.[a] As previously mentioned, Abraham did not tithe on his regular income. When pro-tithers tell Christians they should tithe on their regular incomes because Abraham paid a tithe on recent enemy war spoils, they take Abraham's tithe out of context, and use it as a pretext to raise tithe monies.

Creating False Theological Links

Many tithe supporters tend to lump together all Bible references to tithing. Instead of taking the time to clarify each context, they make sweeping assumptions and create false theological links between tithing and other themes in Scripture such as faith. Here are a few examples:

---

[a] Genesis 14:16; 20c

- "...tithing was a part of the Abrahamic life of faith..."[61]
- "The big mistake we so often make is that we say - if it is in the Old Testament it must be under the law. This is wrong...Men like Abel, Noah, Abraham, Isaac, Jacob, and Joseph did what they did by faith (Hebrews 11:4-22) and this took place before the law came! Not only that; men like Moses, Joshua, Gideon, Samuel, and David did what they did by faith (Hebrews 11:23-32) and this took place after the law came!"[62]
- "The tithe was given before the law of Moses and is a theme of our faith, not of the law."[63]

These claims assert Christians should tithe because they are people of faith. Such false theological links, however, function only as catchphrases because they lack a biblical basis. In addition to this problem, there are several other difficulties with this line of thinking.

First, it is true the book of Hebrews says the eleven heroes mentioned in the second claim above "did what they did by faith."[64] We cannot, however, translate these Old Testament examples into New Testament exhortations to tithe. Out of all those listed, only Abraham and Jacob are associated with the giving or the promising of a tenth. Neither testament compliments any of these heroes of faith for tithing or for vowing to tithe.

Second, Hebrews shows most of these eleven heroes lived with a faith not in tithing but in the specific promises God gave to them about their own futures. Noah had faith "about things not yet seen;"[a] Abraham trusted God "not knowing where he was going;"[b] Isaac had faith "regarding things to come;"[c] by faith, Jacob "blessed each of the sons of Joseph;"[d] Joseph trusted God with his future, and "gave orders concerning his bones;"[e] Moses exercised faith in "looking to the reward"[f] and Joshua moved in faith by having the trumpets sound, after the walls of Jericho "had been

---

[a] Hebrews 11:7, NASB
[b] Hebrews 11:8, NASB
[c] Hebrews 11:20, NASB
[d] Hebrews 11:21, NASB
[e] Hebrews 11:22, NASB
[f] Hebrews 11:26, NASB

encircled for seven days."ᵃ This fact undercuts any attempt to link the faith of these Old Testament saints with tithing then or now.

Third, the Scriptures never describe Jacob's tithe vow or Abraham's tithe as acts of faith. Contrary to the second claim, Jacob did not have the necessary faith to believe God and his promises; his lack of trust was one of the reasons he made a vow/bargain at Bethel, which included the promise of a tithe.ᵇ Concerning Abraham's tithe to Melchizedek, Hebrews chapter 7, describes it not as a sign of faith but as a sign of inferiority.ᶜ The patriarch's willingness to obey God's call to Canaan while "not knowing where he was going"ᵈ was the true sign of his faith, and the kind Hebrews wants believers to emulate.ᵉ

Finally, for tithing to be a significant "theme of our faith,"[65] it would have to be a subject of critical importance in the New Testament both "dominant and recurring."[66] It is true that the New Testament mentions the Greek forms for tithing (*apodekatoo, dekaté, dekatoó*) ten times,ᶠ but 70% of these occurrences appear in the same chapter.ᵍ It is also true that faith is a dominant and recurring element in both the gospels and epistles,ʰ but the New Testament never connects it with tithing.

Forming Unfounded Historical Connections

To interpret any Old Testament text correctly, according to Stuart, we need to ask if the focus of a passage is the "past, present, or future, or a combination of these."[67] The following tithe advocate forms an unfounded historical connection between Abraham and the prophet Malachi,[68] when he writes:

- "Now why did Abraham start tithing? I want to show you some things. Go to the Book of Malachi. We are going to see

---

ᵃ Hebrews 11:30, NASB
ᵇ Genesis 28:13-15; 20 22
ᶜ Hebrews 7:6-7
ᵈ Hebrews 12:8e, NASB
ᵉ Compare Hebrews 11:1-2, 16, 25-26, 39-40 and Romans 4:3 = Genesis 15:6.

ᶠ Matthew 23:23 = Luke 11:42; 18:12; Hebrews 7:2,4,5,6,8,9(2x)
ᵍ Hebrews 7:2,4,5,6,8,9(2x)
ʰ Matthew 6:30-34; 8:10; 9:2; Romans 1:5; 4:1-20; Galatians 2:16; Ephesians 6:16

that there are seven specific blessings that come to the man that tithes...Abraham recognized the benefits for the person who paid tithes. Now here is what Abraham found as penned hundreds of years later by Malachi (Malachi 3:10-12)."[69]

According to this pro-tither, Abraham began to tithe regularly because he observed that when he did, he received the same seven blessings God promised the people of Judah in Malachi's day.[a] In addition to the fact God blessed Abraham greatly before he ever gave a tithe to the king of Salem,[b] there are other difficulties with this statement.

First, this tithe advocate claims we can understand why Abraham tithed to Melchizedek in the first book of the Old Testament, by looking at Malachi's promise to the Judeans in the last book of the Old Testament. In historical context, however, Malachi's prophecy that YHWH would bless the people, if they would pay their full dues to the temple, contains no historical connection with Abraham's tithe. Malachi's prophecy (460-450 B.C.[70]) did not relate to the distant past or future; it only related to what was happening at the present. Not only did the prophet prophesy many centuries after Abraham,[71] but the priests, rituals and temple he addressed were not a part of the patriarch's faith and were not needed for him to obtain divine blessings.

Second, when this tithe supporter asserts Abraham knew he would receive the "seven specific blessings"[72] spoken by Malachi,[c] he falls prey to the fallacy of motivation. This fallacy assumes knowledge of what is unknown and oversimplifies the personal decision-making process. D. Fischer observes, "Historians have often used motivational explanations in their work. Almost always, they have used them badly. Problems of motive in academic historiography tend to be hopelessly mired in a sort of simple-minded moralizing..."[73] D. Carson notes, "In the worst cases, it is an attempt to psychoanalyze one or more of the

---

[a] Malachi 3:8-12
[b] Genesis 12:16,20; 13:1-2,6; 14:14-15
[c] Malachi 3:10-12

participants in a past event, without having access to the patient..."⁷⁴

Third, when read in historical context, most, if not all, of the seven blessings in Malachi 3:10-12 have to do with agriculture. Abraham, however, was not a sedentary farmer; he was a semi-nomadic shepherd of flocks and herds.[a] I demonstrate in future chapters how the patriarch gave a tithe to Melchizedek not to obtain better crops but for two entirely different reasons.[b]

Lastly, quoting Stuart, "The goal of exegesis is to know neither less nor more than the information actually contained in the passage. Exegesis, in other words, places no premium on speculation or inventiveness; novelty in interpretation is not prized."⁷⁵ Similarly, according to G. Stählin, in his first letter to Timothy, Paul condemned all forms of conjecture in the use of the Old Testament.[c] Here the apostle criticized the method of interpretation used by false teachers, probably Jewish Christians influenced by Gnosticism. These teachers exploited ancient stories, including those of the Old Testament,⁷⁶ by adding their own speculations to them. Stählin calls these additions "speculative exploitation."⁷⁷ Even though Paul does not mention tithing, he warns against how false teachers exploit Jewish stories about God, angels,⁷⁸ nature and/or "the origin and future of the soul."⁷⁹ All in all, the apostle condemned Old Testament speculation, especially when it came to exploiting Old Testament stories for the sake of financial gain.[d]

Moralizing from Narratives

When pro-tithers apply Abraham's tithe and Jacob's tithe vow to Christians, they tend to moralize them, that is, draw out principles of ethical behavior.⁸⁰ According to Stuart, such moralizing is one of the most common errors in Old Testament interpretation. Since Abraham's tithe and Jacob's tithe vow both appear in narrative contexts, we need to take this scholar's warning

---

[a] Genesis 13:5; 24:35
[b] See chapters 4, 5 and 6.
[c] I Timothy 1:8
[d] Titus 1:11. Compare I Timothy 6:5.

seriously: "Narratives tell what happened, and are not designed to provide hidden ethical norms."[81]

In addition to moralizing the patriarchs' tithe episodes, Stuart advises Christians against "universal personalizing of ad hoc circumstances."[82] The Latin, ad hoc, means "for this"[83] or "to this." By "ad hoc circumstances,"[84] Stuart refers to unique or special instances in the Old Testament, which do not apply to anyone else. When Abraham gave a tithe to Melchizedek, for example, he found himself in a one-of-a-kind situation in which he gave a tithe of recent war spoils to a Canaanite king,[a] who, as far as we know, he never saw again. Jacob's tithe vow was no less unique. When the patriarch promised YHWH a tithe, he was running away from his older brother, Esau, whom he feared might kill him before he reached his destination.[b] From these highly individualized narrative contexts, we conclude the Abraham and Jacob tithe episodes were unique to them, and, therefore, cannot and should not be applied to believers.

Conclusion

In this chapter, I introduced some of the hermeneutical principles used throughout the rest of the book. I explained that when tithe advocates do not properly exegete the tithe episodes in Genesis, they eisegete them, reading into the text what is not there. If pro-tithers would use the tools of biblical scholarship to understand the historical, literary, theological and biblical contexts of the patriarchs' tithes, they would have to conclude there is nothing in these passages to suggest that God calls New Testament believers to tithe.

---

[a] Genesis 14:20   [b] Genesis 27:41-43

2
Tithing Before the Law

Many tithe advocates continue to assert that God commands New Testament believers to tithe since the word "tenth" appears in the narratives of Abraham and Jacob centuries before YHWH gave the Law to Moses on Sinai/Horeb. Here are some claims:

- "Tithes and offerings are not of the law. They preceded the law...Tithes and offerings were not abolished at the cross...the whole matter of giving of tithes and offerings moves through the cross to a higher level than previous dispensations."[85]
- "The law of Moses made tithing 'legal.' This in itself is a fairly strong hint how seriously God takes tithing...Tithing was practiced by Abraham before the law came along."[86]
- "People say to me, 'Pastor, tithing was taught under the Law, and the Law has been done away with...' Tithing was taught in the Bible 430 years before Moses lived. It is not a dispensational principle. It is a divine principle."[87]

It is true the tithe appears two times before the Law,[a] but this does not automatically mean Christians must tithe. In this chapter, we will explore what significance the patriarchs' tithe episodes have in relation to the New covenant, since both traditionally represent ages of grace not law. In my view, there is no valid hermeneutical (interpretational) basis to support the "before the

---

[a] Genesis 14:20c; 28:22c

Law" argument because it contains the following fallacies: (1) the oversimplification fallacy; (2) the lonely fact fallacy; (3) the unwarranted generalization fallacy and (4) the equivocation fallacy.

The Oversimplification Fallacy

The claims above give readers the impression that because tithing is mentioned in the lives of the patriarchs, it is also applicable to believers. One tithe supporter, for example, told me he believed tithing was one of the "many things," which passed through the cross into the Christian life. There are, however, at least seven practices before the Law the New covenant has either spiritualized or revoked. Even though some scholars hold that more than one of these seven pre-law traditions were later insertions from priestly writers, for the sake of the present discussion, I will take them at face value. They are: (1) firstfruit/firstling offerings;[a] (2) material altars;[b] (3) polygyny;[c]/88 (4) concubinage;[d]/89 (5) clean/unclean foods;[e] (6) animal sacrifices[f] and (7) physical/covenantal circumcision.[g] I could demonstrate how the New covenant made a critical difference in each of these areas, but I have chosen only to address the last three.

First, in Genesis 7:2-3, God commanded Noah to take more

---

[a] Contrast Genesis 4:1-8 (especially verses 3-5) with Romans 8:23; I Corinthians 15:20,23; 16:15; James 1:18; Revelation 14:4.
[b] Contrast Genesis 8:20; 12:7; 13:18; 26:25 with Hebrews 13:10.
[c] Contrast Genesis 4:19, 23; 32:22 with Matthew 19:5-6; Luke 16:18; I Corinthians 7:33; Ephesians 5:31; I Timothy 3:2,12; 5:9; Titus 1:6. Polygyny is the practice of a man having more than one wife. Polygamy is a broader term; it means the practice of having more than one spouse.
[d] Contrast Genesis 16:1-15; 25:12; 30:1-13; 36:12 with Matthew 19:5-6; Luke 16:18; I Corinthians 7:33; Ephesians 5:31; I Timothy 3:2,12; 5:9; Titus 1:6.
[e] Contrast Genesis 7:2-3; 8-9; 8:20 (compare Leviticus 11:47) with Romans 14:14, 20; I Timothy 4:3-4.
[f] Contrast Genesis 8:20; 15:9-11 with Hebrews 9:12-14; 10:5-10.
[g] Contrast Genesis 17:11 with Romans 2:25-29; 4:11; I Corinthians 7:18-19; Galatians 5:6; 6:15; Ephesians 2:11-16; Philippians 3:2-3; Colossians 2:11; Titus 1:10-11.

"clean" than "unclean" creatures into the ark.[a] After the flood waters abated, Noah offered "clean" birds and animals to YHWH.[b] The Lord smelled the "soothing aroma"[c] and promised never again to "curse the ground on account of man..."[d] This implies two things. First, God required "clean" sacrifices. Second, Noah and his family were to eat only "clean" foods, a tradition later emphasized in the Torah.[e] Under the New covenant, however, Jesus, Paul and Hebrews each abolished such food distinctions along with their social and religious importance.[f]

Second, both Abraham and Jacob offered animal sacrifices to YHWH; the former at his request and the latter out of fear.[g] Even before the exodus, Moses pleaded with Pharaoh, "We must go a three days' journey into the wilderness and sacrifice to the Lord our God as He commands us."[h] Under the New covenant, however, God abolished the need for all such offerings. To obtain God's favor or protection from danger, as well as for the forgiveness of sins, Jesus himself became the final and perfect sacrifice.[i]

Third, in Genesis chapter 17, God commanded Abraham to circumcise himself, along with the males of his household, as a sign of the covenant he had made with the patriarch and his descendants (verses 9-14; 23-26). The chapter uses the phrase "in your flesh for an everlasting covenant"[j] to describe the ongoing importance of circumcision, which later became a part of the Law.[k] Stephen, the church's first martyr in Acts,[l] understood God as the one who had given circumcision to the Jews when he

---

[a] Genesis 7:8-9; 8:20-21
[b] Genesis 8:20-21
[c] Genesis 8:21, NASB. Compare Exodus 29:18,25. Contrast Ephesians 5:2.
[d] Genesis 8:21, NASB
[e] Compare Deuteronomy chapter 14; Leviticus chapter 11.
[f] Mark 7:14-23; Romans 14:14-17; Colossians 2:16; Hebrews 9:10; 13:9

[g] Genesis 22:13; 46:1
[h] Exodus 8:27, NASB. Compare 10:25.
[i] Romans 5:9; Hebrews 7:26; 10:1-18
[j] Genesis 17:13
[k] Exodus 12:44,48; Leviticus 12:3
[l] Acts 7:54-60

described the Abrahamic covenant as "the covenant of circumcision."[a] In spite of this, and even though John the Baptist,[b] Jesus,[c] Paul[d] and Timothy[e] were all circumcised, the New Testament declares the ritual as no longer necessary,[f] since the New covenant replaced physical circumcision with spiritual.[g]

Finally, I have demonstrated how the New covenant annulled three pre-Mosaic practices. Therefore, the mere appearance of anything "before the Law," including the tithe, does not automatically prove it continues into the New covenant. Tithe advocates who hold Christians have a duty to tithe because the word "tenth" appears in the lives of the patriarchs commit the fallacy of oversimplification, and, thereby, mislead believers.

The Lonely Fact Fallacy

The above claims assume Abraham and Jacob's tithe episodes demonstrate they were regular tithers. This reasoning falls prey to a more specific fallacy of oversimplification called the "fallacy of the lonely fact."[90] According to D. Fischer, this fallacy is a "statistical generalization from a single case;"[91] it occurs when someone exaggerates one fact into a full-blown pattern. There is no biblical evidence Abraham gave more than a one-time tithe to a Canaanite king,[h] or Jacob fulfilled the one tithe promise he made to YHWH.[i] As previously noted, both of these tithe episodes are stand-alone, ad hoc instances. According to A. Pagolu, Abraham's tithe "...appears to be a unique action..."[92] and Jacob's tithe vow "a single obligation."[93] Fischer holds that the only safeguard against the lonely fact fallacy is in-depth research,[94] which I demonstrate throughout this book is something pro-tithers consistently fail to provide.

---

[a] Acts 7:8, NASB
[b] Luke 1:59
[c] Luke 2:21
[d] Philippians 3:5
[e] Acts 16:3
[f] Romans 2:25-29; 3:30; 4:9-12; Philippians 3:2-7; Colossians 2:11; 3:11; I Corinthians 7:18-19; Galatians 2:3; 5:2-11; 6:12-15; Titus 1:10-11; Acts 15:1,5,28-29
[g] Romans 2:28-29. Compare Colossians 2:11.
[h] Genesis 14:20c
[i] Genesis 28:22c

Although there is no textual evidence to support the claim that tithing was a regular practice of Abraham and Jacob, tithing did occur in other cultures of the ancient Near East before YHWH gave the Law to Moses on Mt. Sinai.[a] Even though knowledge of the ancient Near East is essential to our understanding of Genesis,[95] the New Testament should serve as the basis for Christian doctrine and practice not the customs of ancient cultures.

The Unwarranted Generalization Fallacy

At the beginning of this chapter, one pro-tither claims tithing was not a "dispensational principle"[96] but a "divine"[97] one, a timeless expression of God's will, which would also apply to Christians. This claim suffers from what D. Carson refers to as the fallacy of the "unwarranted generalization,"[98] and here is why:

First, when this tithe advocate asserts we are to understand the narrative episodes of the patriarchs' tithes as addressing all followers of Jesus, he opens the door to maintaining that all Old Testament stories contain immediate life lessons. According to Carson, however, it is dangerous for Christians to assume they can apply any story from the Bible to their lives as a literal or straight-across-the-board model to follow.[99] What principle of Bible interpretation do preachers use to support their view that we should apply Abraham's tithe and Jacob's tithe vow to our lives while ignoring the patriarchs' building of altars,[b] anointing of stones with oil[c] and planting of trees to mark locations of divine favor?[d/100]

Second, we cannot say God taught the patriarchs to tithe because we have no record of God ever commanding them to do so. To claim tithing is a "divine principle"[101] that applies to Christians means we should be able to find specific verses in the Bible in which God tells not only the patriarchs to tithe but also the followers of Jesus, but we cannot.[e] Therefore, how can tithe

---

[a] See Overview & Approach.
[b] Genesis 12:7; 13:4,18
[c] Genesis 28:18; 35:14
[d] Genesis 21:33

[e] Jesus told the Pharisees, who were still under the Law, to tithe not his followers (Matthew 23:23 = Luke 11:42).

advocates use the patriarchs' tithe episodes to teach Christians to tithe when we fail to find any verse in the Bible in which God tells either to do so?

Lastly, YHWH commanded Abraham to circumcise all the members of his household as a sign "throughout your generations for an everlasting covenant,"[a] but he says nothing of this sort concerning Abraham's tithe to Melchizedek or Jacob's tithe vow. Since the word "tenth" appears in the lives of both patriarchs, we can assume the narrator(s) wanted to encourage their Jewish contemporaries to tithe to their respective sanctuaries (Salem/Jerusalem in the southern kingdom of Judah and Bethel in the northern kingdom of Israel). Although the New Testament encourages believers to give material assistance to teachers,[b] missionaries[c] and the poor,[d] as members of a new covenant, Christians no longer need to pay a precise percentage of their wages to a temple, priest and ritual system to maintain their relationship with God.[e]

The Equivocation Fallacy

The equivocation fallacy occurs when a word or concept is used in an argument as always having the same meaning or function, when, in reality, its meaning or function changes.[102] Pro-tithers who associate Abraham's tithe to Melchizedek with Israelite and Christian tithes fall prey to this fallacy. Although the same Hebrew words (*ma'asar; asar*) that are translated "tithe" or "tenth" before the Law are also translated in the same way under the Law,[f] the assumption that these words carry the same meaning in every context is false.[103] When we compare the

---

[a] Genesis 17:7, NASB
[b] Galatians 6:6
[c] Philippians 4:15-20
[d] Galatians 2:10; 2 Corinthians 8:14; 9:9,12
[e] Hebrews 7:23-28; 8:2,13; 9:12. See Book 2 in *The Tithing Series*.
[f] The noun for Abraham's tithe (*ma'aser*) in Genesis 14:20c also occurs in Numbers 18:21, 26 and Nehemiah 10:38. The verb for Jacob's tithe vow (*asar*) in Genesis 28:22c also appears in Deuteronomy 14:22; 26:12; I Samuel 8:15, 17 and Nehemiah 10:37-38. *ma'aser* and *asar* come from the same Hebrew stem, *eser*, meaning ten or tenth.

meaning and function of the tithe in the patriarchal period with that of the Israelites, we discover they are different. In contrast to tithes under the Law, Abraham's tithe and Jacob's tithe vow were both: (1) spontaneous; (2) voluntary; (3) conditional and (4) free of temple obligations.

Spontaneous

The tithe episodes of the patriarchs were unplanned, unforced and unrepeated events, which occurred at the spur of the moment. Without premeditation, for example, Abraham gave a tithe of enemy plunder to Melchizedek.[a] Similarly, Jacob spontaneously made a vow to YHWH, part of which involved the promise of a tithe,[b] after he awoke from a unique dream. Most tithe advocates, however, do not present Abraham's tithe or Jacob's tithe vow as unplanned or spontaneous. Instead, they ignore their contexts and equate them with tithes under the Law, which were a mandated income stream for the state of Israel.[c] They were a regular tax, which supported the central temple,[d] those who traveled to festivals in Jerusalem[e] and the landless poor in the rural villages.[f]

Voluntary

According to several pro-tithers, Christians have no right to exercise any personal choice in the matter of their tithes.[104] Such a view, however, is contrary to the text. When Abraham gave a tithe to the Canaanite king, he was not obeying a divine command; he was voluntarily responding to a peace initiative to which he could have either refused to reciprocate or could have chosen to respond with a different gift. Likewise, Jacob's tithe vow was his own idea.[g] YHWH did not command him to promise a tithe in exchange for his covenant promises. On the contrary, tithing

---

[a] Genesis 14:17-20
[b] Genesis 28:22c
[c] See Book 2 in *The Tithing Series*.
[d] Note "priest" in Leviticus 27:8, 11-14, 18, 21, 23, 30-33.

Also see Deuteronomy 12:5,11,21; 26:2.
[e] Deuteronomy 12:5-7; 10-14; 17-19; 14:22-29
[f] Deuteronomy 14:27-29; 26:12-15
[g] See chapters 13 and 14.

under the Law was compulsory.[a]/[105] The officials in the Second Temple period, for example, required tithes on all grain, produce and animal products.[b] According to Malachi, the people had no choice but to tithe to avoid drought, locust and plant disease.[c] The fact YHWH never threatened the patriarchs with curses if they did not tithe demonstrates he never commanded them to do so.

Conditional

There are several points in the text which demonstrate Abraham's tithe to Melchizedek was conditional. First, if Melchizedek had not claimed his god, El Elyôn ("God Most High"), was the one who had enabled Abraham to gain victory over his enemies,[d] then the patriarch would not have reciprocated with a tithe of war spoils in tribute.[e] Second, if the king had congratulated Abraham for his victory but had not initiated a peace treaty with gifts of food and drink,[f] the patriarch would never have needed to respond with any sort of gift in return.[g] The conditionality of Jacob's tithe vow is even clearer from the text. Jacob promised he would give YHWH a tenth of all he would obtain on his journey east, if the Lord would grant him a safe return to Canaan.[h] Such a qualification makes Jacob's tithe gift a votive offering (from the Latin, *votum*, vow). According to Leviticus, however, the Israelites had to keep their votive offerings strictly separated from both their produce and animal tithes.[i]/[106]

Free of Temple Obligations

Contrary to the way most tithe advocates apply the patriarchs' tithes to Christians today, neither Abraham nor Jacob regularly tithed to support a central sanctuary. Both Abraham and Jacob were seminomads who sojourned with their flocks and herds, built altars for themselves and worshipped YHWH under the open

---

[a] Leviticus 27:30-33
[b] Malachi 3:10, the "whole" tithe; Nehemiah 10:37-38; 12:44,47; 13:5,10,12
[c] Malachi 3:9,11
[d] Genesis 14:19b,20a,b
[e] Genesis 14:20c
[f] Genesis 14:18a
[g] Genesis 14:20c
[h] Genesis 28:20-22
[i] Leviticus 27:2,8,30-33

sky. Even though Abraham spent more time in some places than others, Genesis describes him as a wanderer, "a stranger and an alien."[a] When Hebrews says Abraham lived "in tents with Isaac and Jacob,"[b] it describes the patriarch's son and grandson as having the same seminomadic lifestyle. All other references to tithes in the Bible involve the giving of them to state sanctuaries.[c/107]

Conclusion

In this chapter, I noted the following significant differences between tithes in the patriarchal period and tithes under the Law: (1) spontaneous vs. regular; (2) voluntary vs. mandatory; (3) conditional vs. unconditional and (4) free of vs. bound to temple obligations. From these comparisons, it is clear the kind of tithe most pro-tithers promote is the type commanded under the Law not the one reflected in the lives of Abraham and Jacob. It is significant how one tithe supporter admits if someone could demonstrate tithing originated under the Old covenant and not with the patriarchs, then he would concede the New covenant had abolished the practice.[108] I applaud such an open mind and submit the contents of this chapter as my answer to his challenge.

---

[a] Genesis 23:4, NRSV. Compare Hebrews 11:9.
[b] Hebrews 11:9, NASB
[c] Note "sanctuary" in Numbers 18:1,3,5,16; "tent" in verses 2,3,4,6,21,22,23,31 and "Aaron" in verses 1,8,20,28. Also see Deuteronomy 12:5-7, 10-14, 17-19; 14:22-29; 26:12-15. Note "priest" in Leviticus 27:8,11,12,14,18,21 and "sanctuary" in verses 3,25. See also 2 Chronicles 31:4-6, 11-12; Amos 4:4; Nehemiah 10:37-38; 12:44,47; 13:5,10,12; Malachi 3:6-18; Matthew 23:23 = Luke 11:42; 18:9-14. See Book 2 in *The Tithing Series*.

3

A Motive Analysis

Five kings of the Cities of the Plain served Chedorlaomer, king of Elam, for twelve years in exchange for military protection.[a/109] In the thirteenth year, Bera, king of Sodom, led a rebellion in which each vassal stopped paying his dues of crops, animals and soldiers.[b/110] The next year, accompanied by three other kings, Chedorlaomer came to collect what was owed him and to punish his vassals for their revolt.[111] As he and his alliance journeyed south, not only did they ravage the surrounding lands[c/112] and steal the goods and food supplies of Sodom and Gomorrah,[d] they also kidnapped Abraham's nephew, Lot, along with his possessions.[e] Although the leaders of the Cities of the Plain counter-attacked, they could not defeat the king of Elam and his forces.[f]

When Abraham heard his nephew had been kidnapped, he, along with 318 of his trained men, pursued the Elamite coalition and defeated them at Dan in an early morning raid.[g] As the patriarch was returning from battle, Bera, king of Sodom, and Melchizedek, ruler of Salem, came out to meet him at the valley of Shaveh also called the King's Valley.[h] There Melchizedek

---

[a] Genesis 14:1-4a
[b] Genesis 14:4b
[c] Genesis 14:5-7
[d] Genesis 14:11
[e] Genesis 14:12
[f] Genesis 14:8-10
[g] Genesis 14:13-16

[h] Genesis 14:17-18. This valley became known as the Kidron Valley, which is located between Jerusalem and the Mt. of Olives (2 Samuel 18:18; May, H. G., 1962., 133).

offered Abraham a treaty gift of bread and wine to which the patriarch reciprocated with a tithe of war spoils.

Many have questioned why Abraham gave a tithe of enemy war plunder to Melchizedek. Did YHWH command him to do so? Answers to questions like these are critical to the tithing debate. Tithe advocates need to provide clear, biblical evidence as to what Abraham's tithe to a Canaanite ruler over 3,000 years ago has to do with Christians paying tithes today. In this chapter, I critique the following five motives pro-tithers give to explain what prompted the patriarch to give a tithe: (1) religious duty; (2) human gratitude; (3) divine jurisdiction; (4) personal conviction and (5) financial gain. Let us now look more closely at each of these.

Religious Duty

One motive tithe supporters use to explain Abraham's tithe is religious duty, that is, he gave a tenth in response to a demand or obligation from God. In their book, two tithe advocates put it this way:

- "Long before the time of Moses, the dedication of the tenth to God was recognized as a duty."[113]

These co-authors claim Abraham viewed tithing as a duty because he understood it as a divine command. We know this because in the same context they ask, "Was tithing commanded in the patriarchal days?"[114] to which they answer "Yes..."[115] The text, however, never tells us God commanded Abraham to tithe or that the patriarch considered tithing a necessity. If Abraham viewed tithing as a duty before God, we would observe him donating tithes on more than one occasion, but we do not. As previously alluded to,[a] God never told Abraham to give a tenth of plunder as tribute for helping him win the battle against the Elamite

---

[a] See the subheads "Spontaneous," "Voluntary," "Conditional," and "Free of Temple Membership Obligations" in Chapter 2.

coalition.[a] Neither did he tell Abraham to make a war vow of self-denial before he rescued Lot.[b] Unfortunately, the voluntary nature of Abraham's tithe to Melchizedek is a fact only a few pro-tithers admit.[116]

Human Gratitude

Tithe advocates also suggest Abraham gave a tithe to Melchizedek out of gratitude. Since El Elyôn/YHWH helped the patriarch to rescue his nephew from kidnappers, he donated a tithe to him as a thank offering. Here is one claim:

- "Abraham gave a tithe in a response to his gratitude to the Lord for what He had done for the victory He had given to him – not because someone forced him to do it or because there was a law requiring him to do so...but just out of gratitude to the Lord...His heart toward God was abundantly clear..."[117]

It is reasonable to assume the patriarch was grateful to God, as anyone would be, for helping him rescue his nephew, Lot. Nevertheless, the text does not tell us what was in Abraham's heart when he gave his tithe. His inner thoughts are not "abundantly clear,"[118] as this tithe advocate claims. The notion Abraham donated a tithe out of gratitude to YHWH makes for a good story,[119] but it falls prey to the aesthetic fallacy, which, according to D. Fischer, "...selects beautiful facts, or facts that can be built into a beautiful story, rather than facts that are functional to the empirical problem at hand."[120] There is no scriptural evidence to demonstrate that tithing out of thankfulness was the intended meaning behind Abraham's tithe. If the narrator's goal had been to teach later Israelites to pay their tithes out of gratitude to the Lord, I think he would have mentioned the concept. In the New Testament, Colossians exhorts Christians to "be thankful"[c] and to sing "with thankfulness in your hearts to

---

[a] Genesis 14:19-20
[b] Genesis 14:22-24
[c] Colossians 3:15, NASB

God;"[a] yet neither of these exhortations, nor any other New Testament verse, encourages Christians to tithe as an expression of gratitude.

Divine Jurisdiction

The third motive is Abraham gave a tithe because he acknowledged YHWH had the legal jurisdiction to collect a tenth of the war spoils. One tithe advocate puts it this way:

- "...Abram declines to take anything for himself, though, as a conqueror, he seems to have recognized that he had no jurisdiction over God's tenth..."[121]

Despite the awkward wording of this claim,[122] its point is Abraham paid Melchizedek a tithe because he admitted he had no lawful jurisdiction or authority over that portion of the plunder. The text, however, never says God had a right over tithes during the patriarchal period, or Abraham thought YHWH did. The claim Abraham "had no jurisdiction over God's tenth,"[123] implies he owed God a temple or municipal tax payable to Melchizedek, ruler of Salem. Such an assertion does not fit the context of patriarchal religion. Abraham was not a citizen of Salem; neither was he a member of its temple. He was a seminomadic chieftain under the direct care of YHWH.[b] If Genesis chapter 14 implies any sort of legal jurisdiction, it would be Abraham's right by custom, as the victorious chieftain, to keep the enemy plunder for himself. In the ancient Near East, according to J. Wevers, "the victor automatically assumed his right to possess anything belonging to the vanquished enemy."[124] This is why Bera tried to negotiate the patriarch out of part of his chieftain's reward,[c] which the king knew Abraham had coming to him.[125]

The "no jurisdiction"[126] argument falls prey to the fallacy of

---

[a] Colossians 3:16, NASB
[b] Compare Genesis 14:22-23; 15:1.
[c] Genesis 14:21

presumptive continuity, in which two events or time periods are connected only by assumption.[127] This pro-tither assumes God required tithes during the patriarchal period, and Abraham honored God's right to collect them as the Israelites recognized God's right to collect tithes under the Sinai covenant. There is no legal or historical continuity between the patriarchs' tithes and the Israelites' tithes.[128] Among other factors, the patriarchs' tithes were voluntary and the Israelites' tithes were compulsory. The literary genre of Genesis chapter 14 is historical narrative not legal prescription. This tithe advocate reads into Genesis the jurisdictional law of the tithe, which did not come into effect until the Sinai covenant[a] or even as an addendum[129] to the later Holiness Code.[b/130]

Personal Conviction

The next motivation implies Abraham donated a tenth of enemy plunder because he had a conviction he needed to tithe at once on any inheritance, material increase or financial profit that came into his life. According to one source:

- "Should I tithe on an inheritance? Yes. An inheritance is an increase. Therefore you must tithe on everything that comes into your possession in that way. When Abraham returned with the spoils of war after the successful defeat of Chedorlaomer and the kings (Genesis 14:17-20), he immediately paid the tithe...Your first calculation is to figure your increase. That might be from a paycheck, bonuses, or the sale of some property...After figuring out how much increase you have received, calculate the tithe, or the tenth."[131]

This claim suggests Abraham promptly paid a tithe of plunder to Melchizedek because he believed it was his responsibility not to delay in calculating a tenth from any material increase; and, as

---

[a] Leviticus 27:30-33. See Book 2 in *The Tithing Series*.

[b] The Holiness Code = Leviticus 17-26; holiness = qodesh

Abraham tithed on the enemy war spoils, so believers should tithe on their financial profits. It is true Abraham was a rich man,[a] and the enemy plunder would have made him even wealthier. Nothing in the story, however, indicates Abraham paid a tithe because he was in the habit of tithing on his material increases, or he considered the plunder as an individual increase, upon which he owed a tithe. Before he rescued Lot, Abraham promised to give away the plunder he might obtain in battle,[b] and, according to Genesis, there is no evidence he ever tithed on any of his material increases[c] including family inheritance,[d] royal gifts,[e] slaves,[f] productive livestock,[g] etc. Because of this fact, it is presumptuous to argue Christians are obliged to tithe on their financial increases because of Abraham's one-time tithe. The patriarch did not give a tithe to the king of Salem because he was under a timely conviction; he gave a tithe for different reasons, which I share in chapters 4, 5 and 6.

Financial Gain

Finally, one pro-tither holds Abraham tithed to Melchizedek because he believed tithing would make him rich. According to him, Abraham quickly figured out tithing was a blessing contract with God, which guaranteed him a lifetime of wealth and prosperity. He claims:

- "If he was not commanded to do it [tithe], why did he do it? Because Abraham was a sharp businessman. He was one of the best...If he tithed when he didn't have to, there had to be a good reason on the part of Abraham to do it. Well, there

---

[a] Genesis 13:2; 24:1,35. See chapters 3, 11.
[b] Genesis 14:22-24
[c] Both testaments record Abraham tithed only once (Genesis 14:20c; Hebrews 7:2a).
[d] Compare Genesis 11:31-32 with 12:5. Neither Isaac nor his brothers tithed on their inheritances (25:5-6).
[e] Genesis 12:16; 20:16
[f] Genesis 12:5,16; 14:14; 17:12,13,27
[g] Genesis 13:2,5; 24:35

was. Abraham recognized the benefits for the person who paid tithes."[132]
- "You must see it [tithing] like Abraham saw it. It is a blessing pack [pact]. It was not a command to Abraham. He did it, because it was right. And look what the man got back. There was no law that made him do it. He just did it because it should have been done and he wound up probably the richest man of his day."[133]
- "If you get this kind of thing going [tithing], who has to 'command' you to do it? ... Once he figured this thing out, nobody could stop him...Why, if you present it the way it really is, you can't stop people from tithing."[134]
- "Now here is what Abraham found as penned hundreds of years later by Malachi (Malachi 3:10-12)...You are beginning to see why Abraham got in on tithing...Abraham was so close to God and he trusted God to the point where he saw the seven blessings involved with tithing...So, he began to tithe."[a/135]

According to this tithe advocate, Abraham was a "sharp businessman,"[136] who, as "one of the best,"[137] noticed whenever he tithed, God blessed him abundantly. As a result, "nobody could stop him," and "he wound up probably the richest man of his day."[138] This tithe supporter presents Abraham as a wealthy investor who discovered his tithes secured him the highest rate of return. Such claims may sound exciting, but they contain serious textual problems.

First, even though Abraham traded with local merchants,[b] Genesis does not portray him as a profit-driven tither who jumped at each opportunity to make money. Instead, it depicts him as a seminomadic herder and trader, who, although wealthy,[c] was a loyal,[d] generous[e] and hospitable[f] chieftain[g] with a reputation

---

[a] Malachi 3:10-12
[b] Compare Genesis 23:10,18. The gate of a city was the place of business.
[c] Genesis 13:2
[d] Note how Abraham honored his allies (Genesis 14:13,24).
[e] Genesis 13:8-9
[f] Genesis 18:1-8
[g] Genesis 14:14-16

of a "mighty prince."ᵃ Abraham cared more about protecting his good reputation and making peace with the locals, than he cared about making money. Instead of a "sharp businessman,"¹³⁹ it would be more accurate to characterize him as an astute peacemaker. We observe Abraham's peacemaking nature in his dealings with Bera,ᵇ the sons of Heth,ᶜ/¹⁴⁰ Ephronᵈ and Abimelech.ᵉ Concerning Bera, after Abraham rescued Lot and others from the Elamite coalition, he told the patriarch to take the goods but return the people to him.ᶠ Unlike what a "sharp businessman"¹⁴¹ might have done, Abraham shared with the king his pre-war vow with YHWH and took nothing.ᵍ Regarding the sons of Heth, after the death of Sarah, they told the patriarch he could have any of their "choicest"ʰ graves. Instead of accepting their gift, the patriarch requested to purchase the cave of Machpelah.¹⁴² If Abraham had been a "sharp businessman,"¹⁴³ always looking for ways to save money, would he not have taken advantage of such a free offer? Concerning Ephron, when the Hittite overheard Abraham's offer to buy his cave for Sarah, he also offered it to him for "free,"ⁱ/¹⁴⁴ along with the field in which it was located,ʲ but again, Abraham refused. Instead, the patriarch bowed before the people and told Ephron he wanted to purchase the field for full price.ᵏ In the end, Abraham bought both cave and field for 400 shekels of silver, which was a "very high price."¹⁴⁵ In this transaction, since Abraham was willing to pay any price for the property¹⁴⁶ without any negotiation,ˡ/¹⁴⁷ it was Ephron not Abraham who was the "sharp businessman."¹⁴⁸ Lastly, when Abraham discovered some of Abimelech's men had stolen one of his wells, he did not act like a "sharp businessman"¹⁴⁹ who would have tried to get his well back without paying anything for it. Instead, Abraham voluntarily initiated the re-purchase of his own

---

ᵃ Genesis 23:6, NASB
ᵇ Genesis 14:17,21-24
ᶜ Genesis 23:3-8,16-20
ᵈ Genesis 23:8-20
ᵉ Genesis 21:22-32
ᶠ Genesis 14:21
ᵍ Genesis 14:22-24
ʰ Genesis 23:6, NASB
ⁱ Genesis 23:11
ʲ Genesis 23:11
ᵏ Genesis 23:12-13
ˡ Genesis 23:13-16

well for the price of seven female sheep.[a]

Second, this tithe supporter tells his readers, "You must see it [tithing] like Abraham saw it."[150] Here he assumes to know what was in Abraham's mind when he gave his tithe to Melchizedek. On the contrary, the text does not tell us how Abraham viewed his tithe. The verses which come closest to doing so are Genesis 14:18a and 22b, which I address in other chapters.[b]

Third, this pro-tither claims Abraham viewed his tithe to Melchizedek as part of a "blessing pack"[151] with God. Unfortunately, however, there is nothing in Genesis to support this assumption. In his covenant with the patriarch, God promised to bless Abraham with the land of Canaan, many descendants, etc., but as previously demonstrated, no verse in Genesis makes such blessings contingent upon Abraham tithing. To his credit, a different tithe advocate rejects the assumption Abraham tithed to get blessed. He explains, "...there is not the slightest indication that Abraham was promised a blessing if he gave one tenth of all. He had already been blessed!"[152] If tithing had brought such great blessing into Abraham's life, and if he had been convinced it was necessary for his descendants to tithe to inherit YHWH's promises, then we would expect to see the patriarch instructing his children and grandchildren about how essential tithing was for their futures. Unfortunately, however, we never see Abraham (or any of the patriarchs) instructing their families about the importance of the tithe.

Fourth, in the same "blessing pack" claim, this tithe supporter makes statements for which he provides no biblical foundation. When he implies, for example, that Abraham gave a tithe because he believed "it was right"[153] and "it should have been done,"[154] he gives no proof from Scripture the patriarch held such a moral or ethical stance toward his tithe. Even if he did, it would still be too much of a hermeneutical leap to conclude tithing is "right" for Christians. The clauses "because it was right" and "because it should have been done" sound more like the pro-tither's personal

---

[a] Genesis 21:28-32 [b] See chapters 3,4,5,6.

opinion. When he says Abraham paid his tithe for moral or ethical reasons, albeit unexplained, he contradicts his own claim that Abraham tithed because it made him rich: "Abraham was a sharp businessman...[who] recognized the benefits of the person who paid tithes...and he wound up probably the richest man of his day."[155] He provides readers with no evidence to support such a statement; he surmises as much because the patriarch was wealthy.[a] The text, however, indicates that tithing was not the cause of Abraham's wealth.[b] At the same time, since Abraham gave a tithe to one of the early rulers of Salem (later Jerusalem), I would not doubt the narrator used the patriarch's tithe to encourage his contemporaries that it was "right"[156] to pay their tithes to the Jerusalem authorities of their day. As previously noted, however, to conclude from this that tithing is therefore "right" for believers today is overreach.

Fifth, since Scripture shows Abraham tithed only once,[c] it is false to state or imply he tithed as many times as would have been necessary for him to have "figured this [tithing] thing out."[157] In the same assertion, this tithe advocate claims, "...if you present it [tithing] the way it really is you can't stop people from tithing."[158] To him, "the way it really is"[159] means if leaders would present tithing as a guaranteed way to get rich, they would not be able to stop their supporters from practicing it.[160] Even though such a statement may sound profitable to tithers as well as those who receive tithes, it is impossible to substantiate. If tithing lived up to its reputation as a means of guaranteed financial gain, I submit all believers would tithe without hesitation.

Finally, to the question, "Why did Abraham start tithing?" this tithe advocate claims it was because Abraham experienced the same seven blessings "...penned hundreds of years later by Malachi (Malachi 3:10-12)...he [Abraham] saw the seven blessings involved with tithing..."[161] He writes:

---

[a] Genesis 13:2
[b] See Chapter 11.

[c] Genesis 14:20c is the only mention of the tithe in Abraham's life.

- "Now what are the seven blessings? ... Notice verse 10 says 'Bring all the tithes into the storehouse that there may be meat [food] in my house and test me now by this' saith the Lord, 'if I will not do seven fantastic things for you.'...God here asks us to test Him by doing one thing and then watching Him do seven things in response to it...A seven for one return, and He says, 'Test Me in this'!... 'Test Me. I am going to do seven things in return.' Now does that sound like a pretty good return? In this day of meager rates of return on your savings accounts in your bank, if you found a place that had an iron clad guarantee that would pay you back seven times more than you put in, and you had confidence in the bank and the banker, would you take your money out of an account where they were paying you only 3½% and place it in the place where they would give you 700%?"[162]

This pro-tither identifies Malachi's seven blessings as:[163] (1) opened windows of heaven; (2) blessing; (3) surplus; (4) devourer prevention; (5) fruit protection; (6) vine preservation and (7) delightful land. Before we can agree with his assertions, however, we must first examine each of these blessings to see if Abraham truly experienced them as claimed.

Opened Windows of Heaven: In Malachi 3:10, God promised the people of Judah he would open for them the "windows of heaven,"[a] if they would bring their full tithes and offerings to the temple. This tithe advocate applies this verse to how God made Abraham rich because he tithed. Even though it is beyond question God blessed Abraham materially,[b] I demonstrate in Chapter 11 that the reason for his prosperity was something entirely different than his tithe(s). In the story of Abraham, there is no mention of the windows of heaven or the need to use tithes and offerings to open them.

Blessing: The same tithe supporter defines the word "blessing" (*berakah*) in Malachi 3:10 as "well-being in every area of a

---

[a] NASB   [b] Genesis 13:2

person's life."[164] If we allow such a definition, it is true Abraham experienced spiritual,[a] material[b] and physical blessings,[c] which also included miracles,[d] healings in answer to his prayers[e] and the success of his many children.[f] The text, however, never associates Abraham's tithe to Melchizedek as the cause of any of these.

Surplus: This pro-tither takes the crop surplus in Malachi 3:10 to mean there were "no limits"[165] on the number of divine blessings Abraham experienced because of his faithfulness to tithe. The text, however, demonstrates Abraham not only was given the covenant promises[g] but also became rich[h] well before he ever gave a tithe to Melchizedek.[i]

Devourer Prevention: In Malachi 3:11, this tithe advocate understands the "devourer" as the devil who Abraham overcame through tithing;[166] he concludes, "Is it any wonder Abraham was a tither?"[167] Unfortunately, however, he produces no evidence from Abraham's life to support his statement. In addition, he claims Christians will not be able to overcome the devil unless they tithe. After writing at length about the bad things the devil wants to do to believers, he says, "So just start tithing."[168] Regrettably, he produces no New Testament basis for such a recommendation. If Jesus knew his disciples would not be able to overcome Satan unless they tithed, he would have told them as much, but we search in vain for any evidence he ever did.

Fruit Protection: In Malachi 3:11, God promised the Judeans the locusts would "not destroy the fruits of the ground,"[j] if they would bring their full tithes and offerings to the temple. Similarly, this tithe advocate claims tithing preserved Abraham's livelihood.[169] The patriarch, however, was a wealthy tribesman[170] *before* he ever met Melchizedek.[k] Thus, to argue Abraham's tithe caused his wealth up to that point in his life finds no basis in the

---

[a] Genesis 15:6 = James 2:23
[b] Genesis 13:2; 24:35
[c] Genesis 18:9-15; 25:8; Romans 4:19
[d] Genesis 21:2,7
[e] Genesis 20:17
[f] Genesis 17:20; 24:27, 52-67

[g] Genesis 12:1-3
[h] Genesis 12:16; 13:2
[i] Genesis 14:20c
[j] NASB
[k] Compare Genesis 13:2 with 14:20c. Compare 14:23.

text. Furthermore, Genesis makes no connection between Abraham's tithe to the local ruler and the wealth he obtained *after* giving it.

Vine Preservation: God also promised the Judeans who tithed to the temple their grape vines would be healthy. The text says, "...nor will your vine in the field cast its grapes..."[a] This pro-tither describes Judah's grapevines as "the very source"[171] of their support. He then claims God protected the sources of Abraham's wealth because he was a tither. Such a conclusion is wishful thinking. Genesis never says Abraham's tithe to Melchizedek safeguarded any of his sources of wealth - not his flocks,[b] herds,[c] camels,[d] donkeys,[e] gold,[f] silver,[g] wives,[h] grandchildren,[i] slaves[j] or maids.[k] Furthermore, if Abraham had been a regular or lifetime tither, as many pro-tithers would have us believe,[172] his tithes failed to protect him against the famine which forced him to go to Egypt for food.[l] Essential to Abraham's livestock was regular access to water, but, again, Abraham's tithe to Melchizedek did not prevent Abimelech's servants from stealing one of his wells at Beersheba.[m] Therefore, it is false to claim that Malachi's promise to preserve the "very source"[173] of the Judeans' income applies to the patriarch.

Delightful Land: Finally, Malachi's last promise to the Judeans, if they would pay their full temple dues, was, "All the nations will call you blessed, for you shall be a delightful land."[n] "Delightful land" (*chephets erets*) refers to a place of agricultural abundance. This tithe supporter is unclear about how he applies this promise

---

[a] Malachi 3:11c, NASB
[b] Genesis 13:2; 20:14; 24:35
[c] Genesis 13:2; 20:14; 24:35
[d] Genesis 24:35
[e] Genesis 24:35
[f] Genesis 13:2; 24:35
[g] Genesis 13:2; 24:35
[h] Sarah (Genesis 11:29); Keturah (25:1-4); Hagar (16:3)
[i] Compare Genesis 25:1-4.
[j] Genesis 14:14 refers to Abraham's 318 "trained men" (NASB) or domestic slaves. This would be a low number in light of the likelihood of many, if not most, of these men being married with children, who would also be in Abraham's service. Compare 20:14.
[k] Genesis 24:35
[l] Genesis 12:10
[m] Genesis 21:25
[n] Malachi 3:12, NASB

to Abraham. I assume he makes one of two points. The first possibility is that Abraham's tithe to Melchizedek caused him to find fertile pastures for his flocks and herds. (Again, there is nothing in the text to indicate such a connection.[a]) The second possibility is Abraham's tithe to the ruler of Salem caused the people of Canaan to call him blessed. None of the accounts of the Canaanite rulers who acknowledged Abraham's greatness connect the divine blessing upon his life with his tithe to Melchizedek. Melchizedek, for example, called Abraham blessed because the patriarch, with God's help, defeated their common enemy, the Elamite coalition, led by Chedorlaomer.[b] Abimelech, king of Gerar, acknowledged the divine blessing on the patriarch[c] because God spoke to the ruler in a dream,[d] and because God healed the king and the women of his household through Abraham's prayers.[e] Ephron, a Canaanite property owner and merchant near Hebron, blessed Abraham as a "mighty prince"[f] (*elohim nasiy'*) because of the patriarch's reputation. Thus, there is no biblical evidence for the claim that the Canaanites called Abraham blessed because the patriarch gave a tithe to one of their kings.

Conclusion

In this chapter, I demonstrated the falsity of five motives various pro-tithers claim Abraham had when he gave a tithe to the ruler of Salem. "Human gratitude" came closest to the text, but, upon closer examination, this motive turned out to be more of a kind of tribute to El Elyôn than an expression of human thankfulness. I also exposed the claim that Abraham was a "sharp businessman"[174] to whom tithing was a "blessing pack."[175] This statement turned out to be false in two ways. First, Genesis shows Abraham to be more of a peacemaker than a businessman; in fact,

---

[a] See Genesis 13:2 and 14:20c.
[b] Connect Genesis 14:17a with verse 19a,b.
[c] Genesis 21:22, NRSV
[d] Genesis 20:3-7
[e] Genesis 20:7, 17-18
[f] Genesis 23:6, NASB. Compare "my lord" (*adon*) in verses 6,11,15.

he made some poor business decisions. Second, since Abraham tithed only once, there is no biblical foundation to assert he had the opportunity to observe the results of tithing over time. Finally, I showed that Genesis does not support the claim that Abraham paid a tithe because he experienced the blessings that Malachi promised to the Judeans centuries later. The way this tithe advocate applies Malachi's blessings to Abraham is an example of gross eisegesis. He attempts not only to read Abraham's mind but also denies the patriarch's relationship of grace with YHWH when he places him under the law of Moses by the way he claims Abraham experienced the same benefits as later Judeans, who were promised blessing only if they obeyed the law of the temple tithe.

4

A Vow for a Safe Rescue

When Abraham lived in Mamre, a messenger informed him Chedorlaomer and the Elamite coalition had ravaged Sodom and Gomorrah and captured his nephew, Lot.[a/176] Even though Chedorlaomer's forces consisted of only four kings,[b] they were still able to defeat the vassal coalition of five. It appears Abraham concluded from this that he would need supernatural assistance to aid him in any rescue attempt. To obtain divine help, he made a vow/bargain with God in which he promised he would deny himself his right to the war spoils, if YHWH would grant him the victory.[c] This story highlights Abraham's loyalty to kin rather than his support of a wicked city.[d] Bera plays a major role in the story because he was the ruler of Sodom, the place where Abraham's nephew resided.[e] He was probably the leader of the vassal rebellion because he appears first in the list of the five coalition partners.[f]

After Abraham successfully rescued Lot, Bera tried to negotiate with him over the distribution of the recovered goods and people.[g] He said to the patriarch, "Give the people to me and take the goods for yourself."[h] In response, Abraham shared with the king the vow he had previously made to YHWH before he

---

[a] Genesis 14:11-13
[b] Genesis 14:9
[c] Genesis 14:22-24
[d] Genesis 13:13; 18:20
[e] Genesis 14:12
[f] Genesis 14:2,8
[g] Genesis 14:21
[h] Genesis 14:21, NASB

went in pursuit of their common enemy. This is what Abraham told Bera:

> "With raised hand I have sworn an oath to the LORD, God Most High, Creator of heaven and earth, that I will accept nothing belonging to you, not even a thread or the strap of a sandal, so that you will never be able to say, 'I made Abram rich.' I will accept nothing but what my men have eaten and the share that belongs to the men who went with me—to Aner, Eshkol and Mamre. Let them have their share."[a]

Here the patriarch responds that he could not take any of Bera's goods or people for himself, lest he break the war vow he made with YHWH. It seems the king of Sodom did not attempt to negotiate with Abraham over the Elamite plunder itself. The patriarch's action of giving a tenth of the war spoils to Melchizedek prior to Bera's offer demonstrates he had become its sole and rightful owner.

Previous to Abraham's tithe episode, YHWH promised the patriarch he would curse anyone who cursed him.[b] Despite this promise of divine protection, Abraham was not always perfect in his trust in YHWH;[c] he lived much of his life in fear and doubt instead of faith and confidence.[d/177] This made him prone to ask for reassuring signs.[178] When God told him that he and his descendants were going to possess the land of Canaan, for example, Abraham asked for some tangible evidence, saying, "O Lord God, how am I to know that I shall possess it?"[e] YHWH responded with a supernatural experience which involved both "terror and great darkness."[f] In light of Abraham's insecurities about the future, it is understandable that before he led his men into battle, he made a war vow to YHWH to add weight to his prayer for a safe rescue of Lot.[179]

---

[a] Genesis 14:22-24, NIV. Instead of "sworn," the NET has "vowed."
[b] Genesis 12:3b
[c] Compare Genesis 12:13,18-19 and 20:2,9-12. Compare 15:4 with 16:4; 17:16,18; 18:10,14; 21:1-2. See also 15:1b.
[d] Compare Genesis 17:18 and 20:11.
[e] Genesis 15:8, NRSV
[f] Genesis 15:12

The Characteristics of Abraham's Vow

In his self-initiated and conditional war vow, Abraham said, "I raised my hand to the Lord..."[a] According to J. Schneider, "In swearing the hand was lifted up to heaven, hence 'to lift up the hand' means 'to give a sworn assurance...'"[b/180] To Westermann, Abraham's vow was "a solemn oath,"[181] a serious and formal contract with YHWH.[182] Abraham's tithe to Melchizedek was a gift to El Elyôn/YHWH and his sanctuary in Salem, commemorating how the deity had assisted him in the rescue of Lot and his allies. I will now address the following six aspects of Abraham's war vow: (1) self-initiated; (2) conditional; (3) self-denying; (4) pre-battle; (5) bargain for victory and (6) commemorative.

Self-initiated

Abraham took the initiative to make a bargain with YHWH. The verb in his statement, "I have sworn..."[c] has a *hiphil* stem.[183] This indicates the verb is causative:[184] the subject of the sentence is the one who causes or initiates the action. In other words, the Lord did not command Abraham to promise to give Melchizedek a tenth of the war spoils if he helped him to rescue Lot;[d] neither did the Lord instruct the patriarch to refuse to take any of the vassal coalition's recovered goods, people or any of the plunder. The bargain was not God's idea; it was Abraham's.

Conditional

Abraham's bargain with God was also conditional. C. Westermann points out that the stem of the Hebrew word translated "sworn,"[e] which is comprised of the Hebrew consonants *aleph* and *samech*, "indicates the conditioned self-cursing: may this and this happen to me if [I do not fulfill my part

---

[a] Genesis 14:22b, NET
[b] Compare Deuteronomy 32:40, NASB.
[c] Genesis 14:22, NASB
[d] Later in this chapter see, "Abraham's Tithe of War Spoils to Melchizedek" under "The Threefold Fulfillment of Abraham's Vow."
[e] Genesis 14:22, NASB

of the vow]..."[185] J. Kohlenberger agrees; he translates the patriarch's vow as, "May God punish me *if* I accept anything from you."[a/186] B. Davidson also concurs; to him the stem can mean "to bind an oath upon oneself, that is, bind oneself by an oath."[187] In other words, if YHWH fulfilled his end of the bargain, but Abraham failed to keep his part, then the patriarch invited God to curse him.[b/188] Since Abraham's self-curse was not based on a divine command, it was different from the curse with which Malachi threatened the Judeans during the Second Temple period for not bringing their full tithes and offerings into the Jerusalem temple.[c]

Self-denying

Abraham's war vow was one of self-denial. The patriarch told Bera, "...I will accept nothing belonging to you, not even a thread or the strap of a sandal, so that you will never be able to say, 'I made Abram rich.'"[d] Abraham's war contract re-affirmed his sole dependence upon God,[e/189] keeping him, and YHWH's reputation, free from obligation to any Canaanite king,[f] a situation in which the patriarch found himself more than once.[g] To take even the smallest compensation in footwear or clothing would have been contrary to the patriarch's vow.[h] According to G. Davies, Abraham was to "...gain no advantage of spoil or renown from the battle..."[190]

---

[a] Genesis 14:22-23 (emphasis Kohlenberger)
[b] Even if Abraham had failed to fulfill his war vow, it is doubtful that YHWH would have cursed the patriarch since the text frequently grants the patriarchs preferential treatment despite their moral failings. When Abraham told Sarah to lie to protect himself, he sold his wife into Pharaoh's harem for a profitable price (Genesis 12:15-16). Compare 26:9-14. Compare also 25:29-34 and 27:18-42 with 33:4,12,15.

Ironically, in Genesis 15:1-21 (especially verses 10,12,17-21), it is God who puts himself under a self-curse, if he does not fulfill his promise to Abraham and his descendants. See the critical commentaries.
[c] Malachi 3:9
[d] Genesis 14:23, NIV
[e] Compare Genesis 15:1c; 22:8,14.
[f] Compare Chapter 5.
[g] Genesis 12:10-20. Compare 20:1-18 with 21:22-34.
[h] Genesis 14:23a, NIV

Pre-Battle

Ancient war vows were bargains combatants made with their gods before battle, which attempted to influence the outcome in their favor. Prior to war, soldiers and commanders also frequently offered animal sacrifices to their deities to obtain their assistance. Even though the text does not mention Abraham's war vow until he informs the king of Sodom of it after the fact,[a] we can safely assume Abraham made his vow before he pursued the Elamite coalition for several reasons. First, after his rescue of Lot, Abraham refused Bera's offer due to his vow of self-denial. The only way such a vow could make sense would be if the patriarch had made it with YHWH before (or during) the battle. Matthews and Benjamin explain: "Before going into battle, warriors in the world of the Bible vowed all or a portion of their anticipated prisoners and plunder to Yahweh Sabbaoth."[191] S. Niditch agrees: "The warriors promise the deity something of value in return for his assistance in war."[192] Second, the Hebrew verb in Abraham's statement, "I raised my hand to the Lord..."[b] (*rum yad*) is in the perfect state, which, in this context, indicates a completed action.[c/193] It is evident the patriarch made his vow before he spoke with Bera, and the most logical moment would have been before the patriarch went to war. Finally, the idea Abraham made his war vow before his battle with the Elamite coalition fits the context of other Old Testament war vows, which were made before the enemy was engaged.[d/194] For Abraham to have made a vow after the battle would be inconsistent with the military context of ancient war vows.

---

[a] Genesis 14:22-24
[b] Genesis 14:22b, NET
[c] Some modern paraphrases of the Bible, however, do not keep the verb's perfect or past state in mind when they translate the Hebrew verb. See Genesis 14:22 in *The New Living Translation* and *The Message*.
[d] Compare Mizpah (Judges 11:30-33) and Hormah (Numbers 21:1-3). Compare Jericho (Joshua 6:19,24).

Bargain for Victory

Abraham's war vow was similar to other Old Testament war vows. At Mizpah, Jephthah, an Israelite military leader in the time of the Judges, made a war vow to motivate God to give him victory over the Ammonites.[a/195] He bargained, "If You will indeed give the sons of Ammon into my hand, then it shall be that whatever [or "whoever" [196]] comes out of the doors of my house to meet me when I return in peace from the sons of Ammon, it shall be the Lord's, and I will offer it up as a burnt offering."[b] Unfortunately, the first thing or person to come out of the doors of his house to greet Jephthah after his victory was his daughter.[c] According to J. Schofield, Jephthah "...vows to make a human sacrifice to the Lord as an incentive to the Lord to give him victory."[d/197] Such a notion may seem repugnant, but we dare not read modern sentiments into Scripture lest we distort the text. At Hormah, the Israelites made a war vow to persuade God to give them the victory over the Canaanite king of Arad,[e] who had kidnapped some of their relatives.[f] Israel bargained, "If You will indeed deliver this people into my hand, then I will utterly destroy their cities."[g] The text continues: "The Lord heard the voice of Israel and delivered up the Canaanites; then they utterly destroyed them and their cities. Thus the name of the place was called Hormah ['devotion'[198]]."[h/199]

Although not identical, Abraham's war vow is also similar to the war vow of *h'erem* (the ban) Israel made before the battle of Jericho in that both involved a promise of self-denial. According to N. Fox, whenever Israel vowed to put an enemy under the ban, it meant for their total destruction "with the booty dedicated to the sanctuary."[200] In Joshua 6:1-5, it was not God but Joshua who

---

[a] Judges 11:29-40, especially verses 30-31
[b] Judges 11:30-31, NASB
[c] Judges 11:39
[d] We observe this same phenomenon with Mesha, king of Moab (2 Kings 3:26-27), Ahaz, king of Judah (16:3) and possibly Hiel, a resident of Bethel (I Kings 16:34).
[e] Arad was a village in the southern Negeb of Judah.
[f] Numbers 21:1-2
[g] Numbers 21:2, NASB
[h] Numbers 21:3, NASB

put Jericho under the ban.[a] To influence God to help Israel,[b] he declared, "all the silver and gold and articles of bronze and iron are holy to the Lord; they shall go into the treasury of the Lord."[c] To M. Coogan, the purpose of Joshua chapter 6 is "to describe for its Israelite audience the ideal conduct of war."[201] J. Wevers explains how Israel used the ban in an effort to obtain divine favor for battle:

"In special cases no spoil might be taken. Prior to an assault a city or tribe might be 'devoted' to God. Such a vow meant everything animate was to be destroyed, all precious metals and objects given to God, and the remainder, including the city with its dwellings and surrounding fields, burned or otherwise made useless. Jericho was placed under the ban, devoted to destruction, at the time of the Conquest.[d/202] ...Since war was believed to be a sacred duty, divine favor might be assured by declaring the *h'erem*, a pact with the deity by which everything animate was devoted for destruction. Breaking such a promise was a major sacrilege and might involve defeat, as in the story of Achan."[e/203]

When Abraham made his war bargain, he did not promise to destroy all that belonged to the Elamite coalition. He did, however, vow to put the plunder, along with the recovered goods and people, under a self-imposed ban, which disallowed him any personal benefit from his defeat of Chedorlaomer's forces.

Commemorative

Abraham's tithe of war spoils to the Salem sanctuary was a spontaneous votive offering, which commemorated El-Elyôn/YHWH's victory over the Elamite coalition.[f] Votive offerings were payments made to deities after they answered

---

[a] Joshua 6:1-16,20. Concerning divine judgment, contrast 7:1,10-26.
[b] Joshua 6:17-19, 24
[c] Joshua 6:19, NASB. Compare verse 24.
[d] Joshua 6:17-19 (per Wevers)
[e] Joshua 7:1-26 (per Wevers)
[f] Genesis 14:20a,b

their suppliants' prayers for assistance. The patriarch's commemorative tithe is similar to the offering of Midianite plunder made by the officers of Israel's army in Moses' day. They brought their war spoil offerings to the Lord at the tent of meeting, and the offerings consisted of "articles of gold, armlets and bracelets, signet rings, earrings and necklaces...all kinds of wrought articles."[a] Moses and Eleazar, the high priest, received the plunder from the military leaders and then "brought it to the tent of meeting as a memorial for the sons of Israel before the Lord."[b] In the opinion of T. Fretheim, Moses and Eleazar used the many metallic articles from the spoils to manufacture and decorate the furnishings of the tabernacle.[204] To Fox, the gold was used in the tabernacle as a "continual ritual reminder..."[205] of YHWH's victory over Midian, during which no Israelite soldier was killed.[c]

According to S. Eitrem and J. Croon, votive offerings were normally gifts made to divine beings and were of a "permanent character;"[206] they were normally not sacrifices that were consumed.[207] They explain: "...the object dedicated is not destroyed; it remains as a perpetual glory to the dedicant, and more specifically to his community..."[208] According to these scholars, "For the gods they may mean an increase of their authority: the gift and its publicity 'magnify' the gods, at the same time intensifying the feeling of connexion [connection] and sympathy on both sides."[209] One of the earliest meanings of the word "glory"[210] (*kabod*) was "weight and substance;"[211] it was often associated with the visible wealth and power of palaces and temples.[d] Thus, when we view Genesis chapter 14 as a seamless narrative, the war plunder Abraham donated to the Salem sanctuary became a permanent symbol of liberation from Chedorlaomer and a perpetual glory to El-Elyôn/YHWH, which did not commemorate a regular practice of the patriarch but Abraham's one-time rescue of his nephew.

---

[a] Numbers 31:50-51, NASB
[b] Numbers 31:54, NASB. Compare Exodus 30:16.
[c] Numbers 31:48-49
[d] Haggai 2:3,7,9; Zechariah 2:8; 12:7

The Threefold Fulfillment of Abraham's Vow

If we view the story of Abraham's war vow and tithe as not containing any later additions, the narrative presents readers with three ways in which the patriarch fulfilled his promise of self-denial. They are: (1) his tithe of war spoils to Melchizedek; (2) his return of stolen goods and people to Bera and (3) his distribution of the recovered food supplies to his trained men and the remainder of the plunder to his Amorite allies. I will now look at each of these more closely.

Abraham's Tithe of War Spoils to Melchizedek

It is possible the narrator desired his audience to view Abraham's tithe to Melchizedek as the first way the patriarch fulfilled his war vow. If correct, even though Abraham did not promise YHWH a tenth of the war spoils, when approached by Melchizedek with treaty gifts, he made a spontaneous, on-the-spot decision to part with a tithe of the enemy plunder, which he, by custom, deserved to keep.[212] Such a view of Abraham's tithe is similar to the numerous votive war tithes made by soldiers and commanders in the ancient world. We find votive war tithes in Egypt[213] as well as in Persia.[214] In Greece, along with other examples,[215] was a military commander whose name was Cyrus, who, probably in the middle of a military crisis,[216] persuaded his soldiers to promise a tenth of the plunder to Zeus, if he would help them win the battle.[217] In Rome, victorious commanders often set aside a tenth of the war spoils to make images, statues or flasks for the temples of the gods for whom they fought.[218]

According to W. R. Smith, "...in old times, the spoils of war were chief sources of votive offerings."[219] We observe such war vows in the ancient Near East,[220] the Greco-Roman period[221] as well as in modern Arabia and other Islamic nations.[222] In addition to donating plunder like shields, weapons and chariots, those making war bargains with their gods would promise to give to their temples items such as statues, clothing for idols, images, thrones, mangers, crowns, offerings, sacrifices, colonnades, inscriptions, golden animals and temple pillars.[223] Those with greater means might promise to build entire temples,[a] construct new altars or dedicate athletic games to the gods who answered their prayers.[224]

War spoils were also common votive offerings in Israel.[b/225] According to J. Milgrom, many of the voluntary votive offerings, which the Israelites donated to the sanctuary priests in Leviticus 27:1-13,[c] consisted of the spoils of war. He concludes this on account of their similarities to the mandatory war offerings levied in Numbers chapter 31.[d/226] To him, "Historical sources also attest that captured vessels were dedicated to the Temple,[e] including precious weapons."[f/227] David, for example, donated his enemy plunder to the Jerusalem temple; he took "the shields of gold which were carried by the servants of Hadadezer [king of Aramea] and brought them to Jerusalem."[g] David also dedicated some of the "silver and gold...from all the nations which he had subdued,"[h] that is, from Aram, Moab, Ammon, Philistia, Edom and Zobah.[i] We assume most of the war spoils David donated to the temple were votive offerings, since the king attributed his military victories to the Lord.[j] There are many references to votive offerings in the Psalms,[k/228] a book which contains many songs composed by the king. Wevers writes, "In temple times

---

[a] Compare the second promise in Jacob's journey vow (Genesis 28:22a,b,c).
[b] Compare Micah 4:13; Isaiah 60:9; Haggai 2:7-9.
[c] Contrast "vow" (Leviticus 27:2) with "tax" and "levy" (Numbers 31:28,37,38,39,40,41).
[d] Compare: people (Leviticus 27:2-8; Numbers 31:26,28,29,35,40,46,47); women (Numbers 31:17b; note virgins in verse 35); male children (Numbers 31:17a); animals (Leviticus 27:9-13; Numbers 31:26,28,30,32-34,36-39,43-45) and precious metals (Numbers 31:22,50). In Leviticus chapter 27, the offering of houses (verses 14-15) and lands (verses 16-25) reflect a sedentary life.
[e] 2 Samuel 8:9-12; I Kings 7:51; 15:15; I Chronicles 18:9-11; 26:26-28
[f] 2 Samuel 8:7; I Kings 14:25-28; 2 Kings 11:10 (per Milgrom).
[g] 2 Samuel 8:7 = I Chronicles 18:7, NASB. See also 2 Kings 11:10, NASB. Compare I Samuel 21:9; 22:10.
[h] 2 Samuel 8:11, NASB
[i] 2 Samuel 8:12, NASB
[j] Compare I Samuel 17:37, 46-47.
[k] Psalms 56:12-13; 22:25; 50:14; 61:5,8; 65:1; 66:13-15; 116:14,18-19

parts of the spoil won in battle were dedicated 'for the maintenance of the house of the Lord'..."ª/²²⁹ According to K. Van Der Toorn, vows "that had been made far away from the temple were none the less valid...when the god had provided a way out of trouble, the vows were to be paid in the sanctuary..."²³⁰ The collection of war vow payments was one of the ways ancient temples, including the one in Jerusalem, accumulated wealth and became prime targets for thieves and enemy kings.[b]

Even though Abraham's war vow did not specifically include the promise of a tithe to a sanctuary,[c] we can safely assume when the patriarch gave a tithe to Melchizedek, he gave it to the one in Salem,[d] since Melchizedek was not only the king of the city,[e] but also, according to Hebrews, the high priest of its temple.[f] With his tithe of war spoils, the patriarch acknowledged "the true hero of the victorious campaign" was not himself "but the Lord."²³¹ This is not to say, however, that Abraham was a member of the Salem sanctuary or needed to pay tithes to a temple or high priest as part of his worship of YHWH. To some scholars, the main purpose of Abraham's tithe to the Salem sanctuary was to legitimate, many centuries later, the paying of tithes to the Jerusalem temple.[g]/²³²

Abraham's Return of Stolen Goods and People to Bera

Abraham also fulfilled his war vow by returning to Bera all that Chedorlaomer's forces had stolen.[h] Speaking of the armies of the Elamite coalition, the text states, "...they took all the goods of Sodom and Gomorrah and all their food supply..."[i] and of Abraham it says he "...brought back all the goods, and also brought back his relative Lot with his possessions, and also the women, and the people."[j] As previously noted, all the recovered goods and

---

[a] I Chronicles 26:27, NRSV
[b] Compare 2 Samuel 8:9-12.
[c] Genesis 14:19-24
[d] Salem was later Jerusalem (Psalm 76:2).
[e] Genesis 14:18a
[f] Compare Hebrews 5:10; 6:20; 7:1.

[g] Salem = Zion/Jerusalem (Psalm 76:2).
[h] Genesis 14:22-23. Compare verses 11,16.
[i] Genesis 14:11, NASB
[j] Genesis 14:16, NASB

people belonged to Abraham as the victorious chieftain, but instead of keeping them, he returned them to Bera, the head of the vassal coalition, to honor his war vow.

Abraham's Distribution of Food and Plunder to his Men and Allies

The final way the patriarch honored his war vow of self-denial was in the first and second exceptions he gave to Bera, which involved food and plunder. When the patriarch defined these exceptions, he exercised his right to do whatever he wanted with them. He allowed his trained men[a] to eat some of Sodom and Gomorrah's recovered food supplies[b] and he allowed his three Amorite allies (Aner, Eshcol and Mamre) to "take their share"[c] of the spoil. Consequently, Abraham did not personally profit from his rescue of Lot. Instead, he fulfilled his war vow of self-denial by giving away to others what he, by custom, had the right to retain.

Conclusion

No tithe advocate I have read mentions the fact that Abraham's tithe appears in the same historical context as his war vow. This oversight is not without significance. Even though the text does not say Abraham vowed a tithe to Melchizedek before he rescued Lot, when we view Genesis chapter 14 as a seamless narrative, the patriarch's tithe appears in the story as the first way in which he fulfilled his war vow of self-denial. As such, Abraham's tithe functioned as a votive offering, which he was not obliged to pay, unless God first answered his prayer for a safe rescue of his nephew. Thus, we observe that both occurrences of the tithe before the Law, Abraham's tithe to

---

[a] Genesis 14:24a. I understand the "young men" in verse 24 to be Abraham's 318 trained servants mentioned in verse 14. The reference might also refer to some of the males rescued from the Elamite coalition.
[b] Genesis 14:11,24
[c] Genesis 14:24, NASB

Melchizedek as well as Jacob's tithe vow at Bethel,[a] involved conditional promises and had nothing to do with the regular or mandatory payment of tithes.

---

[a] Genesis 28:20-22. See Chapter 14.

5

A Treaty Between Equals

Of the four main treaty types in the ancient Near East,[233] suzerainty and parity are the most relevant to our study. A suzerainty treaty was one in which a superior party, the overlord or suzerain, agreed to provide military protection to an inferior party, the vassal. In exchange for crops, soldiers and/or taxes, which sometimes were collected in the form of tithes and might involve a vassal's pledge of loyalty to his overlord's god, a vassal expected to receive his suzerain's help whenever threatened by an enemy. If the agreement between Abraham and Melchizedek was a suzerainty treaty, then Abraham's tithe to Melchizedek was one of many regular payments to the king of Salem in exchange for his protection. In contrast, in a parity treaty, both parties were equal; neither was superior to the other. I submit parity best describes the treaty Abraham and Melchizedek made in Genesis 14:18-20. If correct, then Abraham's tithe to the king of Salem was a one-time treaty gift, which sealed their peace alliance.

In this chapter, I address two claims, both of which give the impression Abraham's tithe to Melchizedek was a suzerainty payment. Tithe advocates do not use the technical terms "parity" or "suzerainty," but when they teach that Christians should follow the example of Abraham's tithe to Melchizedek, they describe the general characteristics of a suzerainty treaty. To them, Abraham tithed to Melchizedek to receive his protection, and, likewise, Christians need to tithe to receive God's protection. I will now challenge both of these assumptions and present evidence from the text, which demonstrates that the Abraham and Melchizedek treaty was not one of suzerainty but one of equality. Here is the first claim:

- "Abram initiated the tithe to King Melchizedek. The tithe will protect you financially."[234]

This pro-tither asserts Abraham gave his tithe to Melchizedek without any suggestion or prior initiation from the king. He infers Christians should be pro-active in their payment of tithes. It is accurate to say Melchizedek did not ask Abraham for a tithe of the war spoils. It is false, however, to say or imply the patriarch initiated his tithe to Melchizedek without any prior action on the part of the king. According to the story, Melchizedek was the one who took the initiative to form a treaty with Abraham when he first offered the patriarch gifts of bread and wine.[a] According to the text, Abraham responded with a tithe of enemy plunder only after Melchizedek offered him food and drink.[b]

Another way this tithe advocate implies Abraham's tithe was a suzerainty payment is in the way he capitalizes the word "King."[235] Such an emphasis suggests Melchizedek was not only the king to which the patriarch willingly paid a tithe but he was Jesus; in both instances, indicating Abraham's inferiority.[c]

The second sentence in the above claim insinuates Abraham gave a tithe to Melchizedek to obtain the king's financial protection. Unfortunately, its wording is muddled because the subject of the first sentence is "Abram" while the subject of the next sentence is the tithe and is directed toward readers. Even though this pro-tither did not write, "Abraham tithed to Melchizedek to obtain the ruler's financial protection," he certainly suggests it. In my view, when he writes, "The tithe will

---

[a] Genesis 14:18, NASB
[b] Genesis 14:20c
[c] I address the question as to whether Melchizedek was

Jesus in Book 4 of *The Tithing Series*.

protect you financially,"²³⁶ he wants his readers to conclude they need to tithe to obtain the same protection from God as he implies Abraham received from Melchizedek. Such a claim remains unconvincing for the following reasons:

First, the benefit to a vassal for forming an alliance with a suzerain was not financial assistance. According to T. Mafico, "in return for their loyalty and tribute," ²³⁷ often in the form of crops, soldiers and/or taxes, suzerains agreed to provide their vassals with armed forces. The text, however, does not indicate Abraham exchanged his tithe for Melchizedek's military protection. The patriarch did not give any crops, soldiers and/or taxes to the king in return for a promise of safekeeping. His tithe to Melchizedek was not a seasonal crop tithe; it was a one-time, ad hoc treaty gift of recent war spoils.

Second, in the story of Abraham's rescue of Lot, the patriarch was the one who functioned as the suzerain, since he was the one who defeated the Elamite coalition,[a] an enemy Bera and his allies could not defeat. Thus, if either party could have offered the other military protection, it would have been Abraham who could have offered Melchizedek and his allies such a service not vice versa.

Third, Abraham was a rich chieftain[b] who did not need Melchizedek's financial protection. God blessed the patriarch financially before he gave a tithe.[c] If Abraham had needed Melchizedek's financial protection, it would not make sense for him to have made a war vow, which, in the end, left him nothing.[d] The patriarch's vow makes it clear he did not seek to be enriched by any Canaanite king. Genesis 15:1 states YHWH himself was Abraham's "shield."[e] According to J. Kohlenberger, the word "shield" in this verse means "sovereign."²³⁸ As a king would protect and provide for his subjects, even so YHWH, Abraham's sovereign, would do the same for the patriarch.²³⁹ Even though Westermann views Genesis 15:1 as "a stylized formula,"²⁴⁰ there

---

[a] Genesis 14:15-16
[b] See Chapter 11.
[c] Genesis 12:16,20
[d] Genesis 14:22-24

[e] Genesis 15:1, NASB, KJV, NKJV, NIV, ESV. NLT says, "I will protect you."

is a theological connection between YHWH being Abraham's "shield"[a] and the patriarch's refusal to look to Melchizedek, or his ally, Bera,[b] for financial protection.

Lastly, there is no evidence in the New Testament upholding the idea that tithing financially protects Christians.[c]

Another tithe advocate claims Abraham lived under a kind of suzerainty treaty with Melchizedek, in which the patriarch was the inferior party. He writes:

- "...Abram was not a lone ecclesiastical agent. He was under ecclesiastical authority. The mark of his subordination was his payment of a tithe to Melchizedek, the king-priest of Salem..."[241]

According to this assertion, Abraham demonstrated his submission to the priestly authority of Melchizedek by paying him a tithe of war spoils.[242] It is true Abraham donated a tithe of the Elamite coalition's war plunder to him, who, in turn, probably donated it to the Salem temple to commemorate El-Elyôn's victory over Chedorlaomer's deity, Napirisa.[243] Nevertheless, this claim is seriously flawed for the following reasons:

First, it is correct to say that Hebrews describes Abraham's tithe to Melchizedek as a sign of the patriarch's inferiority when it says, "the lesser is blessed by the greater."[d] However, the writer does not describe Abraham as the inferior party in a suzerainty treaty, in which he owes the king regular tithes. Instead, he calls him "the lesser"[e] in comparison to Melchizedek as a type of Christ.[f] Some may argue Abraham gave a tithe to Melchizedek because he viewed him as a literal manifestation of Jesus.[g] No matter how edifying such a thought might be, the text gives no indication Abraham saw Melchizedek as a messianic or futuristic

---

[a] Genesis 15:1, NASB
[b] Genesis 14:21-24
[c] See Book 4 in *The Tithing Series*.
[d] Hebrews 7:7b, NASB
[e] Hebrews 7:7b, NASB
[f] Note "like" in Hebrews 7:3 and "likeness" in verse 15 (NASB).
[g] Compare Hebrews 7:8.

figure. The point of Hebrews chapter 7 is that the Levitical priesthood is now inferior to Christ's priesthood.[a] Since God changed the priesthood, the Levites no longer have a right to use the Law to collect tithes from the people.[b] Second, if Abraham had lived under Melchizedek's "ecclesiastical authority,"[244] he would not only have been a member of El-Elyôn's temple, over which Melchizedek ruled as king-priest, but also a citizen of Salem, since there was no real separation in Abraham's day between "church" and "state." As such, he would have submitted himself and his household to the political and religious jurisdiction of Melchizedek. The patriarch would not have been a free man in direct and immediate relationship with YHWH; he could not have followed YHWH wherever he led him. At least by implication, if Abraham had been an "ecclesiastical agent"[245] of Melchizedek, not only would the patriarch have had to obtain Melchizedek's permission for all things religious, he would have had to worship El-Elyôn, the chief god of the Canaanite pantheon, whose name or title was gradually adopted into Israelite religion as a description of YHWH.[246] After Melchizedek praised his god, El-Elyôn, for giving Abraham the victory, the patriarch gave the king a tithe of plunder without linking El-Elyôn's name to YHWH's,[c] something he did with Bera later in the story.[d] Even though C. Hayes disagrees,[247] such acknowledgement does not automatically mean Abraham worshipped El-Elyôn.

Since faiths were more fluid in the patriarchal days and the patriarch's intention was to form a peace treaty with the Canaanite king, Abraham used the gift of a tithe to cement an agreement with him in the presence of his new ally's god, El-Elyôn. According to A. Kirk Grayson, ancient treaty making did not always require the vanquished to abandon their god(s) and serve the god(s) of the victor.[248] Westermann addresses the theological awkwardness of this polytheistic context in this way:

---

[a] Hebrews 7:11-28
[b] Hebrews 7:5; 11-12; 18-19
[c] Genesis 14:18-20
[d] Genesis 14:22. "Lord" = YHWH.

"The purpose is to designate the god of a Canaanite shrine, but at the same time to speak of him in such a way that Abraham can acknowledge him."[249]

Lastly, this claim is an example of eisegesis; the pro-tither reads into the text his own notion of church, an entity which did not exist in Abraham's day. The word "ecclesiastical" comes from the Greek word, *ecclesia*, which is translated "church." In the New Testament, *ecclesia* refers to an "assembly"[250] or "community of believers...gathered by God through Christ"[251] from all ethnicities. In the Old Testament, *ecclesia* translates the Hebrew *qahal*[252] and means a "meeting or gathering"[253] for various purposes. *qahal* is not used in Genesis chapter 14. To assert Abraham was under Melchizedek's "ecclesiastical authority,"[254] and he functioned as Melchizedek's "ecclesiastical agent,"[255] lacks textual support and falls under the fallacy of anachronism, which, according to D. Fischer, "consists in the description, analysis, or judgment of an event as if it occurred at some point in time other than when it actually happened."[256]

The idea that Abraham's tithe was "the mark of his subordination"[257] to Melchizedek, implies, at least, Abraham was Melchizedek's vassal. There are, however, several problems with this view as well.

First, to view Abraham's tithe as a "mark of his subordination"[258] to an ancient Canaanite ruler implies YHWH commanded Abraham to submit to Melchizedek's authority and pay him a tithe. There is no biblical proof for such a claim. Furthermore, Abraham's tithe was not a regular payment. He gave it only because of a unique set of circumstances, which, according to the text, never happened again. This fact indicates Abraham had no former or ongoing tithe obligation to the king.

Second, treaty banquets, such as the one Melchizedek initiated with Abraham, did not always indicate the formation of suzerainty treaties; they were also used to seal parity treaties.[a/259]

Third, self-curses were an important part of ancient suzerainty

---

[a] Compare Genesis 26:30-31.

treaties.[260] The weight of such curses fell more upon disobedient vassals than on negligent suzerains. A suzerain retained the right to reprove a vassal for any betrayal of their covenant,[a] which was, little doubt, why Chedorlaomer, the former overlord of the vassal coalition, punished the Cities of the Plain for declaring their independence.[b] According to the text, neither Abraham nor Melchizedek made a self-curse as a part of their treaty. The only self-curse in the story is the one inherent in the war vow Abraham made exclusively with YHWH.[c/261] With this, the narrator probably wanted to convey that YHWH was Abraham's only overlord - not Bera, Melchizedek or any other Canaanite king.[262]

Finally, when Bera tried to negotiate with Abraham over the recovered goods and people,[d] the patriarch did not submit to his request.[e] According to G. Mendenhall, "In suzerainty covenants, a superior binds an inferior to obligations defined by the superior."[f/263] If the tithe Abraham gave to Melchizedek indicated the formation of a suzerainty treaty in which he was the inferior party, and if Melchizedek was an ally of Bera, which the text seems to indicate,[g] aside from his war vow, I submit that Abraham would have been more cooperative with Bera's offer and would have allowed him to define the distribution of plunder.

Since the recovered goods and people belonged to Abraham as victor,[264] if he would have complied with Bera's request, it would have given leverage to the king of Sodom and his partners, with which they could have treated Abraham as a dependent or inferior. C. Westermann agrees: "...some sort of obligation would follow from this, which he rejects."[265] To prevent being put into a vassal-like position of obligation, Abraham informed Bera he was obligated to honor the war vow he previously made to YHWH and not take any of the recovered goods or people for himself.[h] In his vow, Abraham denied himself even the smallest part of the

---

[a] Genesis 14:5-7,11 12. Compare 2 Kings 3:4-9.
[b] Genesis 14:4
[c] Genesis 14:22
[d] Genesis 14:21
[e] Genesis 14:21-24
[f] Ezekiel 17:13. Compare 2 Kings 24:17.
[g] Compare Genesis 14:17,18a,21a.
[h] Genesis 14:22-24

plunder. He told Bera, "I will take nothing, from a thread to a sandal strap...lest you should say, 'I have made Abram rich...'"[a] The patriarch did not want to place himself in a position of financial dependence. According to V. Matthews and D. Benjamin: "He keeps nothing for himself. Abram is a client [vassal] of the God Most High; to accept goods or land from Sodom would create a conflict of interest and make him a client of Sodom. Yahweh, the God Most High, alone provides Abraham with goods and land."[266]

When Abraham declined to divide the recovered goods and people according to Bera's suggestion, he maintained his independence from him and the rest of the vassal coalition, which included Melchizedek. Abraham was a free man under YHWH, and he planned to keep it that way. According to O. Procksch, "...the pride of a free man is speaking..."[267] According to M. Barré, when Abraham maintained his independence from Bera, he "...created a state of amicable relations between the contracting parties...[that] translated into mutual nonaggression and agreement on respective spheres of influence."[268] Abraham's assertion of independence from Bera implies he maintained the same independence when he made a parity treaty with his ally, Melchizedek. YHWH alone was Abraham's suzerain or overlord; the patriarch was no man's vassal.[b]

Abraham and Suzerainty Treaties

Abraham's refusal to form a suzerainty treaty with Melchizedek or Bera was probably because he had learned a lesson about how to deal with local rulers when he previously lived for a while in Egypt. Speaking of Abraham's experience there, Clifford and Murphy write: "He learns a hard lesson from his encounter with Pharaoh (12:10-13:1); only God can enrich him."[c/269]

Another example of Abraham learning through experience that God did not want him to become obligated to local rulers was

---

[a] Genesis 14:23, NKJV. The NKJV italicizes "will" "take" and "is."

[b] Genesis 14:23
[c] "12:10-13:1" = Genesis 12:10–13:1

his interaction with Abimelech, king of Gerar.[a] At Beersheba, Abraham confronted the king about how some of his servants had plugged up one of his wells. In Abimelech's reply, the ruler partially blamed the patriarch for the incident, when he said: "I do not know who has done this; you did not tell me, and I have not heard of it until today."[b] According to Westermann, the king was clearly being "evasive..."[270]

Such a slippery response on the part of Abimelech, however, should not surprise readers. Abraham had previously deceived Abimelech by telling him a half-truth about his wife, Sarah.[c] Abraham and Sarah's deception caused God to threaten the life of the king and his family,[d] sending barrenness to his wife and concubines.[e] In the end, in spite of both being "partners in crime,"[f] the king sent Abraham and Sarah out of his house with many undeserved gifts (animals,[g] slaves,[h] "freedom of movement throughout the land"[i/271] and one thousand pieces of silver,[j] which was, "a fabulously large sum"[272]). When Abraham confronted Abimelech about his stolen well, it appears the king expected him to return the favor he had previously given to the patriarch by allowing his men to take the well without objection. Such an expectation is evident in what the king told Abraham: "...swear to me here by God that you will not deal falsely with me or with my offspring or with my posterity, but according to the kindness that I have shown to you, you shall show to me and to the land in which you have sojourned."[k] In response, Abraham said, "I swear it,"[l] and so sealed their parity treaty.

Little doubt, Abraham felt the king's pressure to acknowledge he owed him a big favor relative to the release of his wife, Sarah. To prevent himself from becoming any more indebted to Abimelech, however, he "shrewdly maneuvers him to

---

[a] Compare Genesis 20:14-16 with 21:22-32.
[b] Genesis 21:26, NRSV
[c] Genesis 20:2,12
[d] Genesis 20:3,7
[e] Genesis 20:17-18
[f] Genesis 20:2,5
[g] Genesis 20:14
[h] Genesis 20:14
[i] Genesis 20:15
[j] Genesis 20:16
[k] Genesis 21:23, NASB
[l] Genesis 21:24, NASB

acknowledge his right of possession"[273] by purchasing his own well back from the king with a payment from his flock.[a] Abraham's hard lesson was that he should allow his riches to come from God alone and not from a Canaanite king, lest he find himself obligated and open to future manipulation.[b]

The patriarch's formation of a parity treaty with Abimelech is consistent with the one he made with Melchizedek. In the former, both parties exchanged oaths,[c] which is one of the signs of a covenant between equals; in the latter, both parties exchanged gifts, which functioned as a verbal commitment between them.[d]

Abraham's parity treaty with Abimelech is also consistent with Isaac's parity treaty with the king, in which there was also a mutual exchange of oaths.[e] According to Matthews, Isaac formed a "parity treaty"[274] with Abimelech that granted him "grazing rights and the use of wells within his territory."[275] In spite of Isaac's treaty with the king, however, local herdsmen from Gerar continued to quarrel with his herdsmen over water rights.[f] With each dispute, Isaac moved to another location instead of creating conflict,[g] a response that mirrored his own father's peaceful approach to inheriting the land. He did this not because he was the inferior vassal to Abimelech; the text makes it clear YHWH blessed Isaac[h] so much that it was out of envy that the king asked him to leave the city.[i] In the end, it was YHWH who led him to a place where he could finally settle down in peace and continue to prosper.[j]

Both Abraham and Isaac made parity treaties with Canaanite kings. Though they showed respect to local rulers, they did not unnecessarily subject themselves to their claims, authority or manipulations. As Abraham and his son sojourned in the land their descendants were going to inherit, they did not embroil themselves in suzerainty treaties, which might have compromised their walk with YHWH and the faith of future generations.

---

[a] Genesis 21:28-32
[b] Compare Genesis 26:29.
[c] Genesis 21:23,24,27,31,32a
[d] See Chapter 6.
[e] Genesis 26:31
[f] Genesis 26:18-21
[g] Genesis 26:17,21,22
[h] Genesis 26:12-14
[i] Genesis 26:14,16
[j] Genesis 26:22,25

Conclusion

In this chapter, I demonstrated that the Abraham-Melchizedek treaty was a parity agreement between equals and not one of suzerainty, in which Abraham was the inferior party. This is a significant point in the discussion of mandatory tithes. Since Abraham's tithe to Melchizedek was not a compulsory payment of crops, soldiers and/or taxes to obtain or maintain the military or financial protection of an overlord, pro-tithers have no hermeneutical basis to use it to collect regular or obligatory tithes from Christians. Similarly, the idea that tithing brought Abraham financial protection, and that it will do the same for Christians, finds no basis in the text and is contrary to the New covenant.

6
A Gift Exchange

Genesis chapter 14 reflects the gradual fulfilling of YHWH's land promises to Abraham and his descendants through the patriarch's ability to keep commitments to family members and forge new ones with local rulers. Consequently, Abraham's tithe to Melchizedek is only a small part of this much larger story and should not be viewed as the main focus of the chapter. V. Matthews and D. Benjamin explain: "The story of Abram and Lot is an ancestor story which celebrates the household of Abram and Sarah for knowing not only how to make covenants but also how to keep them...[It] celebrates Abram for fulfilling his covenant with Lot and for making a new covenant with Melchizedek."[276] In this chapter, we see Abraham as a peacemaker, treaty maker and treaty keeper, whose tithe to Melchizedek was a one-time treaty gift.

Peacemaker

Abraham was a man of peace, whether it was with kin or local kings. When he made a treaty with his nephew, Lot, to prevent their respective herdsmen from quarreling over land and water rights,[a/277] he told his nephew, "Please let there be no strife between you and me, nor between my herdsmen and your herdsmen, for we are brothers."[b] In these words, we hear the

---

[a] Genesis 13:8-12   [b] Genesis 13:8, NASB

patriarch's heart for peaceful relationships. When Abraham knew he was going to have to separate from Lot, he kindly allowed him to have first pick of the land.[a]

Since Abraham was a peacemaker, not a man of war, it may seem surprising when he appears in Genesis chapter 14 as a powerful chieftain who spoke "on equal terms with kings and the Pharaoh..."[b/278] However, when Abraham armed 318 of his trained men to rescue kin and allies from the Elamite coalition, he did not act out of aggression but self-defense. After his victory, he returned home to Mamre instead of invading the coalition's territory.[c/279]

Treaty Maker

Although he was a wealthy, seminomadic chieftain with a small household army at his disposal,[d] Abraham knew he was still an outsider in the land and so resolved conflicts quickly,[e] forthrightly, wisely and non-violently. When the patriarch, for instance, went to protect one of his water wells, which had fallen into dispute with the Philistines, he made a sacrificial in-kind payment to Abimelech, king of Gerar, as a witness that he himself had dug the well.[f] Afterward, the two men swore an oath that the well belonged to the patriarch. His politically shrewd gift defused a potentially violent incident through deferring to the king and giving him the benefit of the doubt. Abraham did not need to pay Abimelech for the well because he already owned it; when he chose to do so, he formed a treaty with another local king like he did with Melchizedek.[280]

Treaty Keeper

Abraham respected his covenants and treaties even when they involved personal risk. Genesis chapter 14 "celebrates Abram for fulfilling his covenant with Lot..."[281] As soon as he learned of Lot's

---

[a] Genesis 13:8-9
[b] Genesis 12:10-20. Compare 14:17-18; 20:2; 21:22.
[c] Genesis 14:15
[d] Genesis 14:14
[e] Genesis 13:7-8
[f] Genesis 21:22-32

abduction, he mounted an armed rescue.ᵃ/²⁸² When Abraham led his men on the mission, he also honored his covenant with three Amorite allies, Aner, Eshcol and Mamre, whose land Chedorlaomer had also ravaged.ᵇ

"Abram does not wage war," observe two scholars, "he defends Sodom, his covenant [treaty] partner."²⁸³ There are two reasons why the patriarch defended a notoriously wicked city. First, the same contentious lines of orthodoxy found later in Israel did not exist during the patriarchal period.²⁸⁴ Second, the five Cities of the Plain, which included Sodom and Gomorrah, were automatically Abraham's allies because Lot, the patriarch's nephew, was a citizen of Sodom if not one of its leaders.ᶜ According to ancient custom, Abraham was obliged to treat as kin, whoever was bound to Lot through the bond or covenant of salt or table fellowship. To W. Smith, "...the practical test of kinship is that the whole kin is answerable for the life of each of its members...Such is, in fact, the law of the desert; when any member of a clan receives an outsider through the bond of salt, the whole clan is bound by his act, and must, while the engagement lasts, receive the stranger as one of themselves."²⁸⁵ While the patriarch's nephew was a resident of Sodom and enjoyed the hospitality of its people, the patriarch was obligated to treat them as kin.

Isaac and Jacob followed Abraham's example of honoring treaties with kin and non-kin.ᵈ/²⁸⁶ For instance, when Isaac sealed an agreement with Abimelech, the patriarch showed he was a man of peace. S. Walters observes, "Isaac's prosperity under divine blessing led to envy and to contention over water rights; he had to move several times, thereby surrendering valuable excavated wells in the process, before finding 'space'...this [showed his] sacrificial determination to occupy the land amicably..."ᵉ/²⁸⁷

ᵃ Genesis 13:8-12; 14:12-16
ᵇ Genesis 14:7,13,24
ᶜ Genesis 19:1a

ᵈ Genesis 26:26-31; 31:43-55
ᵉ Genesis 26:15-21,22

Ancient Treaty Ceremonies

An ancient treaty ceremony commonly involved: (1) a treaty banquet; (2) a gift exchange and (3) a deity witness. Let us now look at each of these aspects to see if the interaction between Abraham and Melchizedek fits the general characteristics of an ancient treaty.

Treaty Banquet

Ancient Near Eastern treaties involved specific ceremonial acts. Although the rituals were not always the same,[a] according to G. Mendenhall and G. Herion, some specific ritual action was "regarded as essential to the ratification of the binding promise."[288] When Melchizedek, ruler of Salem, offered bread and wine to Abraham,[b] his gift entailed more than providing physical refreshment, a reward for heroism or typical Near Eastern hospitality. According to P. King and L. Stager, Melchizedek's common meal bonded him with Abraham in a mutual sense of friendship and "moral obligation."[289] In the opinion of R. Clifford and R. Murphy, Melchizedek's overture of sharing a common meal with Abraham was an attempt "to win the goodwill of so favored a personage"[290] through an act of "covenant loyalty in table fellowship..."[291]

Little doubt, the ruler had been told of Abraham's recent military success over the Elamite coalition and wanted to make a peace treaty with such a great chieftain, who had proven to be a powerful ally against Chedorlaomer, the vassal coalition's former overlord. Thus, when Melchizedek brought out the gifts of bread and wine, he offered Abraham the opportunity to form an official alliance with him through partaking together in a treaty banquet or "covenant meal."[292] According to M. Silver, meal sharing established a "social contract"[293] between two parties, during which loyalty oaths could be exchanged. For Melchizedek and

---

[a] Contrast Genesis 14:18 with 21:27.

[b] Genesis 14:18. On Abraham's Amorite allies see Genesis 14:7,13,24.

Abraham to have formed a legitimate treaty, however, they would not have had to verbalize loyalty oaths to each other; the meal itself would have sufficed.[294]

The Mari documents, over 20,000 texts from the Old Babylonia period,[a/295] refer to the custom of eating bread and drinking wine as symbolic actions that resolved animosities and finalized legal treaties.[b/296] According to Silver, a certain Mari land sale contract ends with the statement that the two parties had not only consecrated each other with oil but had also eaten from the same plate and drunk from the same cup.[297] To A. Millard, the Mari texts also mention "treaties between city rulers and tribes,"[298] which supports the notion that Melchizedek, the ruler of the city of Salem, could have made a treaty with Abraham, a tribal leader. In one Amarna letter,[c] the king of Egypt rebukes his vassal, king Aziru of Amurru, for breaking his loyalty oath and siding with his Hittite enemy "by eating and drinking with him..."[299]

The consumption of bread and wine was also associated with the internalization of a vassal's obligations to his suzerain (overlord) in Assyrian loyalty oaths: "Just as bread and wine enter the intestines, so may the [gods] let this oath enter your intestines."[300] Though centuries after Abraham, the Assyrian king, Esarhaddon,[d] son of Sennacherib, concluded his treaties not only by touching chests and applying oil and water but also by sharing common meals.[301] Mendenhall and Herion write, "Eating and drinking together has been such a universal expression of social solidarities of various sorts that it is not surprising to find common meals appearing frequently in connection with the creation of covenants, both in the ANE[e] and in the biblical narratives."[302] According to Smith, "The Old Testament records many cases where a covenant was sealed by the parties eating and

---

[a] the Old Babylonia period = approximately 2000-1600 B.C.
[b] See Chapter 9.
[c] the Amarna letters = texts from ancient Egypt approximately 1300–1200 B.C.

[d] Esarhaddon ruled Assyria approximately 681-669 B.C. (Freedman, D. N., 1992., volume 2, 574).
[e] ANE = ancient Near East

drinking together."[303] Some examples are: Isaac and Abimelech,[a] Laban and Jacob,[b] Yahweh and Israel[c] and Israel and the Gibeonites.[d/304] Abraham would not have given a tithe to El-Elyôn's temple, if he had not first accepted Melchizedek's covenant overture and participated in a common meal offered him by this local ruler. According to ancient honor customs, such a refusal would have been a serious insult and an outright rejection of Melchizedek's treaty initiation.

Gift Exchange

Ancient Near Eastern treaties also involved the exchange of gifts. Valuable presents of various kinds "were part of the covenant ceremony"[e/305] and symbolized each party's willingness to conform to the terms of the agreement. Political allies, as well as those who wished to be allies, presented gifts of plunder to one another's temples.[306] Such temple gifts formed political connections between mother cities and their outlying settlements.[307] Plunder was one of the most frequently dedicated gifts, and, according to T. Herman, it was a major source of revenue for Syro-Palestinian temples.[308] To P. Schmitz, even in Solomon's day, [f/309] gifts of plunder were "...an important element of interstate relations."[310] When Abraham gave a tithe in response to Melchizedek's blessing,[g/311] he not only commemorated El-Elyôn/YHWH's victory over the Elamite coalition with a permanent gift to the Salem sanctuary,[312] he also increased its material assets and acknowledged Melchizedek as an ally.[313] According to T. Gaster, with his plunder tithe, Abraham "cemented an alliance with Melchizedek."[314]

Deity Witness

In the ancient Near East, including Sumeria,[315] Egypt[316] and Israel,[h/317] every tribe, city and nation had a god(s) to whom it

---

[a] Genesis 26:26-31
[b] Genesis 29:22; 31:54
[c] Exodus 24:9-11
[d] Joshua 9:14-15
[e] Genesis 21:27; I Kings 15:19; Isaiah 30:1-7
[f] Compare I Kings 10:2,10.
[g] Genesis 14:20c
[h] Deuteronomy 20:4; Judges 5:19-23; I Samuel 30:23; 2 Samuel 5:22-25

attributed its military victories.[318] This is why many treaties were signed near or on the premises of a temple, the place where the deity(ies) was thought to dwell.[319] According to Smith, when two contracting parties made a treaty in or near a temple, they believed they were making a "compact under their [gods'] protection."[320] Mendenhall writes, "...all covenants were normally sworn by appeal to deity as witness."[321] Before Abraham sealed a covenant with Melchizedek with his gift of a tithe, the ruler of Salem invoked El-Elyôn as witness to their mutual treaty ceremony by praising him for helping Abraham defeat Chedorlaomer.[a]

Conclusion

In this chapter, I demonstrated that Genesis chapter 14 presents Abraham as a man of peace who honored covenants with kin, allies and rulers of the land, even when it involved risk and sacrifice. I also showed that Abraham's tithe to Melchizedek reflects the attributes of an ancient ceremony which sealed a covenant between them. In light of this historical fact, pro-tithers have no basis to apply Abraham's treaty gift to Christians.

---

[a] Genesis 14:20

7

The Melchizedek Priesthood

Some tithe advocates state and/or imply Abraham used his tithe to hire Melchizedek to mediate his covenant with God. Here are several claims:

- The "Priesthood of Melchisedek"[322] served as a "Mediator of the Covenant."[323]
- "The second feature in Jacob's tenth differing from that of his grandfather [Abraham], is, that no part of Jacob's tithe is mentioned as paid [paying] for the use of a priesthood."[324]
- "It seems, moreover, exceedingly probable that the priestly acts which Melchizedek performed for Abram were simply such as this priest-king would from time to time perform for any Canaanitish chief returning from a victorious expedition, as also perhaps when his people paid their tithes on ordinary occasions...we need not at all conclude that this was either the first or the last occasion on which Abram paid a tenth of his increase to Melchizedek. If the patriarch did so annually, it would be only in keeping with the practice of his Babylonian ancestors..."[325]
- "...tithing was under Abraham and the only priesthood he knew about, which was Melchisedek. The believer is under the New Covenant, and the Melchisedek Priesthood...thus tithing continues in the New Covenant community."[326]

The main point of the above claims is that Christians are obligated to tithe to Christ since Abraham gave a tithe to the Melchizedek priesthood in his day. Many Christians tend to accept such a statement automatically because they are told that the Melchizedek to whom Abraham gave a tithe was Jesus in the flesh, even though, in the final analysis, Hebrews contradicts such a notion.[327] Some pro-tithers attempt to link Abraham's tithe to the priesthood of Melchizedek as well as the Abrahamic covenant so they can claim his tithe is a model for Christians who inherit the spiritual promises of that covenant. It is true that both the old and new testaments use the phrase, "the order of Melchizedek,"[a] but this fact does not validate the claim that Abraham used his tithe to purchase the priestly services of Melchizedek, or under the New covenant, God expects Christians to tithe. Here are the reasons why:

First, according to the text, the Melchizedek priesthood never mediated God's covenant to Abraham. Melchizedek never acted as Abraham's priest, and before he ever met Abraham, God had already begun communicating with the patriarch his covenantal promises.[b] In Chapter 9, I demonstrate how Melchizedek had nothing to do with Abraham's reception of these promises, and how Abraham's tithe was unrelated to the Abrahamic covenant.

Second, the main function of a priest was to pray or intercede with God for others because they were either too fearful or unworthy to approach the deity for themselves. In this case, Abraham was neither too afraid nor too sinful to have a direct relationship with God because God chose him for his own covenantal purposes. Furthermore, there is no evidence to support the idea that Melchizedek prayed for Abraham's protection while he and his men risked their lives to rescue Lot. Melchizedek's only priestly action was his blessing of Abraham.[c] According to later times, to bless the people meant to invoke the name (person) of the Lord upon them with the words: "The Lord bless you, and keep you; The Lord make His face to shine on you,

---

[a] Psalm 110:4; Hebrews 5:6,10; 6:20; 7:11,17 per NASB

[b] Genesis 12:1-4
[c] Genesis 14:19

and be gracious to you; The Lord lift up his countenance on you, and give you peace."ᵃ According to the text, however, Melchizedek never invoked the name or blessing of YHWH upon Abraham. He did not say, "The Lord bless you," as if he was imparting divine favor to the patriarch. He said, "Blessed be Abram by God Most High,"ᵇ merely recognizing how El-Elyôn himself had already blessed Abraham when he enabled him to defeat the forces of Chedorlaomer. Similarly, the second part of Melchizedek's blessing was praise directed to El-Elyôn for giving Abraham victory over the Elamite coalition.ᶜ Therefore, neither of the two parts of Melchizedek's blessing indicates the role of a priest helping the patriarch to merit or receive God's help, favor or forgiveness. Such priestly blessings remind us of a much later time when God gave Aaron and his sons the power to bless the people of Israelᵈ not the religion of the patriarchs in which God blessed them directly,ᵉ and fathers as well as brothers blessed their own sons and daughters.ᶠ

One of the pro-tithers above claims Abraham's tithe "paid for the use of a priesthood;"[328] his tithe hired the "priestly acts"[329] of Melchizedek. According to another tithe advocate, in addition to that of blessing him,[330] Melchizedek's priestly services to Abraham included serving him holy or sacramental communion[331] and collecting his tithes.[332] In Chapter 8, however, I demonstrate that the bread and wine Melchizedek served Abraham cannot be equated with the elements used for communion in the church today. In addition, in chapters 5 and 6, I explained why Christians should not identify Abraham's tithe with the traditional tithe.

According to R. Abba, a priest was: (1) a symbol of sanctity and service;[333] (2) a servant who stood for others before God[334] and (3) a ritualist who helped others maintain covenant with God

---

ᵃ Numbers 6:24-27, NASB
ᵇ Genesis 14:19b, NRSV
ᶜ Genesis 14:20a,b
ᵈ Numbers 6:22-27; Leviticus 9:22-23; Deuteronomy 10:8; 21:5

ᵉ Genesis 25:11; 26:12; 30:30; 35:9; 48:3
ᶠ Compare Genesis 24:50,60; 27:23,27,29,33,41; 28:1,6; 31:55; 48:15,20,28.

through atonement rites.³³⁵ Melchizedek, however, never functioned as a symbol of sanctity and service to Abraham. The patriarch showed respect to the king because he was one of the rulers of Canaan with whom he wanted to live in peace not because he admired his priestly or religious relationship with El-Elyôn. From what we are told, Abraham never viewed Melchizedek as a servant of YHWH from whom he heard the word of God. He did not need Melchizedek to stand before God on his behalf and make atonement for his sins; Abraham did not require a priest to protect him from "the anger of the gods."³³⁶ Completely apart from a priest, the patriarch: (a) built his own altars and offered prayers and sacrifices;[a] (b) saw supernatural visions;[b] (c) received the word of the Lord;[c] (d) obtained faith righteousness[d] and (e) personally dialogued with YHWH.[e] It is therefore not surprising that, in Westermann's view, the traditional notion of a priest is foreign to the religion of the patriarchs.³³⁷

Third, there was no "Melchizedek priesthood"³³⁸ in Abraham's day. There was only one king-priest whose name was Melchizedek. It was not until later that Psalm 110:4 broadened Melchizedek into an order or dynasty of king-priests by its use of the statement, "You are a priest forever according to the order of Melchizedek,"[f] spoken over Davidic kings on the day of their coronation³³⁹ to strengthen their authority over the Jerusalem temple. According to Hebrews, the only person who belongs to the Melchizedek priesthood is Christ himself due to his unique resurrection from the dead.[g] The writer compares Jesus and Melchizedek to prove the superiority of Christ's priesthood over those of Levi and Aaron.[h]

Fourth, each of the above claims assumes Melchizedek was Abraham's intercessor with YHWH; none, however, provides us with any textual proof. As we look carefully at the use of the divine names referred to in Abraham's interaction with

---

[a] Genesis 12:7,8; 13:4,18; 22:9
[b] Genesis 15:1
[c] Genesis 15:4
[d] Genesis 15:6
[e] Genesis 12:1-4a,7; 13:14,18; 15:7-11,13
[f] NASB
[g] Hebrews 7:16-18, 24
[h] Hebrews 7:9,11

Melchizedek, the king-priest blesses his god, El-Elyôn,[a] while Abraham alone acknowledges YHWH.[b] Strictly speaking, aside from later theological developments involving the names of God, Melchizedek could not have been an intercessor for Abraham with YHWH, since YHWH was not his god.[c]

Finally, as previously noted, and contrary to the third claim above, there is no biblical evidence Abraham interacted with Melchizedek outside of Genesis 14:18-20. Therefore, to state or imply Abraham regularly tithed to the Salem sanctuary cannot be maintained.

Conclusion

In this chapter, I quoted several pro-tithers who suggest Abraham's tithe to Melchizedek was a payment for priestly services. Even though these claims contain many textual, historical, theological and Christological problems, believers are expected to feel obligated to pay tithes for their pastor/leaders' "priestly services." In Genesis chapter 14, we find that Melchizedek's descriptive blessing of Abraham, his serving of bread and wine as a treaty banquet and his receiving of a one-time tithe of enemy plunder do not accurately reflect the traditional role of a priest. Even if they did, because YHWH spoke with Abraham directly, the patriarch never needed intercessory services. Finally, Hebrews describes Melchizedek as a prefiguration of Christ,[d] but it never places pastor/leaders into a contemporary Melchizedek priesthood, as if they were somehow entitled to collect believers' tithes.

---

[a] Genesis 14:20a, NASB
[b] Genesis 14:22, NASB. "Lord" = YHWH
[c] See Chapter 5.
[d] Hebrews 7:3 ("like"); 15 ("likeness") per NASB

8

The Lord's Table

After Abraham and his men defeated the Elamite coalition, they passed by the city of Salem on their way home to Mamre/Hebron. As they did, Melchizedek, the city's ruler, came out of the town with "bread and wine."[a] After he declared how it was El-Elyôn who had given Abraham his recent military victory,[b] the patriarch gave him a tenth of the war spoils.[c] Some pro-tithers assert that as Abraham tithed to Melchizedek in exchange for his gifts of bread and wine, so Christians should tithe to God when they partake of communion at the Lord's Table.[d] Here are some claims:

- "The New Covenant's communion meal is the restoration of the Old Covenant's covenantal feast of Salem."[340]
- "Melchizedek ministered Bread and Wine to Abraham at the receiving of tithes (Genesis 14:18). This is the first specific account of 'communion' in Scripture and it is significant that it is with the father of all believers and the priesthood of Melchizedek (Hebrews 7). It was covenant time."[341]
- "Can we claim to be children of Abraham and claim the

---

[a] Genesis 14:18, NASB, NRSV, KJV, NKJV, NIV
[b] Genesis 14:20a,b
[c] Genesis 14:20c
[d] The Lord's Table is also referred to as the Lord's Supper, the Eucharist, breaking of bread, (Holy) Communion, the Blessed Sacrament, fellowship or community meal and Agape.

communion and the priesthood of Jesus and still neglect to give tithes in this covenantal relationship?"[342]

On the surface, these claims might seem plausible. The phrase "bread and wine" brings to mind the bread and cup Jesus gave to his disciples at the Last Supper,[a] and which were also shared at the Lord's Table in Corinth.[b] To interpret Abraham's tithe as a response to Melchizedek for serving him some sort of sacramental meal comparable to the Lord's Table, however, reads too much into the text. Here are some reasons why:

First, in both old and new testaments, bread and wine were common staples in daily meals.[c] Consequently, when a tithe advocate argues that Melchizedek's serving of bread and wine to Abraham is "the first specific account of 'communion' in Scripture,"[343] he commits the fallacy of equivocation. According to D. Fischer, this fallacy happens "whenever a term is used in two or more senses within a single argument, so that a conclusion appears to follow when in fact it does not."[344] The "bread and wine" in Genesis 14:18 and the bread and cup in I Corinthians 11:26 hold two different meanings. The former were everyday foods that were used to facilitate an ancient treaty meal and victors' banquet between a Canaanite ruler (Melchizedek) and a resident alien (Abraham). The latter is a meal that recalls the death of Jesus.[d] Ancient treaty "ritual food"[345] is not synonymous with later "sacramental food."

Second, in Chapter 6, I demonstrated that the bread and wine

---

[a] Mark 14:22-25 = Matthew 26:26-29 = Luke 22:15-20
[b] I Corinthians 11:26-27. NRSV uses "bread" and "cup." Verse 21 mentions that some of the Corinthians were drunk at the Lord's Table, which indicates the consumption of wine.
[c] OT: Deuteronomy 29:6; Judges 19:19; I Samuel 10:3; 16:20; 25:18; 2 Samuel 16:1-2; 2 Kings 18:32; Nehemiah 5:15; Ecclesiastes 9:7; Haggai 2:12; Isaiah 36:17. NT: Matthew 6:11; 15:2 (NASB); 16:5; 21:33; Mark 6:8; Luke 1:15; 7:33; 15:17; John 2:3,9,10; 21:13; Acts 2:42,46; 20:7; Romans 14:21; 2 Corinthians 9:10; Ephesians 5:18; 2 Thessalonians 3:8; I Timothy 3:3; 5:23; Titus 1:7; 2:3
[d] I Corinthians 11:26

that Melchizedek brought out to Abraham was a treaty gift to which the patriarch responded with a tithe-gift of plunder. If the food and drink mentioned in Genesis chapter 14 had been offered to the gods of El-Elyôn and/or YHWH in a ritual covenantal act, we would see Abraham and/or Melchizedek giving their gifts directly to their gods and communing with them not to each other. It is true that in ancient Mesopotamia, worshippers entered the presence of their gods on certain occasions with offerings of food and drink.[346] Ancient "acts of communion between the god and his worshippers" [347] regularly involved the consumption of meat not merely bread and wine. Melchizedek offered bread and wine to Abraham – not to El-Elyôn. He did not greet his god personally;[a] neither did he praise him directly.[b] Abraham and Melchizedek ate their covenant meal *before* their gods as covenant witnesses,[c] not *with* their gods as a means of communion or fellowship with them. These factors indicate Melchizedek formed a treaty with Abraham on a human level; neither man formed or renewed a covenant with his god. The formation of the Abraham-Melchizedek treaty, therefore, was "sacramental" only in the sense that all such treaties between leaders in the ancient Near East were sworn before the leaders' gods in a world thought to be governed by them.

Third, one tithe advocate asserts the Lord's Table "is the restoration of the Old Covenant's covenantal feast of Salem."[348] I understand him to say that the Lord's Table brings to mind the treaty meal Melchizedek shared with Abraham in Genesis chapter 14. To say the Lord's Table restores the "Old Covenant's covenantal feast of Salem,"[349] however, is an error of fact. Melchizedek and Abraham were not under the Old covenant. The "covenantal feast of Salem"[350] in Genesis chapter 14, occurred long before the Old covenant was inaugurated on Mt. Sinai,[d] and, therefore, the two are completely unrelated. According to the New Testament, the purpose of the Lord's Table is not to

---

[a] Genesis 14:20a,b
[b] Genesis 14:20a,b
[c] See *Deity Witness* in Chapter 6.
[d] Exodus chapters 19-20

remember the Abraham-Melchizedek treaty but to "proclaim the Lord's death until He comes."[a]

Fourth, the word "covenantal" in the phrase "covenantal feast of Salem,"[351] can only refer to the treaty meal between Melchizedek and Abraham that occurred near the city of Salem. In context, the word "covenantal" cannot refer to any other covenant including the Abrahamic, Mosaic or New.

Fifth, the fact Melchizedek was a priest does not automatically give a sacramental meaning to Genesis 14:18, as some believers understand the Lord's Table. The verse that refers to Melchizedek as "priest" also refers to him as "king," and, in ancient times, it was characteristic of kings - not priests - to distribute bread to those in their domains as a demonstration of their monarchical benevolence.[b/352] In addition, in the New Testament church, there were no priests who presided over the Lord's Table to give the bread and cup an official or sacred blessing. In Corinth, for example, it was the people who blessed the bread and cup.[c] Special priestly blessings were Old Testament traditions which crept into the church much later.[353] It is not without significance that Melchizedek did not bless or pray over the bread and wine, as pastors or priests would do in many church liturgies; he only blessed Abraham and El-Elyôn.[d]

Sixth, Melchizedek governed at a time when individual rulers held both political and religious offices; it was an era when there was little or no separation between sacred and secular or temple and palace. Aside from the messianic implications of Melchizedek's dual office of king-priest,[e] Abraham gave a tithe to a ruler who exercised a theocratic rule under which there was no separation of "church" and "state." Therefore, if we accept the tithe advocates' suggestion that Christians should tithe to Jesus because Abraham tithed to Melchizedek, then we would also have to accept the notion that Christians should tithe to a state church.[f]

---

[a] I Corinthians 11:26, NASB
[b] Compare John 6:1-15 (especially verses 11,15).
[c] I Corinthians 10:16
[d] Genesis 14:19a,b; 20a

[e] For the question, "Was Melchizedek Jesus?" see Book 4 in *The Tithing Series*.
[f] See Book 2 in *The Tithing Series*.

Seventh, it is possible Melchizedek's gifts of bread and wine were similar to soldiers' wages given in units of food and drink. "The Egyptians expressed payment in units of bread and beer," notes E. Bleiberg, "the main components of their diet."[354] The potential parallel between Egyptian units of payment in bread and beer and Melchizedek's units of payment in bread and wine is not without significance. Until scholars began deciphering the ancient languages of the pictographic symbols (hieroglyphs) of Egypt and the wedge-shaped alphabet (cuneiform) of Mesopotamia, many Bible teachers believed the Scripture was "its own best interpreter."[355] Today, however, according to J. LeMon, "the very opposite is the case;"[356] scholars have discovered that it is impossible to understand the Bible at many points without understanding the various cultures that influenced it.

Eighth, the second claim above capitalizes the words "Bread" and "Wine,"[357] emphasizing their divine or sacramental significance. According to M. Bourke, however, Melchizedek's blessing of Abraham, "does not necessarily indicate that Melchizedek's offering of food and drink to Abram was a cultic [ritual] act."[358] F. Bruce agrees with Bourke and provides us with a New Testament observation about the author of Hebrews: "...the one feature in the Melchizedek narrative of Genesis 14:18-20 which he [the writer of Hebrews] passes over in silence is Melchizedek's bringing bread and wine to Abraham."[359] This omission leads Bruce to the opinion the bread and wine in Genesis 14:18 was not a "sacrificial offering."[360] Thus, neither Bourke nor Bruce agrees with the claim that Melchizedek's bread and wine is comparable to the Lord's Table.

Ninth, another difference between the covenant meal in Genesis chapter 14 and the Lord's Table in Corinth is that those who partook of the Lord's Table examined their consciences before partaking.[a] Paul rebuked the believers there because they continued their class divisions between rich and poor.[b] The rich would arrive at the meetings first, consume their food and drink

---

[a] I Corinthians 11:28   [b] I Corinthians 11:18,33

and not wait to share them with the poor.[a] In these selfish ways, the Corinthians failed to "judge the body rightly."[b] We find no such preliminary examination of conscience in Genesis chapter 14.

Finally, the third claim implies Christians disqualify themselves from partaking of the Lord's Table if they do not tithe.[361] The phrase "claim the communion"[362] lacks clarity, but it probably refers to the notion that tithing believers can draw upon certain benefits of the Lord's Table, whereas non-tithing believers cannot or should not. There is nothing in the New Testament, however, to support such a claim. Jesus did not ask the Twelve to tithe to him or to the Jerusalem temple when he served them bread and wine at the Last Supper.[c] Paul never required the Corinthians to tithe to their house church leaders when they partook of the communion.[d] When the apostle described the kind of behavior that was "unworthy"[e] of the Lord's Table, he never mentioned non-tithing. Even though one of the strongest promoters of the mandatory tithe holds that non-tithing Christians should be denied church membership and voting rights, refreshingly, he also believes they "...should not be required to pay for access to the Lord's Table."[363]

Conclusion

There is little doubt Abraham and his men were hungry and tired when they returned from their rescue of Lot, having traveled approximately 158 miles[364] one way from Mamre[f]/Hebron to Hobah[g] ten miles east of Damascus.[365] In spite of their condition, when Melchizedek greeted them in the Shaveh Valley[h] near Salem, his gifts of bread and wine went beyond mere "physical refreshment"[366] or a "sign of hospitality..."[367] Melchizedek served the refreshments in a victory banquet that celebrated Abraham's

---

[a] I Corinthians 11:21,22,33,34a
[b] I Corinthians 14:29, NASB
[c] Matthew 26:26-29 = Mark 14:22-25 = Luke 22:15-20
[d] I Corinthians 10:16-22; 11:17-34
[e] I Corinthians 11:27, NRSV. Compare verse 22.
[f] Genesis 14:13
[g] Genesis 14:15
[h] Genesis 14:17

defeat of Chedorlaomer, the overlord the vassal coalition had been unable to defeat.[a]

The claim that Abraham's tithe to Melchizedek was a payment for the king's gifts of bread and wine, and, thus, a call for Christians to tithe at the Lord's Table in payment for the benefits of the New covenant is a clear rush to judgment. Since the context of Genesis 14:18-20 is a political and military one in which Melchizedek and Abraham formally agree to become allies, the episode cannot be applied to the Lord's Table without serious distortions to the text. A patriarch's tithe of enemy war spoils to a Canaanite king can hardly be applied to a Christian's tithe of weekly income to a local church or ministry because of the familiar catchphrase "bread and wine."

Most importantly, the New Testament never connects the treaty that Melchizedek initiated with Abraham to the New covenant, Melchizedek's bread and wine to the elements of the Lord's Table or Abraham's tithe to the notion of a Christian's tithe. Even if tithe advocates could find such endorsement from the New Testament, they would still lack a valid hermeneutical basis to show Abraham's tithe obliges Christians to tithe on an ongoing basis, since, as previously mentioned, Abraham's tithe to Melchizedek was a one-time, voluntary act.

---

[a] Genesis 14:8-12

9

The Abrahamic Covenant

The "Abrahamic covenant" refers to the oath YHWH made to Abraham and his descendants. Along with other blessings,[a] its major promise was the land of Canaan.[b] It is one of the most significant covenants in the Bible because of the way the New Testament writers use its themes of grace, faith and promise to point to the coming of Jesus and the spread of the gospel.[c/368] For this reason, pro-tithers attempt to connect Abraham's tithe to the Abrahamic covenant to provide greater theological approval for tithing.

In this chapter, I address the following questions: (1) Was tithing a part of the Abrahamic covenant? If so, on what textual basis and in what way(s)? (2) What was the relationship between Jacob's tithe vow and the Abrahamic covenant? (3) Did the Abrahamic covenant impart moneymaking power to Abraham's tithe? and (4) Did tithing flow from the Abrahamic covenant into the New covenant?

---

[a] See Genesis 12:1-4; 13:14-18; 18:17-19; 21:12; 22:17-18; 26:3-5,24; 46:3-4.
[b] Genesis 15:1-21, especially verses 7,18; 17:1-27, especially verse 8; 28:4

[c] Compare Genesis 12:3; 26:4 and 28:14 with Acts 3:25 and Galatians 3:8. Compare Romans 4:13-14.

Was tithing a part of the Abrahamic covenant?

The following claims are from pro-tithers who believe tithing was somehow connected with God's covenant with Abraham:

- "...because churches reject the continuing validity of the Mosaic law, they reject the binding character of tithing. But tithing precedes the Mosaic law...Tithing is grounded on the Abrahamic covenant. Churches today pay no attention."[369]
- "...Abraham gave tithes before the Law Covenant even existed...Tithing here is connected to the Abrahamic Covenant."[370]
- "Tithing is...the same...covenant act that Abraham and his descendants performed some four hundred and thirty years before the law was ever given to Moses...It was an act of faith and covenant with God. And so it is for the 'seed of Abraham' today."[371]
- "...tithing was under Abraham..."[372]
- "Tithes cannot be separated from Covenantal relationship. This is seen in the Abrahamic, Mosaic and New Covenants..."[373]

These claims assert that tithing was an integral component of the covenant YHWH made with Abraham and his descendants. Some pro-tithers hold that God required tithing in the Abrahamic covenant while others do not. Either way, the direct implication of any position that attempts to connect tithing to this covenant maintains that it was necessary for Abraham and his descendants to receive the covenant's blessings. This means if any of the patriarchs had stopped tithing, if any were in fact tithing at all, they would have damaged or broken their covenantal relationship with YHWH. Such an idea finds no support in the text. These claims fail to provide any textual or theological proof for their position, as the following reasons demonstrate:

First, several of the above claims seem to rely on vagueness and vacuity. When we read, "Tithing here is connected to the Abrahamic Covenant,"[374] how exactly was tithing connected to it? or "Tithing is grounded on the Abrahamic covenant,"[375] what text demonstrates this? or "tithing was under Abraham,"[376] what is meant by "under Abraham"? Pro-tithers are unable to provide us with any textual evidence which links the Abrahamic covenant with tithing; all they put forward is the verse that tells us Abraham gave a tithe to Melchizedek (Genesis 14:20), which, by itself, does not demonstrate such a connection. Not everything that happened "under Abraham,"[377] still or automatically applies to Christians. Circumcision,[a] animal sacrifices,[b] sacred space,[c] concubines[d] and vows[e] all existed "under Abraham,"[378] but the New covenant has abolished them all.[f]

Second, the Hebrew term *berith* ("covenant") is used in Genesis chapter 14 where Abraham gave a tithe to Melchizedek, as it is used in Genesis chapters 15 and 17,[g] the two passages that address, respectively, the oath and sign of the Abrahamic covenant. In Genesis chapter 14, however, *berith* does not refer to YHWH's covenant with the patriarch; it refers to Abraham's covenant with three Amorite brothers who were his allies.[h] Even though Abraham and Melchizedek made their peace alliance in the presence of deity,[i] Abraham's tithe did not form or secure any sort of covenant with YHWH.

Third, because Abraham's tithe to Melchizedek sealed a human covenant and not a divine one,[j] it is critical to the pro-tithing case to identify Melchizedek as Jesus.[k] Without this identification, it is nearly impossible for tithe advocates to claim that a patriarch's one-time, voluntary tithe composed of enemy plunder and made to a Canaanite ruler, could obligate Christians, thousands of years later,

---

[a] Contrast Genesis 17:10 with Romans 2:28-29; I Corinthians 7:19; Galatians 5:6.
[b] Contrast Genesis 22:13 with Hebrews chapters 9-10.
[c] Contrast Genesis 28:16-17 with John 4.22-24.
[d] Contrast Genesis 16:3; 22:23-24; 25:5-6; 30:3-4,9; 35:22; 36:12 with Matthew 19:3-9; Luke 16:18; I Timothy 3:2,12; 5:9; Titus 1:6.
[e] Contrast Genesis 14:22-24 and 28:20-22 with Matthew 5:33-37.
[f] See chapters 1, 2, 19.
[g] Genesis 15:18; 17:2,4,7,9,10,11,13,14,19,21
[h] In Genesis 14:13, "allies" (per NASB) = *berith*.
[i] Genesis 14:19-20
[j] See chapters 5 and 6.
[k] See Book 4 in *The Tithing Series*.

to pay tithes to their places of fellowship. Even if we held, as some pro-tithers do,³⁷⁹ that when Abraham gave a tithe to Melchizedek he gave a tithe to Jesus incarnate,ᵃ we still could not validly conclude that Abraham's tithe was a facet of the Abrahamic covenant because, according to the text, Melchizedek had nothing to do with its formation or development.

Fourth, since Genesis chapter 14 is the only place the tithe is mentioned in Abraham's life, and, since Abraham was the covenant bearer, if tithing was an element of the covenant, we should see God reiterate at least one of the covenant promises to the patriarch when he gave his tithe to Melchizedek,ᵇ but we do not.

Fifth, the original covenant oath YHWH gave to Abraham does not contain any reference to the tithe.ᶜ Genesis 15:18 is the first time the word covenant (*berith*) is applied to Abraham's relationship with YHWH. It says, "On that day, the Lord made a covenant [*berith*] with Abram, saying, 'To your descendants I have given this land, from the river of Egypt [Nile] as far as the great river, the river Euphrates...'"ᵈ If we take Genesis chapters 14 and 15 to be in chronological order, Abraham tithed to Melchizedekᵉ before YHWH ever formally gave his unconditional oath to the patriarch. Be that as it may, there is no clear, direct or necessary connection between Abraham's tithe to Melchizedek in Genesis 14:20c and God's oath to Abraham in Genesis 15:18. According to R. Clifford and R. Murphy, even though Genesis chapter 15:1 begins with the transitional phrase, "After these things,"ᶠ the two chapters are not associated. To these scholars, chapter 15 clearly "marks a new episode"³⁸⁰ in the life of Abraham. This means that Abraham's covenant with Melchizedek in chapter 14 was a different covenant than the one that YHWH made with the patriarch in the following chapter. Among other factors, Abraham's covenant with Melchizedek was conditional; it could have been

---

ᵃ Compare Hebrews 7:3,8.
ᵇ Compare Genesis 12:1-3; 15:1-20; 17:1-8,19,21.
ᶜ Genesis 15:1-21
ᵈ Genesis 15:18, NASB

ᵉ Genesis 14:20c
ᶠ NASB, NRSV. See also Genesis 21:34 - 22:1 and 22:19-20.

broken if either party had breached its part of the agreement. In contrast, according to J. Milgrom, YHWH's original covenant with Abraham had no terms or conditions.[381] In Genesis chapter 15, YHWH used an ancient covenant ritual in which he bound himself to fulfill the covenant promises no matter what Abraham and his descendants did or did not do.[a] During the ceremony, YHWH took upon himself the full responsibility of fulfilling the covenant when he alone passed between the animal carcasses laid out upon the ground and did not require Abraham also to walk between the pieces.[b] Through this symbolic act, he said, analogously of course, "May death also happen to me, if I do not fulfill my oath to you in this covenant." The Lord completed the covenant ritual while Abraham was asleep;[c] the patriarch's passive posture further emphasizes the one-sided and unconditional nature of the covenant.

In Genesis chapter 15, YHWH gave Abraham the following six promises:[d] (1) reward; (2) heir; (3) many offspring; (4) land; (5) deliverance of descendants from future bondage and (6) personal longevity. Theologically, the most important promise of the covenant was probably that of the land. Genesis 15:18 describes YHWH's oath to the patriarch and his lineage as unconditional by the use of the *qal* perfect state, understood here as the English past tense, in the promise: "I have given [*nathan*] this land" to you. In YHWH's mind, the action was already complete.[382] In this verse, YHWH did not require Abraham or his descendants to tithe to inherit Canaan; for that matter, he did not make any of his promises contingent upon tithing. Moreover, when the apostle Paul spoke to the Galatians about God's covenant promises to Abraham, he reassured them his promises were not based on obedience to the Law but upon YHWH's original oath. In Galatians 3:15, Paul makes the point that whether he is talking about human contracts or the one God made with Abraham, once either has been properly "ratified, no one sets it aside or adds conditions to

---

[a] Compare Genesis 15:9-11 with Jeremiah 34:18-20.
[b] Genesis 15:17-18
[c] Genesis 15:12,18
[d] Genesis 15:1-7; 13-16; 18-21

it."[a] The pro-tithers who claim that tithing was a feature of the Abrahamic covenant contradict Paul's words when they add the condition of tithing to a covenant that was originally based solely on promise.

Sixth, even though the version of the Abrahamic covenant in Genesis chapter 17 contains three of the six covenant promises that were in the oath of the covenant in Genesis chapter 15 (descendants, land, heir),[b] it differs in that it adds to the covenant the stipulation of circumcision.[c/383] C. Westermann views the command to circumcise in Genesis 17:10-14 as distinct from the divine oath in Genesis 15:18 because it is a different literary style.[384] In his view, a later editor took the unconditional promises in Genesis chapter 15[d] and reshaped them into promises dependent upon circumcision.[385] G. Mendenhall maintains that the covenant contained absolutely "no obligations."[386] He does not view circumcision as a requirement of the covenant but a sign[e] in the same sense the rainbow was a sign of God's covenant with Noah;[f] one that did not demand of him any behavioral change or obedience to a set of commands.[387]

In Genesis chapter 17, YHWH made the following covenant promises to the patriarch:[g] (1) covenant; (2) descendants; (3) nations; (4) kings; (5) land and (6) heir. The first eight verses of this chapter are dominated by divine sovereignty and unconditionality, typified by the words: "I will establish My covenant between Me and you and your descendants..."[h] The rest of the chapter is controlled by human responsibility and conditionality, embodied in the verses: "As for you, you shall keep my covenant, you and your offspring after you throughout their generations. This is my covenant, which you shall keep, between me and you and your offspring after you: Every male among you shall be circumcised...But an uncircumcised male who is not circumcised in the flesh of his foreskin, that person shall be cut

---

[a] Galatians 3:15c,d,e, NASB
[b] Genesis 15:4,5,7,16,18-21
[c] Genesis 17:10
[d] Genesis 15:1-21, especially verses 7,13,14,16,17-21
[e] Genesis 17:11
[f] Genesis 9:8-17
[g] Genesis 17:2-21
[h] Genesis 17:7a, NASB. Compare verses 2a, 4a.

off from his people; he has broken My covenant."ᵃ Genesis chapter 17 makes no mention of the tithe; it is thus impossible to claim that tithing was the means for any of these six Abrahamic promises to be fulfilled. Since we do not find tithing in either of the two classic chapters of the Abrahamic covenant,ᵇ if tithing was indeed an element of the covenant, we should be able to find it mentioned in one or more of the promise passages outside of these chapters, but we do not.ᶜ

Seventh, it is not without significance that even though the New Testament mentions the Abrahamic covenant and/or its promises at least twelve times,ᵈ not one of its writers links it with tithing.

Finally, the third pro-tither above claims Christians should tithe because they "are the seed of Abraham."[388] Another tithe advocate agrees.[389] Because the patriarch gave a tithe to Melchizedek and the New Testament refers to believers as Abraham's spiritual children, Christians also should tithe. Such thinking opens a theological Pandora's box. As the "seed of Abraham,"[390] what other practices of Abraham's should Christians perform? It is true that, either directly or indirectly, John, Jesus, Paul and Peter all refer to believers as the seed of Abraham;ᵉ however, none of these references promotes the idea Christians should tithe let alone that they should tithe because they are spiritually related to Abraham.

What was the relationship between Jacob's tithe vow and the Abrahamic covenant?

Some tithe advocates make a point about the Abrahamic covenant being the theological context of Jacob's tithe vow.ᶠ They claim that since Jacob made his tithe vow while he was living under the

---

ᵃ Genesis 17:9-10 (NRSV), 14 (NASB)
ᵇ Genesis chapters 15, 17
ᶜ Genesis 12:1-3; 13:14-18; 18:17-19; 22:15-19; 26:1-5; 28:13-15
ᵈ Luke 1:55,73; Acts 3:25; 7:8; Romans 4:13-16; 9:4-13;

Galatians 3:16-18,29; 4:28; Hebrews 6:13-15; 7:6-10; 11:17-19
ᵉ Matthew 3:7-10; John 8:39; Romans 4:16; 9:7; Galatians 3:7,9,14,16,29; 4:21-31. Compare Acts 3:25; I Peter 3:6.
ᶠ Genesis 28:20-22

Abrahamic and not the Sinai covenant, it is incumbent upon Christians to tithe because they are recipients of that same covenant in Christ. Here are some claims which mention Jacob:

- "The tithe, although found in the later mosaic law, originated with the earliest patriarchs, Abraham and Jacob. Therefore, the tithe is part of the Abrahamic covenant, not a part of the covenant of 'works.'"[391]
- "Again, it should be noted clearly, that, this vow of tithing was before the Law was given. Jacob was not under law but under grace. Jacob was in the Abrahamic Covenant, not the Mosaic Covenant."[392]
- "After Jacob had seen an open Heaven, and seen the abundance of what was in Heaven, he fully realized all that God's covenant promises held for him. 'Then Jacob made a vow saying, "If God will be with me, and keep me in this way that I am going...I will surely give a tenth to you"' (Genesis 28:20-22)."[393]

There are several problems with the claim that Jacob's tithe vow at Bethel indicates that tithing was a part of the Abrahamic covenant.

First, the second pro-tither above says, "Jacob was in the Abrahamic covenant."[394] Jacob did make a promise to give a tithe to YHWH while living under the covenant that God made with his grandfather, Abraham. It is also correct to say that when he made such a vow he was not under the Law or Sinai covenant. Nevertheless, it does not follow from this that God expects or obligates believers to tithe.[a] To jump to such a conclusion from the fact that Jacob lived "in the Abrahamic covenant"[395] is like claiming Christian men have the right to have more than one wife because Jacob was "in the Abrahamic covenant"[396] when he married Leah and Rachel.[b]

Second, in Genesis 28:12-15, YHWH appeared to Jacob at

---

[a] See Chapter 2.   [b] Genesis 29:23,28

Bethel in a dream, as he was, like his grandfather,[a] in a passive state of sleep, and reiterated to him the following covenant promises:[b] (1) land; (2) descendants; (3) geographical expansion and (4) global blessing. He then told the patriarch he would protect him on his journey to Haran and eventually bring him back to Canaan.[c] After Jacob heard YHWH tell him the promises of the Abrahamic covenant, the patriarch made a vow,[d] which included the promise of a tithe.[e] It is impossible to claim Jacob's tithe vow was a stipulation of the Abrahamic covenant, since Jacob vowed a tithe on his own initiative and not at YHWH's command or request.[f] In Jacob's dream, YHWH did not tell the patriarch he and his descendants would need to make and keep tithe vows to experience the promises of the covenant.[g]

Finally, the last pro-tither above implies Jacob made a tithe vow to obtain "all that God's covenant promises held for him."[397] By "covenant promises,"[398] he admits he refers to those given in the Abrahamic covenant.[399] On the contrary, this was not the reason Jacob made his vow. According to the text, he vowed to motivate YHWH to grant him four specific requests that pertained to his trip to Haran: (a) Presence; (b) protection; (c) provision and (d) safe return.[h]

Did the Abrahamic covenant impart moneymaking power to Abraham's tithe?

One tithe advocate considers the connection between Abraham's tithe, wealth accumulation and the patriarch's covenant with YHWH so clear, he published the same material under two different titles: *How to Amass Abrahamic Wealth for Yourself and Your Family*[400] and *How to Claim the Abrahamic Covenant.*[401] These two titles for the same book attempt to convince Christians that they can become as rich as Abraham, if they learn how to

---

[a] Genesis 15:12; 28:12
[b] Genesis 28:13-15. Compare verse 4.
[c] Genesis 28:15
[d] Genesis 28:13-15; 22c

[e] Genesis 28:22c
[f] Genesis 28:20a
[g] Genesis 28:12-15
[h] Genesis 28:20-22. See Chapter 14.

"claim the Abrahamic covenant"[402] through, among other items, the regular giving of tithes and offerings. This pro-tither not only believes tithing was a component of the Abrahamic covenant, he also holds that the covenant itself imparted to the patriarch's tithes and offerings an intrinsic, supernatural power to multiply into many financial blessings.

Here is his claim:

- "This [enlivening power] was true of the deadness of Abraham's body after child bearing age. Paul said in Romans 4:17 that 'God giveth life to the dead, and calleth those things which are not, as though they were...' But what was true concerning Abraham's body is also true of tithing and offering inanimate, lifeless pieces of money. With the supernatural, Abrahamic blessing power God promised and gave in His covenant with Abraham, He gives life to the inanimate money when you tithe it and give it in the form of offerings so that it reproduces itself."[403]

This claim asserts the Abrahamic covenant contained a supernatural power to rejuvenate Abraham's impotent body as well as financially multiply "lifeless"[404] tithes and offerings. It also alleges that the acts of tithing and giving contain a supernatural power which guarantee financial prosperity. Here are some of the problems with such ideas:

First, the pro-tither takes Romans 4:17 out of context to make his point about the inherent moneymaking power of tithes and offerings under the Abrahamic covenant. This verse does not refer to money but to Isaac, who was born of divine promise to parents who were past childbearing age.[a]

Second, the Abrahamic covenant itself did not contain the power to cause Abraham and Sarah to have a child; it was the God of the covenant who spoke a personal promise to the couple that

---

[a] Romans 4:16-25

wielded such ability.ᵃ If the covenant had indeed contained such fertility powers, then Abraham and Sarah would not have needed to wait for "the appointed time"ᵇ to see the promise fulfilled.ᶜ Similarly, when Rebekah, Isaac's wife, was barren, it was not enough for her to be living under the Abrahamic covenant; Isaac had to pray for her to become pregnant.ᵈ When Jacob's wife, Leah, was unable to have children, the Lord "opened her womb" with four sons not because the Abrahamic covenant contained reproductive powers but because God saw she "was unloved" and "looked on her affliction."ᵉ If fertility was an integral part of the Abrahamic covenant and was automatically incorporated into the New, then no woman associated with either covenant would be infertile.

Finally, the same pro-tither also contends the Abrahamic covenant supernaturally enlivened Abraham's tithe to Melchizedek to reproduce itself[405] and will do the same with Christians' tithes and offerings. This claim suffers from the "pathetic fallacy," which, according to D. Fischer, is the "ascription of animate behavior to inanimate objects." [406] This tithe advocate applies the animate behavior of the miracle birth of Isaac to the inanimate object of war plunder. There is no biblical evidence to support the notion that Abraham's tithe inherently contained the power to reproduce itself financially either for Abraham or his descendants.ᶠ

This claim turns the Abrahamic covenant into a magical formula. According to I. Mendelsohn, magic is "an inactive power independent of gods and men, but which could be activized by the aid of incantations and rituals to accomplish supernatural deeds."[407] According to this pro-tither, "...in His covenant with Abraham, He [God] gives life to the inanimate money when you tithe it and give it in the form of offerings so that it reproduces itself."[408] In his view, it is God who gives reproductive power to

---

ᵃ Genesis 15:4; 18:10; 21:1-2
ᵇ Genesis 18:14, NASB. Compare 17:21; 18:10.
ᶜ Compare Genesis 17:17; 21:5; Romans 4:19.
ᵈ Genesis 25:21
ᵉ Genesis 29:31-33, NASB/NRSV
ᶠ See Chapter 11.

"inanimate money" through his covenant, but it is the repetition of the tithe/give ritual which causes him to do so. The tithe advocate adds no biblical or theological qualifiers that might hinder or stop God from such lucrative responses. Therefore, if it is the case that God "has no choice"[409] but to make each believer who has made a habit of the tithe/give ritual "extremely wealthy,"[410] then I fear we have left behind the free and sovereign God of the Bible, whose concern penetrates more deeply than outward deeds[a] and have entered the realm of magical rituals.

Let us now look at another pro-tither's claim:

- "Tithing is...the same dynamic and supernatural covenant act that Abraham and his descendants performed some four hundred and thirty years before the law was ever given to Moses."[411]

Contrary to what this statement maintains, Abraham's tithe was not a "covenant act"[412] between him and God; it was a covenant act between him and Melchizedek.[b] When this tithe advocate claims "Abraham and his descendants performed"[413] their covenant act of tithing "some four hundred and thirty years before the law was ever given to Moses,"[414] he gives the impression that since Abraham's descendants were beneficiaries of the Abrahamic covenant, they tithed. Such a claim is based on pure speculation. As noted earlier, the only occurrences of the word "tithe" before the Sinai covenant are Abraham's one-time tithe to Melchizedek[c] and Jacob's one-time tithe promise to YHWH.[d] Genesis records no tithe for Isaac or any of Jacob's twelve sons or grandchildren.

The same pro-tither also alleges Abraham's tithe was a "supernatural"[415] act. To some Christians, the idea of tithing being a "supernatural"[416] act seems justifiable because it coincides with the sermons they have heard about how tithing can miraculously

---

[a] Matthew 5:8,28
[b] See Chapter 6.
[c] Genesis 14:20c
[d] Genesis 28:22c

attract financial blessing including getting believers out of debt. Upon closer examination, however, there was nothing supernatural about Abraham's tithe to Melchizedek. The only supernatural act in the story was YHWH's defeat of the Elamite coalition.[a]

Here is another claim that further misinterprets Scripture:

- "The power to get wealth was the only thing given to us for us to know that He has, of a certainty, continued the Abrahamic system with us...He prospers us to establish with us the Abrahamic covenant. Actually, He has no choice but to make us prosper because if he doesn't he has made the Abrahamic covenant invalid (Deuteronomy 8:18)...God had to give them [Israelites] the blessing power to get wealth because he promised it to The Abrahamic Seed Group in His covenant with Abraham. He had no choice...So he gave us the Abrahamic power to get wealth...Tithing and giving offerings causes a supernatural reproduction of what you 'sowed,' and this supernatural ability to reproduce was given to us by God in order to 'continue' The Abrahamic Covenant with us. In addition to his love for God, this is the reason Abraham paid tithes and gave offerings."[417]

This tithe advocate assumes it was Abraham's tithes and offerings, given under the canopy of the Abrahamic covenant, that made him rich. Based on this assumption, he claims God "had no choice"[418] but to give both Israelites and Christians the same "power to get wealth,"[419] since, in his view, God promised this power to them through the same covenant of which both are heirs. If God had not given this power to them, he would have invalidated his covenant. To this tithe supporter, the only sign God gave to Christians to know he has continued the Abrahamic covenant with them is their power to get rich. He also claims that

---

[a] See Chapter 4.

the universal key to unlocking this "supernatural ability to reproduce"[420] wealth is the giving of tithes and offerings. Here are the problems I see with his line of thinking:

First, as I demonstrated earlier in this chapter, tithes and/or offerings were never a stipulation of the original covenant oath made to Abraham.[a] This fact makes the claim fail whether applied to Abraham, Israel or Christians. Concerning Abraham, it was not tithes and offerings that made him rich.[b] We need to keep in mind what N. Lohfink and others point out: unlike the Sinai covenant, the Abrahamic covenant was "pure promise instead of a contract."[421]

As to Israel, he misinterprets Deuteronomy 8:18, which says, "But you shall remember the Lord your God, for it is He who is giving you power to make wealth, that He may confirm His covenant which He swore to your fathers, as it is this day."[c] In this verse, he is correct to identify the Abrahamic covenant, but he is incorrect to interpret it as a moneymaking one. According to the text, the covenant's focus was not upon riches per se but land and descendants.[d] As God enabled the Israelites to inhabit the land he promised to their fathers, he wanted them to keep in mind that he alone was their ultimate source of wealth. Verse 17 bears this out: "Otherwise, you may say in your heart, 'My power and the strength of my hand made me this wealth.'"[e/422] On this point, at least without giving us further explanation, this pro-tither seems to contradict himself. On the one hand, he claims it was God who gave the Israelites the power to make wealth, as he did with the patriarchs, but, on the other, he claims the Israelites caused themselves to get wealth through their giving of tithes and offerings.

It is helpful to keep in mind that Deuteronomy contains two theological themes: grace and law. These two themes reflect the book's creative interweaving of both the Abrahamic and Sinai covenants on how the Israelites were to inherit the land. We see

---

[a] Genesis 15:1-21
[b] See Chapter 11.
[c] NASB
[d] land: Genesis 12:1; 13:15; 15:18; 17:8; descendants: Genesis 12:7; 13:15-16; 15:5,18; 16:10
[e] NASB

the message of grace in God promising the Israelites a land for which they did not work: "...great and splendid cities which you did not build, and houses full of all good things which you did not fill, and hewn cisterns which you did not dig, vineyards and olive trees which you did not plant."[a] They will not inherit the land through their own efforts or piety: "It is not for your righteousness or for the uprightness of your heart that you are going to possess the land, but it is because of the wickedness of these nations that the Lord is driving them out before you, in order to confirm the oath which the Lord swore to your fathers, to Abraham, Isaac and Jacob."[b]

We also see the message of law in God making obedience to his commands necessary for them to inherit the land: "All the commandments that I am commanding you today you shall be careful to do, that you may live and multiply, and go in and possess the land which the Lord swore to give to your forefathers."[c] Deuteronomy chapter 8, the chapter from which this tithe supporter takes his proof text of verse 18, is a good example of both strands.[d] The pro-tither ignores the theme of grace in the chapter, represented by its references to the Abrahamic covenant oath and the miracles in the desert,[e] and focuses on the theme of law (tithes and offerings) even though neither are mentioned in the chapter.

Regarding Christians, the same tithe advocate cannot legitimately hold that believers have to give tithes and offerings to receive the material blessings of God's covenant with Abraham, since such an idea ignores the covenant's original unconditionality[f] as well as the fact that the New covenant spiritualizes its material blessings.[g]

Second, although God blessed Abraham with silver and gold,[h]

---

[a] Deuteronomy 6:10-11, NASB
[b] Deuteronomy 9:5, NASB. See verses 4-6.
[c] Deuteronomy 8:1, NASB
[d] law = Deuteronomy 8:1,2,6,11,20; grace = Deuteronomy 8:3,4,15,16

[e] Note the oath (Deuteronomy 8:1,18) and the desert miracles (verses 3,4,15,16).
[f] Genesis 15:1-21; 26:3,24; 28:4; Isaiah 51:2-3; Hebrews 6:13-20
[g] Galatians 3:8,16; Hebrews 11:16
[h] Genesis 13:2; 24:35,53

the blessings of the Abrahamic covenant did not revolve around great amounts of cash or money. The main focus of the blessings was land (Canaan) and children (descendants).[a] Both land and children were forms of wealth in Abraham's day, but Genesis does not promise super-abundant monies to Abraham's descendants, as this tithe advocate leads us to believe. Even though Deuteronomy 8:13 says God was going to allow the same blessing of gold and silver to come to Israel, the meaning of the words "bless" and "blessing" in the Bible changed over time.

Under the Sinai covenant, the main point of blessing was that of "material prosperity."[b/423] However, according to J. Campbell, as we approach the New Testament, "There seems...to be a progressive tendency toward a more spiritual conception of blessedness."[424] We observe this in the Beatitudes,[c] the book of James[d] and the first letter of Peter.[e] The sense of "blessing" as well-being is generally consistent between the two testaments, but "the nature of this well-being"[425] is viewed differently at various times "and can be determined only from the context."[426] To apostles like Luke and Paul, it is the gospel that brings to the nations the spiritual and moral blessings promised to Abraham and fulfilled in Christ.[f] This is not to deny the fact that the gospel includes the principles of honesty, generosity, frugality and hard work which may, sooner or later, benefit believers financially;[g] however, from a New Testament perspective, it is beyond dispute that the intent of the Abrahamic covenant was never to impart the "power to get wealth"[427] but to impart to believers the spirit of Jesus Christ.[h]

Finally, even though God has promised to meet the basic needs

---

[a] Note Abraham: land (Genesis 12:7; 13:15,16,18; 24:7) and descendants (15:5); Isaac: land (26:4) and descendants (26:4,24) and Jacob: land (28:4,13; 35:12; 48:4) and descendants (28:14; 32:12; 48:4,19).
[b] Deuteronomy 28:1-14
[c] Matthew 5:3-12. Compare Luke 6:20-26.
[d] James 1:12. Compare 5:11.
[e] I Peter 3:14; 4:14
[f] Acts 3:25-26; Galatians 3:8
[g] Compare 2 Thessalonians 3:10.
[h] Galatians 3:14. Compare verses 2-7.

of believers who seek his kingdom first,[a] and, at times, to bless abundantly those who give sacrificially,[b] the New Testament makes it clear that "the power to get wealth"[428] is not the factor which indicates the Abrahamic covenant has continued into the New covenant. To Paul, the gifts of faith righteousness and the indwelling Spirit are the true signs of the Abrahamic covenant being fulfilled in the lives of believers.[c] The notion that Christians have to give tithes and offerings to "claim the Abrahamic covenant" is nowhere to be found in the New Testament. It is not without significance that our tithe advocate uses the phrase "Abrahamic system"[429] to describe the Abrahamic covenant as if the theological depth and richness of its promises in Christ could be reduced to a step-by-step method of how to get rich.[430]

Did tithing flow from the Abrahamic covenant into the New covenant?

The following pro-tither specifically links the Abrahamic covenant with the New covenant in an effort to support the position that Christians should tithe. Here is his claim:

- "The New Covenant continues the Abrahamic Covenant in Christ...tithing was under Abraham...thus tithing continues in the New Covenant community."[431]

The statement, "tithing was under Abraham" is both false and misleading. According to the text, as I consistently note: Abraham gave a tithe only once, Isaac never tithed and Jacob made a one-time tithe vow he never fulfilled.[d] Along with the tithe advocate's undefined use of the word "continues," [432] his claim also declines to take into account both the uniqueness and superiority of the New covenant over the Abrahamic. The New covenant is unique; it is based on the death and resurrection of the Son of God who

---

[a] Matthew 6:33
[b] Mark 12:41-44; 2 Corinthians 9:6-14
[c] Romans 4:1-25; Galatians 3:13-14
[d] On Jacob's tithe vow see Chapter 15.

now lives "according to the power of an indestructible life."[a] Its superiority over the Abrahamic covenant is founded upon the historical fact that Jesus, as risen Lord, is inherently and eternally God's final and definitive word to Abraham,[b] Jacob[c] and their descendants not only in his person but also in the Spirit he imparts to everyone who follows him.[d]

The New covenant is based on "better promises,"[e] including that of eternal life.[f] It demonstrated its superiority to the Abrahamic covenant when it authoritatively reinterpreted its promises in light of the gospel.[433] It annulled physical circumcision, which the Old Testament describes as the sign of the Abrahamic covenant,[g] and replaced it with circumcision of the heart.[h] The promised "seed" of Abraham is Jesus;[i] his true descendants are no longer biological Jews[j] but the Jews and non-Jews (Gentiles) who follow Christ.[k/434] The blessing of Abraham is no longer financial prosperity or a piece of Palestinian real estate[l/435] but a heavenly country, whose first installation is the gift of the Spirit.[m]

How could the New covenant spiritualize covenantal circumcision, Jewish lineage and the land of promise but still require a literal tithe, which, under the Sinai covenant, came from the agricultural products of the same land it spiritualizes? To do so, would make no theological or covenantal[436] sense. Through

---

[a] Hebrews 7:16b, NASB
[b] John 8:58; Hebrews 7:4,6-7
[c] John 4:12-14
[d] Galatians 3:5,14; Romans 8:9-11,15,16
[e] Hebrews 8:6
[f] John 3:16,36; 4:14,36; 17:2,3. Compare Hebrews 7:16.
[g] Genesis 17:7,9,12. Compare Genesis 17:10-27 with Romans 4:9-12.
[h] Romans 2:28-29; I Corinthians 7:18-19; Philippians 3:3; Colossians 2:11; 3:11

[i] Galatians 3:16,19. Compare verse 8.
[j] John 8:37-47; Romans 2:28-29; 4:9-25; 9:6-13; Galatians 3:7-9,29. Compare Matthew 3:9 = Luke 3:8; John 8:39.
[k] Romans 3:29; 9:24; Galatians 5:6; 6:15
[l] Contrast Genesis 15:17-21 with Hebrews 11:13-16; Genesis 28:4 with Galatians 3:14; Deuteronomy 3:20 with Hebrews 4:8-11; and Numbers 26:53-55 with Hebrews 9:15 and I Peter 1:4.
[m] Galatians 3:14

the death and resurrection of Jesus Christ, God introduced a new,[a] supernatural[b] and eternal[c] covenant, which reinterprets the significance of the Abrahamic covenant in light of the coming of Jesus. In addition, since the New covenant does not tell its members to tithe,[d] how can pro-tithers tell Christians to tithe when they base their claims on the Abrahamic covenant, which contains no tithing stipulation?

Conclusion

In this chapter, I showed that tithing was not a part of the Abrahamic covenant since Abraham's tithe to Melchizedek had nothing to do with YHWH's covenant with the patriarch. Neither can we say that Jacob's tithe vow demonstrates tithing was a part of the same covenant since the idea to vow a tithe did not come from God but from Jacob himself.[e] As the context makes clear, Jacob made his tithe promise only as a one-time journey vow.[f] I also exposed the erroneous assertion that God's covenant with Abraham imparted a special moneymaking power to his one-time tithe. The text never draws a connection between the patriarch's tithe and his subsequent wealth, nor does it indicate any of Abraham's wealth prior to his interaction with Melchizedek was dependent upon a tithe. Finally, since the two major chapters in Genesis that address the Abrahamic covenant,[g] along with the covenant's separate promise passages,[h] never mention the tithe, we must conclude that tithing never flowed through the Abrahamic covenant into the New since there is no textual evidence that it was ever a part of God's covenant with Abraham in the first place.

---

[a] Luke 22:20; I Corinthians 11:25; 2 Corinthians 3:6; Hebrews 8:7-13; 9:1,15; 12:24. Compare 10:20.
[b] Hebrews 7:16,25; 8:1-2; 9:24
[c] Hebrews 9:12,14,15; 13:20
[d] See Book 4 in *The Tithing Series*.
[e] Genesis 28:20a
[f] Genesis 28:20-22
[g] Genesis chapters 15 and 17
[h] Genesis 12:1-3; 13:14-18; 18:17-19; 22:15-19; 26:1-5; 28:13-15

10

The 'Covenant of Blessings'

In this chapter, I address the 'Covenant of Blessings' presented by Clive Pick,[437] whose pro-tithing influence has been increasing in churches across North America. In spite of the fact Mr. Pick's website, at the time of my initial research,[438] described the book from which his 'Covenant of Blessings' is taken as "revelatory and biblically based," I consider his treatment of God's covenant with Abraham to be a clear and serious distortion of the text which needs to be vigorously challenged. He not only gives readers the false impression tithing was a part of the Abrahamic covenant,[a/439] he also forsakes YHWH's unconditional covenant with Abraham (Genesis chapters 15 and 17) as he forms the conditions for his own covenant of Christian prosperity.[440] Pick uses three unrelated episodes from Abraham's life[b] to create what he calls the "covenant pattern of Abraham"[441] or the 'Covenant of Blessings.'[442] He states:

- "Abraham is our pattern, and if we follow exactly what God told Abraham to do, we will then by inheritance, receive Abraham's blessings. The pattern was in this order, firstly to tithe, secondly to walk blameless before God and finally to give an offering. I know that if we, the children of God, follow this pattern, we will indeed receive our rightful inheritance

---

[a] See Chapter 9.   [b] Genesis 14:18-20; 17:1d,e; 22:1-2,18

(Galatians 3:29). To re-establish or to activate this covenant you need to understand, and be totally obedient to the three parts of the covenant...By making a covenant with Abraham, God has promised to bless his descendants and to make them His special people. Abraham's part of the covenant, like ours, was to remain faithful and obedient to God and his word..."[443]

In his claim, this tithe advocate mentions three requirements he believes Christians must fulfill to receive material blessings from God. They are: "firstly to tithe, secondly to walk blameless before God and finally to give an offering."[444] I abbreviate these three requirements as "tithe, walk and give" not to detract from their substance but to make for smoother reading. I address the problems I have with Pick's claim under the following divisions: (1) Abraham and the 'Covenant of Blessings;' (2) Christian Inheritance and the 'Covenant of Blessings' and (3) The Three Requirements of the 'Covenant of Blessings.'

Abraham and the 'Covenant of Blessings'

First, this pro-tither states, "Abraham is our pattern."[445] By "pattern" he means if Christians will follow precisely what God commanded Abraham to do in the verses from Genesis he highlights, the Lord will give to believers the same blessings he gave to the patriarch. Such a statement suffers from the fallacy of over-generalization. The New Testament ignores Abraham's material blessings and interprets his life of faith in terms of the spiritual blessings of righteousness,[a] obedience[b] and the gift of the Spirit.[c] In addition, he focuses on the wrong person. Under the New covenant, Christ is our pattern. Even though Jesus told the Jews who sought to kill him to "do the deeds of Abraham,"[d] the "deeds" to which he referred did not include tithing but believing

---

[a] Romans 4:1-25. "Blessed" (*makarios*) and "blessedness" (*makarismos*) are used 4x in verses 6-9.

[b] Hebrews 11:8-10, 17-19
[c] Galatians 3:13-14
[d] John 8:39, NASB

in the true word of God.ᵃ Jesus did not tell his disciples to follow Abraham, he told them, "Follow Me,"ᵇ a command he used throughout his ministry.ᶜ Similarly, Paul does not say in his letters, "Follow me, as I follow Abraham," he says, "Follow me, as I follow Christ."ᵈ Furthermore, Hebrews does not refer to Abraham's tithe to Melchizedek as any sort of "covenant pattern"ᵉ/⁴⁴⁶ for believers to follow; it uses tithing to demonstrate Abraham's inferiority to Christ.ᶠ

Second, Pick implies he took "tithe, walk and give" from the Abrahamic covenant; his use of both Old and New covenant verses at the beginning of his book are completely jumbled.⁴⁴⁷ In his 'Covenant of Blessings,' he asserts that these three steps were the patriarch's "part of the covenant,"⁴⁴⁸ and Christians are also to follow them. On the contrary, God's covenant with Abraham never required any of these steps for the patriarch to receive divine blessing.ᵍ The Abrahamic covenant never made "tithe, walk and give" a "covenant pattern"⁴⁴⁹ for Jews or Christians to follow since the original covenant had no conditions.ʰ/⁴⁵⁰ It was later editors who added Torah obedienceⁱ/⁴⁵¹ and circumcisionʲ as stipulations to the covenant.ᵏ Speaking of the moment circumcision was added to the Abrahamic covenant, R. N. Whybray observes, "There is now for the first time in the Abraham story a warning against the breach of the covenant, which will entail exclusion from its privileges and from the new special relationship with God..."ˡ/⁴⁵² When Pick implies (or adds) "tithe, walk and give" to God's covenant with Abraham, he turns the unconditional covenant of grace⁴⁵³ into a conditional covenant of works.

ᵃ Compare John 8:40 with Genesis 15:1-6; 18:1-8. See also John 6:28-29.
ᵇ John 1:43; 21:19,22, NASB
ᶜ Matthew 4:19; 8:22; 9:9; 16:24; 19:21,28; Mark 1:17; 2:14; 8:34; 10:21; Luke 5:27; 9:23; 9:59; 18:22; John 8:12; 10:27; 12:26
ᵈ Compare I Corinthians 11:1 in various translations.

ᵉ Hebrews 7:2,4
ᶠ Hebrews 7:6-7. See Book 4 in *The Tithing Series*.
ᵍ See Chapter 9.
ʰ Genesis 15:1-21
ⁱ Genesis 18:19; 26:3-5
ʲ Genesis 17:9-14
ᵏ See Chapter 9.
ˡ Genesis 17:14

Instead of accepting this tithe advocate's subjective creation of a prosperity covenant under the guise of the Abrahamic covenant, Christians should look to the New Testament to show them how Old Testament covenant promises apply to them. Paul, for example, says all believers benefit from God's promises to Abraham by believing in Jesus.[a] Galatians 3:29 states, "...if you belong to Christ, then are you Abraham's offspring, heirs according to the promise."[b] Paul does not say, "If you belong to Christ *and* faithfully tithe, walk in financial integrity and give offerings above your tithes, then are you Abraham's offspring and heirs according to the promise." J. B. Phillips makes the same point in his translation of Galatians 3:18: "For if the receiving of the promised blessing were now made to depend on the Law, that would amount to a cancellation of the original 'contract' which God made with Abraham as a promise..."[454] In other words, if the promises of the Abrahamic covenant to Christians now depend on the laws of "tithe, walk and give," that would cancel the original unconditional promises God made to the patriarch and the way the New Testament writers understand their fulfillment in Christians' lives through the new birth.

Third, when this pro-tither describes his 'Covenant of Blessings,' he says to "re-establish or to activate this covenant you need to understand, and be totally obedient to the three parts of the covenant."[455] Here he uses the verbs "re-establish" and "activate," which reveal he leaves both the Abrahamic and New covenants far behind and presents to readers a covenant of his own making. If he was accurately referring to the Abrahamic or New covenant, then the words "activate"[456] and "re-establish"[457] (re-activate) would not apply since both the Abrahamic and New covenants have been fulfilled in Jesus' death and resurrection and are now fully available to all believers. Neither covenant has to be activated or re-activated by obedience to certain conditions. Pick ignores the present reality of the New covenant, which is the

---

[a] Compare Romans 4:1-25, especially verses 5-15 and Galatians 3:7,13-14.

[b] NRSV

ultimate fulfillment of the promises made to Abraham. Paul makes it clear the blessing of Abraham has already come to the Gentiles in the gospel, and it is not the blessing of financial prosperity but the promise of the indwelling Spirit.[a]

Finally, referring to his 'Covenant of Blessings,' Pick states, "Abraham's part of the covenant, like ours, was to remain faithful and obedient to God and his word...,"[458] that is, faithfully obey "tithe, walk and give." When he uses the phrase, "Abraham's part of the covenant, like ours,"[459] he alleges as Abraham obeyed "tithe, walk and give," so Christians need to do the same. Here this tithe advocate makes two errors.

First, he gives the false impression Abraham fully obeyed "tithe, walk and give." He did not. We find only one time in Scripture that the patriarch gave a tithe; he may or may not have walked in financial integrity (he certainly did not always walk in ethical integrity[b]); and the only offering that he is said to have made was a ram substitute for his son (Isaac), which, contrary to this pro-tither's emphasis, had nothing to do with making sure his offering was over and above the tithe he had previously given to Melchizedek.[c]

Second, concerning his requirement of "tithe" for believers: the book of Hebrews abolishes the mandatory tithe.[d] Regarding Pick's requirement of "walk:" the New covenant agrees Christians should be financially honest,[e] but it never tells them tithing is a part of their being honest. As to his requirement of "give:" the New Testament agrees believers should give to support teachers,[f] needy believers[g] and the poor,[h] but it never tells believers to tithe to do so. Similarly, contrary to many pro-tithers, the New Testament does not endorse the notion that for offerings to be true "offerings," they need to be above the tithe.

---

[a] Galatians 3:14
[b] Genesis 12:18; 20:9-11
[c] Genesis 22:12
[d] Hebrews 7:1-28, especially verses 5, 11-12, 18-19. See Book 4 in *The Tithing Series*.
[e] Compare Luke 19:8. Paul condemns "thieves" and "swindlers" in I Corinthians 6:10.
[f] Galatians 6:6; I Corinthians 9:1-14
[g] Acts 2:45; 4:34; 2 Corinthians chapters 8-9
[h] Matthew 6:3; 19:21. Compare I Corinthians 13:3.

Christian Inheritance and the 'Covenant of Blessings'

Pick claims believers must "tithe, walk and give" to receive from God their financial or material inheritance. He tells believers: "...if we follow exactly what God told Abraham to do, we will then by inheritance, receive Abraham's blessings...I know that if we, the children of God, follow this pattern, we will indeed receive our rightful inheritance..."[460] This pro-tither is not always clear in the way he uses terms. In this instance, I understand his reference to "Abraham's blessings"[461] to be synonymous with believers' "rightful inheritance"[462] in the New covenant. His claim, however, is a serious misinterpretation of Scripture for the following reasons:

First, according to the New Testament, Christians do not receive their inheritance in Christ because they merit it through "tithe, walk and give," but because God freely gives it to them in the gospel.[a] Paul says, "For if the inheritance is based on law, it is no longer based on a promise; but God has granted it to Abraham by means of a promise."[b] He also writes: "For the promise to Abraham or to his descendants that he would be heir of the world was not through the Law, but through the righteousness of faith. For if those who are of the Law are heirs, faith is made void and the promise is nullified..."[c] This tithe advocate may think his claim escapes these verses on Christian liberty because he uses episodes from the book of Genesis ("before the Law") to support his "tithe, walk and give" requirements. The way he applies them to believers, however, is the same way the Old covenant applied them to the ancient Israelites; they are legal requirements for divine blessing.[463] Even though the New covenant says God blesses godliness[d] along with generosity,[e] it is the Old covenant that makes God's material blessings dependent upon laws such as "tithe, walk and give."[f]

---

[a] Ephesians 1:11,14; Colossians 1:12; 3:24; Hebrews 9:15
[b] Galatians 3:18, NASB
[c] Romans 4:13-14, NASB
[d] I Timothy 4:8
[e] Luke 6:38; 2 Corinthians 9:6
[f] tithe (Malachi 3:8-12); walk in perfect financial integrity (Leviticus 19:35-36; Deuteronomy 25:13-16 [compare 26:12-15 with verses 18-19]; Proverbs 11:1; 16:11; 20:10; 20:23; Micah 6:11); give offerings above the tithe (Malachi 3:8-12)

Second, in his comments about believers and their inheritance in Christ, this tithe supporter points out that he refers only to Christians' material inheritance and not to their spiritual or eternal one.[464] It is clear he does not want to be accused of using "tithe, walk and give" to buy salvation or eternal life. His distinction between material and spiritual inheritance, however, worsens the problem. According to the New Testament, Christians have only one covenant with God and that is the New covenant.[a] Even though there are various viewpoints concerning material blessings evidenced by the New Testament writers,[b] it is the New covenant which dominates both the material and spiritual aspects of the Christian life. Under the New covenant, there is no separate covenant for "material" blessings.

As this pro-tither divides Christian inheritance, he departs from New Testament theology, justifies his creation of an extrabiblical 'Covenant of Blessings' and claims it is the only way to receive God's financial favor. He begins with the idea that Christians receive their inheritance through Christ[465], but then adds that for them to receive their material inheritance, they must "tithe, walk and give."[466] Such a subtle change in emphasis is misleading and dangerous. The New Testament does not condone a "tithe, walk and give" covenant. The material blessings Jesus promised to his followers were never dependent upon these three conditions. God promises to meet people's basic needs as they enter his kingdom and put its interests first.[c]

Lastly, Pick alleges Christians will receive their "...rightful inheritance (Galatians 3:29)," if they will follow the "tithe, walk and give" pattern. Galatians 3:29 says, "And if you are Christ's, then you are Abraham's seed, and heirs according to the promise."[d] Paul's point here is the opposite of "tithe, walk and

---

[a] Luke 22:20; I Corinthians 11:25; 2 Corinthians 3:6; Galatians 4:21-31; Hebrews 8:13; 9:15; 12:24
[b] Compare Matthew 6:26 ("do not sow") with 2 Corinthians 9:6 ("who sows sparingly").
See Book 4 in *The Tithing Series*.
[c] Matthew 6:33; Matthew 19:27-30 = Mark 10:29-31 = Luke 18:28-30. Compare Acts 4:32-35.
[d] NKJV

give."ª The apostle affirms that Christians, like Abraham, are justified before God by faith and not works,[b] and, therefore, no longer have to obey the Law to receive their inheritance. Pick ignores the content of Galatians 3:29 and uses it to proof text his point about "tithe, walk and give" playing on the catchword "inheritance."

The Three Requirements of the 'Covenant of Blessings'

Requirement 1: Tithe

The first requirement of Pick's 'Covenant of Blessings' is tithing.[467] He tells Christians to tithe on "any financial increase which comes into your life...This must be done weekly or monthly, including December!"[468] To prove this, he cites Abraham's tithe to Melchizedek (Genesis 14:18-20)[469] and claims only as believers tithe, will they activate the 'Covenant of Blessings.' To him, if believers neglect to tithe on any of their income streams, they will forfeit God's financial blessings and suffer loss. He asserts:

- "The pattern was in this order, firstly to tithe..."[470]
- "Abram initiated the tithe to King Melchizedek. The tithe will protect you financially."[471]
- "First repent of not tithing, and start to tithe in to the church where you worship."[472]
- "...the tithe is a covenant token [or payment] that God needs to release the blessings...When we tithe, we say to Father, 'We choose to come into covenant with you.'...Now, we're not buying God's favor, but God has structured this covenant to operate through the exchange of money. That's how it's activated...We have to exchange [give] money to God first to activate the covenant - which is the tithe...Covenant is one of the strongest relationships that can be!... Whenever

---

[a] Compare Galatians 3:25; 4:1-7. See Book 4 in *The Tithing Series*.

[b] Galatians 3:6,11,26

covenant is entered into, there is always an exchange, for example, when I married Esther, there was an exchange of rings. The wedding ring should be on a certain hand and finger to show everyone that I am married."[473]

Here this pro-tither describes the tithe as a "covenant token,"[474] which Christians need to continue to pay, if they expect to receive God's material blessings. To him, the word "token"[475] means a covenantally-prescribed medium of "exchange,"[476] a term which he uses three times in his last claim above. To Pick, believers exchange their tithes for material blessings like newlyweds exchange rings for conjugal blessings. There are, however, several difficulties with his reasoning.

First, he reduces Christians' reception of God's material blessings to a quid pro quo[a] business transaction: as long as believers tithe, God will send them financial favor; if they stop tithing, he will withhold his blessing. Such a notion, however, comes from the Old covenant not the New. It was under the Old covenant that the prophet Malachi told the Judeans God would bless their crops if they would bring their tithes and offerings into the temple.[b] Christians, however, are no longer under the quid pro quo dealings of the Old covenant. They enjoy a new covenant[c] which reveals God as a generous Father who sends rain even upon those who do not deserve it[d] instead of a shrewd businessman who forms a "covenant to operate through the exchange of money."[477]

According to Matthew, to receive material blessings from their heavenly Father, all his children have to do is ask.[e] In Luke, Jesus does not tell his disciples to fear divine deprivation if they do not

---

[a] The Latin, quid pro quo = something for something.
[b] Malachi 3:10-12
[c] Jeremiah 31:31; Luke 22:20; I Corinthians 11:25; 2 Corinthians 3:6; Hebrews 8:7-8,13; 9:1,15; 12:24
[d] Matthew 5:45; Matthew 6:26 = Luke 12:24. Compare "they neither toil nor spin" in Luke 12:27 = Matthew 6:28 (NASB). Matthew 6:25-33.
[e] Matthew 7:7-11. Compare Luke 11:13. See Book 4 in *The Tithing Series*.

tithe, he tells them, "...seek His kingdom, and these things [food, drink, clothes] will be added to you."[a] This tithe advocate ignores the important roles prayer[b] and grace[c/478] play in the financial lives of New covenant believers.

Similarly, in the Abrahamic covenant, to which Pick inaccurately links his 'Covenant of Blessings,' there was no financial exchange. As I previously demonstrated, Abraham's tithe to Melchizedek had nothing to do with the formation of YHWH's covenant with the patriarch or his reception of divine blessings.[d] Therefore, whether viewed as under the Abrahamic or New covenant, it is clear God does not require Christians to exchange tithes for material blessings.

Second, this tithe advocate describes the tithe as a payment "...that God needs to release the blessings..."[479] Here tithing is not about Christians learning financial discipline or good stewardship, but about God himself needing their tithes before he is able to release earthly blessings to them. On the surface, this claim may seem biblical because it sounds like another way of applying Malachi 3:8-12, in which the prophet told the Judeans during the Second Temple period that God had cursed their crops because they had neglected to bring their tithes and offerings into the sanctuary. Despite its similarity with Malachi, however, this is one of the most unbiblical statements Pick makes about God. To begin with, he assumes because tithing was a law under the Sinai covenant, which was the tradition in which Malachi was written, God has forever bound himself to its strict enforcement, whether to the Jerusalem temple or to the Christian church.

Such an assumption ignores the fact that Jesus introduced a new covenant which stands opposed in many ways to the Sinai covenant in both principle and substance.[e] Also, he neglects the

---

[a] Luke 12:31, NASB. See verses 13-34.
[b] Matthew 7:7-11; 6:8; 6:11 = Luke 11:3
[c] Matthew 6:25-33; 10:29-31; 12:12. Compare Psalm 104:27-28.
[d] See Chapter 9.
[e] Galatians 4:1-31; 2 Corinthians 3:1-18; Romans 14:14,20; I Timothy 4:3; Hebrews 12:18-24. Compare Mark 7:14-23.

point that God has the freedom to change any of the stipulations of the Sinai covenant since he was its author. Hebrews 7:12, for example, says, "For when the priesthood is changed, of necessity there takes place a change of law also."[a] Here God changes the priesthoods of Levi and Aaron, to whom the Law gave the right to collect the people's tithes,[b] to that of his Son when he introduces the New covenant.[c] As a result of this change, God abolished the laws surrounding the two former priesthoods, including the law of the tithe, which supported both of them.[d]

In addition, the notion "God needs" the tithe before he can bless his people is not supported by the lives of the patriarchs or early Israel. God did not need Abraham to tithe to Melchizedek before he blessed him with livestock, silver and gold.[e] God did not need Isaac to tithe before he blessed his crops one hundredfold;[f] the text never says Isaac ever tithed.[g] God did not need Jacob to make a tithe vow before he allowed him to obtain the majority share of his father's estate.[h] Lastly, God blessed Israel with riches as they came out of Egypt, even though they did not tithe to earn such a blessing.[i]

Third, Pick claims when Christians commit to tithe, they say to God, "We choose to come into covenant with you." [480] When this pro-tither calls tithing a "covenant" with God,[481] he does what the leaders of the LDS[j] do in their use of this theologically-loaded term. B. McConkie, for example, a former member of the Quorum of the Twelve Apostles of The Church of Jesus Christ of Latter-day Saints from 1972 until his death in 1985, agrees with Pick that tithing is a covenant. He writes, "Tithing is a covenant by conformity to which men are assured temporal and spiritual blessings (Malachi 3:7-12; *Doctrine and Covenants*, 119)."[482] LDS leaders describe more than one of their doctrines as a

---

[a] NASB
[b] Hebrews 7:5
[c] Hebrews 7:23-24
[d] Hebrews 7:1-28, especially verses 5,11-12,18-19. See Book 4 in *The Tithing Series*.
[e] Genesis 13:2
[f] Genesis 26:12-14
[g] See Chapter 12.
[h] Genesis 25:27-34; 27:18-29; 28:22c
[i] Exodus 12:35-36
[j] LDS = The Church of Jesus Christ of Latter-day Saints

"covenant."[483] When leaders of any group use the biblical term covenant in this way, they not only highlight the seriousness of certain doctrines, they also increase their power to leverage the people's behavior in ways which benefit their institution. Even though various leaders agree with Pick's claim that tithing is a covenant with God, we search in vain for any New Testament writer to do likewise.

Fourth, this tithe advocate argues that even though it is Christians' tithes which enable God to send them material blessings, their tithes are "not buying God's favor [because]...God has structured this covenant to operate through the exchange [giving] of money."[484] Pick's thought is that since it was God himself and not a human source who created the covenant, no one can question its requirements. I have already demonstrated that Pick's 'Covenant of Blessings' is a covenant of his own invention, and God had nothing to do with its formation. The title is not a biblical one, and it certainly functions as a means of "buying God's favor."[485] Its humanly-inspired name ('Covenant of *Blessings*'[a]) reveals its true function: a supposedly "guaranteed"[486] way to purchase God's material favors through the ceaseless habit of "tithe, walk and give."

Finally, this pro-tither asserts, "We have to exchange [give] money to God first to activate the covenant - which is the tithe...Whenever covenant is entered into, there is always an exchange, for example, when I married Esther, there was an exchange of rings."[487] To Pick, as a woman legally qualifies herself to share in her groom's material possessions when she gives him a wedding band, so Christians qualify themselves to share in God's material blessings when they give him their tithes. Even though "marriage by purchase"[b/488] still dominates many ancient Near Eastern cultures, the Christian life is not to be guided by primitive or modern marriage customs. It is to be governed by the New covenant.

---

[a] Emphasis mine.

[b] Compare Genesis 29:20,27-28; 31:15; 34:11-12.

Jesus,[a] John[b] and Paul[c] all use marriage to describe Christ's relationship with his followers, but none of them relates the tithe to marrying Jesus or it being necessary to obtain his blessings. According to Paul, people enter into a marriage covenant with God when they turn to Christ[d] and become one with him in the Spirit.[e] To him, the marriage to their new husband (Christ) produces "fruit for God,"[f] that is, new and visible evidence of the divine nature.[g/489] Though Paul also says Christians are now engaged to Christ and awaiting marriage to him in the future,[h] neither his engagement nor marriage metaphor requires the payment of tithes.

Consequently, Pick is not justified in using the tithe/ring metaphor to support his notion that the New covenant[490] requires believers to tithe to receive God's financial favor. He fails to demonstrate where Jesus or the apostles required a tithe from the early Christians to "activate" [491] their reception of the Father's material blessings under the New covenant. He uses the words "tithe(s),"[492] "offering(s),"[493] "covenant," [494] "inheritance" [495] and "blessing(s)"[496] as popular catchwords without any clear New Testament anchors. By necessitating his own 'Covenant of Blessings,' he falsely implies that the New covenant does not sufficiently address believers' material needs or their reception of its tangible benefits, which it does.[i]

Requirement 2: Walk

According to Pick's 'Covenant of Blessings,' being current on one's tithes does not qualify a Christian to receive God's earthly blessings. A believer must also "walk blameless before God."[497]

---

[a] Matthew 9:15 = Mark 2:19-20 = Luke 5:34-35. Compare Matthew 22:1-14; 25:1-13; Luke 12:36.
[b] John 3:29; Revelation 19:7-8; 21:2,9; 22:17
[c] Ephesians 5:25-32
[d] Romans 7:1-6; Ephesians 5:23
[e] I Corinthians 6:17
[f] Romans 7:4, NASB
[g] 2 Peter 1:4; 2 Corinthians 5:17
[h] 2 Corinthians 11:2; Ephesians 5:27; Revelation 19:7-9; 21:2,9
[i] Matthew 6:33; 19:29 = Mark 10:29-30; Luke 18:29; Acts 2:43-47; 4:32,37; I Timothy 5:3-16; 2 Corinthians 8:13-15

Here are his claims:

- "The pattern was in this order...secondly to walk blameless before God..."[498]
- "Secondly repent of financial unrighteousness and purpose in your heart to be accurate in your handling of money."[499]
- "God asks for a blameless walk."[500]
- "Before God asked Abram for an offering, He asked him to walk before Him blameless..."[a/501]

To create the second requirement of his 'Covenant of Blessings,' Pick uses part of God's word to Abraham in Genesis 17:1-4, which says:

"Now when Abram was ninety-nine years old, the Lord appeared to Abram and said to him, 'I am God Almighty; Walk before Me, and be blameless. I will establish My covenant between Me and you, And I will multiply you exceedingly.' Abram fell on his face, and God talked to him, saying, 'As for Me, behold, My covenant is with you, And you will be the father of a multitude of nations.'"[b]

To this pro-tither, walking blamelessly before the Lord means for Christians to handle their finances with complete honesty. According to him, "Your integrity will position you financially"[502] and "Financial integrity will attract wealth to you."[503] Even though the New Testament encourages financial uprightness, the second requirement of his 'Covenant of Blessings' reveals several errors:

First, this tithe advocate ignores the vast majority of Genesis chapter 17, and, instead, focuses exclusively on verse 1d,e,[504] which, according to C. Westermann, is a part of the prologue of the chapter. Its lack of similarity with the rest of the chapter's contents cause him to conclude verses 1-3a was the tradition the writer had in front of him when he wrote the rest of the narrative about covenantal circumcision.[c/505] Be that as it may, the chapter

---

[a] Compare Genesis 17:1d,e with 22:1-2.
[b] NASB
[c] Genesis 17:9-14; 23-27

begins with a list of God's promises to Abraham:ª (1) covenant; (2) descendants; (3) nations; (4) kings and (5) land. In Genesis chapter 17, God gives three commands to the patriarch:[b] (1) walk before Me; (2) be blameless and (3) circumcise all males. Of these three, Pick combines the first two into one and ignores the third. Here again, he overlooks the verses which do not support his point and leaves the Abrahamic covenant far behind.

Second, contrary to Pick's claim, when the Lord said to the patriarch, "Walk before Me, and be blameless,"[c] he was not speaking of Abraham's financial integrity. This sentence involves two Hebrew imperatives. The first command is to walk with YHWH. When God said, "Walk before Me" (*halakh panim*), according to Westermann, he meant for Abraham to "live his life...in such a way that every single step is made with reference to God and every day experiences him close at hand. This is not meant to be some sort of lofty demand; it is something quite natural..."[506] According to this scholar, "...God's commands are no longer simple, concrete, and hence limited instructions, but are directed to one's very existence as a whole."[507] Thus, he translates the verse: "Live always in my presence..."[d/508] Even though God's command to the patriarch to live in his presence included Abraham's wealth, this divine imperative addresses a much deeper and broader view of Abraham's life than Pick's narrow focus on money leads us to believe. He reads financial righteousness into the text to create his covenant's "Walk" requirement.

God's second command to Abraham was to be blameless (*tamim*), which Westermann translates as "...be perfect..."[509] The only other time *tamim* is used in Genesis is where it refers to Noah's walk with God as "blameless [*tamim*] in his time."[e] According to the same scholar, *tamim* "...has neither moral nor religious echo, but is consciously secular. The nearest approach to the Hebrew would be something like 'and be whole (complete)...'"[510] The

---

ª See Genesis 17:1-8.
[b] Genesis 17:1d,e,10
[c] Genesis 17:1d,e, NASB

[d] Compare also Genesis 17:7b; 8c.
[e] Genesis 6:9, NASB

author's message is, "belonging to God is in proper order only when it is without reservation and unconditional,"[511] something Abraham demonstrated in Genesis chapter 22 when he bound his son upon an altar of sacrifice.[a] Thus, this pro-tither also misinterprets God's second command to Abraham in his attempt to use Genesis 17:1d,e to support the "Walk" requirement of his prosperity covenant.

Requirement 3: Give

To Pick, Christians must do more than keep current on their tithes and walk in complete financial integrity to experience God's financial blessings. They must also give divinely designated offerings above their tithes.[512] Here are his claims:

- "...if we follow exactly what God told Abraham to do, we will then...receive Abraham's blessings. The pattern was in this order...finally to give an offering."[513]
- "Thirdly do pray about the amount of offering that you should give..."[514]
- "God asks for an offering. The offering will increase you financially."[515]

This tithe advocate bases the third requirement of his 'Covenant of Blessings' upon Abraham's offering of Isaac in Genesis 22:2,15-18. He states, "When God asked Abraham for an offering, He actually asked Abraham for his son. It was quite clear what God wanted."[516] Here are the relevant verses:

"The angel of the Lord called to Abraham a second time from heaven, and said, 'By myself I have sworn, says the Lord: Because you have done this, and have not withheld your son, your only son, I will indeed bless you, and I will make your offspring as numerous as the stars of heaven and as the sand that is on the seashore. And your offspring shall possess the gate of their enemies, and by your offspring shall all

---

[a] Genesis 22:1-19

the nations of the earth gain blessing for themselves, because you have obeyed my voice.'"[a]

Verses 16b ("Because you have done this...") and 18c ("because you have obeyed my voice") make God's covenant blessings dependent upon Abraham's offering of Isaac. Here this tithe supporter wants his readers to believe not only that Abraham received God's covenant blessings because he offered Isaac at God's request,[517] but also that Christians will only receive God's material blessings if they give offerings above their tithes.[518] This view is lop-sided. Any attempt to connect the offering of Isaac with Christian offerings is clearly strained for the following reasons:

First, Pick's claim falls prey to the fallacy of "selective attention," which, according to B. Bennett, involves "focusing attention on certain aspects of the argument while completely ignoring or missing other parts."[519] When this tithe advocate uses the binding of Isaac to make his point about how offerings "will increase you financially,"[520] he misses the central message of the passage, which is not material prosperity but Abraham's offspring.[521] In Genesis 22:17-18, the Hebrew word translated "seed" or "offspring" (*zera*) is used three times.[b] It is through many offspring, whether rich or poor, the future nation of Israel will be able to overcome its enemies and bless the nations. Also, to Paul, "in your seed" applies to Christ and "all the nations will be blessed in you" to the spiritual riches of the gospel not to material wealth.[c]

Second, the text does not link Abraham's one-time tithe to the offering of his son, Isaac, as if they were two requirements in a three-step prosperity covenant. To claim these two events are connected and reveal a "covenant pattern"[522] of blessing for Christians falls prey to the fallacy of proof-texting, which "is the practice of using isolated, out-of-context quotations from a document to establish a proposition..."[523] Because God reiterated

---

[a] Genesis 22:15-18, NRSV
[b] Genesis 22:17(2x),18
[c] Galatians 3:8,16, NASB

covenant promises to Abraham in the story of the binding of Isaac does not mean whatever Abraham was doing at the time would automatically apply to Christians.[a] We cannot read the giving of church offerings by Christians into such a personal and unusual test of faith. Contrary to what this tithe supporter implies, YHWH did not compliment Abraham for his willingness to offer Isaac as one of a series of regular, special offerings – let alone an offering above his tithe.[524]

Third, in as much as Pick desires his readers to associate his 'Covenant of Blessings' with the Abrahamic covenant, the idea of giving an offering above one's tithe was never a part of either of its two foundational chapters in Genesis.[b/525] In Genesis chapter 15, which records the original oath of the covenant, Abraham killed a heifer, goat and ram at God's request.[c] Nothing in the text indicates that God commanded Abraham to offer any of these animals as offerings above his tithe to Melchizedek. In Genesis chapter 17, which commands circumcision as the sign of the covenant, Abraham made no offering,[d] unless one considers the foreskins of his male family members to be a primitive type of blood offering.[526] According to G. Mendenhall, the removal of foreskins was an external sign of covenant membership not an offering to ensure the continued reception of the covenant's benefits.[527] According to these two chapters, therefore, it is impossible to hold God wanted Abraham to give a special offering above his tithe to guarantee his reception of the material blessings God promised the patriarch and his descendants.

Fourth, to prove his claim, Pick quotes Genesis 22:16b-17a,18 which read, "...because you have done this thing and have not withheld your son, your only son, indeed I will greatly bless you..."[e] and "In your seed all the nations of the earth shall be blessed, because you have obeyed My voice."[f/528] He uses these verses to try to prove that as God attached the fulfillment of his covenant promises to Abraham's offering of Isaac, so he also

---

[a] Genesis 22:15-18
[b] Genesis chapters 15 and 17
[c] Genesis 15:9-10
[d] Genesis 17:9-27
[e] NASB
[f] NKJV

expects Christians to give offerings above their tithes to qualify for earthly blessings.

The text, however, reveals the offering of Isaac was never a condition of Abraham's reception of material blessings. Abraham was rich before he ever offered Isaac.[a] Also, Genesis 22:15-18 reveals a different tradition of the Abrahamic covenant promises than the earliest record found in Genesis chapter 15, which attaches no conditions to them like later renderings of the covenant do: (1) Genesis 17:9-14 adds the command to circumcise to the unconditional covenant promises given in verses 1-8; (2) Genesis 18:19 adds to the covenant the command to do "righteousness and justice" and (3) Genesis 26:5 adds to the covenant the command to obey God's "charge," "commandments," "statutes," and "laws." The words "righteousness," "justice," "charge," "commandments," "statutes," and "laws" are all terms from the book of Deuteronomy[b] and are foreign to the religion of the patriarchs. Westermann, in agreement with Genesis 15:1-21, points out the promises of the Abrahamic covenant were "originally unconditional"[529] and "...in essence, free assurances from God."[530] Concerning Genesis 22:15-18 and the offering of Isaac, he says, "To ground them [the covenant promises], as here, on Abraham's achievement is to alter the understanding of them. The Deuteronomic theology with its conditioned promise is presupposed."[531]

Fifth, when the angel ordered the patriarch to cease from fulfilling God's initial command,[c] he provided a ram as a substitute to offer in Isaac's place.[d] If we take the ram as an example of God meeting Abraham's material need at the moment, it was not as Abraham *completed* his offering that his need was met,[e] it was as God saw the patriarch was *willing* to make his offering that the Lord intervened. This raises a good question: How can Pick base the third and final requirement of his 'Covenant of Blessings'

---

[a] Compare Genesis 13:2 with 22:1-2.
[b] Note: righteousness (Dt. 6:25; 24:13), justice (10:18; 16:19,20; 24:17; 33:21), charge, commandments, statutes, and laws (11:1. Compare 5:31; 6:2,17; 26:17; 28:15; 30:16).
[c] Genesis 22:11-12
[d] Genesis 22:13
[e] Genesis 22:2

upon an incident in the life of Abraham God himself prevented from happening? Would Christians still satisfy this third requirement, if they started to give an offering above their tithe but did not complete it? In addition, as in the case of Abraham, what would this tithe supporter think if those same believers claimed an angel stopped them from giving the offerings God originally commanded? Would their good intentions be enough?

Sixth, when this tithe advocate makes the offering of Isaac the third stipulation in his 'Covenant of Blessings,' he asks Christians to view Abraham's offering of his son as what YHWH required the patriarch to do "above his tithe" to receive the covenant promises. To Pick, if Abraham had not been willing to offer his son to God as a human sacrifice, he would not have merited God's material blessings. In my opinion, such an interpretation is a vulgar commercialization of a rare and potentially heartbreaking episode involving human sacrifice. There are two references in the New Testament to the offering of Isaac.[a] Both describe the event as a foreshadowing of the sacrifice of Christ; neither uses it to refer to the notion that believers should give offerings above their tithes.

Finally, to Pick, for God to send his people material blessings, Christians must practice "tithe, walk, and give" in their exact order.[532] Following this order or pattern guarantees results.[533] Such a claim is one of this pro-tither's most outlandish. Under the New covenant, Christians can give offerings before they voluntarily tithe because the New Testament never asks believers to tithe in the first place. God may financially bless Christians for walking with financial integrity, even if they do not tithe or give special offerings above their tithes. Should not financial integrity be first on this tithe supporter's list instead of second? Should not believers have financial integrity before they tithe? Pick's insistence on exact order is a clear money grab: tithing is the first on his list even before financial integrity. Such a legalism contradicts the freedom of the Spirit inherent in the New covenant, but it is similar to the *Hallah* ritual in Jewish halakhah,

---

[a] Hebrews 11:17; James 2:21

which tells Jews how they should tithe on pieces of bread dough. For the tithes of bread dough to earn the sacred status of "tithe," a person must perform his tithing ritual "in the order and correct sequencing of its various parts..."[534] The correct order is so important that "when the order changes, the ritual status vanishes;"[535] in such cases, tithers do not have to tithe on their bread dough.[536] According to this pro-tither, however, if Christians do not follow the exact order of the 'Covenant of Blessings,' they still must tithe, if they do not want to be cursed.[537]

Conclusion

In this chapter, I demonstrated that Clive Pick's 'Covenant of Blessings' is not a biblical, God-ordained covenant but one of his own making. At the same time, under the New covenant, "tithe, walk and give" are acceptable practices, as long as we strip them of the legalisms with which this pro-tither surrounds them. In my view, if Christians freely choose to tithe, it should be: (1) voluntarily; (2) anonymously[a] (free from group pressure and leadership scrutiny); (3) confidently (exempt from the fear God will curse them if they do not tithe[b]) and (4) knowingly (fully aware the New covenant does not demand from them any kind of percentage giving). Although the New covenant encourages honesty and integrity in all financial dealings,[c] to conclude from this that God will never bless Christians with money or possessions until they are perfect in this area, as this tithe advocate promotes,[538] is a clear exaggeration. It is true the New covenant encourages the giving of offerings, but it does not even remotely imply - let alone require - that those offerings be given only after one tithes.

---

[a] Compare Matthew 6:2-4.
[b] Contrast Malachi 3:9 with Galatians 3:10-14; Romans 8:1,15,33-34 and Hebrews 7:5,11-12, 18-19; 13:9-10. See Book 4 in *The Tithing Series*.
[c] Compare Romans 13:8.

11

Did Tithing Make Abraham Rich?

When Abraham entered Canaan with his nephew, Lot, the text says he "...was very rich in livestock, in silver and in gold."[a] He owned so much livestock he had to part company with his nephew.[b] Later, when Abraham sent his servant, Eliezer, to obtain a wife for his son, Isaac,[c] he endowed him with a large bridal gift for Bethuel, the father of his son's future bride,[539] which included ten camels, a gold nose-ring, two gold bracelets[d] and "all kinds of choice gifts."[e] When the patriarch died, he left his estate to Isaac[f] while also taking "...care to provide for Isaac's half-brothers so that his patrimony [ancestry] should not diminish..."[g/540] Although tithe advocates readily admit Abraham was wealthy, many falsely assume tithing was what made him rich. In this chapter, I address the following claims and provide evidence that Abraham's prosperity did not derive from his tithe to Melchizedek or from any other offerings he may have given to YHWH.

- "The first of the two things that he [Abraham] did to 'begin and maintain' the flow of provision to himself was he gave a tithe."[541]

---

[a] Genesis 13:2. Compare 24:35.
[b] Genesis 13:8-12
[c] Genesis 24:1-61
[d] Genesis 24:22,30,47, NASB. Compare verse 35.
[e] Genesis 24:10, ESV
[f] Genesis 24:36; 25:5
[g] Genesis 25:6. Compare 17:18,21.

- "He [Abraham] gave tithes to this high priest named Melchisedek and the blessings began to flow."[542]
- "Here's a historical fact: throughout the Old Testament, when God's people were in harmony with God, they tithed, prospered greatly and became wealthy. Genesis 13:2 says that Abraham was very rich."[543]

These claims do not provide any causal link between Abraham's tithe and the patriarch's wealth. Instead of tithing, Genesis makes it clear that YHWH used the following seven ways to make Abraham rich: (1) family of origin; (2) urban business opportunities; (3) gifts from political rulers; (4) productive livestock; (5) substantial posterity; (6) water rights and (7) good trade relations. At the end of this chapter, I look at the ultimate cause of Abraham's wealth.

Family of Origin

Abraham grew up in a family of some wealth because they were "associated with [the] city life"[544] of Ur, which was located on the Euphrates in SE Mesopotamia (present-day Iraq). According to J. Marks, "...in Abraham's time [Ur] was still a city of notable wealth and culture."[545] While living in Ur, Abraham's father, Terah, had three sons: Abram, Nahor and Haran, and Haran became the father of Lot.[a] Haran (*haran*) died in Ur, but the rest of the family moved west to a city called by the same name, Haran (*kharan*).[b] There Terah died,[c] and Abraham inherited his father's estate since he was the eldest son.[d] This statement is based on the general pattern of inheritance during the patriarchal period.[e] The writer's description, "...all their possessions which they had accumulated, and the persons which they had acquired in Haran..."[f] helps to explain Abraham's wealth prior to his entering Canaan.

---

[a] Genesis 11:27
[b] Genesis 11:28
[c] Genesis 11:32
[d] Genesis 11:26-27. The firstborn is usually mentioned first in the list of children's names (24:36; 25:5).
[e] Genesis 25:5,31-34; 27:37; 29:26. Compare Deuteronomy 21:15-17.
[f] Genesis 12:5, NASB

Urban Business Opportunities

Abraham enjoyed profitable business opportunities in both Ur and Haran. According to J. Margueron, Ur was a "prodigious urban capital"[546] and a "great Sumerian metropolis, which was a real key in Mesopotamian commercial relations with the countries of the Persian Gulf and undoubtedly with the Indus valley as well."[547] As its domestic architecture demonstrates, Ur had the rich as well as the poor.[548] It is most famous for its royal tombs.[549] Margueron writes, "An exceptional collection of precious objects has been found in these tombs: jewelry, golden weapons (helmets, daggers, swords), musical instruments (harps and lyres encrusted with mother-of-pearl), game tables, vases of precious materials and the famous 'standard of Ur.' All of this attests to the extraordinary riches that one can doubtlessly link with Ur's role in the Persian Gulf trade."[550]

Haran was also a prosperous trade center located in the beltway of the Euphrates.[551] Terah and his family settled there long enough that Abraham came to call the Haran region "my country."[a/552] In Haran, Abraham not only accumulated more material possessions, he also purchased additional slaves.[b] According to C. Gordon, from cuneiform tablets it is clear "the Haran neighborhood was the scene of commercial colonies...Ezekiel lists Haran among the famous commercial cities [that traded with Tyre on the Phoenician coast]..."[c/553] According to Y. Kobayashi, the city was "an important crossroads,"[554] and Margueron describes it as "a great caravan site..."[555]

Gifts from Political Rulers

Generous gifts from Canaanite "kings and the Pharaoh"[556] also contributed to Abraham's net worth.[d/557] The Pharaoh of Egypt gave Abraham "sheep and oxen and donkeys and male and female servants and female donkeys and camels"[e] to make restitution for

---

[a] Genesis 24:4
[b] Genesis 12:5c
[c] Ezekiel 27:23

[d] Genesis 12:15-16; 20:2,14-16; 21:22-24
[e] Genesis 12:16b, NASB

taking Sarah into his harem.[a] In a similar incident,[558] Abimelech, king of Gerar, gave Abraham "sheep and oxen and male and female servants..."[b] as well as "a thousand pieces of silver."[c] According to C. Westermann, such an amount of silver was a "fabulously large sum."[559]

Productive Livestock

As previously noted, the text describes Abraham as "...very rich in livestock..."[d] The patriarch's large flocks and herds created a constant income stream for him and his household. Millard recognizes this when he says, "Wealth flowed to him through his herds..."[560] As a seminomadic herdsman, Abraham profited wherever he went through the sale and trade of his livestock. G. Barrois writes, "Livestock was offered [sold] principally by nomads and seminomads, and by those peasants who owned extensive pastures or pasture lands...The trade in saddle or pack animals was naturally limited, while the sale of oxen, sheep, and goats, went on extensively..."[561] In Abraham's day, a "head of cattle constituted the basic standard of value."[562] The patriarch's large number of livestock made him a wealthy man, which enabled him to trade his flocks and herds for other goods and services. Abraham not only profited from the high demand for livestock wherever he traveled, he also benefited from the demand for the products derived from them. Whereas the demand for sheep and goats reached its peak in the spring "when lambs and kids were brought to market,"[563] Barrois also explains, "Dairy products, such as milk (sweet and sour), cheese, [and] butter fat, were sold to city people the year around."[564] From their productive flocks and herds, Abraham and Sarah were readily able to serve visitors meat and bread along with "curds and milk."[e]

---

[a] Genesis 12:15,17-20
[b] Genesis 20:14, NASB
[c] Genesis 20:16, NASB
[d] Genesis 13:2, NRSV
[e] Genesis 18:8a, NASB

Substantial Posterity

Another source of Abraham's wealth was his large family to which each member (immediate and extended) contributed directly or indirectly. Over his lifetime, Abraham had two wives, Sarah[a] and Keturah[b] (although some refer to Hagar as a third[c/565]) along with concubines,[d] children[e] and grandchildren.[f] The text makes a point about Abraham's large posterity through Keturah when it observes, "All these were the sons of Keturah."[g] E. Knauf notes Abraham's children and grandchildren by Keturah "...were prominent Arabian or Aramean tribes or cities...Medan, Midian, Dedan and Sheba/Saba were situated along the 'incense route' through W Arabia, and Shuah was involved in Sabean commerce..."[566]

Abraham also had twelve grandchildren through his son, Ishmael, who he conceived through Hagar.[h] Four of these twelve grandsons had a direct connection to wealth: Nebaioth, Kedar, Dumah and Tema. The descendants of Nebaioth became "breeders of small stock *par excellence.*"[i/567] The tribe of Kedar also became known for its flocks and herds[j] as well as its kings and queens.[k] The lineage of Dumah was linked with a political and religious center of the Qedarites (Kedarites),[568] and the tribe of Tema was associated with "a major trade center in N Arabia."[l]

Water Rights

Another cause of Abraham's prosperity was his ownership of water wells.[m] W. Reed notes, "...wells have always been important in Bible lands...They were especially important in a nomadic society (Genesis 26:18), supplying water for both families and flocks

---

[a] Genesis 11:29
[b] Genesis 25:1
[c] Genesis 16:6
[d] Genesis 25:6a
[e] Genesis 16:4,15-16; 21:2-3; 25:1-5
[f] Genesis 25:3-4
[g] Genesis 25:4, NASB
[h] Genesis 25:12-16
[i] Isaiah 60:7b
[j] Isaiah 60:7a; Jeremiah 49;29,32
[k] Isaiah 21:16-17; Ezekiel 27:21. Compare Jeremiah 49:28-33.
[l] Jeremiah 25:23-24; Isaiah 21:13-15; Job 6:19
[m] Genesis 21:25; 26:15

(Genesis 29:2)."[569] Westermann explains, "Because of the scarcity of rainfall...the very existence of the group of people and their herds depended on the watering places. This is the reason why the itineraries [in Genesis] with their information about the wells are handed down; the location of the wells along the route, together with their names, had to be preserved for the next migration; knowledge of this could be a matter of life and death."[570] Because of their critical importance for survival, some of the locals stole one of Abraham's wells.[a] As previously mentioned, to retain his source of water, prevent further theft[571] and avoid conflict, Abraham purchased back his well using some of his flocks as payment.[b] With such water rights,[c] Abraham saw his livestock flourish.

Good Trade Relations

When God called Abraham to leave Haran for Canaan, he called him to exchange his "urban-based life for the seminomadic style of the pastoralist with no permanent home, living in tents."[d/572] Nevertheless, Abraham frequently visited the region between Ai and Bethel[e] and lived in certain locales for longer periods of time like Mamre-Hebron,[f/573] Beersheba[g] and Philistia,[h] where he enjoyed favorable trade relations. According to Millard, in addition to livestock, Abraham "may have traded in other goods, for he knew the language of the marketplace (Genesis 23)."[574] The patriarch also formed nonaggression treaties with communities like Salem.[i/575] Each treaty he formed with local leaders or groups would have further solidified his commercial contacts and income.

The Ultimate Source of Abraham's Wealth

One tithe advocate above claims, "The first of the two things that he [Abraham] did to 'begin and maintain' the flow of provision to himself was he gave a tithe."[576] This statement makes tithing one

---

[a] Genesis 21:25. Compare 26:15.
[b] Genesis 21:25-34
[c] Compare Genesis 26:15.
[d] Genesis 12:8; 13:3,18; 18:1. Compare Hebrews 11:9.
[e] Genesis 12:8; 13:3-4
[f] Genesis 13:18; 18:1; 23:2,19-20.
[g] Genesis 22:19
[h] Genesis 21:34
[i] Genesis 14:18-20

of the major causes of Abraham's reception of God's promises, namely:[a] (1) land; (2) great nation; (3) divine blessing; (4) great name; (5) blessing to others; (6) blessings on those who bless him and (7) curses on those who curse him. If the above assertion was true, then the text should support the notion that Abraham did not receive any of these promises before he gave a tithe to Melchizedek and his tithe to Melchizedek was the direct cause of his reception of each blessing. If we understand the phrase "flow of provision"[577] to include Abraham's experience of some of the covenant promises given to him before he gave a tithe to Melchizedek, the claim is false. There is no evidence to indicate Abraham received any of these seven blessings due to his tithe. The three specific promises of "land," "divine blessing" and "curses..." indicate just the opposite. Concerning the promise of "land," before Abraham ever gave a tithe, he started to possess the territory of Canaan in Mamre.[b] About the promise of "blessing," if we understand it to mean material or financial favor, God extended such blessings to Abraham earlier than his giving of a tithe to the ruler of Salem.[c] Regarding the promise of "curses...," we find it was prior to Abraham giving a tithe to Melchizedek that God cursed Pharaoh for taking the patriarch's wife, Sarah, into his harem.[d] Thus, according to the text, it was plainly not Abraham's tithe that was his "first step to receiving the promises."[578] God began his "flow of provision"[579] to the patriarch as soon as he left Haran[e] if not sooner.

Instead of his tithe to Melchizedek being the beginning, let alone the maintaining, of Abraham's reception of wealth, it is clear the ultimate source of the patriarch's prosperity was his divine call and the unconditional covenant YHWH made with him and his descendants.[f] In light of this, we need to view Abraham's sources of income as a result of his call and covenant. The main promise of the covenant was the land of Canaan, and its

---

[a] Genesis 12:1-3; 13:14-17
[b] Genesis 13:18; 14:13; 18:1. Compare 23:17,19; 25:9; 35:27.
[c] Genesis 12:16; 13:2
[d] Genesis 12:17
[e] Genesis 12:4. Compare 12:1-3 with 12:16; 12:7 with 12:8-9 and 13:14-17 with 13:18.
[f] Genesis 12:1-3; 15:1-21

theological thrust is summed up in the statement, "I will *give* it to you."[a] This is language similar to ancient Near Eastern royal land grants in which kings gave part of their domains freely to whoever they chose.[b]

Because YHWH made an unconditional covenant with Abraham and his descendants, he financially blessed them despite their faults and sins.[c/580] According to J. Milgrom, the covenant did not contain any formal threats of punishment for unsavory behavior.[581] More than once, for example, Abraham deceived a local ruler and put his wife in grave danger.[d] Because he was under the protection of a covenant without qualification, however, God preserved both of their lives, and, in spite of his self-centered actions, each time gave him an unmerited financial blessing.[e] Abimelech, king of Gerar, and Phicol, the commander of his army, recognized this supernatural blessing on Abraham when they told him, "God is with you in all that you do."[f] The text, however, does not attribute this divine blessing to Abraham's tithe to Melchizedek. Similarly, even though Jacob lied to his father, Isaac,[g] exploited and misled his older brother, Esau,[h] and misused the name of YHWH,[i/582] God continued to send angels into his life to bless, protect and direct him because he was a member of the covenant family.[j]

---

[a] Genesis 13:15,17. Compare 12:7; 15:7,18; 17:8; 24:7; 26:3; 28:4,13; 35:12; 48:4. Emphasis mine.
[b] Compare I Samuel 8:14; 22:7; 2 Samuel 9:7-13; I Kings 21:7; Esther 5:3,6 and Mark 6:23.
[c] Abraham (Genesis 12:18; 20:9); Isaac (26:6-11); Jacob (see Chapter 17); Joseph (See attending note. Compare Deuteronomy 9:27.)
[d] Pharaoh (Genesis 12) and Abimelech (Genesis 20)
[e] Genesis 12:16; 20:14-16
[f] Genesis 21:22, NASB
[g] Genesis 27:18-19,20,24
[h] Genesis 25:29-33; 27:36; 33:12-17
[i] Genesis 27:20
[j] Genesis 28:12; 31:11-13; 32:1-2; 48:16. Compare God's words to Isaac, "I will bless you...for the sake of My servant Abraham" (26:24e. Compare 19:29.).

Conclusion

The focus of this chapter has been the sources of Abraham's wealth. Although many pro-tithers assert tithing made the patriarch rich, the evidence I have presented here shows otherwise. It is obvious that YHWH prospered Abraham because of his divine call and unconditional covenant. With such a clear textual basis, we can confidently reject all claims that Abraham was wealthy because he tithed. Such sentiments are based on pro-tithing agendas not Scripture. To assert that Abraham and/or his posterity up to the time of the Sinai covenant became rich due to their paying of tithes is pure tithing propaganda.

12

Did Tithing Make Isaac Rich?

Abraham was not the only wealthy patriarch; his son, Isaac, was also prosperous. Genesis 26:12-14 describes him in this way:

"Now Isaac sowed in that land and reaped in the same year a hundredfold. And the Lord blessed him, and the man became rich, and continued to grow richer until he became very wealthy; for he had possessions of flocks and herds and a great household, so that the Philistines envied him..."[a]

Many of the pro-tithers who refer to the wealth of the patriarchs in an effort to inspire Christians to tithe focus their attention upon Abraham. This makes sense because, according to Scripture, Abraham was the only patriarch who ever gave a tithe.[b] In spite of this fact, however, some tithe advocates still insist God made Isaac rich because he tithed. Others hold Isaac became rich because his father, Abraham, was a tither. The following two assertions reflect the latter view:

- "The Tithing and obedience of Abraham produced blessing for his son, Isaac...(Genesis 26:12-14)."[583]
- "Abraham gave ten percent of his income back as proof and

---

[a] Genesis 26:12-14, NASB
[b] Genesis 14:20c. Jacob promised a tithe (28:22c), but there is no textual evidence he paid it (35:1-7).

evidence that he honored God as his Provider and was blessed incredibly for it (Genesis 13:2). Isaac, his son, continued to reap from the life of obedience (Genesis 26:12-14). It happened for the children of Abraham (Genesis 26:24). When you tithe, you create a financial flow for several generations after you."[584]

These two claims hold that God materially blessed Isaac because his father, Abraham, was a tither. According to them, Abraham's tithes not only caused God to bless his son, Isaac, with wealth, they also caused God to bless "several generations"[585] after him. There are, however, several problems with these statements.

First, in the second claim above, the tithe supporter uses Genesis 13:2 to support his contention that Abraham "was blessed incredibly"[586] because of his payment of tithes. This is an error of fact. It is true this verse says, "Abram was very rich in livestock, in silver, and in gold,"[a] but the text does not indicate he received any of these blessings because he was a tither. Abraham did not pay a tithe until the next chapter after he rescued Lot from the Elamite coalition (Genesis 14:20).

Second, the same pro-tither holds Genesis 26:24 proves God materially blessed Abraham's descendants "for several generations"[587] because Abraham tithed. In this verse, God tells Isaac, "I am the God of your father Abraham; do not be afraid, for I am with you and will bless you and make your offspring numerous for my servant Abraham's sake."[b] Even if we understood the phrase, "My servant,"[c] as not referring to the faith or covenant of Abraham but to his deeds of obedience, we still could not conclude God blessed Isaac and the generations after him because of Abraham's tithe or tithes. The fact is God never commanded Abraham to tithe,[d] and, according to Scripture, he tithed only once.[e]

Third, as previously stated, the text draws no causal

---

[a] NKJV. The original verse has "*was*."
[b] NRSV
[c] Genesis 26:24e, NRSV
[d] See Genesis 14:18-20.
[e] Genesis 14:20c

relationship between Abraham's one-time tithe and his own material wealth.[a] Therefore, we should not be surprised to discover that it does not connect Abraham's tithe to his son's "hundredfold"[b] blessing. The pro-tither provides no direct link between his proof texts and his claims that tithing made Abraham rich[c/588] or that Abraham's tithe made Isaac rich.[d]

Fourth, according to this tithe supporter, the parent (Abraham) caused his son (Isaac) to be materially blessed because he (the parent) tithed. So, without tithing, Isaac became wealthier than his father,[e] who, if we go by Scripture, tithed only once.[f] If Abraham could make his son wealthier than himself by tithing once, why could not Christian parents who tithed one or more times do the same for their children? If they could, then the children of tithing parents would never have to tithe to get rich because their wealth, like Isaac's, would already be a "hundredfold"[g] greater than that of their parents.

Finally, according to Paul, all believers are not only the spiritual children of Abraham,[h] they also, "like Isaac, are children of promise."[i] Since this is the case, why wouldn't Abraham's tithe automatically make all Christians rich like what is claimed to have happened to Isaac?

The next two pro-tithers maintain that Isaac was a tither, and that tithing made him rich. Here are their claims:

- Tithing "is the same dynamic and supernatural covenant act that Abraham and his descendants performed some four hundred and thirty years before the law."[589]
- "The actual act of tithing has great spiritual ramifications...When we are obedient to the word of God [and tithe], we are protected (Psalm 91:1). Absolutely

---

[a] Genesis 14:20c; 13:2; 24:1,35
[b] Genesis 26:12
[c] Genesis 13:2 per M. Murdock
[d] Genesis 26:12-14; 26:24 per M. Murdock
[e] Compare "hundredfold" in Genesis 26:12.
[f] Genesis 14:20c
[g] Genesis 26:12, NASB
[h] Galatians 3:7
[i] Galatians 4:28, NASB

nothing can touch us when we are in the shadow of God's protection...In drought, in hard times, you will still get your crop (Genesis 26:1-3; 12-13)."[590]

Even though neither of the claims above contains the name "Isaac," they both refer to him. The first asserts that both Abraham "and his descendants"[591] tithed, and Isaac was one of the descendants of Abraham. The second also refers to Isaac because it uses verses about his experience of drought and prosperity.[a/592] There is, however, a critical problem with these claims. Scripture does not show that Isaac tithed. Neither the verb (*asar*) nor the noun (*ma'aser*) translated "tithe" or "tenth" ever appears in the Isaac narrative.[b/593] Therefore, it is impossible to hold that, in difficult times, it was tithing that enabled Isaac to "still get [his] crop."[594]

The logic of the second claim above also demonstrates that Isaac never tithed. According to it, when anyone tithes, "Absolutely nothing can touch us when we are in the shadow of God's protection."[595] Unfortunately, however, in Genesis chapter 26, Isaac experienced four distinct evils. First, a famine forced him to move out of the land of promise to Gerar.[c] Second, the herdsmen from the town stopped up the wells he inherited from his father.[d] Third, Abimelech, king of Gerar, who previously had shown kindness to Isaac, told him to move out of town permanently.[e] Finally, even after Isaac moved away from the city, herdsmen continued to quarrel with him over his water rights.[f] Thus, how could this tithe advocate's claim be correct and Isaac have been a tither when so many evils befell him?

The Abrahamic Covenant

To form their claim that tithing made Isaac rich, pro-tithers disconnect Genesis 26:12-14 from its context and read tithing into the verses. For example, Genesis 26:12a says, "Now Isaac sowed

---

[a] Genesis 26:1-3; 12-13 per Clive Pick
[b] Genesis chapters 21 – 27; Isaac's death (35:28-29)
[c] Genesis 26:1
[d] Genesis 26:15,18
[e] Genesis 26:16
[f] Genesis 26:19-21

in that land and reaped in the same year a hundredfold."ᵃ While tithe advocates use this verse to support their assumption that tithing made Isaac rich,ᵇ they neglect the main point of the verse contained in the expression "a hundredfold,"ᶜ which indicates nothing more than YHWH's supernatural blessing. The context never mentions tithing; it ascribes Isaac's wealth to the Lord's blessing upon him with the words, "And the Lord blessed him, and the man became rich..."ᵈ The most biblical way of understanding such blessing is through the Abrahamic covenant.ᵉ

When Isaac moved to Beersheba, for example, YHWH told him, "Do not fear, for I am with you. I will bless you, and multiply your descendants, for the sake of My servant Abraham."ᶠ When understood covenantally, the phrase "for the sake of My servant Abraham"ᵍ annuls any claim that God blessed Isaac for how he may have tithed. Some may understand the term "servant" (*'abdî*) as a nod to his obedience rather than his covenantal election, connecting the phrase with the terms in verse 5 that are foreign to the patriarchal period.ʰ However, to be consistent with Genesis 26:3d, which connects Isaac's blessings to "the oath which I swore to your father Abraham,"ⁱ I think it best to understand "My servant" as one chosen by YHWH. According to C. Westermann, the introductory blessing given by God to Isaac in Genesis 26:3-5, "makes Isaac the heir of the promise to Abraham."[596] Genesis scholars R. Friedman and S. Hooke agree that YHWH blessed him for no other reason than that he was the bearer of the covenant promise originally given to his father.[597] As such, Isaac's wealth was due to his being covenantally "under divine blessing."[598]

ᵃ NASB
ᵇ See the claims at the beginning of this chapter.
ᶜ Genesis 26:12, NASB
ᵈ Genesis 26:12b-13a, NASB
ᵉ Genesis 12:2-3; 14:19-20; 17:16; 24:1,35

ᶠ Genesis 26:24c,d,e, NASB
ᵍ Genesis 26:24e, NASB. Compare verse 3.
ʰ On the Hebrew terms used in Genesis 26:5 see Chapter 9.
ⁱ NASB

The Sources of Isaac's Wealth

The ultimate source of Isaac's wealth was the Abrahamic covenant,[a] which contained no command to tithe.[b] Under the canopy of this covenant, the text reveals that YHWH used the following factors to make Isaac prosperous: (1) family inheritance; (2) obedience to divine command; (3) royal protection and (4) royal treaty.

Family Inheritance

One of the major sources of Isaac's wealth was his father, Abraham's, large estate, which Eliezer, Abraham's servant, described in these terms: "The Lord has greatly blessed my master, so that he has become rich; and He has given him flocks and herds, and silver and gold, and servants and maids, and camels and donkeys."[c] Abraham's estate was so sizable that during his lifetime he was able to give many gifts to Isaac's half-brothers.[d]/599 Upon his death, however, Abraham bequeathed his assets to his son, Isaac,[e] which included valuable water wells.[f] Through Isaac's eventual marriage to Rebekah, he also inherited a family nurse as well as more servants.[g]

Obedience to Divine Command

For some time, Isaac lived in the large, fertile area of Gerar that was "an important city and district near the Mediterranean Sea south and southwest of the southern border of Canaan."[h]/600 During a famine, YHWH appeared to Isaac and told him to remain in that place and not travel to Egypt for help,[i] as his father had done when he had been in a similar situation.[j] Isaac's obedience to YHWH's command to stay in Gerar allowed him to continue to receive God's material blessings.[k]

---

[a] See Genesis 26:3c, 24e.
[b] See Chapter 9.
[c] Genesis 24:35, NASB. Compare verse 1.
[d] Genesis 25:6. Compare 17:18.
[e] Genesis 24:35-36; 25:5
[f] Genesis 26:15,18
[g] Genesis 24:59,61; 35:8
[h] Genesis 26:6
[i] Genesis 26:2
[j] Genesis 12:10
[k] Genesis 26:11-14

Royal Protection

As Isaac lived in Gerar, the men noticed the beauty of his wife, Rebekah, and asked him if she was available.[a] As his father had done in a similar circumstance to save his own life,[b] Isaac lied and told the men that Rebekah was his sister.[c] To protect her from suitors, YHWH intervened in the natural course of affairs and allowed the king to see that she was indeed Isaac's wife.[d] Such an observation was not a coincidence; it was a providential moment that God used to protect Isaac and his increasing prosperity while in Gerar.[e] Since the couple had been living there for a long time, terror and anger gripped the king when he realized that by then many men of the city were desiring to have her.[f] He immediately extended to the couple his royal protection with the warning, "He who touches this man or his wife shall surely be put to death."[g] According to V. Matthews, "Abimelech...is forced (through embarrassment and fear) to grant to him, in the form of a parity treaty, grazing rights and the use of wells within his territory."[601] At least for a while, Isaac produced crops and herds without interference due to the royal protection given him by Abimelech.[h] Though Isaac deceived the men of the town,[i] the Lord still used the situation to put the king into a position where he felt indebted to the patriarch. Like Abraham and Jacob,[j] being blessed in spite of unsavory behavior illustrates how the unconditional covenant that YHWH made with Isaac's father also worked in his favor.

Royal Treaty

Many residents of Gerar envied Isaac's prosperity,[k] and some of them filled up the patriarch's water wells with dirt to force him to find water elsewhere.[l] It appears that some herdsmen complained so much to Abimelech about Isaac's success that the king finally

---

[a] Genesis 26:7
[b] Genesis 12:13; 20:2,5,12
[c] Genesis 26:7,9
[d] Genesis 26:8-9
[e] Genesis 26:11-14
[f] Genesis 26:10
[g] Genesis 26:11, NASB
[h] Genesis 26:11-14
[i] Compare Genesis 26:7,9.
[j] Genesis 15:4; 16:1-4; 17:18. Compare 20:9. Concerning Jacob, see Chapter 17.
[k] Genesis 26:14
[l] Genesis 26:15-17

ordered the patriarch to leave the city altogether.[a] Even though Isaac left and settled in the valley[b] where his uncanny ability to find water[c] continued his "agricultural prosperity,"[602] the locals still contested his water rights.[d] Since he was a man of peace like his father, he moved on and dug other wells.[e] The ease at which Isaac was able to find new water sources attests to the presence of a supernatural power in his life.[f] This divine ability was so clear to Abimelech that he initiated a peace treaty with Isaac to avoid any future conflict.[g] He and his advisors told the patriarch, "We see plainly that the Lord has been with you...You are now the blessed of the Lord."[h] The text attributes Isaac's blessing to YHWH's presence being with him and not as a result of anyone's tithe.

Conclusion

In this chapter, I demonstrated that we cannot account for Isaac's wealth through his having tithed, since no verse states that he ever did. Similarly, when Isaac built an altar and called upon the name of the Lord, he never offered any first fruits offering out of his abundant crops.[i] We also cannot maintain that Isaac became rich through his father's one-time tithe to Melchizedek since the text makes no such causal connection. Genesis provides us with only one factor to account for Isaac's riches, and that is the Abrahamic covenant of which he was an heir.

---

[a] Genesis 26:16-17. Compare verses 20-21.
[b] Genesis 26:17
[c] Genesis 26:19,21a,22a,32-33
[d] Genesis 26:20-21
[e] Genesis 26:19-22
[f] Genesis 26:15,18,20-22; 32-33
[g] Genesis 26:26-31
[h] Genesis 26:28a,29d
[i] Genesis 26:12,25

13

A Tithe for a Safe Return

The second and last reference to the tithe before the Law appears in the life of Jacob,[a] the most famous of Abraham's grandsons. He was the youngest son of Isaac and Rebekah, the twin brother of Esau and the father of the twelve tribes of Israel.[603] After he and Esau became adults, Jacob manipulated his brother out of his birthright as the firstborn.[b] Later, Jacob deceived his father, Isaac, into giving him Esau's paternal blessing,[c] which led to his brother's plot to kill him.[d] To remove Jacob out of harm's way,[e] Rebekah informed her favorite son[f] of the plot[g] and persuaded her husband to send him to her brother Laban's estate in Haran[h/604] to obtain a wife.[i]

On his journey, Jacob spent the night at Luz,[j] where YHWH appeared to him in a dream and confirmed the promises of the Abrahamic covenant.[k] When Jacob awoke, he was awe-struck and changed the name of the place from Luz to Bethel, which means "house of God."[l/605] Fearing his brother's retaliation, he made a vow/bargain with YHWH to secure for himself a safe journey.

---

[a] Genesis 28:22c
[b] Genesis 25:27-34
[c] Genesis 27:18-40
[d] Genesis 27:41
[e] Genesis 27:43-45
[f] Genesis 25:28
[g] Genesis 27:42
[h] Genesis 27:43; 28:10; 29:4. Haran (also Paddan-aram, 28:7) was located in NW Mesopotamia now modern Turkey.
[i] Genesis 27:46 - 28:1-7
[j] Genesis 28:11,19
[k] Genesis 28:12-15
[l] Genesis 28:17,19,22

Here is the account:

"Then Jacob made a vow, saying, 'If God will be with me, and keep me in this way that I am going, and give me bread to eat and clothing to put on, so that I come back to my father's house in peace, then the Lord shall be my God. And this stone which I have set as a pillar shall be God's house, and of all that You give me I will surely give a tenth to You.'"[a]

Jacob the Bargain Maker

The way that many tithe advocates refer to Jacob's tithe vow gives the impression that when the patriarch made his vow, he paid a tithe.[606] This idea finds no foundation in the text. Jacob's tithe vow was not a record of Jacob *paying* a tithe to the Bethel sanctuary; it was an account of the patriarch *promising* to pay a tithe, if God first met his conditions.[b] The conditionality of Jacob's statement, "If God will be with me...then the Lord shall be my God,"[c] makes it clear that he was making a bargain.

Upon close examination, we find that bargaining was the patriarch's modus operandi[d] not only in this instance, but also in the way that he related to other people. Here are five examples, which I have paraphrased: (1) When Esau asked his brother for something to eat after he came in famished from hunting, Jacob replied: "If you will first sell me your birthright, then I will give you some fresh bread and lentil stew."[e] (2) When Jacob was in Haran looking for a bride from his mother's side of the family, he fell in love with Rachel and said to his uncle: "If you will give me Rachel for a wife, I will work for you for the next seven years."[f] (3) When Laban persuaded Jacob to work for him longer than the patriarch wanted, Jacob bargained: "If you will give me your irregular sheep and goats as my wages, then I will continue to

---

[a] Genesis 28:18-22, NKJV
[b] See Chapter 14.
[c] Genesis 28:20-21
[d] *modus operandi* (Latin) = a way, method, procedure or mode of living, working or operating
[e] Compare Genesis 25:32-34.
[f] Genesis 29:18

shepherd your livestock."ᵃ (4) When Jacob wrestled with a man at the Jabbok River and discovered how insistent he was to be released from the patriarch's grip before dawn, Jacob laid out his terms: "If you will bless me, then I will let you go."[b/607] and (5) When Jacob reconciled with Esau, his older brother, and discovered how he wanted him to follow him to Seir [Edom], Jacob replied: "If you will go on before us, then my family and I will meet you there a little later."ᶜ Since Jacob was in the habit of bargaining with others to get what he wanted, it should not surprise us that he would also bargain with YHWH.

The Nature of Jacob's Vow

To some readers, the idea of Jacob making a "bargain" with YHWH might seem out of character. How could a Bible patriarch "cut a deal" with God? Speaking of Jacob's vow, A. Pagolu explains, "The vow language [of 'if...then'] was probably borrowed from the social and business transaction of the bargain..."[608] According to G. Davies, bargains were a common type of Old Testament vow (*neder*), and the kind that Jacob made at Bethel.[609] When pro-tithers refer to Jacob's tithe vow, however, they rarely, if ever, mention this fact. The reason appears to be quite pragmatic: How could tithe advocates tell their financial supporters that they needed to tithe only if God first met their demands, as it was with Jacob? Such a conditional approach to tithing would certainly threaten the stability of the revenue streams tithe supporters seek to establish through their regular collection of tithes. This would especially be true in those churches that expect their members to sign tithing covenants as part of their membership requirements.[610] Contrary to the bargain that Jacob made to ensure his safe return to his father's house, Christians do not have to cut deals with God.ᵈ Because of the finished work of Christ, believers stand before him in a position of favor.ᵉ They can enjoy daily access to

---

ᵃ Genesis 30:31-33
ᵇ Genesis 32:26
ᶜ Compare Genesis 33:12-17.
ᵈ See Chapter 19.
ᵉ Romans 5:2; 8:1; I Corinthians 15:1

God's "presence, protection, provision"[a]/[611] without having to strike bargains.

The Characteristics of Jacob's Vow

Jacob's vow was a (1) tripart; (2) one-time; (3) one-place and (4) fear-based journey vow. It was a bargain, and, as such, disqualifies itself as a valid, biblical basis for the collection of Christians' tithes.

Tripart

Jacob's bargain with God contained three parts, which I refer to as "worship, shrine, and tithe." I borrowed these three terms from G. Davies, who writes, "In return for God's presence, protection, [and] provision, etc., Jacob at Bethel promised worship, shrine, and tithe (Genesis 28:20-22)."[612] I use such terminology frequently because it succinctly summarizes the three commitments that Jacob made to YHWH. Jacob's "worship" promise was "the Lord shall be my God."[b] His "shrine" promise was "this stone, which I have set up for a pillar, shall be God's house"[c] and his "tithe" promise was "of all that you give me I will surely give one-tenth to you."[d]

When tithe advocates refer to Jacob's vow, they usually ignore its first two promises ("worship" and "shrine") and focus exclusively on its third ("tithe").[613] Such inattention to context is typical of the way that most refer to Jacob's tithe vow. If readers exposed themselves to nothing but pro-tithing sources on Jacob's vow, they would have little or no clue that his vow was conditional and that it involved much more than a promise to pay a tithe. Because Jacob's vow was composed of three parts or promises,[e] tithe supporters have no hermeneutical basis to isolate its third part ("tithe") from the other two ("worship" and "shrine").

One possible reason that pro-tithers might isolate Jacob's

---

[a] Hebrews 10:19-22
[b] Genesis 28:21b, NRSV
[c] Genesis 28:22a,b,c, NRSV
[d] Genesis 28:22b, NRSV
[e] Compare Genesis 28:20a; 31:13a,b,c with 28:20-22.

"tithe" promise could stem from the fact that his other two promises are much more difficult to apply to Christians. In contrast to Jacob's promise of "worship," believers do not tell YHWH that if he will first give them what they want, then they will make him their God. According to the Synoptic gospels, Jesus is the one who set the conditions for his disciples to follow him not vice versa.[a] Unlike Jacob's promise of "shrine," followers of Christ are not expected to set up a stone pillar or marker wherever they have a divine visitation, pour oil on top of it, and then come back later to use it as an altar or sanctuary.[614] The New covenant dispenses with the Old covenant notion of sacred or ritual space.[b] Christians themselves are now God's house or sanctuary both corporately[c] and individually.[d] Therefore, since the first two promises of Jacob's bargain with God, "worship" and "shrine," cannot be applied to believers, neither can the third promise of "tithe."

One-time

Besides being a tripart vow, Jacob's bargain with God included the promise of a one-time tithe. Many tithe advocates, however, ignore this fact and characterize the patriarch as a lifetime tither. Here are some claims:

- Jacob was "a tither."[615]
- Jacob honored his "vow of tithes" and his "vow of tithing."[616]
- "Jacob's vow was manifestly to be continued throughout his lifetime and was not framed for the occasion or the journey only."[617]

The above claims state or imply either that Jacob was already a lifetime tither when he arrived at Luz/Bethel, or that he became one by the time he returned to the land. There are, however,

---

[a] Matthew 8:22; 10:38; 16:24; 19:21
[b] Compare Matthew 27:51 with Hebrews 6:19; 10:20.
[c] Ephesians 2:19,22
[d] I Corinthians 3:16-17; 6:19

several problems with these assertions.

First, the claim that Jacob was "a tither" [618] is not supported by Scripture. We know, for example, that Jacob built altars at Shechem,[a] Beersheba[b] and Bethel,[c] but there is no record of him ever offering up a tithe on any of them. Furthermore, if Jacob had been a regular tither when he came to Luz/Bethel, what reason would there have been for him to make a tithe vow?

Second, the above claims hold that Jacob honored his "vow of tithes"[619] and his "vow of tithing"[620] by paying multiple tithes. According to the text, however, Jacob vowed, "I will surely give a tenth to You"[d] (singular); he did not promise more than one tithe. Therefore, when this pro-tither applies his misinterpretation to Christians,[621] he reads his own tithing agenda into the text.

Third, according to N. Sarna, "...Jacob's vow was a single obligation..."[622] because "...the vows of the ancient Near East...were all concerned with immediate circumstances, such as sickness, childlessness, flood or attack of the enemy..."[623] In Jacob's case, he faced an imminent attack from his own brother, Esau, who plotted to kill him for stealing his birthright and paternal blessing.[e] Because the patriarch did not fully trust YHWH's promise to protect him on his journey,[f] in an effort to obtain additional reassurance, he initiated his bargain.[g]

Fourth, the preconditions that Jacob required God to meet before he agreed to pay him a tithe also indicate that the patriarch only intended to pay YHWH a one-time tithe upon his safe return to the land. His requirements were: (1) Presence ("If God will be with me...")[h]; (2) protection ("and will keep me on this journey...")[i]; (3) provision ("and will give me food to eat and garments to wear...")[j] and (4) safe return ("and I return to my

---

[a] Genesis 33:18-20
[b] Genesis 46:1 (by implication)
[c] Genesis 35:1,3,7
[d] Genesis 28:22c
[e] Genesis 27:41,43-45; 28:21a
[f] Genesis 28:15 says, "...will keep you wherever you go..." (NASB).
[g] Compare Genesis 35:1,7 with 28:21 ("in safety").
[h] Genesis 28:20b, NASB
[i] Genesis 28:20c, NASB
[j] Genesis 28:20d,e, NASB

father's house in safety"ª). These four qualifications all related to Jacob's immediate journey to his uncle's estate in Haran and his safe return to Canaan.

Finally, Jacob promised that if YHWH would return him safely to his father's house, the stone pillar, which marked the place of his divine visitation, would be "God's house,"ᵇ that is, a sanctuary for YHWH. Jacob did not promise to sustain this sanctuary with lifetime tithes; nowhere does Genesis indicate that Jacob intended to live at Bethel indefinitely or to pay God any more than a one-time tithe to the shrine. It would have been impractical for him to have made such a promise since, according to Aharoni and Avi-yonah,[624] in addition to the possibility of him living for a while in Ephrath (Bethlehem),[c/625] Jacob lived in locations that ranged from 20 to 200 miles from Bethel.ᵈ There is no evidence to support the notion that Jacob traveled regularly from any of these locations to Bethel to tithe. As a seminomadic shepherd,ᵉ Jacob needed to move from one pasturage to another to sustain his flocks and herds.[626] On his way back from Haran, for example, he required "extensive pasturage"[627] for his livestock not only in Gilead[628] but also in the central mountains of Palestine.[629]

One-place

When pro-tithers claim that Jacob was "a tither,"[630] they fail to provide any biblical evidence as to where the patriarch regularly tithed. The text indicates that Jacob intended his vow to be fulfilled at only one place (Bethel), not at many different sanctuaries or to YHWH in the desert. Jacob eventually returned to Bethel to honor YHWH as "the God of Bethel,"ᶠ who was not only the source of the patriarch's revelatory dream but also the deity of that place.

ª Genesis 28:21a, NASB
ᵇ Genesis 28:22, NASB
ᶜ Genesis 35:16-21
ᵈ Succoth (Genesis 33:17) = 40 miles northeast; Shechem (Genesis 33:18-20) = 20 miles north; Beersheba (Genesis 46:1) = 30 miles south and Goshen (Genesis 45:10; 47:1,6) = 200 miles south
ᵉ Note Jacob's tents (Genesis 33:19; 35:21; Hebrews 11:9), livestock (30:42-43; 31:18; 33:17) and eventual land purchase (33:19).
ᶠ Genesis 31:13

In Jacob's vow fulfillment section (Genesis 35:1-7), "Bethel" is used three times,[a] "El-bethel" once[b] and "the place" once.[c] The narrator's use of the word "there"[d] also indicates an emphasis upon the place itself. After Jacob returned to Bethel, he built an altar and re-named the site "El-bethel."[e] Technically, "El" is not a divine name but a familiar Semitic designation for "the divinity."[631] According to M. Rose, for humans to make contact with this divinity, "El" needed to be rooted in a specific location;[632] in Jacob's case, it was Luz/Bethel. The reason that Jacob renamed the site was "because there God had revealed Himself to him when he fled from his brother."[f]

"Bethel" as the Church

The Hebrew meaning of Bethel is "house of God."[633] Because the New Testament also uses this phrase to describe the church, some pro-tithers inaccurately compare the Old Testament "Bethel" with the New Testament body of believers, as if they were interchangeable. One of the tithe advocates that I quoted earlier in this chapter, for instance, believes that Christians should make and fulfill their tithing vows in and to their local or home churches. When he describes such a practice, he writes: "This will be done at Bethel, the house of God."[634]

I represent his line of reasoning in this four-point syllogism:

- Jacob vowed to pay a tithe at Bethel;[g]
- Bethel means "house of God;"[635]
- The New Testament refers to the local church as "the house of God;"[h]
- Therefore, Christians should vow and pay tithes to their local churches.[636]

---

[a] Genesis 35:1,3,6. Compare "Bethel" in verses 8,15,16.
[b] Genesis 35:7, NASB
[c] Genesis 35:7, NASB. Compare "the place" in verses 13-15.
[d] Compare Genesis 35:1,3.
[e] Genesis 35:7, NASB
[f] Genesis 35:7c, NASB
[g] Genesis 28:19,22
[h] Hebrews 10:21. Compare Ephesians 2:19; I Peter 4:17.

On the surface, such a conclusion might sound reasonable, but it contains several logical and biblical errors.

First, since this tithe advocate expects Christians to pay tithes to their local churches because Jacob promised to pay a tithe to the Bethel sanctuary, does he also expect them, as Jacob did, to set up stone pillars,[a]/[637] pour oil on them[b] and rename the sites of their divine revelations?[c] Upon what hermeneutical basis can he isolate Jacob's tithe vow from the other rituals that the patriarch performed at Bethel?

Second, at first, catch phrases like "Bethel = house of God = church" may seem theologically synonymous, but when we examine them more closely, we discover that, more times than not, their contents and contexts contradict one another. Jacob's "house of God," for example, was not the same as Christ's "house of God." The Bethel sanctuary that Jacob was supposed to have initiated with his tithe became one of the state sanctuaries of Jeroboam I (922-901, B.C.), after he split from the southern kingdom of Judah.[638] Amos 7:13 calls it "the king's sanctuary."[d] In contrast, the Body of Christ is not a state sanctuary under the control of an earthly monarch; it is a spiritual household,[e] a religious and moral family of Jesus followers under the authority of a heavenly king.[f] Since the "house of God" that was eventually built at Bethel was a completely different entity than the "house of God" referred to in the New Testament, Jacob's tithe vow should not be used to leverage tithes from Christians, as if funding one was the same thing as funding the other.[g]

Third, under the Old covenant, the Jerusalem temple was also referred to as the "house of God."[h] The people brought their tithes and offerings into the temple to support a hereditary priesthood

---

[a] Genesis 28:18
[b] Genesis 28:18
[c] Genesis 28:19
[d] NRSV
[e] I Peter 2:5; I Timothy 3:15. Compare verse 5.
[f] Compare Christ as "head of the church" (Ephesians 5:23; Colossians 1:18) and "king of kings" (I Timothy 6:15; Revelation 17:14; 19:16).
[g] See Book 2 in *The Tithing Series*.
[h] I Chronicles 6:48; Ezra 5:14; Psalm 42:4 per NRSV

headed by a high priest,[a] who offered annual atonement sacrifices for the sins of the nation.[b] Full-time singers were also among the staff that lived on its premises.[c] In the New covenant, however, Jesus replaces the old "house of God" with a new entity; one which is comprised of a new temple, new priesthood and new covenant.[d]

Lastly, even though the New Testament refers to Jacob approximately 25 times, no New Testament writer tells believers to follow the example of the patriarch's tithe vow.

Fear-based

The most obvious emotion behind Jacob's tithe vow was fear. Nevertheless, pro-tithers never mention it. Instead, they assert Jacob tithed or promised to tithe either as an act of (1) homage; (2) natural inclination; (3) spontaneous love; (4) joy; (5) blessing or (6) heartfelt gratitude. All neglect to mention the fear that Jacob felt when YHWH appeared to him at Bethel. Here are their claims:

- "Jacob's tithe-paying is presented to us as an act of homage to God."[639]
- "Jacob was brought up in the faith of his grandfather... What, then, could be more natural than that Jacob should avow himself ready to practice Abraham's righteous observances? ...dedicating to God a tenth of all he should receive."[640]
- "Tithing began as a spontaneous act of love in...Jacob's life and not as a commandment from God!"[641]
- Jacob tithed "out of joy."[642]

---

[a] Note the sons of Aaron (Exodus 27:21; 28:1; I Chronicles 6:49-57; 24:1) and the sons of Levi (I Chronicles 9:14-18).
[b] Leviticus 16:6,11,17,24; Hebrews 5:1-3; 7:27; 9:6-10
[c] I Chronicles 9:33. Compare Psalm 134:1.
[d] Note the new temple (1 Corinthians 3:16; 2 Corinthians 6:16; Ephesians 2:21); the new priesthood (Hebrews 7:11-20) and the new covenant (Luke 22:20; Galatians 4:21-31; 2 Corinthians 3:6,14; Hebrews 8:8,13; 9:15-16; 12:24).

- "Jacob wanted to bless Him. It was a heart thing."[643]
- Jacob tithed "from a heart filled with gratitude."[644]

These statements are based on two false assumptions: the first is that Jacob tithed; the second is that these pro-tithers know why he did. The truth is that the text never tells us that Jacob ever followed through with his promise to pay a tithe,[a] but it does tell us why he made his tithe vow.[b] In this section, I explore whether Genesis chapter 28 supports any of the positive motivations provided in the above claims. According to S. Walters, Bethel was "the first time that Jacob shows an interest whatsoever in the religious side of his family tradition."[645] W. Baker views Jacob's vow as reflecting some type of conversion experience if not the moment of his "salvation."[646] Whether a moment of genuine conversion or not, we will now review, in order of their appearance, each of the aforementioned motives in light of the text.

Homage

The first assertion alleges that Jacob tithed "as an act of homage to God."[647] I agree that when Jacob poured oil over the stone pillar, he demonstrated a certain degree of homage.[c/648] However, when YHWH commanded him to return to Bethel, there is no biblical evidence that he ever fulfilled the tithe portion of his vow.[d] This observation, along with the fact that Jacob did not initiate his return to Bethel,[e] cast doubt on how much genuine homage was in his heart when he first made his vow.

Natural Inclination

The second claim holds that since Jacob was raised "in the faith of his grandfather,"[649] it was instinctive for him to make a tithe vow

---

[a] Genesis 35:1-7. See chapters 15 and 16.
[b] Compare Genesis 27:42-45 with 28:21 and 28:17 with verse 22.
[c] Genesis 28:18
[d] Genesis 35:1-7
[e] Genesis 35:1

to show how he was "ready to practice Abraham's righteous observances."[650] When this tithe advocate asks, "What, then, could be more natural?,"[651] he wants readers to think that Jacob made his tithe vow because tithing was a normal, everyday practice, if not habit, of Abraham and his descendants. According to the text, however, Abraham tithed only once;[a] Isaac never tithed,[b] and, only when Jacob was under extreme duress,[c] did he promise to give a one-time tithe, which he never paid.[d] The truth is that it was not at all "natural"[652] for Jacob to vow to practice his grandfather's "righteous observances;"[653] as I illustrate in Chapter 16, he was much more naturally inclined to use deception and manipulation to serve his own interests.[e]

Spontaneous Love

The third statement asserts that Jacob tithed as a "spontaneous act of love."[654] It is accurate to say that Jacob's vow was spontaneous, since he made it right after his revelatory dream[f] "early the next morning."[g] It is inaccurate, however, to hold that Jacob made it out of love for YHWH or his covenant promises. It is more likely that Jacob made his vow as a defensive move because he felt surprised,[h] if not overwhelmed,[655] by his dream. He not only felt shocked that YHWH was in a place like Luz,[i] he did not take God's promise, "I will not leave you until I have done what I have promised you"[j] as personally comforting or trustworthy. Jacob turned YHWH's free promise into a bargain on his own terms to make sure that after he lived a while in Haran, he would return safely to his father's estate. If Jacob vowed a tithe as a "spontaneous act of love,"[656] which would normally involve

---

[a] Genesis 14:20
[b] Compare Genesis 26:12-14.
[c] Connect Genesis 27:42-43 with 28:1-3,10-22, especially verse 22c.
[d] Genesis 35:1-7. See chapters 15 and 16.
[e] Jacob made YHWH's interests contingent first upon getting what he wanted (Genesis 28:20-22). Compare 25:31; 27:18-19. See Chapter 16.
[f] Genesis 28:12-16
[g] Genesis 28:18a, NASB. Did Jacob go back to sleep after Genesis 28:16a or is verse16a simultaneous with verse 18a?
[h] Genesis 28:16
[i] Genesis 28:16-17
[j] Genesis 28:15, NRSV

genuine trust, then why did he turn the Lord's unconditional promise of a safe return to the land into a precondition of his own vow?[a]

Joy

The fourth claim alleges that Jacob tithed "out of joy."[657] Nothing in the text, however, supports such a statement. It is true that Jacob saw YHWH standing at the top of a heavenly staircase and heard him reiterate his covenant promises to him;[b] it is also accurate to say that he observed YHWH's angels going up and down on that staircase as divine messengers who continually ministered to his needs.[c] But the narrative makes it clear that Jacob did not make his tithe vow "out of joy"[658] but out of anxiety and dread. The night before Jacob made his tithe vow the text says, "He was afraid...;"[d] apparently, Jacob's dream was so terrifying that it woke him up from sleep.[e] The next morning, nothing indicates that his mood had changed.[f] Westermann agrees: Jacob's setting up of the stone pillar and anointing it with oil the morning he made his vow was "governed by fear of the holiness of the place..."[659] According to this Genesis scholar, when Jacob declared that Luz was not only the "house of God"[g] but also the "gate of heaven,"[h/660] "...it can only mean that this place is forbidden to humans because God dwells here...the gate does not invite but prohibits entrance; one may not enter the place where God dwells."[661] The text says, "He was afraid and said, 'How dreadful is this place!...'"[i] In this verse, the same Hebrew stem *yare* is translated as both "afraid" and "dreadful." Even though each word has a different state and voice,[662] the *yare* stem in "dreadful" is a *niphal* participle, which indicates in this context that the place of the revelation functions passively,[663] that is, the

---

[a] Contrast Genesis 28:15c with verse 21a.
[b] Genesis 28:13-15. Compare 48:3-4.
[c] Genesis 28:12. Compare Genesis 31:11; 32:1; 48:16 ("The angel" = YHWH?).
[d] Genesis 28:17a, NASB
[e] Genesis 28:16
[f] Genesis 28:18-22
[g] Genesis 28:17, NASB
[h] Genesis 28:17, NASB
[i] Genesis 28:17a,b, KJV

place itself is to be feared.[664] In addition to already fearing his brother's reprisal for stealing his birthright and blessing,[a/665] he now feared having trespassed in the place where God dwelt.[b] Thus, on two levels, Jacob was motivated by fear to make a bargain with YHWH to secure a safe return to the land. During those fearful moments, Jacob did not pray for help.[c] Even after his dream revelation, he "chose to bargain with God"[d/666] instead of confidently thanking him for his covenantal protection.

Unlike the freedom and confidence that Abraham exhibited much of the time when he dialogued with YHWH,[e] Jacob experienced fear and timidity. Jacob's state of fear may have reflected his own sense of alienation from YHWH's unconditional covenant promises. In his dream, YHWH said, "I am the Lord, the God of your father Abraham and the God of Isaac..."[f] In other words, up until his Bethel revelation, Jacob had known YHWH only "in the circle of his father's house."[667] Even though the patriarch was under the blessings of the Abrahamic covenant,[g] he had yet to embrace YHWH and his covenant as his own.[h]

Blessing

The fifth assertion contends that Jacob promised a tithe to "bless the Lord."[668] Such an idea also finds no endorsement in the text. After his dream, Jacob did not want to bless or glorify God; he wanted to use him to get back to the land safely so that he could inherit his father's estate.[i/669] Instead of accepting the free gift that God had to offer,[j] he secured what he was after in a bargain[k] because he "knew" that God would not deny him his desires due to the Lord's commitment to his forefathers.[l]

---

[a] Genesis 27:36
[b] Genesis 28:17. Compare Exodus 19:24.
[c] Contrast Genesis 32:11.
[d] Genesis 28:20-22
[e] Compare Genesis 12:1-3 with 12:4 and 13:14-17 with 13:18. Note also 18:22-33.
[f] Genesis 28:13b, NASB
[g] Compare Genesis 28:4.
[h] Genesis 28:21b
[i] Genesis 25:26,29-34; 27:18-38. Compare 31:30a.
[j] Contrast Genesis 28:13-15 with verses 18-22.
[k] Genesis 28:20-22
[l] Genesis 26:24; 32:9

Heartfelt Gratitude

The sixth and final claim holds that Jacob tithed with "a heart filled with gratitude."[670] I admit that when God commanded Jacob to move to Bethel and build an altar,[a] the patriarch seemed to express a sincere gratitude toward God. He told his family to prepare to go to Bethel because God had "...answered me in the day of my distress and has been with me wherever I have gone."[b] Even though Jacob was grateful for how God had protected him against the wrath of his older brother,[c] a sentiment that he also expressed in his prayer before he met Esau upon his return to the land,[d] there is no evidence that he originally made his tithe vow out of a sense of gratitude.[e]

Genesis reveals that none of these pro-tithers' positive dispositions dominated Jacob when he made his vow. Instead, the text shows us that he was in a state of fear,[f] shock,[g] dread[h] and alienation.[i] I suggest that it was a mixture of these four states of mind that led Jacob to bargain with YHWH instead of accepting his covenant promises outright.[j] Instead of vowing a tithe out of a pure desire to become a lifetime tither and lover of God, he quickly cut a deal to gain divine protection for his round-trip journey to Haran.

Conclusion

In this chapter, I showed that Jacob was a consummate bargain maker, a man who habitually used others to get what he wanted. His ability to manipulate those who were more powerful may have inspired later generations of Israelites to be clever in their own negotiations with others, but if there was any problem with such a hero of faith, it was that Jacob oftentimes conspired and

---

[a] Genesis 35:1
[b] Genesis 35:3c, NASB
[c] Genesis 35:1,3,7
[d] Genesis 32:9-12
[e] Genesis 35:1-7
[f] Genesis 28:17a
[g] Genesis 28:16c
[h] Genesis 28:17b
[i] Genesis 28:17c
[j] Contrast Genesis 28:13-15 with verses 20-22.

deceived to reach his goals. The fact that he frequently made self-serving agreements with others to get what he wanted should help us to understand that when he made a bargain with YHWH, he acted according to his natural instincts.

I also demonstrated that Jacob's tithe promise was only one of three promises in the patriarch's vow. Most tithe advocates ignore the other two promises as they focus almost exclusively on Jacob's promise to "tithe." The fact that Jacob's vow involved only a one-time and one-place kind of tithe flies in the face of all pro-tithers who use it falsely to try to collect lifetime tithes from Christians. Even more unfortunate is how tithe supporters confidently claim that Jacob had positive motivations behind his tithe vow when the text is clear that Jacob made his vow out of fear and desperation. It was Jacob's fear of Esau's revenge, accompanied by a feeling of alienation from God, which led him to promise YHWH "worship, shrine, and tithe" in exchange for a safe return to his father's estate; something he had coveted from birth.[a]

---

[a] Genesis 25:26, 29-34; 27:36

14

A Voluntary & Conditional Tithe

In Jacob's tripart bargain with God, his last promise was to give a tenth of what he obtained in Haran to YHWH in exchange for a safe return to his father's house. This tithe commitment, along with the patriarch's promise to make YHWH his God and dedicate the stone pillar as God's house, was voluntary and conditional. Genesis 28:20-22 states:

"Then Jacob made a vow, saying, 'If God will be with me and will keep me on this journey that I take, and will give me food to eat and garments to wear, and I return to my father's house in safety, then the Lord will be my God. This stone, which I have set up as a pillar, will be God's house, and of all that You give me I will surely give a tenth to You.'"[a]

Voluntary or Involuntary?

The same pro-tithers who claim that YHWH commanded Abraham to tithe also hold that he commanded Jacob to tithe. Here are two examples:

- "Was tithing commanded in the Patriarchal days? Yes, note the following Scriptures: Genesis 14:20; 28:22; Leviticus 27:30,32."[671]

---

[a] NASB

- "Tithe paying is commanded in the Bible. Abraham paid tithes to Melchizedek (Genesis 14:20). Jacob covenanted to 'give the tenth' unto God (Genesis 28:22)."[672]

These assertions claim that it was YHWH who commanded Abraham to give a tithe to Melchizedek and Jacob to make a tithe vow at Bethel. This means that tithing for both patriarchs would have been involuntary. If so, it would be reasonable to assume that if either had disobeyed God's command to tithe, there would probably have been some kind of consequence. There are, however, serious difficulties with these claims.

First, even though the above statements hold that Genesis 14:20 demonstrates that the Lord commanded Abraham to tithe, I have already presented textual evidence to the contrary in previous chapters of this book.

Second, contrary to the claim that God commanded Jacob to tithe, Genesis 28:22 states the opposite. The context demonstrates that it was Jacob who came up with the idea to make a tithe vow: "Then Jacob made a vow, saying..."[a] Nothing here or anywhere else in Genesis indicates that God commanded the patriarch to tithe or make a tithe vow. Jacob's bargain with God was his own personal response to a dream that YHWH had given him. According to one Genesis scholar, "A vow is voluntary; so, the tithe was a free-will offering. Vowing and tithing are an option; no legalistic rule can be legitimately based on this passage."[673] A. Pagolu agrees: "Jacob's vow was a matter of his choice."[674]

Third, in the second claim above, the tithe advocate misquotes Genesis 28:22. He states, "Jacob covenanted to 'give the tenth' unto God...," but the text shows Jacob saying, "...of all that You give me I will surely give a tenth to You." "*The* tenth" implies that the tithe had been practiced previously and regularly by Jacob and/or his forebears; "*a* tenth" means that the patriarch promised only one tithe. In context, he pledged to pay a one-time tithe only upon his safe return.

---

[a] Genesis 28:20a, NRSV.
Compare 31:13a,c, NASB.

Fourth, although the first assertion above states that Leviticus 27:30,32 indicates that God commanded the patriarchs to tithe, we find this to be impossible since the book of Leviticus does not address the patriarchal period.[675] The last verse of Leviticus chapter 27 places the chapter, and possibly the entire book, not in the patriarchal period but in the Sinai period: "These are the commandments which the Lord commanded Moses for the sons of Israel at Mount Sinai."[a] To some scholars, however, Leviticus chapter 27 concerns a time much later than Moses when Israel was to bring its grain, produce and animal tithes to the priests at a central sanctuary.[b/676] Either way, and contrary to this claim, these verses have nothing to do with "the Patriarchal days."[677]

Fifth, outside of Jacob's tithe vow at Bethel, neither the word "tithe" (*ma'aser*) nor the concept of tithing ever appears in the patriarch's life. Jacob's father, Isaac, for example, never said to Jacob, "If you want the blessings of the covenant given to our father, Abraham, then you must tithe."[c] When Jacob asked the man with whom he wrestled at the Jabbok River to bless him, his opponent did not say, "I will not bless you unless you return to Bethel and pay the tithe you promised."[d] The stranger blessed the patriarch with no mention of his tithe vow. Before a wary Jacob met his older brother, Esau, on his way back to Canaan, the patriarch did not pray, "Lord, because I made a tithe vow at Bethel, you must protect me."[e]

Finally, like all ancient vows, Jacob voluntarily initiated his bargain with YHWH. If Jacob had fulfilled his tithe promise, we could refer to what he gave as a votive offering. "Votive" comes from the Latin, *votivus*, something paid to fulfill the promise of a vow (from *votum*, a vow). According to W. R. Smith, the Semites' votive offerings "form a distinct class from offerings at the altar"[678] in that they were all voluntary. It was not until the Sinai covenant that tithes became mandatory. L. Coppes tells readers to

---

[a] Leviticus 27:34, NASB
[b] Leviticus 27 refers to "the priest" (verses 8,11,12,14,18,21,23), his staff (verse 32) and a central sanctuary with a currency standard (verses 3,25).
[c] See Genesis 27:27-29; 28:1-4.
[d] See Genesis 32:26,29.
[e] See Genesis 32:9-12.

"...note the development in the concept of tithing..."[679] from it first being voluntary[a] to it later becoming compulsory.[b] Under the Abrahamic covenant, Jacob was free to promise a tithe as a voluntary, votive offering. Under the Sinai covenant, however, the Law forbad the Israelites from using their tithes as votive offerings.[c] In Leviticus, for instance, the grain, produce and animal tithes,[d] along with every firstling,[e] belonged to God by inherent right, and, therefore, were the property of the priests.[f] Because all vows were voluntary, the Law did not require them. According to Coppes and G. Stob, Old Testament vows "were not commanded,"[680] and, therefore, they were "not a religious duty."[g/681] If some pro-tithers insist on using Jacob's self-initiated tithe vow as a tithing model for believers, they need to be honest with the text and admit that all such tithes would have to be discretionary. As a voluntary offering, it would be up to each believer to decide when or where to pay a tithe.

Conditional or Unconditional?

One tithe advocate asserts that Jacob's tithe vow was unconditional, that is, Jacob did not attach any strings to it that might prevent it from being fulfilled. He presents Jacob's promise not as a vow but as a declaration of gratitude. He says:

- "We read this [Genesis 28:20-22] as if it were a conditional vow, 'If God, then I...,' but it should really be read in the sense of the word 'since,' that is, 'Since God is doing all of these

---

[a] Genesis 14:20c; 28:22c. 31:13c says, "...where *you made a vow to Me*..." Emphasis mine.
[b] In Leviticus 27, the produce and animal tithes (verses 30,32), along with the firstlings (verse 26), are intrinsically and by definition "the Lord's" property.
[c] In Leviticus 27, the voluntarily consecrations (verses 1-25,28-29; note "vow" in verses 2,8) are distinguished from the compulsory offerings of the firstlings (verse 26) and tithes (verses 30,32).
[d] Leviticus 27:30,32
[e] Leviticus 27:26
[f] Note the priest's staff (Leviticus 27:32). Compare Jeremiah 33:13.
[g] Compare Deuteronomy 23:23.

radical things in my life, I want to somehow show my gratitude to him.' He [Jacob] was assuming that God was going to do all of the things that he had promised, and so he wanted to show God his thanks in a very tangible way. Is it not interesting that the way in which he chooses to do this is to give the Lord a tenth of what he has?"[682]

Even though a reputable Old Testament scholar admits that the first sentence in Jacob's vow, "If God be with me..." is "difficult,"[683] and J. Kohlenberger offers "Since God..." as a translation option in a footnote on Genesis 28:20,[684] there are good textual reasons to view Jacob's words as a vow-bargain with YHWH and not his way "to show God his thanks in a very tangible way."[685]

First, many Hebrew scholars support the "if...then" translation of Genesis 28:20.[686] Old Testament expert, R. de Vaux, for example, understands Jacob's vow as a "conditional promise"[687] because of its similarity to other Old Testament provisional vows. He explains:

"A vow (*neder*) is a promise to give or to consecrate to God a person or thing, for example, a tithe (Genesis 28:20), a sacrifice (2 Samuel 15:8), plunder taken in war (Numbers 21:2), [or] a person (Judges 11:30-31; I Samuel 1:11). In all the instances cited, the vow was a conditional promise to give something to God, if God first granted a favour: Jacob promised to pay a tithe if YHWH brought him home safe and sound; Jephthah promised to sacrifice someone if he won a victory; Anna [Hannah] promised to consecrate her child to God if he would grant her a son and so forth. The purpose of these vows was to add force to a prayer by making a kind of contract with God. All the vows in the Old Testament seem to have been of this kind, even when the condition was not openly expressed..."[688]

G. Davies agrees with de Vaux that Jacob's vow was conditional. To him, the patriarch's vow not only parallels the conditional vows of Absalom,[a] Jephthah,[b] Israel,[c] Anna[d] and Jonah's shipmates,[e/689] it also parallels several found in the Psalms. As Jacob uttered his vow to God when he was "in the day of [his] distress,"[f] the songwriter also promises, "...I shall pay You my vows, which my lips uttered and my mouth spoke when I was in distress."[g] According to J. Milgrom,[690] T. Cartledge has clearly demonstrated that "...all vows, biblical and ancient Near Eastern alike, are conditional..."[691]

Second, to translate Genesis 28:20 correctly, we must understand its structure. According to E. Dalglish, the verse introduces a 5-point protasis clause followed by a 3-point apodosis clause.[692] A protasis is "the clause expressing the condition in a conditional sentence"[693] often introduced with the word "if." An apodosis clause is "the clause expressing the consequence in a conditional sentence"[694] often beginning with the word "then." It is true that the Hebrew particle אִם ('IM) is sometimes translated "indeed" or "surely."[695] Most often, however, it is used as the protasis in conditional sentences.[696] According to two Hebrew sources, in Genesis 28:20, 'IM clearly means "if only..."[697] or "if, supposing that..."[698] As is often the case in conditional statements, here the Hebrew letter ו (waw) introduces the apodosis clause.[699] It is the first letter of the word הָיָה (hayah), which means, "then-he-will-be" ("as-God" "to-me").[700] This confirms the idea that Genesis 28:20 is the beginning of a conditional statement.

To translate 'IM as "since," the Hebrew adverb לֹא (LO) would need to accompany it, as it does in Isaiah 5:9 and Psalm 89:34-35,[701] but it does not. The Hebrew LO means no or not,[702] and if it did appear with 'IM in Genesis 28:20, it would form an "emphatic positive"[703] best understood as "indeed," "surely" or "since." How can an adverb that means no or not help to form an "emphatic positive?" Baker and Carpenter inform us that when

---

[a] 2 Samuel 15:8
[b] Judges 11:30-31
[c] Numbers 21:2
[d] I Samuel 1:11
[e] Jonah 1:16

[f] Genesis 35:3c, NASB (adapted)
[g] Psalm 66:13b-14, NASB. Compare Psalm 50:14-15.

LO "is prefixed to a noun or adjective, it negates that word, making it have an opposite or contrary meaning..."[704] A simple equation might help: לֹא (LO) (not) + אִם ('IM) (if) = indeed, surely or since. In other words, the adverb "not" negates the particle "if" to make the sentence an expression of certainty as reflected in the word "since." The point is that when 'IM is used alone in a sentence without LO, it is "used to express an emphatic negative"[705] conveyed by the word "if." Since LO does not appear in Genesis 28:20, 'IM is best translated "if" as an emphatic negative particle, which indicates that the vow that it introduces is conditional.

Third, Genesis 28:20 says, "Jacob vowed (*nadar*) a vow (*neder*)."[706] Here both a verb and a noun use the same Hebrew root, *ndr*. According to Baker and Carpenter, *nadar* "denotes the making of an oral, voluntary promise to give or do something as an expression of consecration or devotion to the service of God. Jacob vowed to return a tenth of all that God bestowed on him if God would protect and preserve him on his journey (Genesis 28:20)."[707] This meaning of *nadar* goes against the notion that Jacob's vow was an expression of thanks because of the votive ("if...then") context in which we find it.[a]

Fourth, most of the verbs in Genesis 28:20-22 are in the imperfect (future) state with one main exception. The first verb in 28:22, "I have set up," is in the perfect (past, completed) state. It refers to the stone pillar that Jacob set up before he made his vow.[b] The other verbs are imperfect, which, in the context, corresponds to the English future,[708] that is, "shall become the house of God," etc.[709] The verb (*hayah*) translated "will be" in Jacob's two statements, "then the Lord will be my God" and "then...this stone...will be God's house" is in the *qal* imperfect, which, according to Baker, indicates "imperfective action"[710] yet to be completed. The proper sense of these verses is thus "contingent action,"[711] that is, Jacob will fulfill his promises, if God does his part first and gives the patriarch the ability and

---

[a] Genesis 28:13-15   [b] Genesis 28:18, 20

opportunity to do his.[712] R. Harris concurs.[713]

Fifth, to deny that Jacob's vow was a conditional promise contradicts the culture of reciprocity in human and divine relations that still dominates the ancient Near East. By a culture of reciprocity, I mean that Party A does a good deed to Party B with the expectation that Party B will return the favor. Party A expects Party B to reciprocate, that is, to "...act, feel or give mutually or in return."[714] "Concern for reciprocity in giving and receiving," observes P. Perkins, "was fundamental to the ethos of the ancient world..."[715] F. Danker agrees: "A basic feature of Mediterranean and Near Eastern culture is reciprocity."[716] Danker goes on to explain that reciprocity in the ancient Near East also applies to people's relationships with their gods: "To confer benefits is the primary obligation of deities, heads of state, and all others who would aspire to a reputation for the highest excellence. Conversely, it is expected that the recipient of bounties will make appropriate acknowledgment."[717] He continues: "To hasten the process, a devotee may assure the deity that if a specific boon [blessing] is granted the recipient will respond in the manner specified in what is termed the vow. The entire arrangement can be summed up in the [Latin] phrase *do ut des* (I am prepared to give in the hope that you will give)."[718] The Latin phrase, quid pro quo ("this for that") also describes such a relationship.

Jacob's reciprocal tithe bargain with YHWH fits with a religious text from ancient Ugarit, a kingdom along the Mediterranean coast of Syria that prospered in the second millennium B.C. Since 1929, archaeologists have discovered at Ugarit important texts written in different languages that disclose "cultural, religious, and mythical traditions from essentially the 14th through the 13th centuries B.C."[719] One of the texts supports the notion that promising a tithe to a deity could motivate him or her to act on one's behalf. Pagolu observes: "A ritual text from Ugarit describes tithing in a religious context, with the Ugaritians advised to vow various offerings such as a bull, a firstborn or tithes, and to seek the help of Baal in the event of an enemy's attack..."[720] As the citizens of Ugarit tithed to Baal in exchange for his protection against their enemies, even so Jacob, as previously noted, vowed a tithe to YHWH in exchange for his protection from the wrath of his brother, Esau, who sought to kill him.[a]

According to Davies, if God would give Jacob a safe return to his father's estate, then the patriarch would give him "worship, shrine, and tithe."[721] M. Herman agrees with Davies that Jacob's tithe bargain with YHWH was of a reciprocal nature. To him, the Old Testament, "...reveals the tithe to be a part of a pattern of reciprocities in which goods are exchanged for divine acceptance, protection, and blessing...the tithe should properly be viewed as a gift... having significant features in common with gift-exchange systems in other cultures."[722] If by "gift" Herman means that even under the Sinai covenant, the tithe continued to be a voluntary, votive offering, I would beg to differ. I agree with Milgrom that, under the Law, the tithe was not a voluntary gift but a compulsory tax.[723] I support, however, Herman's general characterization that the tithe, along with the other sacrifices and offerings of the Old covenant, was an important part of a ritual system[b] intended for Israel to maintain "divine acceptance, protection and blessing."[724]

Sixth, to deny that Jacob's vow was conditional ignores the fact that in Genesis chapter 28 Jacob turned the unconditional Abrahamic covenant promises of grace into the conditional terms of an ancient Near Eastern business transaction. As YHWH had spoken his covenant promises of land, descendants and global blessing to his grandfather, Abraham, without any terms or conditions,[c] so he reiterated them to Jacob.[d] In these verses, we observe the essence of the unconditional nature of the Bethel revelation in the phrases "I am..." and "I will..." When we view YHWH's promises to Jacob (Genesis 28:13-15) and Jacob's response to them (verses 18-22) as a seamless narrative, it appears that Jacob did not accept YHWH's promises at face value and free of obligation. The patriarch agreed to cooperate with

---

[a] Genesis 27:41
[b] See Book 2 in *The Tithing Series*.
[c] Genesis 12:1-3; 13:14-17; 15:7,13-16,18-21
[d] Genesis 28:13-15

YHWH's call upon his family line only if YHWH first gave him what he wanted: a safe return to his father's estate.[a] Jacob "reciprocated the promise by a conditional vow," agrees S. Walters.[725] To him, Jacob "...alters the promise...in subtle ways (for example, 'I [the Lord] will bring you back' becomes 'if I [Jacob] return' and 'this land' becomes 'my father's house'), all of which shows that Jacob wishes to retain the initiative and is more interested in the family estate than the land [of Canaan]. In short, although the Bethel event marks Jacob's awakening to God and to the promise, he is still a 'smooth man,' and his vow appears to be as much a bargain as a commitment."[726] C. Westermann concurs: Jacob took God's promise of a safe return to the land and reshaped it "into the condition of a vow."[727] Upon hearing God's many unconditional promises to him and his family, Jacob re-framed them on his own terms to get what he wanted. At first, this may seem shocking, but such a self-centered response is consistent with Jacob being a trickster.[b]

Lastly, the vow that Jacob made at Luz/Bethel was a journey vow. Journey vows were one of the most common categories of vows in the ancient world, and they were always conditional. Travel was dangerous; poor road conditions and bandits made it hazardous for most travelers and divine protection was often sought. Jacob's journey vow at Bethel was not the only time that the patriarch attempted to purchase divine protection through the exchange of gifts. Toward the end of his life, when Jacob traveled to Egypt to be reunited with his missing son, Joseph, he stopped in Beer-sheba, which was located at the "southern extreme of Israelite territory."[c/728] There he offered "sacrifices to the God of his father Isaac"[d] to secure a safe trip.[e] It appears that the patriarch was apprehensive about what might happen to him and his family, along with their possessions, once they journeyed outside of the land of promise. Soon after Jacob offered sacrifices

---

[a] Genesis 28:21a
[b] See Chapter 17.
[c] Note the phrase, "from Dan to Beersheba" (Judges 20:1; I Samuel 3:20).
[d] Genesis 46:1, NASB
[e] Genesis 46:1-4

to YHWH, the Lord comforted him with the words, "...do not be afraid to go down to Egypt, for I will make you a great nation there. I will go down with you to Egypt, and I will also surely bring you up again; and Joseph will close your eyes."[a] God did not tell Jacob, "Do not be afraid to go down to Egypt because your tithe vow will protect you financially," as one tithe supporter promises believers.[729]

Jacob's journey vow fits other journey vows in the Old Testament like those of Absalom and Jonah. When Absalom asked leave of king David to travel to Hebron, he said, "Please let me go to Hebron and pay the vow that I have made to the Lord. For your servant made a vow while I lived at Geshur in Aram: If the Lord will indeed bring me back to Jerusalem, then I will worship the Lord in Hebron."[b/730] Similarly, Jonah informed his shipmates that he was the cause of the violent storm, which their ship was experiencing at sea.[c] He assured them that if they would toss him overboard, the sea would become calm. At first, they hesitated,[d] but soon they did as the prophet instructed and "the sea stopped its raging."[e] The crew then offered YHWH a sacrifice, probably one of thanksgiving, for answering their prayers for deliverance.[f] They also made journey vows to the Lord hoping to reach their final destination without further incident.[g]

Other journey vows in the ancient world, like those in Sumer and Rome, also remind us of the one Jacob made. In the Sumerian story, "Gilgamesh and the Cedar Forest," Gilgamesh, a monarch said to rule the city of Uruk[h] seeks "to secure permission of safe conduct to cut timber from the god Huwawa, the lord of the forest, by offering him gifts."[731] In Roman culture, vows were often made for the safe return of the emperor or empress.[732] According to S. Eitrem and R. Ogilvie, "Vows for the safe return of the Emperor (from expeditions or war), for his health, his reign, for the delivery of the empress, etc. were customary."[733]

---

[a] Genesis 46:3b-4
[b] 2 Samuel 15:7-8, NRSV
[c] Jonah 1:12
[d] Jonah 1:13
[e] Jonah 1:15, NASB
[f] Jonah 1:14
[g] Jonah 1:16
[h] Uruk was a city in southern Mesopotamia around 2600 B.C.

Jacob's vow was no different than any other journey vow in the ancient world.

Conclusion

I demonstrated in this chapter how Jacob's one-time journey vow was a common ancient Near Eastern bargain with God that was both voluntary (self-initiated) and conditional (contingent upon God's answer to his requests). Because Jacob's tithe promise was both voluntary and conditional, pro-tithers have no hermeneutical basis to claim that Christians are divinely obligated to make similar vows or that they should tithe regardless of whether God has first answered their prayers. Some pro-tithers base their entire "before the Law" argument for Christian tithing on Abraham's tithe to Melchizedek.[734] This may be because when they looked at Jacob's tithe vow more closely, they realized that since it was both voluntary and conditional, it would not provide a good basis for their collection of regular and mandatory tithes. Without specifically mentioning Jacob or his tithe bargain, one tithe advocate states, "...it does not follow that we can bargain with God on the basis of tithing. We can never do this, and should we think it, we must put it out of our minds at once!"[735] The idea of collecting tithes from believers solely on a voluntary basis and that only after God has answered their specific prayer requests, shakes both the doctrinal and financial foundations of the traditional teaching on tithes. To avoid such a nightmare, most tithe advocates ignore Jacob's tithe vow altogether.

15
An Unpaid Tithe

As Jacob traveled to obtain a wife from the household of his mother's brother, Laban, he spent the night at Luz and had his first encounter with YHWH.[a] In a dream, the Lord revealed himself as "...the God of your father Abraham and the God of Isaac..."[b] and repeated to Jacob the promises of land, descendants and global blessing.[c] The implication was that YHWH wanted the patriarch to accept him fully as his own God[d] and embrace his covenant promises. From what we can see in the text, however, Jacob did not immediately do either. Instead, he made his acceptance of YHWH's promises contingent first upon getting what he wanted.[e] In exchange for a safe return to his father's house, Jacob committed himself to three promises, the last of which was that he would pay a tithe of all that the Lord would give him on his journey.[f] Did he, however, fulfill his promise? Here is one example of a pro-tither who believes that he did:

- "... Jacob has a visitation from God and without doubt he kept his vow of tithes...It would be unthinkable that Jacob lied to God and did not keep his vow of the tenth over all these years of the Lord's blessings and dealings with him. Jacob lived to be 147 years of age (Genesis 47:28). Did he not give to God

---

[a] Genesis 28:10-17
[b] Genesis 28:13, NASB
[c] Genesis 28:13-15
[d] Compare Genesis 28:21.
[e] Genesis 28:20-22
[f] Genesis 28:22

his tithes and offerings over these years? Did he not keep his vow of tithes to the Lord? Would God say He is the God of Abraham, Isaac and Jacob if he did not? Once more, we believe the answer should be evident, even though 'chapter and verse' is not given every time he gave to the Lord...[Jacob] undoubtedly kept his *vow of tithes*."[736]

In the above claim, the context of "vow of tithes"[737] indicates that the tithe advocate wants readers to understand Jacob as a lifetime or regular tither[738] who promised to pay more than a one-time tithe upon his safe return to Canaan. The tithe supporter believes so firmly in his claim that he uses language of unquestioning confidence: "without doubt,"[739] "undoubtedly"[740] and "It would be unthinkable..."[741] In my view, he uses such emphasis to remove any question in his readers' minds that Jacob might not have been a practicing tither. This makes sense because of the way that he exhorts his audience to follow Jacob's example and become full-time tithers. He writes:

- "Those who accept the God of Abraham, the God of Isaac and the God of Jacob will also keep their vow of tithes and give back to the Lord a tenth of all He gives them."[742]

If it could be demonstrated from Scripture that Jacob failed to pay his tithe vow, or worse yet, was never a regular tither, it would eliminate the basis for this pro-tither's claim. Furthermore, if it could also be shown that God blessed Jacob financially in spite of the fact that he never tithed, it would damage the pro-tithing case even further. Even though this tithe advocate fails to produce any evidence from the text that Jacob fulfilled his tithe vow and/or that he systematically tithed, he still expects his readers to believe his self-assured statements. I find this amazing. In this chapter, I make the case that Jacob did not fulfill the tithe portion of his vow.

Facts

YHWH honored the covenant promises that he had given to Jacob at Bethel as well as Jacob's requests. The Lord's presence was always with him.[a] He protected the patriarch from violent attacks,[b] gave him ample provisions,[c] and, ultimately, provided him a safe return to his father's house.[d] After God fulfilled his promises, it was then the patriarch's turn to fulfill what he had promised: (1) make YHWH his God ["worship"];[e] (2) consecrate a YHWH sanctuary at Bethel ["shrine"][f] and (3) give a tithe of the goods he obtained on his journey to dedicate this sanctuary ["tithe"].[g]

Genesis scholars J. Levenson and C. Westermann agree that the episode in which Jacob returns to Bethel[h] not only serves to conclude the story of the patriarch,[743] it also attempts to demonstrate that he fulfilled his vow.[744] By "fulfilled," I do not mean that they hold Jacob made good on all three of his promises, but that they recognize that the writer intended to communicate to his audience that the patriarch kept his vow. "The fulfillment of the vow is noted in Genesis 35:1,3,7,"[745] concurs E. Dalglish, since each of these verses mentions Jacob's return to Bethel and the altar that he built there. According to him, when Jacob built an altar at Bethel, he fulfilled all three parts of his vow: "worship, shrine, and tithe."[746] I will now examine Dalglish's opinion more closely by looking at each of the three promises in Jacob's vow to see how many of them he kept. By examining each of the patriarch's commitments, we will better understand Jacob's character as a whole and what were possibly some of the intentions of the original writer(s).

---

[a] Genesis 31:3,5. Compare 28:15a.
[b] Compare Genesis 34:30 with 35:5. See also 31:29,42. Compare 28:15b.
[c] Genesis 33:11. Compare 28:20.
[d] Genesis 33:18. Compare 28:15c, s21a.
[e] Genesis 28:21b
[f] Genesis 28:22a,b,c
[g] Genesis 28:22d
[h] Genesis 35:1-7

Worship

Jacob's first promise to YHWH in exchange for a safe return to his father's estate was, "the Lord [YHWH] will be my God [*hayah ly elohim*]."[a/747] In the ancient Near East, clan leaders adopted a certain god who became the god of the clan;[b/748] sons were expected to worship the same god as their fathers. YHWH had been the god of Jacob's tribe as far back as his grandfather, Abraham,[c] but, apparently, he had yet to make YHWH his own personal God.

Even after Jacob returned to Canaan, his household still utilized or worshipped "foreign gods"[d] (*nechahr elohim*). We assume that these gods included the "household idols" (*teraphim*) that Rachel, who may not have completely broken away from her polytheistic background,[749] stole from her father, Laban, when she and her family secretly fled from his estate.[e] The fact that those under Jacob's authority had foreign images and amulets implies that Jacob may have worshipped or trusted in them as well, and may be one of the reasons why, after his return to the land,[f] he did not immediately or voluntarily return to Bethel to fulfill his vow. Instead, he settled in Succoth,[g] approximately 37 miles northeast of Bethel.[750]

We do not know how long Jacob lived in Succoth, but while there, he built a house for his family and booths for his livestock.[h] When he left and crossed the Jordan into the heartland, he settled in Shechem,[i/751] which is located "in the central highlands of Israel"[752] 25 miles north of Bethel.[753] There Jacob bought some property and built an altar.[j] According to Pagolu, the patriarch

---

[a] Genesis 28:21b, NASB
[b] Compare Genesis 26:24; 31:5,29,42; 32:9; 48:15. Compare also 24:12,27,42,48; 2 Chronicles 11:16; 13:18.
[c] Genesis 28:13; 43:23; 46:1,3; 31:5,29. Compare Genesis 17:7, "...to be God to you...," NASB. Compare 24:27,48; 26:24b; 28:13.
[d] Genesis 35:2,4, NASB
[e] Genesis 31:19,30,32,34,35
[f] Genesis 28:15. Compare verse 21a.
[g] Genesis 33:17
[h] Genesis 33:17
[i] Genesis 33:18-19. Compare 35:4.
[j] Genesis 33:19-20

probably lived in Shechem "for a long time...since Jacob's children were relatively young when they arrived, but were adults when they left..."[a/754]

It appears that Jacob never intended to journey to Bethel to fulfill his vow like he originally promised.[b] When he did return, it was only after God commanded him to do so.[c] Sometime after the Shechem massacre, God told the patriarch, "Arise, go up [*alah*] to Bethel..."[d] According to more than one Genesis scholar, the Hebrew *qal* (plain sense/imperative) of "go up" indicates that God commanded Jacob to make, as it were, a formal, religious pilgrimage.[755] The writer presents Jacob as the founder of the Bethel sanctuary; one who led his family on a holy pilgrimage to a holy site to show his consecration to the holy God, YHWH.[e/756] "The actions of the founder," according to de Vaux, "constituted a ritual which was [later] perpetuated by the faithful...[who] went on pilgrimage there, poured oil on a stele and paid tithes."[757] The phrase "go up" (*alah*) in Genesis 35:1 is also used to describe the Israelites' pilgrimages to the annual feasts in Jerusalem.[f] The use of pilgrimage language in this verse deepens the religious meaning of the patriarch's return to Bethel, but it does not necessarily indicate a deeper commitment on Jacob's part. The concept of sacred pilgrimage was unfamiliar in the patriarchal period. It was the later writers of Genesis who wanted their contemporaries to make pilgrimages to Bethel, and, who, by associating them with Jacob, had a better chance of motivating more Israelites to make the trip.

Before he led his family to the location of his previous theophany,[g] Jacob told his household, "...purify yourselves and change your garments; and let us arise and go up to Bethel..."[h] The

---

[a] Contrast Genesis 33:1,2,13-14 with Genesis 34:16,25,27.
[b] Genesis 28:22a,b,c
[c] Genesis 35:1
[d] Genesis 35:1b, NASB
[e] Compare Genesis 35:4.
[f] Exodus 34:24; I Samuel 1:3. I Samuel 10:3 says, "...up to [*alah*] God at Bethel..." (NASB).
[g] A theophany is an appearance or manifestation of a god to a human being.
[h] Genesis 35:2b-3a, NASB

command to "purify yourselves"[a] had to do with his household washing their bodies with water to prepare to encounter God's presence. Smith writes, "...the primary conception of uncleanness is that of a dangerous infection. Washing and purifications play a great part in Semitic ritual,[758] and were performed with living [running] water, which was as such sacred in some degree."[759] The patriarch's request for his household to change their garments as they were about to pilgrimage to Bethel was similar to the Arabian practice in which the change of garments was also associated with the taking of a pilgrimage to a sacred site.[760] A person's clothes "became taboo...through contact with the holy place and function...[Therefore] a man does not perform a sacred function in his everyday clothes, for fear of making them taboo."[761] According to R. Clifford and R. Murphy, "Jacob's preparations are far more than the building of an altar; this is a preparation for ritual worship..."[762]

It appears that the patriarch prescribed these two purification rituals because of his family's possession of "foreign gods,"[b] which had made the members of his household ritually unclean in both body and garment – unfit to meet with God at the altar that he was going to build upon their arrival at Bethel.[c/763] However, even though Semites did practice body washing and garment changing, I agree with Westermann that neither practice was a part of the religion of the patriarchs.[764] Both, somewhat modified, were a part of the later ritual system of ancient Israel used to purify unclean males,[d] Levites[e] and those exposed to corpses.[f]

Before Jacob moved to Bethel, he buried his family's "foreign gods"[g] and "the rings which were in their ears"[h] under the oak near Shechem.[i] These earrings may have been either the jewelry that household members placed on the ears of the statues for good luck,

---

[a] Genesis 35:2, NASB
[b] Genesis 35:2, NASB
[c] Genesis 35:1,3,7
[d] Leviticus 15:1-18 (especially verses 5-11,13,17); for females (Leviticus 15:19-30, especially verses 21-22,27)
[e] Numbers 8:5-22, especially verses 7, 21
[f] Numbers 19:1-22, especially verses 7,8,10,19,21
[g] Genesis 35:2,4, NASB
[h] Genesis 35:4, NASB
[i] Genesis 35:4

votive offerings to the teraphim for answering their prayers or amulets that household members wore to attract blessing and ward off evil.[765] To Clifford and Murphy, when Jacob called his family to let go of the Aramean[a] gods of the past, "...a new life of service to the God of the fathers is to begin..."[766] According to Levenson, the patriarch's new life of service began "...with a deepened and renewed consecration to the one God..."[767] To S. Walters, Genesis chapter 35 shows "the new Jacob at his best."[768] He now "cares about his people,"[769] exercises "religious leadership"[770] over them and finally shows "...his engagement in religious life..."[771] God changes Jacob's name "as a mark of his...piety."[b/772]

When God commanded Jacob to move to Bethel, he also told him to build an altar.[c] According to Pagolu, the patriarchs built altars for three reasons: (1) to worship the Lord;[773] (2) to commemorate a theophany[774] and/or (3) to claim land for YHWH.[775] The text makes it clear that the main reason that Jacob built an altar was to commemorate his theophany,[d] during which the Lord promised to protect him from the revenge of his older brother.[e] This means that his purpose for building the altar at Bethel was not to offer to God a tithe of his livestock. This becomes all the more significant in light of the fact that it was God who told Jacob to build the altar.[f] In Genesis chapter 46, the narrator still describes Jacob's relationship with YHWH as that of "the God of his father Isaac,"[g] when he writes: "I am God, the God of your father."[h] After this, however, a few verses do appear in Genesis chapters 48 and 49 that seem to indicate that Jacob did finally make YHWH his God and embrace his covenant promises. There is much discussion among scholars as to when these chapters reached their final form;[776] here, however, I take them at face value as showing a positive end to Jacob's life.

In Genesis 48:15-16, Jacob blesses Joseph's two sons, Ephraim and Manasseh, and identifies himself as having walked before the

---

[a] Compare Genesis 25:19-20; 28:4-5; 31:20,24.
[b] Genesis 35:9-10
[c] Genesis 35:1,3,7
[d] Genesis 35:1,3,7
[e] Genesis 28:15. Compare 35:1,3,7.
[f] Genesis 35:1
[g] Genesis 46:1, NASB
[h] Genesis 46:3, NASB

same God as that of his fathers. He admits that it was this same God who led him and protected him from evil as a shepherd would his sheep. He prays that his own name may live on in his grandsons along with the names of his fathers, so that, "they may grow into a multitude in the midst of the earth,"[a] as YHWH previously promised him at Bethel.[b] In Genesis chapter 49, Jacob blesses his son, Joseph, and describes him as a resilient target who has been strengthened "from the hands of the Mighty One of Jacob...from the God of your father who helps you...[and with] the blessings of your father..."[c] Here "your father" refers to Jacob; thus, when the patriarch calls YHWH the "Mighty One of Jacob," he identifies the deity as his own God.[d/777] Therefore, based on Genesis 48:15-16 and 49:24-26, I conclude that, at least eventually, Jacob did make YHWH his God and embrace his covenant promises.

Shrine

The second promise in Jacob's vow was, "This stone, which I have set up as a pillar, will be God's house..."[e] When Jacob said this, did he believe that there was something special about the stone? Was he promising to (1) use it as a down payment or 'cornerstone' for a future sanctuary; (2) venerate it as a dwelling place of God and/or (3) consider it as a witness to his vow?

In support of the first theory, Westermann points out that since Jacob never built a traditional sanctuary at Bethel after he returned to the land, he, or the narrator, must be predicting the building of a YHWH sanctuary there sometime in the future.[778] This Genesis scholar writes, "...a sanctuary is to arise from this stone, or the stone is to be extended into a sanctuary (or acquire the status of a sanctuary) at which the God, Yahweh (verse 21b), is to be worshipped."[779] Westermann, however, misses the fact

---

[a] Genesis 48:16e, NASB
[b] Genesis 28:14
[c] Genesis 49:24c; 25a; 26a, NASB. Compare Psalm 132:2,5; Isaiah 1:24.
[d] Genesis 49:18
[e] Genesis 28:22, NASB

that the patriarch promised that the stone pillar itself would be "God's house."[a] Even though it is true that, centuries later, a sanctuary was built at Bethel,[b] Jacob was not a prophet, and it is clear from the text that his vow meant that once he returned to Canaan, he himself was going to be the one to fulfill his promise.

The second theory is the idea that Jacob believed that YHWH lived inside the stone. Even though Dalglish claims, "There is no suggestion that the stone served as a house for a god…,"[780] we should keep in mind that immediately after Jacob's visitation, he anointed the stone pillar with oil probably indicating that he believed the stone itself somehow contributed to his revelation having slept on or near it during his dream. Along these lines, Smith views Jacob's stone pillar as "more than a mere landmark"[781] because it was "anointed, just as idols were in antiquity."[c/782] Even though this scholar seems to miss the fact that Genesis 28:17 also refers to the Bethel site as the "house of God," he does remind us that Jacob's promise in verse 22 refers to the notion that "…the pillar itself, not the spot on which it stood, is called 'the house of God,' as if the deity were conceived actually to dwell in the stone, or manifest himself therein to his worshippers. And this is the conception that appears to have been associated with sacred stones everywhere."[783]

Before we reject Smith's suggestion that Jacob held an animistic[d] or semi-animistic attitude toward the stone pillar, we should keep in mind that, according to Westermann, when Jacob built an altar at Bethel and changed the name of the place to "El-bethel,"[e] he showed animistic tendencies in that he equated the place with God.[784] If correct, we would understand El-Bethel to mean not "the God of Bethel"[785] but "the El Bethel,"[f/786] that is, the Bethel divinity or the divinity named Bethel.[787] If Jacob did view Bethel as God or a direct manifestation of him, he could have

---

[a] Genesis 28:22, NASB
[b] Judges 20:26-28; I Kings 12:29-33
[c] Genesis 28:18. Compare 35:14.
[d] Animism is the belief that natural objects like plants, rocks, rivers, trees, etc. contain souls or spirits.
[e] Genesis 35:3,7
[f] Compare Genesis 31:13.

easily viewed the stone pillar, which he believed was instrumental in his divine revelation, with similar religious sentiments. Accordingly, Jacob promised that, upon his safe return to Bethel, he would continue to honor the stone pillar as a "house"[a] or living space for YHWH, as he had done when he anointed it with oil after he awoke from his dream.[b] Such an idea is related to the ancient worship of stones and pillars.[788] Assuming that Jacob did have an animistic or semi-animistic attitude toward the Bethel site as well as the stone pillar, it would be consistent with him having a similar attitude toward the household idols (*nekhar*[789]) and amulets (*nozem ozen*[790]), which he allowed in his home up until the time that God commanded him to move to Bethel.[c] There is no denying the fact that when Jacob returned to his father's house from Haran, he "sets foot on the land of Canaan with his own gods."[791] Jacob and his household would have viewed the foreign gods and talismans as having the power to mediate blessing from the divine into the human realm.[792] Jacob's toleration of idols and talismans[d] in his family suggest that one of the reasons why Jacob had such a difficult time making YHWH his God after he returned to Canaan may have been that he had become all too comfortable with the gods of his favorite wife, Rachel, and their former life in Haran.[e]

Jacob's vow fulfillment section (Genesis 35:1-7), however, makes no mention of the stone pillar. From this we could conclude that the author of this passage did not intend for it to be a record of the fulfillment of Jacob's vow. Or, based on the assumption that this portion of Genesis was intended to demonstrate how Jacob honored his vow, we might ask why an altar replaced the stone pillar.[f] One possible reason might be that having Jacob fulfill his vow through the building of an altar brought the fulfillment of the patriarch's vow more in line with the accepted modes of worship in the narrator's day. Sarna holds that "El Bethel" ("the God of Bethel"[793]) in Genesis 35:7 is what

---

[a] Genesis 28:22
[b] Genesis 28:18
[c] Genesis 35:1-2
[d] Genesis 35:2
[e] Genesis 31:19
[f] Genesis 35:1,3,7

Jacob named his altar.ᵃ/⁷⁹⁴ If so, when Jacob named his altar "El Bethel," he would have fulfilled the "shrine" promise of his vow in that he continued to venerate the stone pillar - now a stone altar - as the dwelling or speaking place of YHWH. If true, the patriarch's stone altar would not have been a place of sacrifice but of veneration and consecration.

The third theory is that Jacob's stone functioned as a "witness" to his vow.⁷⁹⁵ An illustration of this idea is the treaty between two ancient kings,ᵇ in which the phrase "houses of the gods" refers to the steles upon which were written the terms of their treaty not to the temple or sanctuary of their respective deities.⁷⁹⁶ In the ancient Near East, stones were used as "witnesses" to agreements involving both men and gods, believing the stone(s) functioned as an all-seeing "abode of the gods."⁷⁹⁷ If one party did not keep his end of the agreement, "The watchful divinity thought to reside in the stone of testimony"⁷⁹⁸ would make sure he suffered the consequences. When Jacob made a non-aggression treaty with Laban concerning his flocks and children, for example, he set up a stone pillar along with a pile of other stones as witness to their agreement.ᶜ Laban observed, "This mound is a witness between you and me today...May the Lord watch between you and me when we are out of each other's sight. If you mistreat my daughters or take other wives, though no one is with us, understand that God will be a witness between you and me...The God of Abraham, and the gods of Nahor - the gods of their father - will judge between us."ᵈ

Similarly, Sarna believes Jacob anointed the stone pillar with oil to seal his vow to God⁷⁹⁹ like a modern signature on a contract. Oil was used in the ancient Near East to seal treaties and business agreements, in which there was an "assumed obligation."⁸⁰⁰ In Genesis 31:13, for example, oil and vow are connected in a

---

ᵃ On the naming of altars after deities, see Genesis 33:20; Exodus 17:15-16; Judges 6:23-24.
ᵇ They were kings Bargayah of KTK and Matiel of Arpad whose treaty is dated approximately 760 B.C.
ᶜ Genesis 31:43-46,52
ᵈ Genesis 31:48-50,53, CSB

context of human obligation. God said to Jacob while the patriarch was still in Haran, "I am the God of Bethel, where you anointed a pillar, where you made a vow to Me; now arise, leave this land, and return to the land of your birth."[a]

Finally, according to Smith, "...new altars or temples [were] erected, only where the godhead has given unmistakable evidence of his presence,"[801] and Jacob's own words confirm as much for Bethel: "Surely the Lord is in this place...This is none other than the house of God..."[b] Smith continues, "...in the earlier parts of the Old Testament a theophany is always taken to be a good reason for sacrificing on the spot."[c/802] Even though we have no evidence Jacob sacrificed at Bethel, he did build an altar at the location where he had previously experienced a theophany. Interestingly, de Vaux regards Jacob's altar as a shrine or sanctuary; he notes, "the phrase 'setting up an altar' means, in effect, founding a sanctuary..."[803] Smith agrees: "In the more advanced type of sanctuary the real meeting-place between man and his god is the altar."[804] If we accept the comments of de Vaux and Smith on this point, Jacob did fulfill the second promise of his vow when he returned to Bethel and built an altar to YHWH.[d] We assume as long as Jacob and his family lived in Bethel, they worshipped at the same altar.[e]

Tithe

The third and final part of Jacob's vow was, "...of all that You give me, I will surely give a tenth to You."[f] Here the patriarch refers to the material blessings, especially livestock, which he hoped God would give him on his round-trip to Haran. According to K. Van Der Toorn, in the ancient Near East, "Vows were usually paid in money or offerings."[805] Money was one of the most common items to be promised to the gods in exchange for their granting of requests.[806] In Jacob's case, however, offering up a tenth of the

---

[a] NASB
[b] Genesis 28:16-17, NASB
[c] Genesis 12:7; 28:13-15,18. Compare Exodus 17:14-16.
[d] Note "to God" in Genesis 35:1,3, NASB.
[e] Genesis 35:1,16
[f] Genesis 28:22c, NASB

livestock God miraculously gave him as in-kind wages while working for his uncle in Haran[a] better fits the context.

Pagolu surmises Bethel's lack of a shrine or sanctuary could have been one of the reasons why the writer of Genesis 35:1-7 did not have Jacob fulfill the tithe portion of his vow when he returned there. Pagolu writes, "...there was no sanctuary or priests to appropriate these things in a manner fitting to the rituals."[807] In other words, the final editor of Genesis 35:1-7 may have preferred to have characterized Jacob as paying a tithe to an official sanctuary, as existed in the day of his contemporaries, instead of an unofficial or seemingly non-existent one.

In Genesis 35:1-7, in spite of the divine command to return to Bethel[b] and the fact the word "altar" appears three times in this section,[c] we find no mention of Jacob fulfilling (paying) his tithe vow. Pagolu concurs that the patriarch "...only built an altar and did not present a tithe."[808] He believes the narrator sought to demonstrate only that Jacob was acquainted with the tithe, not that he was a regular tither so as to normalize the practice.[809] According to Pagolu, if the author had wanted to use Jacob's tithe vow to promote tithing, "...he would surely have added that he also paid it there. This would not only [have] strengthened his case but also [have] portrayed the patriarch in a better light...Therefore there is no reason to think that the author was legitimizing the tithe by the example of the patriarch, especially when the patriarch did not actually pay it."[810] He also observes, "...the text shows no concern that...Jacob ever paid his promised tithes at all...The author is more concerned to show how Jacob escaped near annihilation than to state whether he fulfilled his vow."[811] This last remark accurately refers to the contents of Jacob's vow fulfillment section (Genesis 35:1-7, especially verse 5). The narrator emphasizes how YHWH kept his promise to protect Jacob and bring him safely back to the land,[d] shielding him against the retaliation of the Shechemites'

---

[a] Genesis 31:7-8, 41. Compare 30:28,32,33,43.
[b] Genesis 31:13; 35:1
[c] Genesis 35:1,3,7
[d] Genesis 28:15. Compare verses 20-21.

neighbors[a] and the revenge of his older brother.[b] God did not protect the patriarch and his sons from danger because they tithed or made tithe vows; he protected them because they were Abraham's descendants and heirs of the covenant promises. Thus, the Jacob story does not support the claim that Christians need to tithe for God to protect them.[c]

It is possible Jacob fulfilled the "worship" and "shrine" parts of his vow, but there is no evidence that he fulfilled the promise of his "tithe." This raises difficult questions for pro-tithers. How can some claim Jacob fulfilled his tithe vow when there is no Scriptural evidence he did? How can they assert Jacob was a regular or lifetime tither when the text records he only made a single journey vow which involved the promise of a one-time tithe? In light of these textual challenges, and in all intellectual honesty, tithe advocates cannot use Jacob as an example of how Christians should pay tithes without falling prey to some fallacy.

Fallacies

At the beginning of this chapter, I quoted a pro-tither who asserted Jacob "undoubtedly kept his vow of tithes."[812] When read in its entirety, his claim asserts much more than the notion that after Jacob returned to Canaan, he paid a tithe on his wages or material blessings he had obtained while working for his uncle, Laban. In it, he uses various lines of reasoning to suggest Jacob was a lifetime tither even before he made his tithe vow. Unfortunately, his claim contains the following fallacies: (1) the longevity fallacy; (2) the negative-assumption fallacy; (3) the possible-proof fallacy and (4) the honor-by-association fallacy.

Longevity Fallacy

The tithe advocate's first argument is, "It would be unthinkable that Jacob...did not keep his vow of the tenth over all these

---

[a] Compare Genesis 34:30 with 35:5.
[b] Genesis 35:1,3,7. Compare Genesis 27:42; 32:6-8; 33:1-4.
[c] See Book 4 in *The Tithing Series*.

years...Jacob lived to be 147 years of age...Did he not give to God his tithes and offerings over these years?"[813] This claim falls prey to the longevity fallacy, which makes assumptions based on the passage of time that have no bearing on the truthfulness of the statement. This tithe supporter is correct in stating Jacob lived for 147 years,[a] however, this fact does not prove he ever paid a tithe. Furthermore, if Jacob already was a regular tither when he came to Bethel, why, when he made his vow, did he feel the need to promise an additional tithe?

Negative-Assumption Fallacy

This pro-tither also uses negative repetition to make his point. Five times in his claim, he uses the phrase "did he not?"[814] and presumes readers will agree with his conclusion Jacob honored his tithe vow and was a regular tither. His assumptive negatives, however, rely on a rhetorical use of reiteration and do not prove Jacob tithed.

Possible-Proof Fallacy

This tithe advocate also states, "Once more, we believe the answer should be evident, even though 'chapter and verse' is not given every time he gave to the Lord."[815] Arguments from silence like this are misleading and dangerous. To base an important church doctrine and practice on such a non-existent or questionable foundation falls prey to the fallacy of the "possible proof."[816] This fallacy exists when one tries to establish facts with possibilities. Because Jacob *might* have been a lifetime tither does not mean he *was*. Possibility is not historical reality; in these matters, we must be guided by the text. Since this tithe advocate uses Jacob as an example for Christians to follow, the burden of proof is upon him to provide scriptural evidence not only that Jacob was a regular tither, but also how his tithe vow can validly be applied to believers. Both of these he fails to do. If we are not careful, we could be led astray by false doctrines which have no foundation in Scripture and open a Pandora's box to heresy.

---

[a] Genesis 47:28

Honor-by-Association Fallacy

Concerning whether Jacob was a regular tither, and, thereby, "kept his vow of tithes,"[817] this tithe advocate asks the following question, "Would God say He is the God of Abraham, Isaac and Jacob if he did not?"[818] Here this pro-tither falls prey to a fallacy referred to as "honor by association."[819] Most people are familiar with the concept of "guilt by association," in which an innocent party is incriminated not on the basis of physical evidence but by being associated in some way with the guilty party. Similarly, one commits the fallacy of honor-by-association, when, "one claims that someone or something must be reputable because of the people or organizations that are related to it or otherwise support it."[820] I will now show why we need to examine the facts of Jacob's life more closely before we accept this tithe supporter's line of reasoning.

First, the fact Jacob's name appears in a description of God, sometimes along with the names of his father and grandfather[a] and other times all alone as the "God of Jacob,"[b] need not indicate anything more than he, like Abraham and Isaac, was one of the forefathers of the nation of Israel. Because YHWH admitted Jacob's name into one of his own titles does not prove Jacob fulfilled his tithe vow.

Second, YHWH allowed himself to be called the "God of Abraham" and the "God of Isaac" when the first patriarch tithed only once[c] and the second not at all.[d] As tithing had nothing to do with the inclusion of these patriarchs' names into this divine description, the same applies to Jacob's name.

Third, the claim that the Lord allowed himself to be called the "God of Jacob" because the patriarch fulfilled his tithe vow by being a regular tither contradicts what the prophets Jeremiah,[e/821]

---

[a] Exodus 3:6,15-16; 4:5
[b] 2 Samuel 23:1; Psalms 20:1; 46:7,11; 81:1,4; 94:7; 114:7; 146:5; Isaiah 2:3; Micah 4:2
[c] Genesis 14:20c
[d] See Chapter 12.

[e] In Jeremiah 9:4, the Hebrew verb translated "supplant" (KJV) is ya`· qob, which is a play on the name of Jacob (ya·'ă·qōb). Compare Genesis 27:36.

Isaiah,[a] Hosea[b]/[822] and Malachi[c]/[823] all say about Jacob being a dishonest man.

Fourth, in contrast to this tithe advocate's claim, even though the exact phrase, "the God of Abraham, Isaac and Jacob" is not always used, each book of the Torah (Pentateuch) contains at least one verse that connects YHWH to each of the patriarchs not because of their tithing habits but because of their reception of the same land promise.[d] Deuteronomy 9:5 is a good example: "...you are going to possess their land...in order to confirm the oath which the Lord swore to your fathers, Abraham, Isaac and Jacob."[e]

Lastly, the Psalms encourage the Israelites to call on the "God of Jacob" at various times of need. No psalm mentions tithing or Jacob's tithe vow. For example, when the songwriters or their audiences needed supernatural protection, the same way the patriarch did on his way from Shechem to Bethel,[f] they were to call on the "God of Jacob" as their "stronghold."[g] Likewise, when they needed divine intervention, as God gave to the patriarch when Laban exploited him,[h] they were to invoke the "God of Jacob" as their judge, who exalts the righteous and puts down the wicked.[i] The phrase "God of Jacob" was rooted historically in the life of the patriarch,[j] which meant YHWH would answer the Israelites in their "day of trouble"[k] and help the needy among them.[l] Such a commitment was not because Jacob was a tither but because the Lord desired to protect his descendants in the same way he had protected the patriarch.[824]

---

[a] Isaiah 48:1
[b] Hosea 12:1-4,12
[c] Malachi 3:8-9
[d] Genesis 50:24; Exodus 6:3-4,8; 33:1; Leviticus 26:42; Numbers 32:11; Deuteronomy 1:8; 6:10; 9:5; 30:20; 34:4
[e] Deuteronomy 9:5, NASB
[f] Genesis 35:5
[g] Psalm 46:7b, NASB
[h] Genesis 31:8-13,16,24
[i] Psalm 75:9; 76:6
[j] Genesis 35:3, NASB
[k] Psalm 20:1-2, NASB
[l] Psalm 94:6-7. Compare 146:5.

Conclusion

In this chapter, I focused on the three promises of Jacob's vow summarized as "worship, shrine, and tithe." I demonstrated it is possible to conclude Jacob fulfilled the first two promises of his vow, however, there is no scriptural evidence to support the claim Jacob fulfilled his promise to pay a tithe let alone he was a regular or lifetime tither. If pro-tithers expect Christians to tithe because Jacob supposedly tithed, at the least, they should be able to demonstrate from Scripture that Jacob fulfilled the tithe portion of his vow. Instead, they base their claims on assumption and conjecture.

16

A Deceptive Lifestyle

One pro-tither claims:

- "It would be unthinkable that Jacob lied to God and did not keep his vow of the tenth..."[825]

This assertion implies Jacob's character never interfered with the fulfilling of his tithe vow, and the thought of lying to God would never have entered the patriarch's mind. At least when it comes to his relationship with YHWH, such a black-and-white assumption puts Jacob's integrity beyond question. In his claim, this tithe advocate does not use the word "impossible" or "unbiblical" but "unthinkable."[826] To me, this indicates he might hold a higher view of Jacob in his own mind than the text itself. As previously noted, the patriarch's bargain with YHWH was an exploitation for personal gain instead of an acceptance of the family promises.[a] Instead of submitting to YHWH's plan without hesitation, Jacob immediately made a bargain to cooperate only if YHWH would ensure him a safe return to his father's estate. The fact he turned God's unconditional promises into a self-serving bargain should cause us to examine his character and lifestyle more closely. Scripture highlights Jacob's deceptive nature much more than any positive qualities he may have eventually

---

[a] Genesis 28:13-15

exhibited. Since Jacob lied to his father (Isaac[a]), his uncle (Laban[b]) and his brother (Esau[c]); why not also to YHWH?

Jacob Lies to Isaac

During the patriarchal period, the family name, estate and personality of the father was passed on to the next generation through the firstborn son.[827] The firstborn male was the "principal heir"[828] of the estate and was in line to receive both the family birthright as well as the paternal blessing. Ancient Semites believed the gods held special claim over the firstborn; if a father was to sacrifice his first child as an offering to the deity,[829] he could expect to receive special favors.[d] For this and other reasons, the firstborn was given "preferential treatment."[830] At table, for example, "the sons were seated in order of their ages"[831] with the firstborn at the head.[e] At times, however, fathers chose to bypass their firstborn,[f/832] but since this did not always sit well with families, later lawmakers attempted to stop this arbitrary practice.[g/833]

A father's deathbed blessing to his firstborn son was important to the patriarchs.[h/834] It was a sacred moment, as Isaac expressed to his favorite son,[i] Esau: "...that I might eat and bless you in the presence of the Lord before my death."[j] In the Old Testament, a father passed on to his son not only a material inheritance;[835] he also imparted to him his entire being, that is, his whole "vital power,"[836] which involved all that was spiritual including his life experience.[837] According to C. Westermann, the ancient notion was that "the father's blessing determines the destiny"[k/838] of the son and the rest of the family.

---

[a] Genesis 27:19,20,24
[b] Genesis 31:20,26,27
[c] Genesis 33:14-17
[d] Compare Judges 11:29-40.
[e] Compare Genesis 43:33.
[f] Genesis 17:19-21; 48:17-20; I Kings 1:32-53; 2:15; I Chronicles 3:1-8; 2 Samuel 3:4; I Chronicles 26:10-11

[g] Deuteronomy 21:15-17
[h] Genesis 27:1-40; 48:10-22; 49:1-33. Compare Deuteronomy 33:1-29; Joshua 23:1-16.
[i] Genesis 25:28
[j] Genesis 27:7, NASB
[k] Genesis 27:27-29

Jacob's mother, Rebekah, used her authority in the family[a] to deceive Isaac into giving his paternal blessing (*berakha*[839]) to her best-loved son, Jacob, instead of to Esau.[b] Although Rebekah hatched the plot,[c] Jacob followed along without objection; his only hesitation was a fear of being cursed if exposed.[d/840] On this occasion, Jacob lied three times to his father: twice he identified himself as Esau,[e] and once he attributed to the Lord the speed at which he was able to obtain his father's favorite meal.[f] According to Westermann, "Both mother and son knew that the deception had to come out,"[841] but both were also aware by the time their plot was exposed, it would be too late for Esau to do anything to reverse it.[g] A father could give his blessing only to one son, and he could not take it back once it had been given.[842] This meant the other son(s) did not obtain the same advantages from their father and could easily become jealous and even vengeful.[843] Rebekah, however, never foresaw Esau would get so angry at his brother he would plan on killing the son for whom she had devised the scheme in the first place.[h]

The Lord had previously spoken to Rebekah that Esau ("the older") was going to serve Jacob ("the younger").[i] This fact, however, does not mean YHWH desired Jacob to lie to his father.[j] On this point, scholars are divided as to whether Jacob's statement to his father, "Because the Lord your God caused it to happen to me,"[k] should be considered as "blasphemous audacity"[844] or a description of the "right" actions of providence.[l/845] At any rate, as far as we know, Jacob felt no remorse for lying to his father. Even at the end of his father's life, when Jacob saw him one last time, nothing in the record mentions he sought his father's forgiveness for his lies.[m]

---

[a] Genesis 27:8,13
[b] Genesis 27:1-45
[c] Genesis 27:5-17, especially verse 8
[d] Genesis 27:12
[e] Genesis 27:19,24
[f] Genesis 27:20
[g] Genesis 27:36-38
[h] Genesis 27:41
[i] Genesis 25:23
[j] Genesis 27:19,20,24
[k] Genesis 27:20d, NASB. Compare Exodus 20:7 = Deuteronomy 5:11.
[l] Compare Genesis 25:23e.
[m] Genesis 35:27-29

Jacob Lies to Laban

After twenty years of working for his uncle,[a] Jacob observed that the attitude of Laban and his sons became negative toward him,[b] due to the way God had blessed his flocks and herds more than their own.[c] The Lord then told Jacob to leave Haran and return to the land of his birth.[d] With the support of his wives,[e] the text says, "... Jacob deceived Laban the Aramean by not telling him that he was fleeing. So he fled with all that he had; and he arose and crossed the Euphrates River, and set his face toward the hill country of Gilead."[f] When Laban caught up with Jacob and his family ten days later,[g] he asked his son-in-law, "What have you done by deceiving me and carrying away my daughters like captives of the sword? Why did you flee secretly and deceive me, and did not tell me...?"[h] In these verses, the NASB translation uses some form of the word "deceive" three times to describe Jacob's behavior toward Laban. Jacob knew if he told his uncle he was leaving his estate with his wives and children, he would not have allowed him to go without strong opposition.[i] The last time he told his father-in-law he wanted to leave for Canaan, Laban talked him into staying.[j] This time, instead of telling him it was the Lord who told him to leave,[k] he resorted to his usual approach of deception.

Jacob Lies to Esau

When Jacob met Esau on his return to Canaan, he reconciled with his estranged brother in an emotional embrace.[l] Immediately afterwards, Esau asked Jacob to accompany him back to his home in Seir (Edom).[m/846] To decline his brother's offer graciously, Jacob made up an excuse about the frailty of his livestock and

---

[a] Genesis 31:38,41
[b] Genesis 31:1-2
[c] Genesis 30:37-43, especially verse 42
[d] Genesis 31:3
[e] Genesis 31:14-16
[f] Genesis 31:20-21, NASB, which italicizes "Euphrates."
[g] Genesis 31:22-23
[h] Genesis 31:26-27, NASB
[i] Compare Genesis 31:26-31.
[j] Genesis 30:25-36
[k] Genesis 31:3,11,13
[l] Genesis 33:4
[m] Genesis 33:12,14

children.[a]/847 When Esau offered to leave a military entourage with Jacob, he also declined.[b] Instead of accepting either of his brother's overtures, Jacob insisted Esau travel to Seir ahead of him and promised he would meet him there as soon as he could.[c] Jacob, however, led his household to Succoth,[d] 160 miles in the opposite direction.[848]

Jacob Lies to God

Despite some positive comments about Jacob,[e] Genesis portrays him as a man who not only lied to his own family members (Isaac,[f] Laban[g] and Esau[h]), but as one who also lied to God. He promised YHWH upon his safe return to his father's house, he would travel to Bethel and give him a tenth of the tangible goods he obtained on his journey.[i] Even though the text describes the livestock Jacob brought back from Haran in terms of its quantity ("large flocks"[j]) as well as its quality ("so the feebler were Laban's and the stronger Jacob's"[k]), there is no record he ever paid a tithe on them as he had promised.[l] We do not know exactly what Jacob meant by the phrase, "return to my father's house." Did he have in mind returning to the land of promise, coming back to his family's household or even seeing his father again?[m] Whatever he was thinking, we cannot deny the fact that Jacob never returned to Bethel to fulfill his vow on his own initiative.[n] A. Pagolu refers to Jacob's promise at Bethel as the patriarch's "forgotten vow."[849]/[o] The overall narrative seems to reveal that he promised YHWH a tithe to try to manipulate him into bringing him back to the land so he could inherit the

---

[a] Genesis 33:13-14
[b] Genesis 33:15
[c] Genesis 33:14,16
[d] Genesis 33:17
[e] Genesis 31:42; 32:9-12; 33:4-11
[f] Genesis 27:18-24
[g] Genesis 31:26-28
[h] Genesis 33:12-17
[i] Genesis 28:20-22
[j] Genesis 30:43, NASB. Compare 31:16-18.
[k] Compare Genesis 30:42c, NASB.
[l] Contrast Genesis 28:22c with 35:1-7.
[m] How is Genesis 27:2,7 to be reconciled with 35:29?
[n] Compare Genesis 35:1.
[o] Note the divine reminder in Genesis 31:13.

majority share of his father's estate, which he acquired from his older brother through a series of lies and manipulations.

Fear plays a major role in the development of a habitual liar according to psychologists.[850] Even though the text does not trace each fear in Jacob's life to a lie, the patriarch exhibited many fears, such as: (1) Esau's revenge;[a] (2) being caught and cursed for lying to his father;[b] (3) the anger and power of Laban and his sons;[c] (4) retribution from the Shechemites' allies[d] and (5) the loss of his two favorite sons, Joseph and Benjamin.[e] This kind of anxiety motivated the patriarch to make a covenant with Laban at Mizpah[f] and offer a journey sacrifice at Beersheba as he left the land of promise for Egypt.[g] Jacob's fear of Esau's revenge, however, seems to have dominated his life more than any other;[h] it influenced his prayers,[i] his gifts[j] and even his tithe vow.[k] After YHWH brought Jacob back to the land and removed the Esau threat from his life,[l] it seems his commitment to return to Bethel and fulfill his tithe promise disappeared. It is reasonable to conclude his tithe promise was merely the last part of a bargain vow, which he hoped would help him to escape from danger. Once he was out of harm's way, he gave no thought to his vow until YHWH had to command him to return to Bethel.[m]

Jacob's Negative Reputation

The claim, "It would be unthinkable that Jacob lied to God and did not keep his vow of the tenth...,"[851] is not only inconsistent with

---

[a] Genesis 32:7-8,11
[b] Genesis 27:11-12
[c] Genesis 31:1-2,31,52-53
[d] Genesis 34:30. Compare 35:5.
[e] Joseph (Genesis 37:3-4,33-35; 44:29); Benjamin (42:4,38)
[f] Genesis 31:43-55, especially verse 54
[g] Genesis 46:1-4, especially verse 3
[h] Genesis 27:41; 32:7-12 and possibly 33:12-17
[i] Genesis 32:1-12, especially verses 7-8,11. Compare Genesis 28:20-22. Note the lack of first-person prayer until verse 22c.
[j] Genesis 32:3-5 with 33:8-11
[k] Genesis 27:41-43; 28:21a
[l] Note the theme of safety in Genesis 28:21; 33:18. Genesis 27:41; 32:11; 33:4.
[m] Genesis 35:1

the Jacob narrative, it also contradicts the way the rest of the Old Testament views the patriarch. No verse in the Bible characterizes Jacob as one who regularly tithed or fulfilled his tithe vow. Instead, a negative reputation follows him through the ministries of Jeremiah[a] and Hosea[b] right down to the end of the biblical period where the Lord says in the book of Malachi, "Ought man to defraud God? Yet you are defrauding Me. And you ask, 'How have we been defrauding You?' In tithe and contribution. You are suffering under a curse, yet you go on defrauding Me – the whole nation of you."[c] In these two verses, Malachi uses the Hebrew word *kaba* ("defraud") four times, which is a play on the name *Ya'aqobh* (Jacob).[852] God was saying to his people, "Stop *Jacobing* Me!"[d]

Conclusion

In this chapter, I demonstrated that it would not at all be "unthinkable" for Jacob to have lied to God about his tithe since there is no evidence he ever paid it. The undeniable emphasis of the Bible is that Jacob was a manipulator and liar.[e] To conclude otherwise is to hold a higher view of the patriarch than Scripture. Jacob stands as an example of a man, who, for most of his life, served God on his own terms and for his own ends. His fear, greed, distrust and self-obsession are underscored by his inconsolability[f] along with his vows and prayers of self-interest.[g] It appears he took personal advantage of being a part of God's covenant people. Despite the fact Jacob lied, manipulated, bargained and even used brute force at times to get what he wanted,[h] YHWH did not permit anyone to harm him.[i] At the same time, he did allow him to get a good taste of his own medicine

---

[a] Jeremiah 9:4
[b] Hosea 12:2-6
[c] Malachi 3:8-9, JSB. Compare verses 6-7. See Book 3 in *The Tithing Series*.
[d] Emphasis mine.
[e] manipulation = Genesis 25:27-34

[f] Genesis 37:35; 42:38; 44:29,31
[g] Genesis 28:22c; 32:9-12
[h] Genesis 32:26b. Note Jacob's physical strength (Genesis 29:1-3,10).
[i] Genesis 31:7,29; 34:30; 35:5-6. Compare also 31:43-55; 45:24-28.

while working for his uncle in Haran.[a] Even though Jacob did not deliver on his promised tithe, which he hoped would bring him divine favor, in the end, he was unable to use it to manipulate YHWH. The divine activity in the patriarch's life[b] demonstrates that YHWH continued his unconditional covenant of grace with a sinful Jacob/Israel. YHWH freely chose to love the Israelites, who, like their father, Jacob, did not always keep their word.

---

[a] Compare Genesis 27:18-24,36 with 29:25; 31:7a,42.
[b] Note the supernatural dreams (Genesis 28:12; 31:11,24), angelic visitations (28:12; 31:11; 32:1; 48:16a), divine protection (31:24,29 34:30; 35:5-6), personal prosperity (30:43; 31:9,16), prosperity for others (30:27,30) and answers to prayer (28:21a with 33:18 and 32:11 with 33:4).

17
A Motive Analysis

Jacob had no money or possessions when he left Canaan to seek a bride in Haran.[a] His destitution has led some to speculate he had impure motives when he promised to give God a tithe.[b] Others hold his intentions were pure, and, like Jacob, Christians need to follow his example to receive the blessings of the New covenant. Here are a couple of claims from one tithe advocate:

- "Jacob saw an open Heaven, not because he was righteous but because of God's call and His faithfulness to Abraham. Jacob was the third generation to receive the promises of the Abrahamic covenant. The Lord identified Himself by His previous relationship with Abraham and Isaac (Genesis 28:14). After Jacob had seen an open Heaven, and seen the abundance of what was in Heaven, he fully realized all that God's covenant promises held for him (Genesis 28:20-22). The tithe, although found in the later mosaic law, originated with the earliest patriarchs, Abraham and Jacob."[853]
- "It [the tithe] also shows that we are agreeing to walk trustingly with Him, in our part of His covenant blessings. The church of Jesus Christ has to be able to operate under a 100 percent open Heaven. If only 20 percent of the church

---

[a] Genesis 32:10. Compare 29:18.

[b] Compare chapters 13,14,15 and 16.

worldwide tithe, it means that 80 percent of the windows of heaven are closed over the church."[854]

I understand these claims to mean: (1) Jacob saw an open heaven and great abundance inside; (2) Jacob received YHWH's promises not because he was righteous but because he was under the Abrahamic covenant; (3) Jacob fully realized all that YHWH's promises held for him only after he had seen heaven's abundance; and (4) although not stated clearly, Jacob concluded he needed to make a tithe vow to obtain YHWH's promises.[a/855] I will now examine these statements more closely.

Open Heaven

The pro-tither maintains that during Jacob's dream, the patriarch observed an "open heaven"[856] along with seeing "the abundance of what was in Heaven."[857] I understand this to mean God allowed the patriarch to see his dwelling place above the earth unobstructed, and when he looked inside, he observed heaven's many blessings. As sweet as this may sound, these two claims have several problems with them, which render them less than possible.

First, the word translated "heaven" (*shamayim*) is used twice in the story.[b] The first instance describes the staircase "with its top reaching to heaven."[c] The second identifies the place of the dream as the "gate of heaven."[d] This is the only place the Old Testament uses the phrase "gate of heaven," and here the Hebrew word translated "gate" (*shaar*) could refer to a portal through which Jacob's ministering angels traveled, but, to the patriarch, it did not indicate an "open heaven" because he never described it as such. To R. Clifford and R. Murphy, the gate is "ambiguous; is the gate open or closed?"[858] To C. Westermann, on the other hand, the metaphor refers to the fact the "...place is forbidden to humans because God dwells here."[859] To him, the gate appears

---

[a] Genesis 28:20-22
[b] Genesis 28:12,17 (English translations)
[c] Genesis 28:12, NASB
[d] Genesis 28:17d, NASB

"...in the context of the dividing line between the divine and the human, the line where awe begins."[a/860] Whether the gate invited or prohibited entrance into the house of God or was a portal for angels, the image speaks of a boundary line between heaven and earth not an "open heaven."

Second, this pro-tither adapts his catchphrase "open heaven"[861] from the book of Malachi. He attempts to link the phrase to Jacob's dream and then subsequently to his tithe vow. Such a connection, however, is artificial and anachronistic.[b] Malachi promised the returnees from Babylon God would open the "windows of heaven"[c] for them, that is, provide rain for their crops, if they would bring their full tithes and offerings to the Jerusalem temple. In contrast, when Jacob made his tithe vow, it was the patriarch who was using his vow to try to guarantee himself a safe return to the land not God telling him he would bless him if he would tithe.[d] Malachi chapter 3 is a prophetic book written in the Sinai covenant tradition, whereas Genesis chapter 28 is a patriarchal story written in the Abrahamic covenant tradition. In Jacob's day, there was no Mosaic law, no central temple, no hereditary priesthood and no mandatory tithe needed to obtain the blessings of the covenant.

Finally, this pro-tither also claims Jacob saw "...the abundance of what was in Heaven."[862] According to the text, however, the only objects Jacob saw during his dream were: (1) a staircase connecting earth to heaven;[e] (2) angels ascending and descending on it[f] and (3) the Lord standing at the top.[g] When the Lord stood above the staircase, he probably evoked an image of divine glory so bright any onlooker would not have been able to see anyone or anything beyond him. The Lord, as well as the angels who were simultaneously ascending and descending on the staircase, would

---

[a] Jacob says, "How awesome is this place..." (Genesis 28:17, NASB).
[b] anachronistic = "something or someone that is not in its correct historical or chronological time" (dictionary.com)
[c] Malachi 3:10, NASB
[d] Genesis 28:20-22
[e] Genesis 28:12b
[f] Genesis 28:12c
[g] Genesis 28:13a

have blocked the patriarch's view.

Jacob's prophecy over Joseph, his eleventh son, included the words: "...through the Almighty who will bless you with blessings from heaven above..."[a] Here the patriarch used the same term translated "heaven" (*shamayim*) as appears in his earlier Bethel dream. However, he did not tell his son that he ever observed such blessings let alone that he had seen "the abundance of what was in Heaven."[863]

Abrahamic Covenant

The tithe advocate also claims Jacob saw an open heaven and received the promises of the Abrahamic covenant "not because he was righteous but because of God's call and His faithfulness to Abraham."[864] Here he accurately observes Jacob as the third generation after Abraham and Isaac to be given YHWH's covenant promises. However, when he goes on to state tithing, "...shows that we [Christians] are agreeing to walk trustingly with Him, in *our part* of His covenant blessings,"[865] he commits a serious error. How could Jacob inherit the covenant promises through grace ("not because he was righteous"[866]), but Christians inherit them only by tithing? This tithe supporter implies Jacob saw an open heaven and received YHWH's promises through grace, but to experience them, he had to do *his part*, which was to make a promise to tithe. As I have previously demonstrated, neither Abraham, Isaac nor Jacob needed to tithe to enjoy YHWH's covenant promises.[b] More importantly, nothing in the New Testament says believers have to tithe or make tithe vows to experience the fulfillment of the Abrahamic covenant in Christ.[c] As Paul asks, "...how will he [God] not also with Him [Christ] *freely* give us all things?"[d]

---

[a] Genesis 49:25b,c, MLB
[b] See chapters 9,11,12,15 and 16.
[c] Matthew 23:23 = Luke 11:42 and Luke 18:12 address the Pharisees not believers.
Hebrews 7:5,11-12, 18-19 abolish the mandatory tithe.
[d] Romans 8:32c, NASB. Emphasis mine.

Full Realization

The pro-tither further asserts that in Jacob's dream, the patriarch "fully realized all that God's covenant promises held for him..."[867] Here he attempts to provide a material motive for Jacob's tithe vow. Realistically, how could the promises of land, people, the ability to bless the nations, personal protection, a safe return to Canaan and YHWH's presence be what Jacob somehow observed in heaven?[a] The patriarch did not need to see heaven's contents to understand completely the covenant promises because in his dream God told him clearly what the promises were. Neither did he need to view its abundance to motivate him to make a tithe vow since his self-centered motives were already in his heart, and, according to the text, his focus was solely on ensuring himself a safe trip to and from Haran.[b]

A Tithe for the Promises

This tithe advocate uses Genesis 28:20-22 to support his argument that it was only after Jacob had viewed heaven's abundance he grasped everything God's covenant promises held for him.[868] These verses, however, do not contain the covenant promises; those were given earlier in the chapter (verses 13-15). Genesis 28:20-22 contains only Jacob's vow. So, either the pro-tither made a mistake in using this reference, or he uses it to suggest Jacob made a tithe vow to obtain YHWH's covenant promises. I believe the latter is the case because of his next sentence: "The tithe, although found in the later mosaic law, originated with the earliest patriarchs, Abraham and Jacob."[869] From what I understand him to say, not only did God require these patriarchs to tithe to obtain his covenant blessings,[c/870] but he also requires us as believers to do *"our part* of His covenant blessings."[871] On the contrary, there is no evidence God told Jacob he had to make a tithe vow to receive his covenant promises. YHWH never said to Jacob, "If you will give me 'worship, shrine, and tithe,'[872] then I will bless you."

---

[a] Genesis 28:13-15
[b] See chapters 13,14 and 17.
[c] See chapters 9 and 10.

As I showed in Chapter 14, Jacob's tithe vow was a completely voluntary and conditional promise centered upon his own personal desires.

Much later, Jacob described his Luz/Bethel experience to his son, Joseph, in this way: "God Almighty appeared to me at Luz in the land of Canaan and blessed me, and He said to me, 'Behold, I will make you fruitful and numerous, and I will make you a company of peoples, and will give this land to your descendants after you for an everlasting possession.'"[a] Note the recurrence here of God's promissory phrase "I will...," which indicates YHWH's promises of land and people had no conditions. If Jacob's dream had convinced him that tithing was the only way that he and his descendants were going to be able to receive YHWH's covenant blessings, I submit he would definitely have shared such a vital key not only with Joseph,[b] but with all of his sons, and yet there is no evidence he ever did. When this tithe supporter suggests Jacob tithed or promised to tithe that he and his descendants might receive God's covenant promises, he reads into the text what is not there.

Conclusion

Contrary to what this pro-tither leads Christians to believe,[873] Jacob, like Abraham and Isaac, did not have to tithe to receive God's covenant promises. When God shared his promises with the patriarch in a dream, he used words of assurance instead of images of abundance with a demand for tithes. According to the text, Jacob could not have seen an "open heaven"[874] because the Lord at the top of the staircase, as well as the angels continuously ascending and descending on it, would have blocked his view. As a result, the patriarch could not have gazed upon heaven's abundance or any covenant promises somehow waiting for him there. It is accurate to say that it was after God spoke his promises to Jacob that the patriarch made his tithe vow. However, the conditions Jacob set forth in his vow make it clear he did not

---

[a] Genesis 48:3-4, NASB. Compare verses 1, 21.
[b] Genesis 37:3, NASB

promise a tithe because he thought it would guarantee him material blessings beyond his round-trip to Haran.[a] Along with "worship" and "shrine," the patriarch promised only a one-time, journey tithe. Therefore, we are forced to conclude Jacob did not make his tithe vow so he could receive YHWH's covenant promises since those were given to him freely. He made his vow to add weight to his prayers in an effort to guarantee a safe return to his father's house.

---

[a] Genesis 28:20-22

18

Did Jacob's Tithe Vow Make Him Rich?

The story of Jacob's tithe vow began when his mother, Rebekah, told him his older brother, Esau, planned to murder him for stealing his paternal blessing.[a] To prevent such a fate, Rebekah told her husband she was fearful Jacob would marry a Canaanite woman, unless he sent their son to obtain a wife from her brother's family in Haran.[b] Isaac took his wife's advice, but he sent Jacob away empty-handed without a bride price or provisions for his journey.[c] Such unusual behavior[d] may have occurred because Jacob recently deceived his father into giving him the blessing reserved for Esau,[e] Isaac's favorite son.[f] According to S. Walters, Jacob left Canaan "in naked flight."[875] A. Beck agrees: "Jacob is the poor stranger, his own emissary, a refugee from his brother Esau's wrath, bearing no rich gifts, only his walking staff."[g/876] Thus, when the patriarch arrived at his uncle's estate, he "had to pay in services, the equivalent of seven years' hard labor for a wife."[h/877] It is no wonder, therefore, that Jacob made a bargain with God to cooperate with his covenant, as long as he would provide him not only a safe return to the land but also "food to eat" and "garments to wear" for his journey.[i]

---

[a] Genesis 27:41-45. Compare verse 36.
[b] Genesis 28:1-2. Compare 26:34-35; 27:46.
[c] Genesis 27:43 - 28:9
[d] Contrast Genesis 24:53. Compare verses 10,22,30.
[e] Genesis 27:35,37
[f] Genesis 25:28
[g] Genesis 32:10
[h] Genesis 29:18,21,27,30
[i] Genesis 28:20, NASB

According to Walters, Jacob "...eventually became wealthy in livestock and servants."[878] The patriarch arrived back in Canaan, after being away for twenty years,[a] "exceedingly rich."[b] Jacob himself observed, "...for with my staff only I crossed this Jordan, now I have become two companies."[c] The text refers to such wealth as assets he accumulated while working for his uncle in Haran.[d] Some tithe supporters, however, allege Jacob's tithe vow at Bethel,[e] or tithing in general, was the cause of the patriarch's wealth.[f] Here are two examples:

- "Tithing is God's bedrock way to make his people wealthy. This is as true today as it was when Jacob adapted it."[879]
- "Thus Jacob has a visitation from God and without doubt he kept his vow of tithes. We see how God blessed him throughout his life, in spite of his 'Jacob-nature.'"[880]

Both of these claims are based on assumption; they allege God blessed Jacob because he tithed. I have already demonstrated that it cannot be shown from Scripture Jacob was a tither;[g] as a result, tithing could not have made him rich. Does Genesis, then, uphold the idea God prospered Jacob because the patriarch made a tithe vow at Bethel? Moreover, did God enable Jacob to exploit Laban's livestock for personal gain because he was counting on the patriarch to give him a tenth of his increase when he returned to the land of promise? Even though the answer to both of these questions is no, one tithe advocate asserts God will send financial blessings into believers' lives the moment they *promise* to tithe – even before they make their first tithe payment.[881] In contrast, after Jacob made a tithe vow at Bethel, his life was anything but financially easy.[h] The patriarch was no richer by the time he reached his uncle's estate in Haran, 400 miles away,[882] than he was when he first made his tithe vow. Prior to his

---

[a] Genesis 31:38,41
[b] Genesis 30:43, NRSV. Compare 30:43; 31:18; 32:5,13-21,22; 35:4.
[c] Genesis 32:10, NASB, which italicizes "only."
[d] Genesis 31:17-18
[e] Genesis 28:22c
[f] Contrast Genesis 35:1-7.
[g] See chapters 15 and 16.
[h] Compare Genesis 31:7,41.

arrival, God did not provide the patriarch with a bride price for a wife, nor did he bless him with significant in-kind earnings of his own flocks and herds until the beginning of the fifteenth year of his employment.[a]

It is clear YHWH favored Jacob merely because he was a member of the covenant family. The blessings the patriarch eventually experienced did not come through tithing or his one-time tithe vow at Bethel; instead, they came from: (1) family inheritance from his father; (2) fruitful wives and concubines; (3) divine intervention in childbearing; (4) miraculous reproduction of livestock and (5) Shechemite plunder.

Family Inheritance from His Father

Jacob's possession of the birthright guaranteed him the majority share of the family inheritance.[b] The one who held the family birthright received "...the principal inheritance of property and name. Through him the family line was continued."[883] Thus, we see that Jacob instead of Esau continued Abraham and Isaac's family line. Since Abraham had bequeathed "all that he had to Isaac,"[c] this meant upon Isaac's death, Jacob would inherit the principle share of his grandfather's sizable estate. Later, Jacob lied and also obtained Esau's paternal blessing.[d] The father's blessing was also a part of the firstborn's birthright.[884] Isaac's blessing gave Jacob social precedence over his older brother.[e]

Fruitful Wives and Concubines

During the patriarchal age, the number of wives, concubines, servants and children (especially sons[f]) were all a part of a man's wealth; the greater the number of household members, the greater a man's net worth. After Jacob arrived in Haran, he married Laban's two daughters, Leah and Rachel. As a wedding gift, his uncle gave each of his daughters a maid; to Leah, he gave

---

[a] Genesis 30:31-36; 31:41
[b] Genesis 25:29-34
[c] Genesis 25:5a, NASB
[d] Genesis 27:1-40
[e] Genesis 27:29c,d,40b
[f] Compare Genesis 29:31-35; 30:7-8.

Zilpah[a] and to Rachel, he gave Bilhah.[b] C. Mariottini writes, "...the giving of a maid to a bride was a common practice in ancient Mesopotamia."[885] Besides assisting Jacob's two wives in their daily duties, Zilpah and Bilhah became the patriarch's concubines, who increased his net worth by giving him four more sons.[c] Not only did these sons increase the number of Jacob's descendants ("sixteen descendants of Zilpah are listed among the seventy people who went to Egypt..."[d/886]), they also multiplied their father's wealth in terms of labor as they "tended the flock of their father."[e/887]

Divine Intervention in Childbearing

One pastor, whose wife was childless, told his congregation that the Lord eventually blessed them with children and properties because they had never stopped giving him their tithes and offerings. He, along with other tithe supporters who make similar claims,[888] implied childless Christian couples could move God to give them houses and children, if they would only give the Lord their tithes and offerings.

The story of Jacob and Rachel, however, serves as an example to the contrary. When Rachel was barren, she became jealous of Leah because her older sister gave birth to four sons (Reuben, Simeon, Levi and Judah) before she had delivered one child.[f] Rachel's jealousy toward her sister, Leah, turned into anger toward Jacob; she demanded of him, "Give me children, or else I die."[g] Rachel blamed her husband for her childlessness. Jacob did not take kindly to her accusation, so he replied, "Am I in the place of God, who has withheld from you the fruit of the womb?"[h] If Jacob had believed his tithe vow would have motivated God to make his barren wife pregnant, this would have been Jacob's opportunity to tell Rachel, in effect, "Don't worry, honey, God will give us a child soon because I made a tithe vow back at

---

[a] Genesis 29:24; 30:9
[b] Genesis 29:29; 30:3
[c] Genesis 30:3-13; 35:25-26
[d] Genesis 46:18
[e] Genesis 37:2
[f] Genesis 29:31-35; 30:1-2
[g] Genesis 30:1, NASB
[h] Genesis 30:2, NASB

Bethel," or "Don't get so upset, dear, all we have to do is tithe on our flocks and God will give us a child." The text, however, says nothing like this because tithing had nothing to do with God supernaturally making Rachel fruitful. Jacob admitted there was nothing he could do to produce children; in his mind, conceiving children was up to God.

On the divine level, according to Scripture, what caused Jacob's wives to conceive was a combination of God's sovereignty,[a] his heart for Leah as the unloved wife[b] and his answer to Rachel's prayers.[c] The human level involved the use of mandrakes,[d/889] which were believed to be "an aphrodisiac and an aid to fertility."[890] According to the text, however, it was God who enabled Rachel to conceive both Joseph[e] and Benjamin;[f] the text fails to connect the miraculous birth of either son with Jacob's tithe vow.

Miraculous Reproduction of Livestock

Before Jacob returned to Canaan with his family, he and Laban agreed his wages would consist of the irregulars in his uncle's flocks and herds.[g] Laban separated the irregulars and gave them into the care of his sons, distancing Jacob's in-kind wages a three-day journey from him.[h] Using a creative breeding method,[i] Jacob turned the "regulars" of Laban's livestock into "irregulars," which he then set aside for himself.[j]

Due to Laban's abuse of Jacob,[k] the miraculous was also involved. An angel revealed to the patriarch in a dream,[l] how God was helping to increase his irregulars.[m] Over a period of six years,[n] after Jacob's livestock became stronger and more numerous than

---

[a] Genesis 30:2,6,17,18,20,22,23
[b] Genesis 29:31-33
[c] Genesis 30:6,22-24. God answered Rachel's prayer for a second son (30:24; 35:16-18).
[d] Genesis 30:14-17
[e] Genesis 30:22-23
[f] Connect Genesis 30:24b with 35:16-18.
[g] Genesis 30:31-34
[h] Genesis 30:35-36
[i] Genesis 30:37-42
[j] Genesis 30:39-40
[k] Genesis 31:7,12
[l] Genesis 31:11
[m] Genesis 31:8-12
[n] Genesis 31:41

his uncle's,[a] his cousins angrily observed, "Jacob has taken away all that was our father's, and from what belonged to our father, he has made all his wealth."[b] In similar terms, Leah and Rachel described their newfound prosperity as "...wealth which God has taken away from our father..."[c] Thus, Jacob "became exceedingly prosperous, and had large flocks and female and male servants and camels and donkeys."[d]

Shechemite Plunder

After Jacob and his household returned to the land of promise and settled in Shechem,[e/891] the patriarch also profited from the misbehavior of his sons. When Dinah, Jacob's daughter by Leah, "went out to visit the daughters of the land,"[f] Shechem, the son of Hamor, the Hivite ruler of the area, raped her.[g] After the incident, he asked for Dinah's hand in marriage, for which he was willing to pay any price.[h] When Jacob heard about his daughter's rape, he did not say anything to anybody; instead, he waited until his sons came in from the field.[i] When he told them about how Shechem had violated their sister, the brothers instigated a deceptive plan to avenge her honor. They told the Shechemites they would be glad to intermarry with them and become "one people,"[j] if their males would be circumcised. The men of Shechem agreed, but before they fully recovered from being circumcised:

"Jacob's sons came upon the slain and looted the city, because they had defiled their sister. They took their flocks and their herds and their donkeys, and that which was in the city and that which was in the field; and they captured and looted all their wealth and all their little ones and their wives, even all that was in the houses."[k]

---

[a] Genesis 30:41-42
[b] Genesis 31:1, NASB
[c] Genesis 31:16, NASB
[d] Genesis 30:43, NASB
[e] Genesis 33:18-19
[f] Genesis 34:1, NASB
[g] Genesis 34:2
[h] Genesis 34:4,12
[i] Genesis 34:5
[j] Genesis 34:22, NASB
[k] Genesis 34:27-29, NASB. Compare verse 23. Verse 29 in NASB italicizes "was."

According to L. Toombs, archaeologists[892] have demonstrated the unmistakable signs of Shechem prosperity: a "necklace of crystal and agate beads"[893] found on a small child's remains, an "abundance of luxury items"[894] and the residence of an "exceptionally wealthy citizen."[895] Even though Jacob verbally condemned Simeon and Levi's looting of Shechem,[a] little doubt, he benefited greatly from the plunder.[b]

Conclusion

When Jacob made his tithe vow at Bethel, he was financially destitute. Twenty years later, he was rich, but there is no biblical evidence to show God blessed him because he tithed. Instead, the God of the Abrahamic covenant, of which Jacob was an heir, prospered the patriarch, as he had done for his father and grandfather. Jacob told Laban his financial blessings came from the God of Abraham and Isaac being with him.[c] God did not prosper Laban on account of Jacob the man but on account of Jacob the covenant-bearer. When God told Jacob, "Behold, I am with you...,"[d] he indicated much more than a sure promise of Presence; he revealed the secret to Jacob's riches.

As Jacob returned to Canaan, his older brother, Esau, approached him and his family with four hundred men. Jacob feared for his life and appealed to YHWH, saying, "Deliver me, I pray, from the hand of my brother, from the hand of Esau; for I fear him, that he will come and attack me and the mothers with the children. For You said, 'I will surely prosper you and make your descendants as the sand of the sea, which is too great to be numbered.'"[e] In his prayer, Jacob did not ask God to protect him because he had vowed a tithe. Instead, he appealed to God on the basis of the promises of the Abrahamic covenant. Here Jacob realized he was a covenant heir and did not need to use a tithe to bargain with God.

---

[a] Genesis 34:30
[b] Genesis 34:27-29. Compare 46:6.
[c] Genesis 31:42
[d] Genesis 28:15, NASB
[e] Genesis 32:11-12, NASB. The NASB italicizes "and" in verse 11.

19

Tithing Vows & the New Covenant

Does the fact Jacob made a tithe vow to YHWH[a] obligate Christians to make similar commitments? The following pro-tithers answer yes:

- "Those who accept the God of Abraham, the God of Isaac and the God of Jacob will also keep their vow of tithes and give back to the Lord a tenth of all He gives them...this vow of tithing was before the Law was given."[896]
- "Now repeat after me: 'I repent of the sin of not tithing. I break the curse of not tithing in my own life. I break the curse of not tithing all the way back to my parents, Adam and Eve. I promise to tithe and to give God his ten percent. From this day forward, I will be a tither. I pray this in Jesus' name. Amen.'"[897]
- "...read the following prayer... 'Dear heavenly Father...I am sorry that I have not returned Your tithe to You...from this day on, I commit to tithe on all income that comes into my hands...In Jesus' Name. Amen.'"[898]

What the above quotations have in common is the belief Christians have a duty to make tithing vows, promises or commitments. In this chapter, I demonstrate how and why no

---

[a] Genesis 28:20-22

New Testament writer encourages believers to make any kind of vow.

In the Old Testament, people vowed to the deity personal items of value in the form of sacrifices or offerings in exchange for his favor(s).[899] Some began to make vows without first counting the cost.[a] Israel believed that if a suppliant failed to pay what he had promised, God would hold him to his obligation.[b] As a result, some writers warned against making vows in the first place.[c] M. Weinfeld writes: "The warning against vows and cultic [liturgical] commitments in Deuteronomy 23:21-23 has its parallel in Ecclesiastes 5:1–7...Warnings against rash declarations and vows are a frequent topic of Israelite wisdom (Proverbs 20:25; 18:7)."[900]

The Septuagint (LXX[901]) is typically considered the most ancient Greek version of the Hebrew Bible (Old Testament) and was translated in Alexandria, Egypt two-hundred years before Christ.[902] According to J. Wevers, "The LXX constitutes the bridge between the Old Testament and the New Testament. It provides the thought world and vocabulary for the New Testament writers."[903] Nevertheless, the New Testament does not use the Septuagint phrase, "I will pay my vows to the Lord" (*apodidomi eucheon*).[d]/[904] When Jesus uses similar wording in the Sermon on the Mount, he does not use it to support vows or oaths; he uses it to set up his rejection of them. He says:

> "*Again, you have heard that the ancients were told, 'YOU SHALL NOT MAKE FALSE VOWS, BUT SHALL FULFILL YOUR VOWS TO THE LORD.' But I say to you, make no oath at all, either by heaven, for it is the throne of God, or by the earth, for it is the footstool of His feet, or by Jerusalem, for it is THE CITY OF THE GREAT KING. Nor shall you make*

---

[a] Proverbs 20:25b
[b] Deuteronomy 23:21. Compare James 5:12.
[c] Deuteronomy 23:22; Ecclesiastes 5:5; Proverbs 20:25
[d] The Hebrew noun for vow (*neder*) is found in Psalms 22:25b; 50:14b; 56:12a; 61:5a,8b; 65:1b; 66:13b and 116:14a,18a. The Hebrew verb for vow (*nadar*) is found in Psalm 76:11a and 132:2b.

an oath by your head, for you cannot make one hair white or black. But let your statement be, 'Yes, yes' or 'No, no'; anything beyond these is of evil."[a]

Here Jesus does not distinguish between oaths and vows.[905] According to J. Milgrom, the oath parallels the vow in Psalm 132:2.[906] Numbers chapter 30 also connects the vow and the oath: "If a man makes a vow to the Lord, or takes an oath to bind himself with a binding obligation, he shall not violate his word; he shall do according to all that proceeds out of his mouth."[b] Although others disagree,[907] Milgrom holds, "The common denominator of oaths, vows, and consecrations is that all are statements that invoke the name of God."[908] N. Fox concurs;[909] her main point is whatever is a "sworn statement in the name of God"[910] is binding.[c] In the Law, both "oaths and vows had to be kept."[911] The Mishna, a third century collection of laws fundamental to rabbinic Judaism,[912] places oaths and vows together.[913] Maimonides, the leading intellectual figure of medieval Judaism, who died in 1204 A.D., also combined vow and oath obligations under the single category of keeping one's word.[914]

After addressing vows to God, Jesus turns his attention to oaths to men. He says, "...make no oath *at all*..."[d] Jesus forbids oaths to men because his followers should never need to swear by sacred things (heaven, earth, Jerusalem or oneself) in an effort to convince others they are telling the truth; they are to live honestly.[e] Similarly, Jesus also forbids the making of vows, since they are oaths directed to God. His followers need not bargain with him for their daily necessities; they are to trust their heavenly Father completely.[f] According to S. Laws, when compared with Jewish rabbis and Greek philosophers, Jesus was the only one in the ancient world who put an "absolute ban" [915] on the use of both oaths and vows.

---

[a] Matthew 5:33-37, NASB. See Numbers 30:2; Deuteronomy 23:21-23; Leviticus 19:12.
[b] Numbers 30:2, NASB
[c] Compare Exodus 20:7 = Deuteronomy 5:11.
[d] Matthew 5:34, NASB. Emphasis mine.
[e] Compare James 5:12.
[f] Matthew 6:25-34

In addition to the words of Jesus, there are several other reasons why the New Testament eliminates the need for Christians to make vows:

First, according to H. Hahn, in ancient times, vows were a popular way of "counteracting the anger of the gods."[916] Occasionally, the Israelites made vows to YHWH to end droughts[917] and wars,[a/918] when they interpreted them as judgments for Torah violations.[b] Most tithe advocates hold believers must tithe to escape the wrath of God as expressed in the curse of the prophet Malachi.[c] Due to the finished work of Christ, however, vows are no longer needed to pacify divine wrath.[d]

Second, according to K. Van Der Toorn, throughout ancient Syria and Palestine, many people made vows to "lend force to petitionary prayer."[919] G. Davies agrees: the purpose of a vow was to "strengthen prayer." [e/920] Under the New covenant, however, answers to prayer no longer require believers to make vows to God. Greevan writes, "The distinctive feature of early Christian prayer is the certainty of being heard. This derives directly from faith in the fatherly love of God..."[921] According to Mark 11:24, all that is needed is simple trust.[f/922] Two other New Testament writers concur: Paul says believers "have boldness and confident access [to God] through faith in Him [Jesus];"[g] and Hebrews states all Christians can "draw near with confidence to the throne of grace, so that we may receive mercy and find grace to help in time of need."[h] From these verses, it is clear prayer is not dependent upon vows, bargains or tithes which operate on a quid pro quo basis.

Third, Milgrom observes, "...all vows in the Bible are consecrations to the sanctuary...Jacob promises to build a

---

[a] Compare Psalm 76:3,5-6,11-12; Nahum 1:15.
[b] Compare Deuteronomy 28:25,31,38-40.
[c] Malachi 3:9. See Book 3 in *The Tithing Series*.
[d] John 3:36; Romans 5:9; I Thessalonians 1:10; 5:9. Compare John 19:30.
[e] Compare Proverbs 31:2c; I Samuel 1:11.
[f] Compare Matthew 7:7-11 = Luke 11:9-13.
[g] Ephesians 3:12, NASB
[h] Hebrews 4:16, NASB

sanctuary [at Bethel[a]], Israel consecrates the Canaanite spoils as *herem*[b] [for the Lord's treasury]...Jephthah sacrifices his daughter [at a place which eventually became a sanctuary[c/923]], Hannah dedicates her son to the [Shiloh] sanctuary as a Nazirite,[d] and Absalom offers sacrifices at the Hebron sanctuary."[e/924] Under the New covenant, however, there is no central or institutional sanctuary to which vows are to be paid. The church (*ekklesia*) is God's new temple,[f] and, it is located, in the words of Jesus, "...where two or three have gathered together in My name, I am there in their midst."[g] Therefore, when the New covenant eliminated the central sanctuary, it also removed the need for a place to make and pay vows.

Fourth, archaeologists have discovered thousands of small votive objects throughout the ancient Near East indicating both rich and poor made vows.[925] In ancient Sumeria, for example, "...votive offerings were made by rather prosperous individuals..."[926] The donation of expensive and noticeable votive gifts became a means of personal pride and public recognition. Some first century Jews, for example, gave votive gifts[h] to the temple as symbols of national and personal prestige;[i] Jesus, however, was not impressed.[j] Luke writes: "And while some were talking about the temple, that it was adorned with beautiful stones and votive gifts, He [Jesus] said, 'As for these things which you are looking at, the days will come in which there will not be left

---

[a] Genesis 28:19,22
[b] *herem* = under the ban of extermination; set apart for the Lord's treasury (Joshua 6:19,24). Compare 7:1-26. The cited source does not contain this footnote.
[c] Judges 11:29-40. The reference to Mizpah (verses 29,34) refers either to the Mizpah of Benjamin (Judges 10:17; 11:11; 20:1; I Samuel 7:5-6) or the Mizpah of Gilead (Judges 11:29,34,39-40, especially verse 40).

[d] I Samuel 1:21-22,24. Compare the Nazirite vow and the clause "to the doorway of the tent of meeting" (Numbers 6:2,10,13,18, NASB).
[e] 2 Samuel 15:7-9
[f] I Corinthians 3:17; Ephesians 2:21. Compare Acts 17:24.
[g] Matthew 18:20, NASB
[h] Luke 21:5 has "votive gifts" (NASB).
[i] Compare Matthew 24:1 = Mark 13:1 = Luke 21:5 with Matthew 6:1,5,16; 23:5.
[j] Compare Mark 12:41-44.

one stone upon another which will not be torn down.'"[a]

Fifth, unlike the vows of Abraham and Jacob,[b] the New Testament does not encourage believers to make any sort of vow (war, journey or tithe).[c] It records many different journeys,[d] but, unlike Jacob, no Christian made a journey or tithe vow to ensure his/her safe passage. The apostle Paul, for example, endured at least three dangerous shipwrecks in his ministry,[e] but we have no record he ever made a journey vow similar to Jacob's in an effort to prevent such disasters from occurring.[f] Much of the early church's confidence to travel came not only from Christ's promises about the power of prayer,[g] it also originated from their direct and immediate relationship with the Father whose Spirit would initiate,[h] redirect[i] and protect their travel plans according to his will.[j]

To W. Burkert, "...the practice of vows can be seen as a major human strategy for coping with the future."[927] Jesus, however, told his followers to trust in the providential love of their heavenly Father and to leave the future in his hands.[k] He said, "Do not worry about tomorrow; for tomorrow will care for itself. Each day has enough trouble of its own."[l] Similarly, James, probably the younger brother of Jesus,[928] exhorted the merchants of his community to recognize their future was in God's hands.[m] Like Jesus, he never encouraged those in his fellowship to make any kind of vow to guarantee their security or prosperity.

---

[a] Luke 21:5-6 (NASB) = Matthew 24:1-2 = Mark 13:1-2
[b] Genesis 14:22-24; 28:20-22
[c] Acts 21:23-26 does not exhort believers to make similar vows.
[d] Joseph/Mary: Luke 2:22,39,41-44,51; Jesus: Mark 10:17a; John 4:6; Christ's disciples: Mark 6:8; Matthew 10:9-11; Luke 9:3; 10:7; 22:35; Cornelius' attendants: Acts 10:1-8; Phillip: Acts 8:5,40; Peter/John: Acts 8:14; Peter: Acts 9:32,38; Paul: Acts 13-18
[e] 2 Corinthians 11:25; Acts 27:39-44; 28:1
[f] Most scholars view Paul's vow in Acts 18:18 as a Nazirite instead of a journey vow.
[g] Matthew 6:6; 7:7; 17:20; 21:22; Mark 9:23
[h] God used angels (Matthew 2:13-15,19-22), visions (Acts 10:3,8; 16:9-10) and direct dialogue (10:20).
[i] Matthew 2:12; Acts 16:6-8
[j] Compare Acts 18:21.
[k] Matthew 6:25-34 = Luke 12:22-31
[l] Matthew 6:34, NASB
[m] James 4:13-16

Finally, the New Testament does not encourage believers to make vows because vows in themselves do not transform lives. T. Merton, a late Trappist monk and author of *The Seven Storey Mountain*, said, "It is an illusion to think that by making vows, it makes us a different person."[929] According to the New covenant, it is God who changes people's lives by imparting to them a new heart (nature) through the gospel.[a]

Conclusion

No New Testament writer tells believers to make vows to God, and this includes tithe vows. Tithe supporters who claim Christians should make tithing vows contradict the New covenant both in letter and spirit. According to G. Stob, "Apart from this condemnation of vows wrongly used [Matthew 15:3-9; Mark 7:9-13], it is not evident that Jesus or any of the New Testament writers make significant reference to vows, which are so prominent an expression of Old Testament piety."[930] The making of vows to add weight to one's prayers for divine protection or blessing can easily corrupt a Christian's relationship with God. Vows and vow/bargains change the father/child[b] relationship from grace and trust to bondage and fear.

According to J. McFadyen, "It is not an accident that vows play practically no role at all in the New Testament, where the demand is for a consecration not occasional but continuous, and for a consecration not of gifts but of the entire personality."[932] The true cost of discipleship is illustrated in the Hallmark Channel film, "Though None Go with Me" (2006). As Elizabeth Leroy (played by Cheryl Ladd), dedicates her life to God, she eventually becomes disillusioned because she continues to lose those who are closest to her: first her parents, then her first love, then her son and finally her husband. Even though this is not the end of her story, a friend reminds her: "Elizabeth, you made a commitment to God not a bargain."

---

[a] John 3:3,5; 2; Romans 2:4-5; 2 Corinthians 5:17; I Peter 1:3,23. Compare Ezekiel 11:19; 36:26.

[b] Galatians 4:1-7

I admit God is bigger than my present understanding of the New covenant and vows. He is free to honor *any* vow for his own sovereign purposes, since the goal of the gospel is to draw all people to himself. If a soldier, for example, cries out on the battlefield, "Jesus, if you will keep me safe, then I will serve you," the Lord may answer such a prayer.[931] Or, if a believer vows, "God, if you will get me out of debt, then I will pay tithes for the rest of my life," the Lord, likewise, may answer such a request - not because he requires tithe vows of his children, but because he knows that by answering, he will have this believer's attention and be able subsequently to instruct him/her in how to follow him more completely.

A WORD FROM THE AUTHOR

Dear Reader,

Thank you for taking this journey with me as we explored this critically important issue for the Church. I realize that this study may have disrupted your present understanding of tithing. I respect the concern for not wanting to question such a long-held belief. I invite you to pray over what you have read and consider continuing with me by reading the other three books in this series as they become available. In Book 2, I address questions like, "If the tithe is 'holy' why should believers not be required to pay it?" In Book 3, I look at what the prophet Malachi said about tithes in social and historical context. Finally, in Book 4, we will explore why neither Jesus nor any of the apostles collected tithes, and what the New Testament presents as tithing alternatives. May God bless you as you open your heart in further reflection on this subject.

David G. Mackin
Galatian 5:1

NOTES

OVERVIEW & APPROACH

[1] Pagolu, Augustine, 1998., 171, note 1

[2] Pagolu, Augustine, 1998., 178

[3] Pagolu, Augustine, 1998., 172

[4] Pagolu, Augustine, 1998., 173-175

[5] Pagolu, Augustine, 1998., 175-177. "The Tithe in Ugarit (3.WS.C.1)" in *Context of Scripture Online,* Editor in Chief: W. Hallo. Consulted online on 23 August 2016. Heltzer, Michael, "Village Tithe Payments at Ugarit (3.83)" in *Context of Scripture Online,* Editor in Chief: W. Hallo. Consulted online on 23 August 2016. See also *"Mission de Ras Shamra,* IV, Index, under *masaru, mesertun*; Ras Shamra 1929, v.2: 'sr 'sr" per T. H. Gaster, "Sacrifices and Offerings, Old Testament," Buttrick, G. A., 1962, volume 4, 149.

[6] Pagolu, Augustine, 1998., 175

[7] Pagolu, Augustine, 1998., 175, 183

[8] T. H. Gaster, "Sacrifices and Offerings, Old Testament," Buttrick, G. A., 1962, volume 4, 177-178

[9] J. C. Wilson, "Tithe," Freedman, D. N., 1992., volume 5, 580

[10] J. MacCulloch, "Tithes," Hastings, James, 1913., volume 12, 348

[11] J. MacCulloch, "Tithes," Hastings, James, 1913., volume 12, 349

[12] www.barna.org. The date of the poll was 2007. C. Hansen, "The Ancient Rise and Fall of Tithing," *Christianity Today,* Carol Stream, Illinois, 08/08/2008.

1 HOW TO INTERPRET THE PATRIARCHS' TITHES

[13] Verhoef, Peter A., 1974., 121

[14] Douglas Stuart, "Exegesis," Freedman, D. N., 1992., volume 2, 687

[15] Lansdell, Henry, 1963., 12; 18-19; 20-22; 49-50

[16] Hagee, John, 2005., tape 2; Kendall, R. T., 1982., 29, 76; www.citybusinesschurch.org—atlanta-city-church; Morris, Robert, 2004., 38, 50; Lansdell, Henry, 1963., 50-51; Hinn, Benny, 1997., 128

[17] Hagee, John, 2006.

[18] Hagee, John, 2006., and 12/14/2006; Smith, Wendell, 2005., 183

[19] Hinn, Benny, 1997., 197-237; Conner, Kevin J., 1986., 11-12; 13-15; 21; Bahne, Eric, 2013.; Smith, Wendell, 2005., 74-75; Damazio, Frank and Brott, Rich, 2005., 191-195

[20] Conner, Kevin J., 1993., 10; Lansdell, Henry, 1963., 14-15; 79; 104

[21] D. Stuart, "Exegesis," Freedman, D. N., 1992, volume 2, 682-688

[22] D. Stuart observes, "It may be noted that the exegete, the person who has developed expertise in the passage is in the best position to recommend its proper application, as opposed to someone who has not been involved in the process prior to attempting to determine how the passage might apply" ("Exegesis," Freedman, D. N., 1992, volume 2, 687).

[23] Compare Carson, Donald A., 1996., 32, 53, 57-58; 115-116.

[24] D. Stuart, "Exegesis," Freedman, D. N., 1992., volume 2, 683

[25] D. Stuart, "Exegesis," Freedman, D. N., 1992, volume 2, 683

[26] D. Stuart, "Exegesis," Freedman, D. N., 1992, volume 2, 686

[27] D. Stuart, "Exegesis," Freedman, D. N., 1992., volume 2, 686

[28] D. Stuart, "Exegesis," Freedman, D. N., 1992., volume 2, 686

[29] Lindsay, Gordon, 1959., 29

[30] Lansdell, Henry, 1963., 16

[31] A. R. Millard, "Abraham," Freedman, D. N., 1992., volume 1, 36

[32] Aharoni, Y. and Avi-yonah, M., 1968., 28, map no. 26

[33] Aharoni, Y. and Avi-yonah, M., 1968., 28, map no. 26

[34] Aharoni, Y. and Avi-yonah, M., 1968., 28, map no. 24

[35] Aharoni, Y. and Avi-yonah, M., 1968., 28, map no. 26

[36] J. Zarins, "Camel," Freedman, D. N., 1992., volume 1, 826

[37] Lansdell, Henry, 1963., 17

[38] R. T. Kendall states that "Abraham was a tither" (Kendall, R. T., 1982., 67). Similarly, K. J. Conner writes, "Abraham – a Tither" (Conner, Kevin J., 1982., 274; Conner, Kevin J., 1993., 11).

[39] Snell, Jay, 1995., 8

[40] Hinn, Benny, 1997., 121

[41] Lansdell, Henry, 1963., 7

[42] Damazio, Frank and Brott, Rich, 2005., 175. Compare Smith, Wendell, 2005., 267.

[43] Damazio, Frank and Brott, Rich, 2005.,167. Compare Pick, Clive, 1998., 84.

[44] Damazio, Frank and Brott, Rich, 2005.,162. Compare "tithing was under Abraham" in Conner, Kevin J., 1982., 279.

[45] Durant, Will and Ariel, 1954., volume 4, 556, 668, 683

[46] J. Van Engen, "Scriptural Authority: Biblical Authority in the Medieval Church," Freedman, D. N., 1992., volume 5, 1028

[47] R. Pfeiffer, "Canon of the Old Testament," Buttrick, G. A., 1962., volume 1, 518. See also Henri de Lubac, *Medieval Exegesis: The Four Senses of Scripture*, volumes 1-2, Eerdmans Publishing Co./T & T Clark, Ltd., Edinburgh, Scotland, 1998.

[48] R. Pfeiffer, "Canon of the Old Testament," Buttrick, G. A., 1962., volume 1, 518

[49] Koester, Craig R., 2001., 339. See 32 for examples.

[50] Compare Riché, Pierre and Lobrochon, Guy, 1984., 336, 356, 375, 391, 617.

[51] Hinn, Benny, 1997., 132; Conner, Kevin J., 1993., 10-18; Alcorn, Randy C., 2003., 173-194; Kendall, R. T., 1982., 43-56; Lansdell, Henry, 1963., 23-36

[52] Snell, Jay, 1995., 11-12

[53] Hinn, Benny, 1997., 117-118; Morris, Robert, 2004., 32

[54] Morris, Robert, 2004., 57; Hinn, Benny, 1997., 121; Kendall, R. T., 1982., 69; Hagin, Kenneth E., 1995, 110. Some claim divine revelation on the subject of tithing. About his book on tithing, C. Pick writes, "Father has commissioned me to write this book, and it has been a three-year battle to put 'word to paper'" (Pick, Clive, 1998., 5). He also claims that the Lord told him to go into all the world and tell Christians that they are supposed to pay their tithes to God. K. Copeland writes, "the Lord said... 'If you believe My Word about tithing, if you believe that Jesus will take your money and worship Me with it, why don't you tithe now on the amount you are needing and expecting...?" (Copeland, Kenneth, 1974., 75). The claim, "...Jesus will take your money and worship Me with it," appears to be a serious distortion of Hebrews 7:8 combined with 8:3.

[55] Conner, Kevin J., 1982., 274; Hinn, Benny, 1997., 119, 121

[56] Conner, Kevin J., 1982., 274

[57] Conner, Kevin J., 1982., 274

[58] Three exhaustive Bible concordances in English are: *Strong's Exhaustive Concordance of the Bible*, J. Strong, Hendrickson Publishers, Peabody, Massachusetts, 2007; *The New American Standard Exhaustive Concordance of the Bible*, R. L. Thomas, Holman, Nashville, Tennessee, 1981 and *The NIV Exhaustive Concordance*, E. W. Goodrick and J. R. Kohlenberger, III, Harper Collins, Canada, 1990.

[59] Allis, Oswald T., 1945.

[60] Verhoef, Peter A., 1974., 115

[61] Pick, Clive, 1998., 84

62 Kendall, R. T., 1982., 25

63 Damazio, Frank and Brott, Rich, 2005., 175

64 Kendall, R. T., 1982., 25

65 Damazio, Frank and Brott, Rich, 2005., 175

66 This phrase is used to describe the term "leitmotif" in http://education.yahoo.com/reference/dictionary/.

67 D. Stuart, "Exegesis," Freedman, D. N., 1992., volume 2, 688. The original ends with a question mark.

68 According to A. R. Millard, it is reasonable to place Abraham at about 1200 B.C., "Abraham," Freedman, D. N., 1992., volume 1, 39-40. According to Andrew E. Hill, Malachi's ministry can be placed approximately 500 – 480 B.C., "Malachi," Freedman, D. N., 1992., volume 4, 480.

69 Snell, Jay, 1995., 23-24

70 Buttrick, G. A., 1962., volume 3, 229

71 According to A. R. Millard, it is reasonable to place Abraham at about 1200 B.C., "Abraham," Freedman, D. N., 1992., volume 1, 39-40. According to Andrew E. Hill, Malachi's ministry can be placed approximately 500 – 480 B.C., "Malachi," Freedman, D. N., 1992., volume 4, 480.

72 Snell, Jay, 1995., 23-24. Compare Snell, Jay, 1995., 21-38.

73 Fischer, David H., 1970., 187

74 Carson, Donald A., 1996., 134-135

75 D. Stuart, "Exegesis," Freedman, D. N., 1992., volume 2, 682

76 G. Stählin, "Myth," Kittel, G., 1964., volume 4, 788

77 G. Stählin, "Myth," Kittel, G., 1964., volume 4, 788

78 G. Stählin, "Myth," Kittel, G., 1964., volume 4, 783, note 126

79 G. Stählin, "Myth," Kittel, G., 1964., volume 4,783, note 127

80 D. Stuart, "Exegesis," Freedman, D. N., 1992., volume 2, 688

[81] D. Stuart, "Exegesis," Freedman, D. N., 1992., volume 2, 688

[82] D. Stuart, "Exegesis," Freedman, D. N., 1992., volume 2, 688.

[83] www.dictionary.com

[84] D. Stuart, "Exegesis," Freedman, D. N., 1992., volume 2, 688.

2 TITHING BEFORE THE LAW

[85] Conner, Kevin J., 1993., 38-39

[86] Kendall, R. T., 1982., 68

[87] Hagee, John, 2005., tape no. 0441

[88] V. P. Hamilton, "Marriage (Old Testament and Ancient Near East)," Freedman, D. N., 1992., volume 4, 565

[89] According to O. J. Baab, "A girl in this classification achieved a certain status if she had sons" ("Concubine," Buttrick, G. A., 1962., volume 1, 666).

[90] Fischer, David H., 1970., 109

[91] Fischer, David H., 1970., 109

[92] Pagolu, Augustine, 1998.,189

[93] Pagolu, Augustine, 1998., 190

[94] Fischer, David H., 1970., 109

[95] See Joel LeMon, "Cultures of the Ancient Near East," Gaventa, B. R. and Peterson, D., 2010., 973-978 and its excellent bibliography.

[96] Hagee, John, 2005., tape no. 0441

[97] Hagee, John, 2005., tape no. 0441

[98] Carson, Donald A., 1996., 108

[99] Carson, Donald A., 1996., 141-142

[100] Elizabeth Bloch-Smith, "Burials," Freedman, D. N., 1992., volume 1, 785. Abraham planted a tamarisk tree at the location where he made a treaty with the local Canaanite ruler, Abimelech. Here, Abraham also

called on the name of the Lord because he saw this treaty as part of the fulfillment of YHWH's land promise to him and his descendants.

[101] Hagee, John, 2005., tape no. 0441

[102] Compare Carson, Donald A., 1996., 33-35.

[103] Carson, Donald A., 1996., 33-35. Compare C. R. Taber, "Semantics," Crim, K., 1976., 802.

[104] North, Gary, 1987., 5, 13, 50; Rushdoony, Rousas J. and Powell, Edward A., 1979., 137; Conner, Kevin J., 1982., 275

[105] Jacob Milgrom has successfully argued against the Kaufmann-Haran thesis of a voluntary tithe (Milgrom, Jacob, 2001., 2422-2423; 2426-2431).

[106] The Law also forbad the Israelites from using their ritually pure firstborn animals or their *h'erem* contributions (that which was doomed or under the ban) to fulfill their conditional vows (Leviticus 27:26-29).

[107] On "the place in which the Lord your God will choose for His name to dwell" (NASB, Deuteronomy 12:11) as being Jerusalem see C. Bultmann, "Deuteronomy," Barton, J., and Muddiman, J., 2001., 145; J. Blenkinsopp, "Deuteronomy," in Brown, R.E., Fitzmyer, J. A. and Murphy, R. E., 1990., 101. G.H. Davies says, "...Shiloh and later Jerusalem..." in "Deuteronomy," Black, M. and Rowley, H. H., 1962., 276.

[108] Conner, Kevin J., 1993., 38-39. Compare Conner, Kevin J., 1982., 279

3 A MOTIVE ANALYSIS

[109] Elam was an ancient Near Eastern civilization encompassing modern Iran (F. Vallat, "Elam," [place], Freedman, D. N., 1992., volume 2, 424). The Cities of the Plain were probably near the Dead Sea (Genesis 14:3). For a short, scholarly discussion about the historicity of the four kings in the Elamite coalition in the second millennium see A. R. Millard, "Abraham," Freedman, D. N., 1992., volume 1, 40.

[110] Bera was the leader of the vassal coalition because: (1) his name regularly appears at the beginning of the lists of the four kings (Genesis

14:2,8. Compare verses 10-11.); (2) he was the one who first met Abraham as he was returning from his defeat of the Elamite coalition (14:17) and (3) he was the one who negotiated with Abraham over the war spoils (14:21).

[111] Matthews, Victor H., and Benjamin, Don C., 1993., 207

[112] See "The Campaigns of the Kings of the North, 20th century B.C." in Aharoni, Y. and Avi-yonah, M., 1968., 27, map 24.

[113] Damazio, Frank and Brott, Rich, 2005., 167

[114] Damazio, Frank and Brott, Rich, 2005., 167. The original has the entire sentence in title case.

[115] Damazio, Frank and Brott, Rich, 2005., 167

[116] Kendall, R. T., 1982., 45; Bill Ritchie, http://www.crossroadschurch.net/ > Teaching > Commentary > Old Testament > Malachi > 3:8-18; 45

[117] Bill Ritchie, http://www.crossroadschurch.net/ > Teaching > Commentary > Old Testament > Malachi > 3:8-18. Compare Kendall, R. T., 1982., 47. See also Kendall, R. T., 1982., 48-49.

[118] Bill Ritchie, http://www.crossroadschurch.net/ > Teaching > Commentary > Old Testament > Malachi > 3:8-18. Compare Kendall, R. T., 1982., 47.

[119] Bill Ritchie, http://www.crossroadschurch.net/

[120] Fischer, David H., 1970., 87

[121] Lansdell, Henry, 1963., 16

[122] I wonder how, "...though, as a conqueror..." relates to this pro-tither's main point.

[123] Lansdell, Henry, 1963., 16

[124] J. W. Wevers, "Spoil," Buttrick, G. A., 1962., volume 4, 437

[125] Westermann, Claus, 1995., 202

[126] Lansdell, Henry, 1963., 16

[127] Compare Fischer, David H., 1970., 154-155.

[128] One could argue against this if one adopted the view that both of the patriarchs' tithes were later insertions by editors in the employ of kings whose primary purpose was to exact compulsory tithes from the Israelites at two state sanctuaries: Salem/Jerusalem in southern Israel (Genesis 14:18-20) and Bethel in northern Israel (Genesis 28:20-22). Adopting this view, however, would still not necessitate that Christians would be under obligation to tithe since both editors would have been working under the rubric of the Sinai instead of the New covenant.

[129] B. Levine, "Leviticus, Book of," Freedman, D. N., 1992., volume 4, 318

[130] Henry T. C. Sun, "Holiness Code," Freedman, D. N., 1992, volume 3, 254-257

[131] Damazio, Frank and Brott, Rich, 2005., 172, 168

[132] Snell, Jay, 1995., 23, 24. Compare 26 and Snell, Jay, 1995a.

[133] Snell, Jay, 1995a, Chapter Two, "The First Step You Must Take To Amass Abrahamic Wealth." No page provided.

[134] Snell, Jay, 1995., 27-28

[135] Snell, Jay, 1995., 23-24,30

[136] Snell, Jay, 1995., 23, 24. Compare 26 and Snell, Jay, 1995a.

[137] Snell, Jay, 1995., 23, 24. Compare 26 and Snell, Jay, 1995a.

[138] Snell, Jay, 1995a.; No page provided.

[139] Snell, Jay, 1995., 23, 24. Compare 26 and Snell, Jay, 1995a.

[140] According to David W. Baker, Heth was one of Noah's great-grandsons ("Heth," Freedman, D. N., 1992., volume 3, 188).

[141] Snell, Jay, 1995., 23, 24. Compare 26 and Snell, Jay, 1995a.

[142] LaMoine F. DeVries, "Machpelah," Freedman, D. N., 1992., volume 4, 459

[143] Snell, Jay, 1995., 23, 24. Compare 26 and Snell, Jay, 1995a.

[144] Berlin, A. and Brettler, M. Z., 2004., 48, note on verses 10-16

[145] Dennis T. Olson, "Genesis," Gaventa, B. R. and Peterson, D., 2010., 20. Some scholars believe that Abraham overpaid for the property (Westermann, Claus, 1995., 375; James C. Moyer, "Ephron," Freedman, D. N., 1992., volume 2, 558; Jon D. Levenson, "Genesis," Berlin, A. and Brettler, M. Z., 2004., 48, note on Genesis 23:10-16).

[146] Westermann, Claus, 1995., 375

[147] Westermann, Claus, 1995., 375

[148] Snell, Jay, 1995., 23, 24. Compare 26 and Snell, Jay, 1995a.

[149] Snell, Jay, 1995., 23, 24. Compare 26 and Snell, Jay, 1995a.

[150] Snell, Jay, 1995a, Chapter Two, "The First Step You Must Take To Amass Abrahamic Wealth." No page provided.

[151] Snell, Jay, 1995a, Chapter Two, "The First Step You Must Take To Amass Abrahamic Wealth." No page provided.

[152] Kendall, R. T., 1982., 48-49

[153] Snell, Jay, 1995a, Chapter Two, "The First Step You Must Take To Amass Abrahamic Wealth." No page provided.

[154] Snell, Jay, 1995a, Chapter Two, "The First Step You Must Take To Amass Abrahamic Wealth." No page provided.

[155] Snell, Jay, 1995., 23, 24. Compare 26 and Snell, Jay, 1995a; Snell, Jay, 1995a, Chapter Two, "The First Step You Must Take To Amass Abrahamic Wealth." No page provided.

[156] Snell, Jay, 1995a, Chapter Two, "The First Step You Must Take To Amass Abrahamic Wealth." No page provided.

[157] Snell, Jay, 1995., 24

[158] Snell, Jay, 1995., 28

[159] Snell, Jay, 1995., 28

[160] Snell, Jay, 1995., 28

[161] Snell, Jay, 1995., 23-24,30

[162] Snell, Jay, 1995., 24-25. See also 27-28.

[163] Snell, Jay, 1995., 26-38

[164] Snell, Jay, 1995., 27

[165] Snell, Jay, 1995., 29

[166] Snell, Jay, 1995., 31

[167] Snell, Jay, 1995., 32

[168] Snell, Jay, 1995., 32

[169] Compare Snell, Jay, 1995., 24 and 32. He also applies Malachi's promise to Christians (Snell, Jay, 1995., 33).

[170] A. R. Millard, "Abraham," Freedman, D. N., 1992. volume 1, 38

[171] Snell, Jay, 1995., 33

[172] Snell, Jay, 1995., 12, 27-28; "Christian Wealth," www.jaysnell.org. Compare Snell, Jay, 1995a., Chapter 2, "The First Step You Must Take to Amass Abrahamic Wealth;" Pick, Clive, 1998., 11. Compare 91-93.; Hagee, John, 2005., tape 2; Smith, Wendell, 2005., 39; Lansdell, Henry, 1963., 16; K. Conner calls Abraham "a tither" (Conner, Kevin J., 1982., 274).

[173] Snell, Jay, 1995., 33

[174] Snell, Jay, 1995., 23-24

[175] Snell, Jay, 1995a, Chapter Two, "The First Step You Must Take To Amass Abrahamic Wealth." No page provided.

4 A VOW FOR A SAFE RESCUE

[176] According to Matthews and Benjamin, the "fugitive" of Genesis 14:13a (NASB) was probably, "an official messenger on a diplomatic mission" (Matthews, Victor H., and Benjamin, Don C., 1993., 208).

[177] Some scholars see Genesis 13:1 as the last verse of Genesis chapter 12 (Brown, R.E., Fitzmyer, J. A. and Murphy, R. E., 1990., 20).

[178] Clifford and Murphy, "Genesis," in Brown, R.E., Fitzmyer, J. A. and Murphy, R. E., 1990., 24a

[179] Matthews, Victor H., and Benjamin, Don C., 1993., 209. G. H. Davies says that vows are "...intended to strengthen prayer" ("Vows," Buttrick, G. A., 1962., volume 4, 793).

[180] Kittel, G., 1964., volume 5, 459, note 19

[181] Westermann, Claus, 1995., 202

[182] According to T. H. Gaster, "...the vows themselves could be envisaged either as purely speculative, or as formally contractual" ("Sacrifices and Offerings, Old Testament," Buttrick, G. A., 1962., volume 4, 149).

[183] Associated Publishers and Authors, 1975., 1163; Baker, W., 1994., 38

[184] Harris, R. Laird, 1950., 18

[185] Westermann, Claus, 1995., 202

[186] Kohlenberger, John R., III, 1987., *xxvii*

[187] Davidson, Benjamin, 1993., 38

[188] R.N. Whybray, "Genesis," Barton, J., and Muddiman, J., 2001., 51

[189] Westermann, Claus, 1995., 218

[190] G. H. Davies, "Vows," Buttrick, G. A., 1962., volume 4, 793

[191] Matthews, Victor H., and Benjamin, Don C., 1993., 98. According to C. L. Seow, "Yahweh Sabbaoth" describes the Lord as Israel's king who reigns above all the "gods of the heavenly [war] council" ("Hosts, Lord of," Freedman, D. N., 1992., volume 3, 304).

[192] Susan Niditch, "Judges," Barton, J., and Muddiman, J., 2001., 185

[193] Associated Publishers and Authors, 1975., 1163; Baker, W., 1994., 38

[194] N. Gottwald, "War, holy," Crim, K., 1976., 942.

[195] Black, M. and Rowley, H. H., Peake, A. S., 1962., 312; G. Henton Davies, "Vows," Buttrick, G. A., 1962., volume 4, 792

[196] Brown, R.E., Fitzmyer, J. A. and Murphy, R. E., 1990., 141

[197] Black, M. and Rowley, H. H., Peake, A. S., 1962., 312. Compare Smith, W. Robertson, 1894., 492.

[198] S. Cohen, "Hormah," Buttrick, G. A., 1962., volume 2, 645

[199] According to this tradition, Hormah means "destruction" (J. M. Hamilton, "Hormah," (place), Freedman, D. N., 1992., volume 3, 289).

[200] Nili Fox, "Numbers," Berlin, A. and Brettler, M. Z., 2004., note 1 on 21:1-3, 325; Compare M. H. Pope, "Devoted," Buttrick, G. A., 1962., volume 1, 839.

[201] Michael David Coogan, "Joshua" in Brown, R.E., Fitzmyer, J. A. and Murphy, R. E., 1990., 117

[202] J. W. Wevers, "Spoil," Buttrick, G. A., 1962., volume 4, 437-438

[203] J. W. Wevers, "War, methods of," Buttrick, G. A., 1962., volume 4, 804

[204] T. E. Fretheim, "Numbers," Barton, J., and Muddiman, J., 2001., 132

[205] Nili Fox, "Numbers," Berlin, A. and Brettler, M. Z., 2004., 346, note on Numbers 31:54

[206] Hammond and Scullard, 1970., 1132

[207] Hammond and Scullard, 1970., 1132

[208] Hammond and Scullard, 1970., 1132

[209] Hammond and Scullard, 1970., 1132

[210] Michael David Coogan, "Judges," in Brown, R.E., Fitzmyer, J. A. and Murphy, R. E., 1990., 138

[211] Richardson, Alan, 1962., 175

[212] Compare J. W. Wevers, "Spoil," Buttrick, G. A., 1962., volume 4, 437.

[213] Hastings, James, 1913., volume 12, 347

[214] Hastings, James, 1913., volume 12, 347

[215] Hastings, James, 1913., volume 12, 347, 351; Smith, W. Robertson, 1894., 459-460; Hammond and Scullard, 1970., 1132; Pausania, *Description of Greece, Attica*, XXVIII. Andrew Stewart, *One Hundred Greek Sculptors: Their Careers and Extant Works: The Peloponnese: The Polykleitan School*. War vows were paid in ancient, "Apollonia, Athens,

Boeotia, Branchidae, Crete, Mantinea [Montinea?], Megara, Sparta, Thessaly; at Delphi by Athenians, Caphyes, Cnidians, Liparians, Spartans and Tarentines; [and] at Olympia by Clitorians, Eleans, Messenians, Spartans, Thurians" (Hastings, James, 1913., volume 12, 351). W. Robertson Smith writes, "...in Greece the sacred tithe occurs mainly in the form of a percentage on the spoils of war" (Smith, W. Robertson, 1894., 460).

[216] D. E. W. Wormell., "Cyrus II," Hammond and Scullard, 1970., 308

[217] J. MacCulloch, "Tithes," Hastings, James, 1913., volume 12, 347

[218] Hastings, James, 1913., volume 12, 347

[219] Smith, W. Robertson, 1894., 460

[220] John F. Robertson, "Temples and Sanctuaries, Mesopotamia," Freedman, D. N., 1992., volume 6, 372-76; Smith, W. Robertson, 1894., 460; P. C. Schmitz, "Phoenician Religion," Freedman, D. N., 1992., volume 5, 357; Smith, W. Robertson, 1894., 460; G. L. Mattingly observes that Mesha's "...political and military successes were attributed to the favor of Chemosh (lines 4-5, 9, etc. [of the Moab Stone])" ("Mesha," [person], Freedman, D. N., 1992., volume 4, 707).

[221] Diodorus Siculus, 11.21, Hammond and Scullard, 1970., 1132 (compare 1133). Frederick W. Danker refers to Diodorus Siculus 11.26.7 in, "Ex Voto," Freedman, D. N., 1992., 680.

[222] According to J. W. Wevers, "Muhammad decreed that one fifth of all booty was to be set-aside for Allah (*Quran* VIII.41)" ("Booty," Buttrick, G. A., 1962., volume 1, 458).

[223] Hammond and Scullard, 1970., 1132-33. Compare, "garments, weapons, and treasure" in Smith, W. Robertson, 1894., 218.

[224] Hammond and Scullard, 1970., 1132-33

[225] V. Matthews and D. Benjamin write, "Before going into battle, warriors in the world of the Bible vowed all or a portion of their anticipated prisoners and plunder to Yahweh Sabbaoth..." (Matthews, Victor H., and Benjamin, Don C., 1993., 98). Such prisoners and plunder were under the law of the ban (*h'erem*).

[226] Milgrom, Jacob, 2001., volume 3, 2414

[227] Milgrom, Jacob, 2001., volume 3, 2414

[228] G. H. Davies, "Vows," Buttrick, G. A., 1962., volume 4, 793

[229] J. W. Wevers, "Spoil," Buttrick, G. A., 1962., volume 4, 437

[230] Karel van der Toorn, "Theology, Priests, and Worship in Canaan and Ancient Israel," Sasson, J. M., 1995., volume 3, 2055-56

[231] Berlin, A. and Brettler, M. Z., 2004., 35, note on verses 21-24

[232] Westermann, Claus, 1995., 207-208

5 A TREATY BETWEEN EQUALS

[233] G. E. Mendenhall, "Covenant," Buttrick, G. A., 1962., volume 1, 716-717. The other two treaty types are patron and promissory.

[234] Pick, Clive, 1998., 91

[235] Pick, Clive, 1998., 91

[236] Pick, Clive, 1998., 91

[237] Temba L. J. Mafico, "Ethics, Old Testament" ("The Treaty Formula in the Ancient Near East"), Freedman, D. N., 1992., volume 2, 647

[238] Kohlenberger, John R., III, 1987., 32, note "p" on Genesis 15:1

[239] Westermann, Claus, 1995., 218

[240] Westermann, Claus, 1995., 218

[241] North, Gary, 1994., 1. Compare Lansdell, Henry, 1963., 18; Conner, Kevin J., 1982., 274, 279 and Conner, Kevin J., 1993., 32, 49.

[242] North, Gary, 1994., 1

[243] According to François Vallat, Napirisa was the main deity in the Elamite pantheon during the Middle Elamite Period, approximately 1500-1100 B.C., but other Elamite gods were Insusinak, Awanites, Simaskians and Ansanites ("Elam," Freedman, D. N., 1992., volume 2, 426).

[244] North, Gary, 1994., 1

²⁴⁵ North, Gary, 1994., 1

²⁴⁶ Buttrick, G. A., 1962., "God, names of," volume 2, 412

²⁴⁷ Christine Hayes suggests that Abraham worshipped El-Elyôn and did not know or perceive him as YHWH ("Introduction to the Hebrew Bible," Open Yale Courses, Yale University, New Haven, Connecticut, 2012; www.oyc.yale.edu.).

²⁴⁸ According to A. Kirk Grayson, Persia did not impose its religion(s) upon the peoples it conquered ("Assyria," Freedman, D. N., 1992., volume 4, 754. Compare Ezra 7:1-28).

²⁴⁹ Westermann, Claus, 1995., 204. According to Westermann, "Possessor" (Genesis 14:19) is best understood as "Creator" (Westermann, Claus, 1995., 202, 205), which YHWH was held to be.

²⁵⁰ P. S. Minear, "Church, idea of," Buttrick, G. A., 1962., volume 1, 608

²⁵¹ P. S. Minear, "Church, idea of," Buttrick, G. A., 1962., volume 1, 608

²⁵² P. S. Minear, "Church, idea of," Buttrick, G. A., 1962., volume 1, 608

²⁵³ P. S. Minear, "Church, idea of," Buttrick, G. A., 1962., volume 1, 608

²⁵⁴ North, Gary, 1994., 1

²⁵⁵ North, Gary, 1994., 1

²⁵⁶ Fischer, David H., 1970., 132-133

²⁵⁷ North, Gary, 1994., 1

²⁵⁸ North, Gary, 1994., 1. Compare Lansdell, Henry, 1963., 18; Conner, Kevin J., 1982., 274, 279; Conner, Kevin J., 1993., 32, 49.

²⁵⁹ George E. Mendenhall and Gary A. Herion, "Covenant," Freedman, D. N., 1992., volume 1, 1194

²⁶⁰ George E. Mendenhall and Gary A. Herion, "Covenant," Freedman, D. N., 1992., volume 1, 1181

²⁶¹ Westermann, Claus, 1995., 202

²⁶² Compare D. A. Demarest, "Melchizedek, Salem," Brown, Colin, 1971., volume 2, 590.

263 George E. Mendenhall, "Covenant," Buttrick, G. A., 1962., 716

264 Westermann, Claus, 1995., 202

265 Westermann, Claus, 1995., 202

266 Matthews, Victor H., and Benjamin, Don C., 1993., 210

267 Westermann, Claus, 1995., 202

268 Michael L. Barré, "Treaties of the Ancient Near East," Freedman, D. N., 1992., volume 6, 655. Compare 654.

269 R. J. Clifford and R. E. Murphy, "Genesis," in Brown, R.E., Fitzmyer, J. A. and Murphy, R. E., 1990., 21

270 Westermann, Claus, 1995., 348. Compare 349.

271 Westermann, Claus, 1995., 327

272 Westermann, Claus, 1995., 327

273 Westermann, Claus, 1995., 349

274 Victor H. Matthews, "Abimelech" (person), Freedman, D. N., 1992., volume 1, 20

275 Victor H. Matthews, "Abimelech" (person), Freedman, D. N., 1992., volume 1, 20

6 A GIFT EXCHANGE

276 Matthews, Victor H., and Benjamin, Don C., 1993., 206

277 Westermann, Claus, 1995., 176-177

278 A. R. Millard, "Abraham," Freedman, D. N., 1992., volume 1, 36

279 According to Matthews and Benjamin, Abraham returns to the oaks of Mamre, "without staying to exploit the state he delivers" (Matthews, Victor H., and Benjamin, Don C., 1993., 207, 205).

280 A. R. Millard, "Abraham," Freedman, D. N., 1992., volume 1, 36

281 Matthews, Victor H., and Benjamin, Don C., 1993., 206

[282] Bruckner, James K., 2001., 141 note 46. Compare Matthews, Victor H., and Benjamin, Don C., 1993., 207.

[283] Matthews, Victor H., and Benjamin, Don C., 1993., 206

[284] Westermann, Claus, 1995., 207

[285] Smith, W. Robertson, 1894., 273-274. The original says, "parts."

[286] The Treaty at Mizpah between Jacob and Laban (Genesis 31:43-55) involved setting up a heap of stones as a boundary marker (verse 51), swearing an oath of no harm (verse 53), offering a sacrifice (verse 54), and the two parties sharing in a common meal (verse 54).

[287] S. D. Walters, "Jacob Narrative," Freedman, D. N., 1992., volume 3, 601

[288] George E. Mendenhall and Gary A. Herion, "Covenant: Ancient Near Eastern Treaties," Freedman, D. N., 1992., volume 1, 1180

[289] King, Philip J. and Stager, Lawrence E., 2001., 62

[290] R. J. Clifford and R. E. Murphy, "Genesis," in Brown, R.E., Fitzmyer, J. A. and Murphy, R. E., 1990., 21

[291] R. J. Clifford and R. E. Murphy, "Genesis," in Brown, R.E., Fitzmyer, J. A. and Murphy, R. E., 1990., 25.

[292] Eugene H. Maly, "Genesis," in Brown, R. E., Fitzmyer, J. A. and Murphy, R. E., 1968., 19. Compare George E. Mendenhall and Gary A. Herion, "Covenant: The Covenant Banquet," Freedman, D. N., 1992., volume 1, 1194. Compare 1198.

[293] Silver, Morris, 1995., 39

[294] G. E. Mendenhall and G. A Herion, "Covenant," Freedman, D. N., 1992., volume 1, 1194; Mendenhall, George E., 2001., 227

[295] Jean-Claude Margueron, "Mari," Freedman, D. N., 1992., volume 4, 525

[296] ARMT (Archives royals de Mari: transcriptions et traductions) 8:13 per George E. Mendenhall and Gary A. Herion, "Covenant: The Covenant Banquet," Freedman, D. N., 1992., volume 1, 1194.

Mendenhall and Herion indicate that the mention of the drinking of wine in the Mari documents is "probable." For more information on how ancient Semitic covenants were made with food along with the significance of food for warriors, see Smith, W. Robertson, 1894., 264, 269, 491.

[297] Silver, Morris, 1995., 39 per T. Mettinger, *King and Messiah*, Gleerup Publishing, Lund, Denmark, 1976, 216

[298] A.R. Millard, "Abraham," Freedman, D. N., 1992., volume 1, Freedman, D. N., 1992., 38

[299] Tell el-Amarna tablets 162:22-25 per Knudtzon, J. A.; Weber, O. and Ebeling, E., 1970 per George E. Mendenhall and Gary A. Herion, "Covenant," Freedman, D. N., 1992., volume 1, 1194 and Nadav Na'aman, "Amarna Letters," Freedman, D. N., 1992., volume 1, 176

[300] Pritchard, James B., 1969., 539 per G. E. Mendenhall and G. A Herion, "Covenant," Freedman, D. N., 1992., volume 1, 1198

[301] Pritchard, James B., 1969., 536 per Michael L. Barré, "Treaties in the Ancient Near East," Freedman, D. N., 1992., volume 6, 536, 654

[302] G. E. Mendenhall and G. A Herion, "Covenant," Freedman, D. N., 1992., volume 1, 1194

[303] Smith, W. Robertson, 1894., 271

[304] G. E. Mendenhall and G. A Herion, "Covenant," Freedman, D. N., 1992., volume 1, 1194; Smith, W. Robertson, 1894., 271

[305] Brown, R.E., Fitzmyer, J. A. and Murphy, R. E., 1990., 25

[306] Philip C. Schmitz, "Phoenician Religion," Freedman, D. N., 1992., volume 5, 360

[307] Diodorus Siculus 13.108.4; 17.41.8 per Philip C. Schmitz, "Phoenician Religion," Freedman, D. N., 1992., volume 5, 360

[308] Herman Te Velde, "Theology, Priests, and Worship in Canaan and Ancient Israel," Sasson, J. M., 1995., volume 3, 2051

[309] According to Stephen D. Ricks, the Queen of Sheba visited Solomon to "strengthen trade relations" which the king was potentially

threatening through harboring his fleet of ships at Ezion-geber on the Gulf of Aqaba ("Queen of Sheba," Freedman, D. N., 1992., volume 5, 1171).

[310] Philip C. Schmitz, "Phoenician Religion," Freedman, D. N., 1992., volume 5, 360

[311] Westermann, Claus, 1995., 206

[312] Compare the war spoils gold that the Israelite commanders brought to the priest at the tent of meeting "as a reminder" of their military victory (Numbers 31:9,11,12,54, NRSV). Compare other "continual ritual reminder[s]" in Exodus 30:16 and Numbers 16:39-40 (Nili S. Fox, "Numbers," Berlin, A. and Brettler, M. Z., 2004., 346).

[313] Westermann, Claus, 1995., 206

[314] Compare T. H. Gaster, "Sacrifices and Offerings, Old Testament," Buttrick, G. A., 1962., volume 4, 151.

[315] Samuel Greengus, "Legal and Social Institutions of Ancient Mesopotamia," Sasson, J. M., 1995., volume 1, 470. Compare *Enuma Elish*.

[316] Ronald J. Leprohon, "Royal Ideology and State Administration in Pharaonic Egypt," Sasson, J. M., 1995., volume 1, 274

[317] Matthews, Victor H., and Benjamin, Don C., 1993., 100; G. L. Mattingly, "Mesha," Freedman, D. N., 1992., volume 4, 707. The Exodus story was a battle between opposing deities that YHWH won (Karel van der Toorn, "Theology, Priests, and Worship in Canaan and Ancient Israel," Sasson, J. M., 1995., volume 3, 2056).

[318] Compare the concept of holy war in L. E. Toombs, "War, Ideas of," Buttrick, G. A., 1962., volume 4, 797. See also Frankfort, Henri, Frankfort, H. A., Wilson, J. A. and Jacobsen, T., 1968., 19-21.

[319] According to Edward R. Dalglish, compare: (1) "...in an oath of a certain Menahem it is stated that he swore by '[...], by the temple and by 'Anatya'u' (*CAP* [A. E. Cowley. 1923. *Aramaic Papyri of the Fifth Century* B.C. Oxford] 44.22)" per "Bethel," (deity), Freedman, D. N., 1992., volume 1, 707; and (2) "Malkiah, a person possessing a definite

Yahwistic name, swears an oath before 'Bethel the god' (*CAP* [A. E. Cowley. 1923. *Aramaic Papyri of the Fifth Century* B.C. Oxford] 7:7)..." per "Bethel," (deity), Freedman, D. N., 1992., volume 1, 708. See also Michael L. Barré, "Treaties in the ANE," Freedman, D. N., 1992., volume 6, 653-656.

[320] Smith, W. Robertson, 1894., 316

[321] G. E. Mendenhall, "Covenant," Buttrick, G. A., 1962., volume 1, 716. Compare G. E. Mendenhall and G. A Herion, "Covenant," Freedman, D. N., 1992., volume 1, 1182.

7 THE MELCHIZEDEK PRIESTHOOD

[322] Conner, Kevin J. and Malmin, Ken, 1983., 36

[323] Conner, Kevin J. and Malmin, Ken, 1983., 36. According to the same source, the other mediator of the Abrahamic covenant was the "Priesthood of Abraham" (Conner, Kevin J. and Malmin, Ken, 1983., 37).

[324] Lansdell, Henry, 1963., 18

[325] Lansdell, Henry, 1963., 16

[326] Conner, Kevin J., 1982., 279

[327] Melchizedek was not Jesus in the flesh; Hebrews makes it clear that he was a prototype of Jesus. Note Hebrews 7:3, which says, "made like the Son of God" (NASB) and 7:15, which says, "to the likeness of Melchizedek" (NASB).

[328] Lansdell, Henry, 1963., 18

[329] Lansdell, Henry, 1963., 16

[330] Conner, Kevin J., 1990., 36

[331] Conner, Kevin J., 1990., 52

[332] Conner, Kevin J., 1990., 52

[333] Raymond Abba, "Priests and Levites," Buttrick, G. A., 1962., volume 3, 876-877

[334] Raymond Abba, "Priests and Levites," Buttrick, G. A., 1962., volume 3, 877

[335] Raymond Abba, "Priests and Levites," Buttrick, G. A., 1962., volume 3, 877

[336] Gunnar Landtman, "Priest, Priesthood," Hastings, James, 1913., volume 10, 278-279

[337] Westermann, Claus, 1995., 203

[338] Conner, Kevin J. and Malmin, Ken, 1983., 36; Lansdell, Henry, 1963., 18

[339] John S. Kselman; Michael L. Barré, "Psalms," Brown, R.E., Fitzmyer, J. A. and Murphy, R. E., 1990., 545

8 THE LORD'S TABLE

[340] North, Gary, 1994., 2

[341] Conner, Kevin J., 1982., 290

[342] Conner, Kevin J., 1982., 274

[343] Conner, Kevin J., 1982., 290

[344] Fischer, David H., 1970., 274

[345] Matthews, Victor H., and Benjamin, Don C., 1993., 209. The original says "foods."

[346] F. A. M. Wiggermann, "Theologies, Priests and Worship in Ancient Mesopotamia," Sasson, J. M., 1995., volume 3, 1863

[347] Smith, W. Robertson, 1894., 243. Compare 236-243.

[348] North, Gary, 1994., 2

[349] North, Gary, 1994., 2

[350] North, Gary, 1994., 2

[351] North, Gary, 1994., 2

[352] See Pheme Perkins, "The Gospel According to John," in Brown, R.E., Fitzmyer, J. A. and Murphy, R. E., 1990 on the "true nature of Jesus'

kingship" (961) and Dorothy Ann Lee, "John," Gaventa, B. R. and Peterson, D., 2010 about "the king who feeds his people" (719).

[353] Everett Ferguson, "Agape Meal," Freedman, D. N., 1992., volume 1, 90-91

[354] Edward Bleiberg, "The Economy of Ancient Egypt," Sasson, J. M., 1995., volume 3, 1379

[355] Joel LeMon, "Cultures of the Ancient Near East," Gaventa, B. R. and Peterson, D., 2010., 973

[356] Joel LeMon, "Cultures of the Ancient Near East," Gaventa, B. R. and Peterson, D., 2010., 973

[357] Conner, Kevin J., 1982., 290

[358] Brown, R. E., Fitzmyer, J. A. and Murphy, R. E., 1968., 393

[359] F. F. Bruce, "Altar, NT," Crim, K., 1976, 20. Compare Bruce, F.F., 1964., 135 and Attridge, H. W., 1989., 188.

[360] Bruce, F.F., 1964., 135, note 10

[361] Conner, Kevin J., 1982., 274

[362] Conner, Kevin J., 1982., 274

[363] North, Gary, 1994., 40

[364] May, H. G., 1962., 62-63

[365] Henry O. Thompson, "Hobah," (place), Freedman, D. N., 1992., volume 3, 235

[366] D. A. Demarest, "Melchizedek, Salem," Brown, Colin, 1971., volume 2, 590. See also Westermann, Claus, 1995., 205 and Bruce, F.F., 1964., 135.

[367] King, Philip J. and Stager, Lawrence E., 2001., 62. See also D. A. Demarest, "Melchizedek, Salem," Brown, Colin, 1971., 590 and Westermann, Claus, 1995., 205.

9 THE ABRAHAMIC COVENANT

[368] Jack R. Lundbom, "New Covenant," Freedman, D. N., 1992., volume 4, 1091

[369] North, Gary, 1994., 42

[370] Conner, Kevin J., 1993., 11

[371] Smith, Wendell, 2005., 39

[372] Conner, Kevin J., 1982., 279

[373] Conner, Kevin J., 1982., 280. Compare Conner, Kevin J., 1993., 51, pullout.

[374] Conner, Kevin J., 1993., 11; Conner, Kevin J., 1982., 274

[375] North, Gary, 1994., 42

[376] Conner, Kevin J., 1982., 279

[377] Conner, Kevin J., 1982., 279

[378] Conner, Kevin J., 1982., 279

[379] Conner, Kevin J., 1982., 274. Havis Gabbard, www.citybusinesschurch.org. Compare Pick, Clive, 1998, 85-86.

[380] Brown, R.E., Fitzmyer, J. A. and Murphy, R. E., 1990., 21

[381] Milgrom, Jacob, 2000., 1716

[382] Compare Harris, R. Laird, 1950., 8.

[383] Brown, R.E., Fitzmyer, J. A. and Murphy, R. E., 1990., 21-22

[384] Westermann, Claus, 1995., 264

[385] Westermann, Claus, 1995., 264

[386] G. E. Mendenhall, "Covenant," Buttrick, G. A., 1962., volume 1, 718

[387] G. E. Mendenhall, "Covenant," Buttrick, G. A., 1962., volume 1, 718

[388] Smith, Wendell, 2005., 39

[389] Conner, Kevin J., 1982., 279

390 Smith, Wendell, 2005., 39

391 Pick, Clive, 1998., 88

392 Conner, Kevin J., 1993., 13

393 Pick, Clive, 1998., 88

394 Conner, Kevin J., 1993., 13

395 Conner, Kevin J., 1993., 13

396 Conner, Kevin J., 1993., 13

397 Pick, Clive, 1998., 88

398 Pick, Clive, 1998., 88

399 Pick, Clive, 1998., 88, paragraphs 1 and 5

400 Snell, Jay, 1995., 2

401 Snell, Jay, 1995., 23-88 (on tithing)

402 Snell, Jay, 1995., 23-88 (on tithing)

403 Snell, Jay, 1995, 18

404 Snell, Jay, 1995, 18

405 Snell, Jay, 1995., 13

406 Fischer, David H., 1970., 190

407 Mendelsohn, I., "Magic, Magician," Buttrick, G. A., 1962., volume 3, 223

408 Snell, Jay, 1995, 18

409 Snell, Jay, 1995., 17; Snell, Jay, 1995a., "Two Kinds of Bible Prosperity." www.jaysnell.org.; Snell, Jay, 1995, 18; Snell, Jay, 1995, 18-19.

410 Snell, Jay, 1995a., www.jaysnell.org., "Abraham's Second Step to His Wealth Flow." Compare Snell, Jay, 1995, 18-19.

411 Smith, Wendell, 2005., 39

412 Smith, Wendell, 2005., 39

[413] Smith, Wendell, 2005., 39

[414] Smith, Wendell, 2005., 39

[415] Smith, Wendell, 2005., 39

[416] Smith, Wendell, 2005., 39

[417] Snell, Jay, 1995., 17; Snell, Jay, 1995a., "Two Kinds of Bible Prosperity." www.jaysnell.org.; Snell, Jay, 1995, 18; Snell, Jay, 1995, 18-19.

[418] Snell, Jay, 1995., 17-19, selected; Snell, Jay, 1995a., "Two Kinds of Bible Prosperity." www.jaysnell.org.

[419] Snell, Jay, 1995., 17-19, selected; Snell, Jay, 1995a., "Two Kinds of Bible Prosperity." www.jaysnell.org.

[420] Snell, Jay, 1995., 19

[421] N. Lohfink, "Deuteronomy," Crim, K., 1976., 232

[422] N. K. Gottwald, "Deuteronomy," Laymon, C. M., 1971., 108

[423] J. Y. Campbell, "Blessedness," Buttrick, G. A., 1962., volume 1, 445

[424] J. Y. Campbell, "Blessedness," Buttrick, G. A., 1962., volume 1, 446

[425] J. Y. Campbell, "Blessedness," Buttrick, G. A., 1962., volume 1, 446

[426] J. Y. Campbell, "Blessedness," Buttrick, G. A., 1962., volume 1, 446

[427] Snell, Jay, 1995., 17; Snell, Jay, 1995a., "Two Kinds of Bible Prosperity." www.jaysnell.org.; Snell, Jay, 1995, 18; Snell, Jay, 1995, 18-19.

[428] Snell, Jay, 1995., 17; Snell, Jay, 1995a., "Two Kinds of Bible Prosperity." www.jaysnell.org.; Snell, Jay, 1995, 18; Snell, Jay, 1995, 18-19.

[429] Snell, Jay, 1995., 17

[430] Snell, Jay, 1995., 3

[431] Conner, Kevin J., 1982., 279

[432] Conner, Kevin J., 1982., 279

[433] Compare Allis, Oswald T., 1945.

[434] Compare J. W. Flight, "Nationality," Buttrick, G. A., 1962., volume 3, 514.

[435] For a discussion of both sides of the holy land issue, see Waldemar Janzen, "Land," (Freedman, D. N., 1992., volume 4, 143-154).

[436] Compare Oswald T. Allis' summary critique of Dispensationalism in Allis, Oswald T., 1945., 256-262.

10 THE 'COVENANT OF BLESSINGS'

[437] Clive Pick is a minister, a professional church and ministry fundraiser, a former presenter of "Money Matters" (GOD TV), Ontario, Canada and author of, *Open Heaven: The Transformation* (Crossroads Christian Communications, Inc., Visualeyes Communications, Burlington, Ontario, Canada, 2005 (revised). The former title of the book seems to have been *The Revelation of Financial Renewal* (New Wine Press, 1998).

[438] As of April, 2018, www.clivepick.ca was inactive.

[439] Pick, Clive, 1998., 88-89

[440] Pick, Clive, 1998., 91-93

[441] Pick, Clive, 1998., 94

[442] Pick, Clive, 1998., 11-15; 91-94

[443] Pick, Clive, 1998., 11. Compare 91-93.

[444] Pick, Clive, 1998., 11

[445] Pick, Clive, 1998., 11

[446] Pick, Clive, 1998., 94

[447] Pick, Clive, 1998., 9-11

[448] Pick, Clive, 1998., 14. Read 11-14 and note the conceptual parallel given here between "tithe, walk and give" and God's "covenant with Abraham."

[449] Pick, Clive, 1998., 94

[450] On Genesis 15:17, see Barton, J., and Muddiman, J., 2001., 51.

[451] In Genesis 22:18, by way of comparison, the writer demonstrates that when Abraham spared the life of his firstborn son, he obeyed the Torah (Exodus 13:13,15; 34:20). The slaying of the firstborn was not unknown in Israel (Judges 11:34-40; Ezekiel 20:26; Micah 6:7.).

[452] R. N. Whybray in Barton, J., and Muddiman, J., 2001., 51

[453] Concerning Genesis 15:9-11 and Jeremiah 34:17-22, J. Levenson writes, "...the essence of the ritual is a self-curse: Those walking between the pieces will be like dead animals if they violate the covenant. In the case at hand, remarkably, it is the Lord, symbolized by the 'smoking oven' and 'flaming torch' (15:17) who invokes the self-curse, and nothing is said about any covenantal obligations that Abram is to fulfill. This type of covenant is called a covenant of grant..." (Berlin, A. and Brettler, M. Z., 2004., 35-36, note on verses 9-11). Compare Genesis 12:1-3 and 26:24e.

[454] Galatians 3:18 per J. B. Phillips, *The New Testament from 26 Translations*, Zondervan, Grand Rapids, Michigan, 1967, 851

[455] Pick, Clive, 1998., 11

[456] Pick, Clive, 1998., 11

[457] Pick, Clive, 1998., 11

[458] Pick, Clive, 1998., 14

[459] Pick, Clive, 1998., 14

[460] Pick, Clive, 1998., 11

[461] Pick, Clive, 1998., 11

[462] Pick, Clive, 1998., 11

[463] Compare Pick, Clive, 2005., Disc #1 (36:35, etc.) with Deuteronomy chapters 27 and 28.

[464] Pick, Clive, 1998., 12

[465] Pick, Clive, 1998., 9-11

[466] Pick, Clive, 1998., 10-15

[467] Pick, Clive, 1998., 11

[468] Pick, Clive, 1998., 12

[469] Pick, Clive, 1998., 11, 91

[470] Pick, Clive, 1998., 11

[471] Pick, Clive, 1998., 91

[472] Pick, Clive, 1998., 14

[473] Pick, Clive, 2005., Disc #1 (36:35, etc.)

[474] Pick, Clive, 2005., Disc #1 (36:35, etc.)

[475] Pick, Clive, 2005., Disc #1 (36:35, etc.)

[476] Pick, Clive, 2005., Disc #1 (36:35, etc.)

[477] Pick, Clive, 2005., Disc #1 (36:35, etc.)

[478] For a discussion of how Jesus' exhortation to his disciples of seeking first the kingdom of God and his righteousness in Matthew 6:33 does not turn the grace evident in 6:25-32 into "works-righteousness," see Luz, Ulrich, 1989., 407-408.

[479] Pick, Clive, 2005., Disc #1 (36:35, etc.)

[480] Pick, Clive, 2005., Disc #1 (36:35, etc.)

[481] Pick, Clive, 2005., Disc #1 (36:35, etc.)

[482] McConkie, Bruce R., 1966., 167

[483] McConkie, Bruce R., 1966., 166-168

[484] Pick, Clive, 2005., Disc #1 (36:35, etc.)

[485] Pick, Clive, 2005., Disc #1 (36:35, etc.)

[486] Pick, Clive, 1998., 14

[487] Pick, Clive, 2005., Disc #1 (36:35, etc.)

[488] O. J. Baab, "Marriage," Buttrick, G. A., 1962, volume 3, 283

[489] Edwin Cyril Blackman, "The Letter of Paul to the Romans," Laymon, C. M., 1971., 780

[490] Pick, Clive, 1998., 9-11, especially 10.

[491] Pick, Clive, 1998., 11

[492] Pick, Clive, 1998., 11-2, 29-30, 44, 69, 76-77, 80-82, 91-92, 106, 108, 116

[493] Pick, Clive, 1998., 13-15, 44, 70, 92-93, 106

[494] Pick, Clive, 1998., 9, 11, 89, 91, 94

[495] Pick, Clive, 1998., 10

[496] Pick, Clive, 1998., 9-11, 15, 75, 99, 117

[497] Pick, Clive, 1998., 11

[498] Pick, Clive, 1998., 11

[499] Pick, Clive, 1998., 14

[500] Pick, Clive, 1998., 91

[501] Pick, Clive, 1998., 12

[502] Pick, Clive, 1998., 91

[503] Pick, Clive, 1998., 92

[504] Compare Westermann, Claus, 1995., 255, 257.

[505] Westermann, Claus, 1995., 256-257

[506] Westermann, Claus, 1995., 259

[507] Westermann, Claus, 1995., 259

[508] Westermann, Claus, 1995., 257. Compare 255.

[509] Westermann, Claus, 1995., 257

[510] Westermann, Claus, 1995., 259

[511] Westermann, Claus, 1995., 259. Refer to the academic commentaries on Genesis chapter 15.

[512] Pick, Clive, 1998., 11; 13-15; 92-94

[513] Pick, Clive, 1998., 11

[514] Pick, Clive, 1998., 14

[515] Pick, Clive, 1998., 91. Compare 14.

[516] Pick, Clive, 1998., 92

[517] Pick, Clive, 1998., 93

[518] Pick, Clive, 1998., 93

[519] Bo Bennett, Ph.D., *Logically Fallacious.* www.logicallyfallacious.com

[520] Pick, Clive, 1998., 91. Compare 14.

[521] Westermann, Claus, 1995., 364

[522] Pick, Clive, 1998., 94

[523] "Prooftext," en.wikipedia.org

[524] Pick, Clive, 1998., 11; 13-15; 92-94

[525] Pick, Clive, 1998., 11; 13-15; 92-94

[526] Louis H. Gray, "Circumcision" (Introductory), Hastings, James, 1913., volume 3, 665

[527] G. E. Mendenhall, "Covenant," Buttrick, G. A., 1962., volume 1, 718

[528] Pick, Clive, 1998., 15, 93

[529] Westermann, Claus, 1995., 289

[530] Westermann, Claus, 1995., 363

[531] Westermann, Claus, 1995., 363, Compare 289.

[532] Pick, Clive, 1998., 11,14

[533] Pick, Clive, 1998., 14

[534] Gruenwald, Ithamar, 2003., 170

[535] Gruenwald, Ithamar, 2003., 170

[536] Gruenwald, Ithamar, 2003., 171

[537] Pick, Clive, 1998., 107-108

[538] Clive Pick writes, "Satan is a legalist and any form of robbery however small will block your blessings from God. I firmly believe that a small discrepancy can stop a big blessing...(Song of Songs 2:15)." Pick, Clive, 1998., 13

11 DID TITHING MAKE ABRAHAM RICH?

[539] Concerning Genesis 24:53, C. Westermann remarks, "Rebekah receives the finest presents because it is a real present and not a brideprice" (Westermann, Claus, 1995., 389).

[540] A. R. Millard, "Abraham," (person), Freedman, D. N., 1992., volume 1, 36

[541] Snell, Jay, 1995., 9-10

[542] Snell, Jay, 1995., 30

[543] Hagee, John, 2005., tape 2

[544] A. R. Millard, "Abraham," (person), Freedman, D. N., 1992., volume 1, 35

[545] Laymon, C. M., 1971., 11. Compare T. Jacobsen, "Ur," Buttrick, G. A., 1962., volume 4, 736-737.

[546] J. Margueron, "Ur," (place), Freedman, D. N., 1992., volume 6, 766

[547] J. Margueron, "Ur," (place), Freedman, D. N., 1992., volume 6, 766

[548] J. Margueron, "Ur," (place), Freedman, D. N., 1992., volume 6, 766-767

[549] J. Margueron, "Ur," (place), Freedman, D. N., 1992., volume 6, 767

[550] J. Margueron, "Ur," (place), Freedman, D. N., 1992., volume 6, 767

[551] J. Margueron, "Ur," (place), Freedman, D. N., 1992., volume 6, 766

[552] Yoshitaka Kobayashi, "Haran," Freedman, D. N., 1992., volume 3, 58. Abraham's servant found Rebekah in the city of Nahor (Genesis 24:10), the name of Abraham's brother (verses 15,24,47), and possibly the same city as that of Haran (R. Hess, "Nahor" (place), Freedman, D. N., 1992. 998).

553 C. H. Gordon, "Haran," (place), Buttrick, G. A., 1962., volume 2, 524; Y. Kobayashi, "Haran," (place), Freedman, D. N., 1992., volume 3, 59

554 Yoshitaka Kobayashi, "Haran," Freedman, D. N., 1992., volume 3, 58

555 J. Margueron, "Ur," (place), Freedman, D. N., 1992., volume 6, 766

556 A. R. Millard, "Abraham," (person), Freedman, D. N., 1992., volume 1, 36

557 Compare A. R. Millard, "Abraham," (person), Freedman, D. N., 1992., volume 1, 36.

558 R. J. Clifford and R. E. Murphy, "Genesis," in Brown, R.E., Fitzmyer, J. A. and Murphy, R. E., 1990., 24

559 Westermann, Claus, 1995., 327

560 A. R. Millard, "Abraham," (person), Freedman, D. N., 1992., volume 1, 36

561 G. A. Barrois, "Trade and Commerce," Buttrick, G. A., 1962., volume 4, 678

562 G. A. Barrois, "Trade and Commerce," Buttrick, G. A., 1962., volume 4, 678. According to Barrois, the references to "shekels" in Genesis (23:15-16; 24:22; 37:28) would apply more to the weight of silver than to a developed coinage system as utilized in Greco-Roman times or the modern world.

563 G. A. Barrois, "Trade and Commerce," Buttrick, G. A., 1962., volume 4, 678

564 G. A. Barrois, "Trade and Commerce," Buttrick, G. A., 1962., volume 4, 678

565 Ernst Axel Knauf, "Keturah," (person), Freedman, D. N., 1992., volume 4, 31

566 Ernst Axel Knauf, "Keturah," (person), Freedman, D. N., 1992., volume 4, 31

567 Ernst Axel Knauf, "Ishmaelites," Freedman, D. N., 1992., volume 3, 514

568 Ernst Axel Knauf, "Ishmaelites," Freedman, D. N., 1992., volume 3, 514

569 W. L. Reed, "Wells," Buttrick, G. A., 1962., volume 4, 839. Compare B. W. Anderson, "Water," Buttrick, G. A., 1962., volume 4, 807. Compare Deuteronomy 11:11-12.

570 Westermann, Claus, 1995., 426

571 According to R. K. Harrison, the theft of water wells continues to this day among the nomadic tribes of the Middle East ("Wells," Buttrick, G. A., 1962., volume 4, 839).

572 A. R. Millard, "Abraham," (person), Freedman, D. N., 1992., volume 1, 36

573 A. R. Millard, "Abraham," (person), Freedman, D. N., 1992., volume 1, 36. Abraham was welcome at the city gate, the place of commerce (Genesis 23:10,18).

574 A. R. Millard, "Abraham," (person), Freedman, D. N., 1992., volume 1, 36

575 A. R. Millard, "Abraham," (person), Freedman, D. N., 1992., volume 1, 36

576 Snell, Jay, 1995., 9-10

577 Snell, Jay, 1995., 9-10

578 Snell, Jay, 1995., 9

579 Snell, Jay, 1995., 9-10

580 Compare the competition between Joseph's sons, Ephraim and Manasseh in C.H.J. de Geus, "Manasseh" (place), Freedman, D. N., 1992., 493-494.

581 Milgrom, Jacob, 2000., 1394

582 N. Sarna writes, "Jacob actually invokes God's name in an outright lie!" (Sarna, Nahum M., 1989., 191).

12 DID TITHING MAKE ISAAC RICH?

583 Murdock, Mike, 1997a., 23-24

584 Murdock, Mike, 1997., 141-142

585 Murdock, Mike, 1997., 141-142

586 Murdock, Mike, 1997., 141-142

587 Murdock, Mike, 1997., 141-142

588 Murdock, Mike, 1997., 141-142

589 Smith, Wendell, 2005., 39

590 Pick, Clive, 1998., 114

591 Smith, Wendell, 2005., 39

592 Pick, Clive, 1998., 114

593 L. Hicks, "Isaac," Buttrick, G. A., 1962., 728-731

594 Pick, Clive, 1998., 114

595 Pick, Clive, 1998., 114

596 Westermann, Claus, 1995., 430

597 Richard Elliott Friedman, "Torah (Pentateuch)," Freedman, D. N., 1992., volume 6, 606; S. H. Hooke, "Genesis," Black, M. and Rowley, H. H., Peake, A. S., 1962., 194

598 Stanley D. Walters, "Jacob Narrative," Freedman, D. N., 1992., volume 3, 601

599 Westermann, Claus, 1995., 397

600 S. Cohen, "Gerar," Buttrick, G. A., 1962., volume 2, 381. See also 382.

601 Victor H. Matthews, "Abimelech," (person), Freedman, D. N., 1992., volume 1, 21

602 Stanley D. Walters, "Jacob Narrative," Freedman, D. N., 1992., volume 3, 606

13 A TITHE FOR A SAFE RETURN

[603] S. D. Walters, "Jacob Narrative," Freedman, D. N., 1992., volume 3, 599

[604] Yoshitaka Kobayashi, "Haran," (place) Freedman, D. N., 1992., volume 3, 58

[605] Harold Brodsky, "Bethel," (place) Freedman, D. N., 1992., volume 1, 710

[606] Readers can observe this general tendency as they survey the pro-tithing claims in this chapter.

[607] Westermann, Claus, 1995., 518. To Westermann, Jacob's attacker "transfer[red] some of his superhuman power to the one he could not overcome (a common feature in narratives of this sort)..." (519).

[608] Pagolu, Augustine, 1998., 212

[609] G. Henton Davies, "Vows," Buttrick, G. A., 1962., volume 4, 792-793; T. H. Gaster, "Sacrifices and Offerings, Old Testament," Buttrick, G. A., 1962., volume 4, 149

[610] Mark Strong, *The Lamp Series Step Two Membership Discovering Christian Community Responsibilities and Covenant*, Life Change Christian Center (Portland, Oregon), no publication date provided, 36-40

[611] G. Henton Davies, "Vows," Buttrick, G. A., 1962., volume 4, 792

[612] G. Henton Davies, "Vows," Buttrick, G. A., 1962., volume 4, 792

[613] Lansdell, Henry, 1963., 17-18. Compare 22. Bill Ritchie, Crossroads Community Church, Vancouver, Washington, October, 2003; Bill Ritchie, Crossroads Community Church, Vancouver, Washington, www.crossroadschurch.net/ > Teaching > Commentary > Old Testament > Genesis > Genesis chapter 28; Ray Young per Pick, Clive, 2005; Morris, Robert, 2004., 58; etc.

[614] See E. R. Leach, "3. Ritual Place" in David P. Wright, "Holiness," Freedman, D. N., 1992., volume 3, 248.

[615] Conner, Kevin J., 1993., 12; Conner, Kevin J., 1982., 274

[616] Conner, Kevin J., 1982., 274

[617] Lansdell, Henry, 1963., 17-18. Compare 22.

[618] Conner, Kevin J., 1993., 12; Conner, Kevin J., 1982., 274

[619] Conner, Kevin J., 1982., 274

[620] Conner, Kevin J., 1982., 274

[621] Conner, Kevin J., 1993., 12-13

[622] Pagolu, Augustine, 1998., 190. For a potentially different view of Pagolu's see 209. See also Sarna, Nahum M., 1989., 201 (per Pagolu).

[623] Pagolu, Augustine, 1998., 209

[624] Aharoni, Y. and Avi-yonah, M., 1968., 28, map 26; 29, map 27; 40, map 48

[625] Aharoni, Y. and Avi-yonah, M., 1968., 29, map no. 27

[626] Aharoni, Y. and Avi-yonah, M., 1968., 29

[627] Aharoni, Y. and Avi-yonah, M., 1968., 29

[628] Before he arrived in Canaan, on his return from Haran, Jacob fed his flocks in central Gilead, east of the Jordan (Aharoni, Y. and Avi-yonah, M., 1968., 40, map 47).

[629] The central mountains of Palestine run from Shechem to the north through Hebron and on to the Negeb in the south (Aharoni, Y. and Avi-yonah, M., 1968., 29; 41, map 51).

[630] Conner, Kevin J., 1993., 12; Conner, Kevin J., 1982., 274

[631] See Butterweck, G. J., Ringgren, H., Fabry, H. J., 1974-., volume 1:242-61 per Martin Rose, "Names of God in the Old Testament," Freedman, D. N., 1992., volume 4, 1004.

[632] Martin Rose, "Names of God in the Old Testament," Freedman, D. N., 1992., volume 4, 1004

[633] E. R. Dalglish, "Bethel," (deity), Freedman, D. N., 1992., volume 1, 707; H. Brodsky, "Bethel," (place), Freedman, D. N., 1992., volume 1, 710

634 Conner, Kevin J., 1993., 12-13. Compare Conner, Kevin J., 1982., 274-275.

635 E. R. Dalglish, "Bethel," (deity), Freedman, D. N., 1992., volume 1, 707; H. Brodsky, "Bethel" (place), Freedman, D. N., 1992., volume 1, 710

636 Conner, Kevin J., 1993., 27, 28, 30, 31

637 On the various functions of markers and pillars (*massebah*), see Dale W. Manor, "Massebah," Freedman, D. N., 1992., volume 4, 601.

638 L. J. Hoppe, "Israel, history of," Freedman, D. N., 1992., volume 3, 563

639 Lansdell, Henry, 1963., 18

640 Lansdell, Henry, 1963., 17

641 Bill Ritchie, Crossroads Community Church, Vancouver, Washington, October, 2003

642 Ray Young per Pick, Clive, 2005

643 Morris, Robert, 2004., 58

644 Bill Ritchie, Crossroads Community Church, Vancouver, Washington, http://www.crossroadschurch.net/ > Teaching > Commentary > Old Testament > Genesis > Genesis chapter 28. Robert Morris agrees, "Jacob's vow to tithe came straight from his grateful heart" (Morris, Robert, 2004., 58).

645 Stanley D. Walters, "Jacob Narrative," Freedman, D. N., 1992., volume 3, 603

646 Baker, W., 1994., 79, footnote; Baker, W., 1994., 94, footnote

647 Lansdell, Henry, 1963., 18

648 Compare the sacred stones and pillars in Shechem (Joshua 24:26), Gilead (Genesis 31:45), Gilgal (Joshua 4:5), Mizpeh (I Samuel 7:12), Gibeon (2 Samuel 20:8) and En-rogel (I Kings 1:9) in Smith, W. Robertson, 1894., 203, note 1. In the same source, also compare the *tamassoh* of the ancient Arabians (233).

[649] Lansdell, Henry, 1963., 17

[650] Lansdell, Henry, 1963., 17

[651] Lansdell, Henry, 1963., 17

[652] Lansdell, Henry, 1963., 17

[653] Lansdell, Henry, 1963., 17

[654] Bill Ritchie, Crossroads Community Church, Vancouver, Washington, October, 2003

[655] Westermann, Claus, 1995., 457

[656] Bill Ritchie, Crossroads Community Church, Vancouver, Washington, October, 2003

[657] Ray Young per Pick, Clive, 2005.

[658] Ray Young per Pick, Clive, 2005.

[659] Westermann, Claus, 1995., 457

[660] Westermann, Claus, 1995., 457

[661] Westermann, Claus, 1995., 457

[662] *yare* (often translated "afraid") is a *waw* consecutive with a *qal* imperfect (active, simple voice and imperfect action). *yare* (often translated "awesome") is a *niphal* participle with a passive voice [see W. Baker, editor, Baker, W., 1994., 2278 (no. 57), 2282 (no. 95) and 2283 (no. 105)].

[663] Harris, R. Laird, 1950., 18, 30

[664] Davidson, Benjamin, 1993., 344; Harris, R., Archer, G. and Waltke, B., 1980, volume 1, 400; Westermann, Claus, 1995., 454

[665] Compare Westermann, Claus, 1995., 456.

[666] Pagolu, Augustine, 1998., 212

[667] Westermann, Claus, 1995., 456

[668] Morris, Robert, 2004., 58

669 According to Walter Wink, "...the issue [in Jacob's life] is not merely psychological-developmental but economic as well" (*Psychology and the Bible: A New Way to Read the Scriptures: From Genesis to Apocalytic Vision*, Volume 2, editors, J. Harold Ellens, Wayne Rollins, Praeger Publications, Westport, Connecticut, 2004, 11).

670 Bill Ritchie, Crossroads Community Church, Vancouver, Washington, http://www.crossroadschurch.net/ > Teaching > Commentary > Old Testament > Genesis > Genesis chapter 28. Robert Morris writes, "Jacob's vow to tithe came straight from his grateful heart" (Morris, Robert, 2004., 58).

14 A VOLUNTARY & CONDITIONAL TITHE

671 Damazio, Frank and Brott, Rich, 2005., 167-168

672 Oaks, D. H., 1994., 3

673 Personal correspondence from Paul H. Seely, author, *Inerrant Wisdom: Science and Inerrancy in Biblical Perspective*, Evangelical Reform, Inc., Portland, Oregon, 1989

674 Pagolu, Augustine, 1998., 212. Compare 214.

675 B. J. Schwartz, "Leviticus," Gaventa, B. R. and Peterson, D., 2010., 58

676 Roland J. Faley, "Leviticus," in Brown, R.E., Fitzmyer, J. A. and Murphy, R. E., 1990., 79

677 Damazio, Frank and Brott, Rich, 2005., 167-168

678 Smith, W. Robertson, 1894., 214

679 Harris, R., Archer, G. and Waltke, B., 1980., volume 2, 557

680 Tenney, M. C., 1975., volume 5, 891

681 Harris, R., Archer, G. and Waltke, B., 1980., volume 2, 558

682 Bill Ritchie, Crossroads Community Church, Vancouver, Washington, http://www.crossroadschurch.net/ > Teaching > Commentary > Old Testament > Genesis > Genesis 28

683 Westermann, Claus, 1995., 459

⁶⁸⁴ Kohlenberger, John R., III, 1987., 74

⁶⁸⁵ Bill Ritchie, Crossroads Community Church, Vancouver, Washington, http://www.crossroadschurch.net/ > Teaching > Commentary > Old Testament > Genesis > Genesis 28

⁶⁸⁶ Edward R. Dalglish, "Bethel (deity)," Freedman, D. N., 1992., volume 1, 709; Frederick W. Danker, "Ex Voto," Freedman, D. N., 1992., volume 2, 680-681; Westermann, Claus, 1995., 459; Richard J. Clifford and Roland E. Murphy, "Genesis," in Brown, R.E., Fitzmyer, J. A. and Murphy, R. E., 1990., 30

⁶⁸⁷ de Vaux, Roland, 1965, volume 2., 465

⁶⁸⁸ de Vaux, Roland, 1965, volume 2., 465. On the development of vows into "simple prayers" and sometimes "unconditional promise[s]" see 466.

⁶⁸⁹ G. Henton Davies, "Vows," Buttrick, G. A., 1962, volume 4, 792-793

⁶⁹⁰ Milgrom, Jacob, 2001., 2426

⁶⁹¹ Cartledge, T. W., 1992., 147

⁶⁹² E. R. Dalglish, "Bethel (deity)," Freedman, D. N., 1992., volume 1, 709

⁶⁹³ www.dictionary.com

⁶⁹⁴ www.dictionary.com

⁶⁹⁵ Baker, W. and Carpenter, E., 2003., 66

⁶⁹⁶ Harris, R. Laird, 1950., 74

⁶⁹⁷ Brian Webster on blogs.bible.org. Compare Baker, W. and Carpenter, E., 2003., 66. According to Koehler and Baumgartner, this is true "in desiderative clause[s], with [the imperfect] and [with a] suppressed apodosis," all three of which, in my view, fit the context of Jacob's vow in Genesis 28:20-22 (Koehler, Ludwig, Baumgartner, Walter and Richardson, M.E.J., 1994., volume 1, 60).

⁶⁹⁸ Davidson, Benjamin, 1993., 31

⁶⁹⁹ Davidson, Benjamin, 1993., 74

700 Kohlenberger, John R., III, 1987., 74

701 Baker, W. and Carpenter, E., 2003., 66

702 Kohlenberger, John R., III, 1987., 535

703 Harris, R. Laird, 1950., 74

704 Baker, W. and Carpenter, E., 2003., 535. Compare Harris, R. Laird, 1950., 74.

705 Harris, R. Laird, 1950., 74

706 Associated Publishers and Authors, 1975., 797

707 Baker, W. and Carpenter, E., 2003., 711. Compare Baker, W., 1994., 2338.

708 Koehler, Ludwig, Baumgartner, Walter and Richardson, M.E.J., 1994., volume 1, 797; Wilson, W., 1900., 470

709 E. R. Dalglish, "Bethel (deity)," Freedman, D. N., 1992., volume 1, 709

710 Baker, W., 1994., 2282, #95

711 Baker, W., 1994, 2277, note 43

712 Baker, W., 1994, 2277, note 43

713 R. Harris says, "In general, an imperfect in the protasis expresses a condition of eventuality" (Harris, R. Laird, 1950., 74).

714 www.onelook.com

715 Pheme Perkins, "Ethics, New Testament," Freedman, D. N., 1992., volume 2, 663

716 F. W. Danker, "Ex Voto," Freedman, D. N., 1992., volume 2, 680

717 F. W. Danker, "Ex Voto," Freedman, D. N., 1992., volume 2, 680

718 F. W. Danker, "Ex Voto," Freedman, D. N., 1992., volume 2, 680. To J. Crenshaw, *do ut des* means "I give in order to receive."

719 Marguerite Yon, "Ugarit," Freedman, D. N., 1992., volume 6, 695

[720] Pagolu, Augustine, 1998., 176. The ancients believed that bulls and firstborns held much weight with the gods.

[721] G. Henton Davies, "Vows," Buttrick, G. A., 1962., volume 4, 792

[722] Herman, Menahem, 1991., 1-2. Compare Gray, George Buchanan, 1925.

[723] Milgrom, Jacob, 2001., volume 3, 2426-2431

[724] Herman, Menahem, 1991., 1-2. Compare Gray, George Buchanan, 1925.

[725] Stanley D. Walters, "Jacob Narrative," Freedman, D. N., 1992., volume 3, 602

[726] Stanley D. Walters, "Jacob Narrative," Freedman, D. N., 1992., volume 3, 603

[727] Westermann, Claus, 1995., 459

[728] Dale W. Manor, "Beer-sheba," Freedman, D. N., 1992., volume 1, 641

[729] Clive Pick writes, "...the tithe will protect you financially..." (Pick, Clive, 1998., 14).

[730] According to Claus Westermann, "to serve the Lord" in 2 Samuel 15:8 (NASB) means to offer a ritual sacrifice to God (Westermann, Claus, 1995., 459).

[731] Silver, Morris, 1995., 99

[732] S. Eitrem and R. M. Ogilvie, "Votum," Hammond and Scullard, 1970., 1133

[733] S. Eitrem and R. M. Ogilvie, "Votum," Hammond and Scullard, 1970., 1133

[734] In Chapter 7, "The Principle of the Tithe Before Moses," of his book, *The Biblical Road to Blessing*, Benny Hinn addresses: (a) "Adam and the Tithe (Genesis 2)," 116-118; (b) "Cain and Abel and the Tithe (Genesis 4)," 118-121 and (c) "Abraham & Melchizedek and the Tithe (Genesis 14)," 121-127, but he never mentions Jacob's tithe vow; he does not mention it anywhere in his book (Hinn, Benny, 1997). Similarly, R. T.

Kendall ignores Jacob's tithe vow in Chapter 2, "The Origin of Tithing," (Kendall, R. T., 1982., 43-56); instead, he spends the entire chapter talking about Abraham's tithe to Melchizedek.

[735] Kendall, R. T., 1982., 100

15 AN UNPAID TITHE

[736] Conner, Kevin J., 1993., 12-13 with Conner, Kevin J., 1982., 274

[737] Conner, Kevin J., 1993., 12-13; Conner, Kevin J., 1982., 274

[738] Conner, Kevin J., 1993., 12-13 and Conner, Kevin J., 1982., 274-275

[739] Conner, Kevin J., 1993., 12

[740] Conner, Kevin J., 1982, 274

[741] Conner, Kevin J., 1993., 13

[742] Conner, Kevin J., 1993., 13

[743] Westermann, Claus, 1995., 550; J. D. Levenson, "Genesis," Berlin, A. and Brettler, M. Z., 2004., 71

[744] Westermann, Claus, 1995., 550, 557. Contrast Pagolu, Augustine, 1998, 210.

[745] E. R. Dalglish, "Bethel," (deity), Freedman, D. N., 1992., volume 1, 709

[746] G. H. Davies, "Vows," Buttrick, G. A., 1962., volume 4, 792

[747] Edward R. Dalglish, "Bethel," (deity), Freedman, D. N., 1992., volume 1, 709

[748] Compare Betty Jane Lillie, "Almighty," Freedman, D. N., 1992., volume 1, 160.

[749] Compare the worship of Sin, the Mesopotamian moon-god in Haran (Yoshitaka Kobayashi, "Haran," (place) Freedman, D. N., 1992., volume 3, 58-59).

[750] Aharoni, Y. and Avi-yonah, M., 1968., 29, map #27

[751] Aharoni, Y. and Avi-yonah, M., 1968., 29, map #27

[752] Lawrence E. Toombs, "Shechem" (place), Freedman, D. N., 1992, volume 5, 1174

[753] Aharoni, Y. and Avi-yonah, M., 1968., 22, map no. 17

[754] Pagolu, Augustine, 1998., 210 and note 24. Pagolu's "Genesis 33:23-24" is a typographical error; he probably meant Genesis 33:13-14.

[755] R. J. Clifford and R. E. Murphy, "Genesis," in Brown, R.E., Fitzmyer, J. A. and Murphy, R. E., 1990., 35; Westermann, Claus, 1995., 550

[756] Some readers might doubt this purpose in specific terms because YHWH is not used for the divine name anywhere in Genesis chapter 35. This fact, however, could indicate the presence of a different tradition.

[757] de Vaux, Roland, 1965, Volume 2., 291. Compare E. R. Dalglish, "Bethel," (deity), Freedman, D. N., 1992., volume 1, 709. Note the parallels, mostly from de Vaux, between Jacob's experience at Bethel with those of later Israelites at the same location: the use of pilgrimage language (Genesis 35:1,3; I Samuel 10:3), the promising and/or paying of tithes (Genesis 28:22c; Amos 4:4d), the building of an altar (Genesis 35:1,3,7; Judges 21:2,4) and the place of divine revelation (Genesis 28:13-17; Judges 20:18,26-28).

[758] Semitic is "a subfamily of Afro-asiatic languages that includes Akkadian, Arabic, Aramaic, Ethiopic, Hebrew and Phoenician" (www.dictionary.com).

[759] Smith, W. Robertson, 1894., 184

[760] Smith, W. Robertson, 1894., 485. Compare 451.

[761] Smith, W. Robertson, 1894., 451, 485

[762] R. J. Clifford and R. E. Murphy, "Genesis," in Brown, R.E., Fitzmyer, J. A. and Murphy, R. E., 1990., 35

[763] Compare Pagolu, Augustine, 1998., 214.

[764] Westermann, Claus, 1995., 550

[765] Compare Westermann, Claus, 1995., 551.

[766] R. J. Clifford and R. E. Murphy, "Genesis," in Brown, R.E., Fitzmyer, J. A. and Murphy, R. E., 1990., 35

[767] J. D. Levenson, "Genesis," Berlin, A. and Brettler, M. Z., 2004., 71

[768] S. D. Walters, "Jacob Cycle," Freedman, D. N., 1992., volume 3, 607

[769] S. D. Walters, "Jacob Narrative," Freedman, D. N., 1992., volume 3, 606

[770] S. D. Walters, "Jacob Narrative," Freedman, D. N., 1992., volume 3, 606

[771] S. D. Walters, "Jacob Narrative," Freedman, D. N., 1992., volume 3, 606. Compare 607.

[772] S. D. Walters, "Jacob Narrative," Freedman, D. N., 1992., volume 3, 599

[773] Pagolu, Augustine, 1998., 68

[774] Pagolu, Augustine, 1998., 68. Compare de Vaux, Roland, 1965, Volume 2., 413.

[775] Pagolu, Augustine, 1998., 68. Compare 70.

[776] Black, M. and Rowley, H. H., 1962., 204-206

[777] Compare Buttrick, G. A., 1962., volume 2, 415.

[778] Westermann, Claus, 1995., 459

[779] Westermann, Claus, 1995., 459

[780] E. R. Dalglish, "Bethel," (deity), Freedman, D. N., 1992., volume 1, 709. R. A. Oden, Jr. agrees that the patriarchs do not show animistic tendencies, animism being "the ascription of living souls *(anima)* to everything in nature" ("Myth and Mythology," Freedman, D. N., 1992., volume 4, 950).

[781] Smith, W. Robertson, 1894., 204

[782] Smith, W. Robertson, 1894., 204-205

[783] Smith, W. Robertson, 1894., 204-205. Compare 206-212.

784 Westermann, Claus, 1995., 552. For further discussion of El-Bethel in Genesis 35:7 and the Semitic deity named "Bethel" see Edward R. Dalglish, "Bethel (Deity)," Freedman, D. N., 1992., 706-710.

785 Sarna, Nahum M.,1989., 240

786 B. W. Anderson, "God, names of," Buttrick, G. A., 1962., volume 2, 412. For the versions that read El-Bethel as "El of Bethel," see the same reference. Compare Sarna, Nahum M., 1989., Genesis, 396-397.

787 Daglish calls this interpretation of Genesis 35:7 an "invalid approach" (Freedman, D. N., 1992., volume 1, 709). The idea is also based on an analogy with the deity names of El Olam, El Shaddai and El Elyôn (Buttrick, G. A., 1962., volume 2, 412).

788 G. A. Barrois, "Pillar," Buttrick, G. A., 1962., volume 3, 815

789 To Sarna, "idols" (*nekhar*) refer to non-Israelite "foreignness" (Sarna, Nahum M.,1989., 241).

790 To Sarna, the earrings were "talismans adorned with pagan symbols" (Sarna, Nahum M.,1989., 241).

791 Westermann, Claus, 1995., 529

792 Compare Westermann, Claus, 1995., 550-551.

793 Sarna, Nahum M.,1989., Genesis, 240

794 Sarna, Nahum M.,1989., Genesis, 232, note 15; Genesis, 240

795 To Sarna, Jacob's stone pillar "functions as a witness to the dream" (Sarna, Nahum M.,1989., Genesis, 199).

796 Freedman, D. N., 1992., volume 1, 709

797 Sarna, Nahum M.,1989., Genesis, 200

798 Sarna, Nahum M.,1989., Genesis, 201

799 Sarna, Nahum M.,1989., Genesis, 200

800 Sarna, Nahum M.,1989., Genesis, 200

801 Smith, W. Robertson, 1894., 115

802 Smith, W. Robertson, 1894., 115

[803] de Vaux, Roland, 1965, Volume 2., 406

[804] Smith, W. Robertson, 1894., 200

[805] Karel van der Toorn, "Theology, Priests, and Worship in Canaan and Ancient Israel," Sasson, J. M., 1995., volume 3, 2055-2056

[806] Pagolu, Augustine, 1998., 207

[807] Pagolu, Augustine, 1998., 210, 213. Compare 211.

[808] Pagolu, Augustine, 1998., 189. Compare 171-172. According to Pagolu, Jacob "...did not pay tithes..." (Pagolu, Augustine, 1998., 212). Compare 210.

[809] Pagolu, Augustine, 1998., 171-172

[810] Pagolu, Augustine, 1998., 190

[811] Augustine, 1998., 172, 211. Compare 213.

[812] Conner, Kevin J., 1993., 12-13; Conner, Kevin J., 1982., 274

[813] Conner, Kevin J., 1993., 12-13; Conner, Kevin J., 1982., 274

[814] Conner, Kevin J., 1993., 12-13; Conner, Kevin J., 1982., 274

[815] Conner, Kevin J., 1993., 12-13; Conner, Kevin J., 1982., 274

[816] Fischer, David H., 1970., 53

[817] Conner, Kevin J., 1993., 13; Conner, Kevin J., 1982., 274

[818] Conner, Kevin J., 1993., 13; Conner, Kevin J., 1982., 274

[819] Challies, Tim, 2007., 145. *The Discipline of Spiritual Discernment*, Crossway Books, Wheaton, Illinois

[820] http://en.wikipedia.org/wiki/Association_fallacyl

[821] For a literary commentary on Jeremiah 9:4 (English Bible) or 9:3 (Hebrew Bible), see Stanley D. Walters, "Jacob Narrative," Freedman, D. N., 1992., 608.

[822] According to D. J. McCarthy and R. E. Murphy, in Hosea 12:1-14, Ephraim (Israel) followed the sins of his father, Jacob: deceit, treachery, presumption, insincerity, manipulation, etc. Although there might be a

hint of Jacob's conversion (verse 4c), Jacob is Israel's "first sinner" (Brown, R.E., Fitzmyer, J. A. and Murphy, R. E., 1990., 227).

[823] According to E.B. Zvi, in Malachi 3:8-9, when God told Israel to stop defrauding him, he was saying, "Stop *Jacobing* Me!" ("Malachi," Berlin, A. and Brettler, M. Z., 2004., 1273). Emphasis mine.

[824] Compare the ministry of angels in Jacob's life (Genesis 28:12; 31:11; 32:1; 48:16) with the same in the lives of the Hebrews (Exodus 14:19; 23:20,23; 33:2) and Israelites (2 Samuel 24:16-17; I Kings 13:18; 19:5,7; 2 Kings 1:3,15; 19:35).

16 JACOB'S DECEPTIVE LIFESTYLE

[825] Conner, Kevin J., 1993., 13

[826] Conner, Kevin J., 1993., 13

[827] O. J. Baab, "Family," Buttrick, G. A., 1962., volume 2, 239

[828] Astrid Billes Beck, "Rebekah," (person), Freedman, D. N., 1992., volume 5, 630

[829] V. H. Kooy, "First-born," Buttrick, G. A., 1962., volume 2, 270

[830] V. H. Kooy, "First-born," Buttrick, G. A., 1962., volume 2, 270

[831] O. J. Baab, "Birthright," Buttrick, G. A., 1962., volume, 1, 440

[832] O. J. Baab, "Birthright," Buttrick, G. A., 1962., volume, 1, 440

[833] H. Preserved Smith, "Inheritance (Hebrew)," Hastings, James, 1913., volume 7, 306

[834] Westermann, Claus, 1995., 435, 437

[835] Westermann, Claus, 1995., 437, 444

[836] Westermann, Claus, 1995., 443

[837] Westermann, Claus, 1995., 444

[838] Westermann, Claus, 1995., 444. Compare 440.

[839] J. D. Levenson, "Genesis," Berlin, A. and Brettler, M. Z., 2004., 57, note on Genesis 27:36

[840] Westermann, Claus, 1995., 438

[841] Westermann, Claus, 1995., 442

[842] Westermann, Claus, 1995., 435. Later, the paternal (deathbed) blessing could be given to two grandsons, who legally belonged to the grandfather (Genesis 48:5-6; 8-20) or even to multiple sons (Genesis 49:1-33) (Westermann, Claus, 1995., 438).

[843] Compare all the trouble that Tamar's midwife went to in distinguishing who was the true firstborn of her twins Perez and Zerah (Genesis 38:27-30). Compare Westermann, Claus, 1995., 440, 414.

[844] J. H. Marks, "Genesis," Laymon, C. M., 1971., 21. Compare G. Coats, *Genesis* ("The Forms of the Old Testament Literature 1;" GR, 1983) per R. J. Clifford, R. E. Murphy, "Genesis," in Brown, R.E., Fitzmyer, J. A. and Murphy, R. E., 1990., 29.

[845] R. J. Clifford and R. E. Murphy, "Genesis," in Brown, R.E., Fitzmyer, J. A. and Murphy, R. E., 1990., 29. Compare Raymond F. Collins, "Ten Commandments," Freedman, D. N., 1992., volume 6, 385 and J. H. Marks, "Genesis," Laymon, C. M., 1971., 21. Westermann, however, does not see Isaac's blessing of Esau as a curse (Genesis 27:38-40). To him, "it is rather a daring intimation of the later and extended meaning of the idea of the blessing, the blessing as the promise of vital power: 'you shall live!'" (Westermann, Claus, 1995., 443). Genesis 27:40d, "...you will break his yoke from your neck," seems to confirm Westermann's view.

[846] E. A. Knauf, "Seir," (place), Freedman, D. N., 1992., volume 5, 1072

[847] R. J. Clifford and R. E. Murphy, "Genesis," in Brown, R.E., Fitzmyer, J. A. and Murphy, R. E., 1990., 34

[848] Aharoni, Y. and Avi-yonah, M., 1968., 14, map no. 6; 22, map no. 17; 29, map no. 27

[849] Pagolu, Augustine, 1998., 73

[850] http://depressiond.com/pathological-liar/ 4.2, "Habitual Liar." Compare D. L. Schuurman, "Lying," Benner, David G., 1985., 665.

[851] Conner, Kevin J., 1993., 13

852 E. B. Zvi, "Malachi," in Berlin, A. and Brettler, M. Z., 2004., 1273

17 A MOTIVE ANALYSIS

853 Pick, Clive, 1998., 88. Clive Pick meant Genesis 28:13 not 28:14.

854 Pick, Clive, 1998., 89

855 G. Henton Davies, "Vows," Buttrick, G. A., 1962., volume 4, 792

856 Pick, Clive, 1998., 88

857 Pick, Clive, 1998., 88

858 R. J. Clifford and R. E. Murphy, "Genesis," Brown, R.E., Fitzmyer, J. A. and Murphy, R. E., 1990., 30

859 Westermann, Claus, 1995., 457

860 Westermann, Claus, 1995., 457

861 Pick, Clive, 1998., 88

862 Pick, Clive, 1998., 88

863 Pick, Clive, 1998., 88

864 Pick, Clive, 1998., 88

865 Pick, Clive, 1998., 89. Emphasis mine.

866 Pick, Clive, 1998., 88

867 Pick, Clive, 1998., 88

868 Pick, Clive, 1998., 88

869 Pick, Clive, 1998., 88

870 Pick, Clive, 1998., 88

871 Pick, Clive, 1998., 89. Emphasis mine.

872 G. H. Davies, "Vows," Buttrick, G. A., 1962., volume 4, 792

873 Pick, Clive, 1998., 88

874 Pick, Clive, 1998., 88

18 DID JACOB'S TITHE VOW MAKE HIM RICH?

[875] Stanley D. Walters, "Jacob Narrative," Freedman, D. N., 1992., volume 3, 605

[876] Astrid Billes Beck, "Rachel," (person), Freedman, D. N., 1992., volume 5, 606

[877] Astrid Billes Beck, "Rachel," (person), Freedman, D. N., 1992., volume 5, 606

[878] Stanley D. Walters, "Jacob narrative," Freedman, D. N., 1992., volume 3, 603

[879] jaysnell.org/asgeletters/jacobswealth.html

[880] Conner, Kevin J., 1993., 12. Compare Conner, Kevin J., 1982., 274.

[881] Immediately after Clive Pick provides non-tithers with a prayer of repentance for not tithing, under the heading, "Blessings are on Their Way," he writes: "Brothers and sisters, begin to expect your blessings now" (Pick, Clive, 1998., 117).

[882] Compare Aharoni, Y. and Avi-yonah, M., 1968., 29, map no. 27 with 31, map no. 30.

[883] O. J. Baab, "Birthright," Buttrick, G. A., 1962., volume 1, 440

[884] V. H. Kooy, "First-born," Buttrick, G. A., 1962., volume 2, 271

[885] C. F. Mariottini, "Zilpah," (person), Freedman, D. N., 1992., volume 6, 1094

[886] C. F. Mariottini, "Zilpah," (person), Freedman, D. N., 1992., volume 6, 1094

[887] C. F. Mariottini, "Zilpah," (person), Freedman, D. N., 1992., volume 6, 1094

[888] Pick, Clive, 1998., 31; Paul Crouch and son, local Channel 20, Trinity Broadcasting Network, 05/04/2006; Ray Young per Pick, Clive, 2005.; Damazio, Frank, 1992.; Damazio, Frank and Brott, Rich, 2005., 178, 181; Snell, Jay, 1995., 5, 14; Hinn, Benny, 1997., 171

[889] According to I. Jacob and W. Jacob, "Mandrakes (*Mandragora officinarum*) are...found in stony places. The root resembles a human

figure, which led to its association with fertility rites. The mandrake is a stemless perennial related to the potato. The dark-green, oblong, wrinkled leaves form a rosette; from this rises a flower stalk bearing a bluish-violet, bell-shaped flower followed by a yellow plum-sized berry. The fruit was used as food; the root possesses narcotic properties for which it was esteemed. The plant is slightly poisonous" ("Flora," Freedman, D. N., 1992., volume 2, 812).

[890] Gale A. Yee, "Leah," Freedman, D. N., 1992., volume 4, 268; Compare Gary A. Herion, "Issachar," Freedman, D. N., 1992., volume 3, 577.

[891] L. Toombs states that Shechem was an ancient city located about 40 miles north of Jerusalem in the interior highlands of Israel, the earliest settlement of which dates back as far as the Chalcolithic Period, which was approximately 4500-3200, B.C. ("Shechem," Freedman, D. N., 1992., volume 5, 1179).

[892] According to L. Toombs, the archaeological evidence reveals that Shechem would have been too well defended with walls to be ravaged by Jacob's sons except after the destruction of the city toward the end of the Middle Bronze Age (approximately 1900-1750, B.C.) or at the time of the city's downturn at the end of the Late Bronze Age (approximately 1400-1300, B.C.).

[893] Lawrence E. Toombs, "Shechem," (place), Freedman, D. N., 1992., volume 5, 1180

[894] Lawrence E. Toombs, "Shechem," (place), Freedman, D. N., 1992., volume 5, 1181

[895] Lawrence E. Toombs, "Shechem," (place), Freedman, D. N., 1992., volume 5, 1182

19 TITHING VOWS & THE NEW COVENANT

[896] Conner, Kevin J.,1993.,13; Conner, Kevin J., 1982., 274-275

[897] I recorded this vow/prayer, nearly word-for-word, from a church meeting I attended in Vancouver, Washington (approximately August, 2009). The name of the source and church is being withheld due to the

fact that the church's senior pastor was absent and did not support what was done or said.

[898] Pick, Clive, 1998., 116

[899] Harris, R., Archer, G. and Waltke, B., 1980., 557

[900] M. Weinfeld, "Deuteronomy, book of," Freedman, D. N., 1992, volume 2, 182. The original has, incorrectly, "Proverbs 20:13."

[901] The Septuagint is abbreviated by "LXX" for the seventy or so elders said to have translated the Pentateuch into Greek. According to M. K. H. Peters, the notion that there were exactly "seventy" translators is "now acknowledged to be fictitious" ("Septuagint," Freedman, D. N., 1992., volume 5, 1093).

[902] J. W. Wevers, "Septuagint," Buttrick, G. A., 1962., volume 4, 273

[903] J. W. Wevers, "Septuagint," Buttrick, G. A., 1962., volume 4, 277

[904] Frederick W. Danker, "Ex Voto," Freedman, D. N., 1992, volume 2, 681

[905] Brown, R. E., Fitzmyer, J. A. and Murphy, R. E., 1968., 72

[906] Milgrom, Jacob, 2001., volume 3, 2410

[907] According to Leviticus 19:12, oaths invoke the name of God. According to J. Schneider, "God's name was not invoked in vows, but it was in oaths..." ("Oath," Kittel, G., 1964., volume 10, 178, note 16).

[908] Milgrom, Jacob, 2001., 2409

[909] Nili S. Fox, "Numbers," Berlin, A. and Brettler, M. Z., 2004., 343-344; note on Numbers 30:2-17

[910] Nili S. Fox, "Numbers," Berlin, A. and Brettler, M. Z., 2004., 343; note on Numbers 30:2-17

[911] J. Schneider, "Oath," Kittel, G., 1964., volume 5, 178

[912] Roger Brooks, "Mishnah," Freedman, D. N., 1992, volume 4, 871

[913] *Nedarim* 1:1-2; 2:2, etc.; Ketub. 9:5; Git. 4:3; Sanh. 3:2. See also Mishna tractates *Sebu'ot* and *Nazir*; Diog. Laertius 8.22; Pseudo-

Phocylides 1.16 and 2 Enoch 49.1 per B. T. Viviano, "Matthew," Brown, R.E., Fitzmyer, J. A. and Murphy, R. E., 1990., 643.

[914] Hilknot Nedarim 1:3, www.mhcny.org/parasha/1042.pdf

[915] Sophie Laws, "James, Epistle of," Freedman, D. N., 1992., volume 3, 624-625

[916] H. C. Hahn, "Anger, Wrath," (*orge*), Brown, Colin, 1971., volume 1, 107

[917] Compare Psalm 65:1-2,9-13 (G. W. Anderson, "The Psalms," Black, M. and Rowley, H. H., 1962., 426).

[918] Robin Wakely, "*naœdar; neder*, etc." VanGemeren, W., 1996., volume 3, 37

[919] Karel van der Toorn, "Theology, Priests, and Worship in Canaan and Ancient Israel," Sasson, J. M., 1995., volume 3, 2055-2056

[920] G. H. Davies, "Vows," Buttrick, G. A., 1962., volume 4, 793

[921] H. Greevan, "Vow," (prayer), Kittel, G., 1964., volume 2, 803-804

[922] H. Greeven, "*Euchomai*, etc.," (prayer), Kittel, G. and Friedrich, G., 1985., 284

[923] Patrick M. Arnold, "Mizpah," (place), Freedman, D. N., 1992., 880

[924] Milgrom, Jacob, 2001., 2410

[925] In Freedman, D. N., 1992., see: Donald B. Redford, "Amarna, Tell El-" (volume 1, 181-182); James F. Strange, "Beth-zatha" (volume 1, 701); "Cyprus" (volume 1, 1228-1230); Pauline Albenda, "Art and Architecture" (volume 1, 421) and Edward M. Curtis, "Idol, Idolatry" (volume 3, 377).

[926] "Votive Inscriptions," Household and Family in Early Mesopotamia, Sasson, J. M., 1995., volume 1, 65

[927] Burkert, W., 1986., per Silver, Morris, 1995., 47

[928] F. M. Gillman, "James, Brother of Jesus," Freedman, D. N., 1992, volume 3, 620

[929] Thomas Merton (deceased 1968), O.C.S.O., Trappist monk, "Merton" (Netflix)

[930] G. Stob, "Vows," Tenney, M.C., 2009., volume 5, 891

[931] When Serge A.'s helicopter dropped from the sky into the icy waters of Antarctica, he made several promises to God in exchange for his rescue. Serge was able to pull himself up onto an iceberg and successfully chased away a polar beer; eventually, he was rescued (NPR/OPB, 12/17/2015).

[932] John E. McFadyen, "Vows (Hebrew)," Hastings, James, 1913., volume 12, 656

BIBLIOGRAPHY

Aharoni, Y. and Avi-yonah, M., 1968. *Macmillan Bible Atlas*, Macmillan, New York, New York

Alcorn, Randy C., 2001. *The Treasure Principle*, Multnomah Publishers, Sisters, Oregon

Alcorn, Randy C., 2003. *Money, Possessions and Eternity*, Eternal Perspective Ministries, Tyndale House Publishers, Inc., Carol Stream, Illinois

Allen, A. A., 1953. *The Secret to Scriptural Financial Success*, A. A. Allen, Dallas, Texas

Allis, Oswald T., 1945. *Prophecy and the Church*, Presbyterian and Reformed Publishing Co., Phillipsburg, New Jersey

Angeles, Peter A., 1981. *Dictionary of Philosophy*, Barnes & Noble Books, New York, New York

Apocrypha, The, www.catholic.org

Associated Publishers and Authors, 1975. *The New Englishman's Hebrew and Chaldee Concordance of the Old Testament*, Wilmington, Delaware

Attridge, H. W., 1989. *Hermeneia: Hebrews*, Fortress Press, Minneapolis, Minnesota

Avanzini, John, 1994. *God's Debt-Free Guarantee*, Harrison House, Tulsa, Oklahoma

Bahne, Eric, 2013. LIFE Series, "ID The Important," New Beginnings Church, Portland, Oregon, January 20, 2013

Bahnsen, Greg L., 1977. *Theonomy In Christian Ethics*, Presbyterian & Reformed Publishing Co., Phillipsburg, New Jersey

Bainton, Roland, H., 1950. *Here I Stand: A Life of Martin Luther*, Abingdon Press, New York, New York

Baker, W. and Carpenter, E., 2003. *Complete Word Study Dictionary Old Testament,* AMG Publishers, Chattanooga, Tennessee

Baker, W., 1994. Editor, *The Complete Word Study Old Testament,* AMG Publishers, Chattanooga, Tennessee

Banks, Robert, 1994. *Paul's Idea of Community,* Hendrickson Publishers, Peabody, Massachusetts

Barr, James, 1961. *The Semantics of Biblical Language,* Oxford University Press, Oxford, United Kingdom

Barr, James, 1966. *Old and New in Interpretation: A Study of the Two Testaments,* SCM Press, Ltd., Alva, Scotland

Barr, James, 1977. *Fundamentalism,* The Westminster Press, Philadelphia, Pennsylvania

Barton, J., and Muddiman, J., 2001. Editors, *Oxford Bible Commentary,* Oxford University Press, New York, New York

Bauer, Arndt & Gingrich, 1957. *Greek-English Lexicon of the New Testament and Other Early Christian Literature,* University of Chicago Press, Chicago, Illinois

Benner, David G., 1985. Editor, *Baker Encyclopedia of Psychology,* Baker Book House, Grand Rapids, Michigan

Berlin, A. and Brettler, M. Z., 2004. *Jewish Study Bible,* Jewish Publication Society, Tanakh Translation, Oxford University Press, Oxford, United Kingdom

Bettenson, Henry, 1963. Editor, *Documents of the Christian Church,* Second Edition, Oxford University Press, Oxford, United Kingdom

Black, H. C., 1983. *Black's Law Dictionary,* Fifth Edition, West Publishing, St. Paul, Minnesota

Black, M. and Rowley, H. H., 1962. Editors, *Peake's Commentary on the Bible,* Thomas Nelson, Melbourne, Australia

Borowski, Oded, 1987. *Agriculture in Iron Age Israel,* Eisenbrauns, Winona Lake, Indiana

Botterweck, G. J., Ringgren, H., Fabry, H. J., 1974, etc. Editors, *Theological Dictionary of the Old Testament,* Translators, J. T. Willis, G. W. Bromiley and D. E. Green, Eerdmans, Grand Rapids, Michigan

Brooks, Paula, 2004. "Tithing?" Selah Publishing Group, LLC, Dillsboro, Indiana

Brown, Colin, 1971. Editor, *New International Dictionary of New Testament Theology*, Zondervan, Grand Rapids

Brown, R. E., Fitzmyer, J. A. and Murphy, R. E., 1968. Editors, *Jerome Biblical Commentary*, Prentice-Hall, Inc., Englewood Cliffs, New Jersey

Brown, R.E., Fitzmyer, J. A. and Murphy, R. E., 1990. Editors, *New Jerome Biblical Commentary*, Prentice-Hall, Inc., Englewood Cliffs, New Jersey

Brown, Raymond E., 1966. *The Anchor Bible: The Gospel According to John (1-12)*, Doubleday, Garden City, New York

Brown, Raymond E., 1982. *The Anchor Bible: The Epistles of John*, Doubleday, New York, New York

Bruce, F.F., 1964. *The Epistle to the Hebrews*, Eerdmans, Grand Rapids, Michigan

Bruckner, James K., 2001. *Implied Law in the Abraham Narrative: A Literary and Theological Analysis*, Sheffield Academic Press, New York, New York

Brunner, Emil, 1943. *Truth as Encounter*, The Westminster, Press, Philadelphia, Pennsylvania

Brunner, Emil, 1947. *The Mediator*, The Westminster Press, Philadelphia, Pennsylvania

Brunner, Emil, 1953. *The Misunderstanding of the Church*, The Westminster Press, Philadelphia, Pennsylvania

Buchanan, George Wesley, 1972. *The Anchor Bible: To the Hebrews*, Doubleday & Company, Garden City, New York

Bultmann, Rudolf, 1955. *Theology of the New Testament*, Translator, K. Grobel, Charles Scribner's Sons, New York, New York

Burkert, W., 1986. *Ancient Mystery Cults*, Cambridge, Massachusetts, Harvard University Press

Buttrick, G. A., 1962. *The Interpreter's Dictionary of the Bible*, Abingdon Press, Nashville, Tennessee

Carson, Donald A., 1996. *Exegetical Fallacies*, Second Edition, Baker Academic, Grand Rapids, Michigan

Cartledge, T. W., 1992. "Vows in the Hebrew Bible and the Ancient Near East," *Journal for the Studies of the Old Testament* Press, Sheffield, England

Christensen, Duane L., 1991. *Word Biblical Commentary: Deuteronomy 1-11*, Word Books, Dallas, Texas

Christianity Today, Carol Stream, Illinois

Cockerill, Gareth Lee, 2012. *The New International Commentary on the New Testament: The Epistle to the Hebrews*, Eerdmans, Grand Rapids, Michigan

Conner, Kevin J. and Malmin, Ken, 1983. *The Covenants*, Bible Temple Publishing, Portland, Oregon

Conner, Kevin J. and Malmin, Ken, 1976. *Interpreting the Scriptures*, Bible Press, Portland, Oregon

Conner, Kevin J., 1982. *The Church in the New Testament*, Sovereign World International, Kent, United Kingdom and City Bible Publishing, Portland, Oregon

Conner, Kevin J., 1986. *The Relevance of the Old Testament to a New Testament Church*, KJC Publications, Blackburn South, Victoria, Australia

Conner, Kevin J., 1990. *New Covenant Realities*, KJC Publications, Acacia Press, Pty. Ltd., Blackburn South, Victoria, Australia

Conner, Kevin J., 1993. *Tithes and Offerings or Christian Stewardship*, KJC Publications, Acacia Press, Pty. Ltd., Blackburn South, Victoria, Australia

Conner, Kevin J., 2001. *Foundational Principles of Church Membership*, KJC Publications, Blackburn South, Victoria, Australia

Copeland, Kenneth, 1974. *The Laws of Prosperity*, Harrison House, Tulsa, Oklahoma

Crim, K., 1976. *Interpreter's Dictionary of the Bible, Supplementary Volume*, Abingdon, Nashville, Tennessee

Cross, F. M., 1973. *Canaanite Myth and Hebrew Epic*, The President and Fellows of Harvard College, Cambridge, Massachusetts

Dahood, Mitchell, 1968. *The Anchor Bible: Psalms II: 51-100*, Doubleday & Company, Inc., Garden City, New York

Dahood, Mitchell, 1970. *The Anchor Bible: Psalms III: 101-150*, Doubleday & Company, Inc., Garden City, New York

Damazio, Frank and Brott, Rich, 2005. *Biblical Principles for Releasing Financial Provision! Obtaining the Favor of God in your Personal &*

Business World: Seven Keys to Open Heavens, City Publishing, City Bible Church, Portland, Oregon

Damazio, Frank, 1992. "The No-Sacrifice Tithe," City Publishing, City Bible Church, Portland, Oregon, cassette tape #122-24-052

Damazio, Frank, 1997. "Giving a Faith Harvest Offering," City Christian Publishing, City Bible Church, Portland, Oregon, cassette tape #127-09-111

Damazio, Frank, 2002. *Partnership: A Class for those Seeking to Become a Participating Member*, City Bible Publishing, City Bible Church, Portland, Oregon

Damazio, Frank, 2003. *Empowering the Giving of Your Church*, City Bible Publishing, City Bible Church, Portland, Oregon

Damazio, Frank, 2005. *52 Offering Prayers & Scriptures*, City Bible Publishing, City Bible Church, Portland, Oregon

Dandamayev, M. A., 1979. "State and Temple in Babylonia in the First Millennium, B.C.," in *State and Temple Economy in the Ancient Near East*, Editor, Edward Lipinski, Department of Oriental Studies, University of Leuven, Leuven, Belgium, Volume 2

Davidson, Benjamin, 1993. *Analytical Hebrew and Chaldee Lexicon*, Zondervan, Grand Rapids, Michigan

Davies, W. D. and Allison, D. C., 1988. *International Critical Commentary: Matthew 1-7*, T & T Clark, Ltd., London, England; New York, New York

Davies, W. D., 1952. "Torah in the Messianic Age and/or the Age to Come," *Journal of Biblical Literature, Monograph Series*, Volume VII, Society of Biblical Literature

Davies, W. D., 1974. *The Gospel and the Land: Early Christianity and Jewish Territorial Doctrine*, University of California Press, Berkeley, California

de Vaux, Roland, 1965, Volume 1. *Ancient Israel: Social Institutions*, McGraw-Hill Book Company, New York, New York

de Vaux, Roland, 1965, Volume 2. *Ancient Israel: Religious Institutions*, McGraw-Hill Book Company, New York, New York

DeSilva, Stephen K., 2010. *Money and the Prosperous Soul: Tipping the Scales of Favor and Blessing*, Chosen Books, Grand Rapids, Michigan

Dillenberger, John, 1961. Editor, "The Freedom of a Christian," an Open Letter to Pope Leo X in *Martin Luther: Selections from his Writings*, Anchor Books, Doubleday & Co., Inc., Garden City, New York

Douglas, J. D., 1962. Editor, *The New Bible Dictionary*, Eerdmans, Grand Rapids, Michigan

Douglas, J. D., 1974. Editor, *New International Dictionary of the Christian Church*, Revised Edition, Zondervan, Grand Rapids, Michigan

Douglas, Mary, 1966. *Purity and Danger: An Analysis of Concepts of Pollution and Taboo*, Frederick A. Praeger Publishers, New York, New York

Dunn, James, D. G., 1977. *Unity and Diversity in the New Testament: An Inquiry into the Character of Earliest Christianity*, Westminster Press, Philadelphia, Pennsylvania

Duplantis, Jesse, 1997. *God is not Enough, He's Too Much!* Harrison House, Tulsa, Oklahoma

Durant, Will and Ariel, 1954. *The Story of Civilization* series, Simon and Schuster, New York, New York

Durham, John I., 1987. *Word Biblical Commentary: Exodus*, Word Books, Waco, Texas

Elwell, Walter A., 1984. *The Evangelical Dictionary of Theology*, Baker Book House, Grand Rapids, Michigan

Eskridge, Larry and Noll, Mark A., 2000. Editors, *More Money, More Ministry: Money and Evangelicals in Recent North American History*, Eerdmans, Grand Rapids, Michigan

Fischer, David H., 1970. *Historians' Fallacies: Toward a Logic of Historical Thought*, Harper & Row, New York, New York

Fitzmyer, Joseph A., 1981. *The Anchor Bible: The Gospel According to Luke (I-IX)*, Doubleday, New York, New York

Fitzmyer, Joseph A., 1985. *The Anchor Bible: The Gospel According to Luke (X-XXIV)*, Doubleday, New York, New York

Follett Publishing Company, 1960. *Interlinear Literal Translation of the Greek New Testament*, Chicago, Illinois

Fox, George, 1683. "Tythes, Offerings, and First-fruits Commanded by the Law in the Old Testament Is Not Gospel Neither before the Law nor After..." Imprint: London, United Kingdom; Printed for Benjamin Clark in George-Yard in Lombard-Street, microfilm call number: PR1127.E21384:32, Western Washington University, Bellingham, Washington

Fox, George, 1904. Editor, R. M. Jones, *The Autobiography of George Fox*, Christian Classics Ethereal Library, www.ccel.org

Foxe, John, 1995. *Foxe's Book of Martyrs: An Edition for the People*, prepared by W. Grinton Berry, Baker Book House, Grand Rapids, Michigan (18th printing)

Frankfort, Henri, Frankfort, H. A., Wilson, J. A. and Jacobsen, T., 1968. *Before Philosophy: The Intellectual Adventure of Ancient Man*, Penguin Books, Baltimore, Maryland

Freedman, D. N., 1992. General Editor, *Anchor Bible Dictionary*, Doubleday, New York, New York

Gaventa, B. R. and Peterson, D., 2010. Editors, *New Interpreter's Bible: One-Volume Commentary*, Abingdon, Nashville, Tennessee

Geldenhuys, Norval, 1951. *Commentary on the Gospel of Luke*, Eerdmans, Grand Rapids, Michigan

Gordon, Cyrus H. and Rendsburg, Gary A., 1997. *The Bible and the Ancient Near East*, W. W. Norton & Company, Inc., New York, New York

Gospel Publishing House, 2005. *Perspectives: Managing God's Resources, Principles of Christian Stewardship*, Assemblies of God Office of Public Relations, Springfield, Missouri

Grant, F. C., 1926. *The Economic Background of the Gospels*, Oxford University Press, London, United Kingdom

Gray, George Buchanan, 1925. *Sacrifice in the Old Testament*, Clarendon Press, Oxford, England

Gruenwald, Ithamar, 2003. *Rituals and Ritual Theory in Ancient Israel*, Brill Reference Library of Judaism, Editor, J. Neusner, Volume 10, Leiden, South Holland

Gruyter GmbH, Walter de, 2014. Publisher, The Jerusalem Talmud (Talmud Yerushalmi), Second Order: Mo'ed, Tractates Seqalim, Sukkah, Ros Hashanah and Yom Tov (Besah), Berlin/Boston, 2014

Guggenheimer, Heinrich W., 2003. Editor, The Jerusalem Talmud (Talmud Yerushalmi), First Order: Zeraim Tractates Ma'aser Seni, Hallah, Orlah, and Bikkurim, Walter de Gruyter GmbH & Co. KG, D-10785, Berlin, Germany, 2003

Gundry, Robert H, 1994. *Matthew: A Commentary on his Handbook for a Mixed Church Under Persecution*, Second Edition, Eerdmans, Grand Rapids, Michigan

Gundry, Robert H., 1993. *Mark: A Commentary on His Apology for the Cross*, Eerdmans, Grand Rapids, Michigan

Guthrie, D. and Motyer J.A., 1970. *The New Bible Commentary*, Third Edition, Guideposts Edition, Carmel, New York with Eerdmans, Grand Rapids, Michigan

Hagee, John, 2005. "Seven Secrets of Financial Freedom," John Hagee Ministries, San Antonio, Texas, 05/16/2005 (3 cassettes)

Hagee, John, 2006. *John Hagee Today*, Trinity Broadcasting Network, 12/20/2006

Hagin, Kenneth E., 1995. *Biblical Keys to Financial Prosperity*, Rhema Bible Church, Tulsa, Oklahoma

Hammond and Scullard, 1970. Oxford *Classical Dictionary*, Second Edition, Oxford University Press, Oxford, United Kingdom

Harrelson, W., 2005. "Tithing," *Encyclopedia of Religion*, Second Edition, Editor, L. Jones, Macmillan, Thomson-Gale, New York, New York

Harris, R. Laird, 1950. *Introductory Hebrew Grammar*, Eerdmans, Grand Rapids, Michigan

Harris, R., Archer, G. and Waltke, B., 1980. Editors, *Theological Wordbook of the Old Testament*, Moody Press, Chicago, Illinois

Hastings, James, 1913. Editor, *Encyclopedia of Religion and Ethics*, T & T Clark, Edinburgh, Scotland and Charles Scribner's Sons, New York, New York

Hay, Louise, L., 1991. *The Power is Within You*, Hay House, Inc., Carlsbad, California

Haygood, Edward L., 1979. *Why the Tithe?* Harrison House, Tulsa, Oklahoma

Heidel, William A., 1929. *The Day of Yahweh: A Study of Sacred Days and Ritual Forms in the Ancient Near East*, The Century Company, New York

Hemingway, Colette and Hemingway, Seán, 2000. "Greek Gods and Religious Practices," *Heilbrunn Timeline of Art History*. New York: The Metropolitan Museum of Art, metmuseum.org

Herman, Menahem, 1991. *Tithe as Gift: The Institution in the Pentateuch and in Light of Mauss's Prestation Theory*, Mellen Research University Press, San Francisco, California

Hinn, Benny, 1997. *The Biblical Road to Blessing*, Thomas Nelson, Nashville, Tennessee

Holland, Richard (no copyright date). *Tithing: An Essential Part of a Christian's Walk*, Immanuel Press, Canterbury, Victoria, Australia

Hood, Kregg, 1996. *Take God at His Word*, Sweet Publishing, Fort Worth, Texas

Intellectual Reserve, Inc., 2000. *Scriptures of The Church of Jesus Christ of Latter-day Saints*; scriptures.lds.org.

Jakes, T. D., 1997. *Tithing is a Matter of Love not Law*, Albury Publishing, Tulsa, Oklahoma

Johnson, Bill, globallegacy.com; ibethel.org

Karesh, Sara E. and Hurvitz, Mitchell M., 2008. *Encyclopedia of Judaism*, Checkmark Books, Infobase Publishing, New York, New York

Kendall, R. T., 1982. *Tithing*, Zondervan, Grand Rapids, Michigan

Kidd, D. A., 1962. *Collins Latin Gem Dictionary*, Collins, London, United Kingdom; Glasgow, Scotland

King, Philip J. and Stager, Lawrence E., 2001. *Life in Biblical Israel*, Westminster John Knox Press, Louisville, Kentucky

Kittel, G. and Friedrich, G., 1985. Editors, *Theological Dictionary of the New Testament, Abridged in One Volume* by G. W. Bromiley, Eerdmans, Grand Rapids, Michigan

Kittel, G., 1964. Editor, *Theological Dictionary of the New Testament*, Eerdmans, Grand Rapids, Michigan

Klein, Ernest, 1987. *A Comprehensive Etymological Dictionary of the Hebrew Language for Readers of English*, Carta Jerusalem, The Beatrice & Arthur Minden Foundation & The University of Haifa, Haifa, Israel

Knudtzon, J. A., Weber, O. and Ebeling, E., 1970. *Die El-Amarna Tafeln*, 2 vols., VAB 2, Leipzig, 1915 and A. F. Rainey, *El-Amarna Tablets 359–379: Supplement to J. A. Knudtzon, Die El-Amarna Tafeln*, 2d rev. ed., AOAT 8, Kevelaer and Neukirchen-Vluyn

Koehler, Ludwig; Baumgartner, Walter and Richardson, M.E.J., 1994. *The Hebrew & Aramaic Lexicon of the Old Testament*, E. J. Brill, Leiden, The Netherlands

Koester, Craig R., 2001. *Hebrews: A New Translation with Introduction and Commentary: The Anchor Yale Bible*, Yale University Press, New Haven and London

Kohlenberger, John R., III, 1987. *The Interlinear NIV Hebrew-English Old Testament*, Zondervan, Grand Rapids, Michigan

Kraybill, Donald, 1990. *The Puzzles of Amish Life*, Good Book Publishing, Intercourse, Pennsylvania

Kuehner, Fred C., 1974. "Emphases in Malachi and Modern Thought," *The Law and the Prophets:Old Testament Studies Prepared in Honor of Oswald Thompson Allis*, Editor, John Skilton, Presbyterian and Reformed Publishing, Nutley, New Jersey, 482-493

Lane, William L., 1991. *Word Biblical Commentary: Hebrews 9-13*, Word Books, Dallas, Texas

Lansdell, Henry, 1963. *The Tithe in Scripture*, Baker Book House, Grand Rapids, Michigan

Laymon, C. M., 1971. Editor, *Interpreter's One-Volume Commentary of the Bible*, Abingdon Press, Nashville, Tennessee

LeBlanc, Douglas, 2010. *The Ancient Practices Series: Tithing: Test Me in This*, Thomas Nelson, Nashville, Tennessee

Lindsay, Gordon, 1959. *God's Master Key to Success and Prosperity*, The Voice of Healing, Dallas, Texas

Lipinski, Edward, 1979. Editor, *State and Temple Economy in the Ancient Near East*, Department of Oriental Studies, University of Leuven, Leuven, Belgium

Lubac, Henri de, 1998. *Medieval Exegesis: The Four Senses of Scripture*, Eerdmans, Grand Rapids, Michigan and T & T Clark, Ltd., Edinburgh, Scotland

Luz, Ulrich, 1989. *Matthew 1-7: A Continental Commentary*, Translator, Wilhelm C. Linss, Fortress Press, Minneapolis, Minnesota

Malina, Bruce and Rohrbaugh, Richard L., 1992. *Social Science Commentary on the Synoptic Gospels*, Fortress Press, Minneapolis, Minnesota

Manson, T. W., 1948. *The Teaching of Jesus*, Cambridge University Press, Cambridge, England

Manson, T. W., 1957. *The Sayings of Jesus*, Eerdmans, Grand Rapids, Michigan

Martin, Ralph P., 1974. *Worship in the Early Church*, Eerdmans, Grand Rapids, Michigan

Matthews, Victor H., and Benjamin, Don C., 1993. *Social World of Ancient Israel 1250-587 BCE*, Hendrickson Publishers, Peabody, Massachusetts

May, H. G., 1962. Editor, *The Oxford Bible Atlas*, Second Edition, Oxford University Press, London, United Kingdom

McComiskey, T. E., 1974. "The Religion of the Patriarchs: An Analysis of The God of the Fathers by Albrecht Alt," *The Law and the Prophets: Old Testament Studies Prepared in Honor of Oswald Thompson Allis*, Editor, John Skilton, Presbyterian and Reformed Publishing, Nutley, New Jersey, 195-206

McConkie, Bruce R., 1966. *Mormon Doctrine*, Second Edition, Bookcraft, Salt Lake City, Utah

Melton, J. Gordon, 1978. Editor, *The Encyclopedia of American Religions*, McGrath Publishing Co., Wilmington, North Carolina

Mendenhall, George E., 2001. *Ancient Israel's Faith and History: An Introduction to the Bible in Context*, Westminster John Knox Press, Louisville, Kentucky

Metzger, B. M. and Coogan, Michael D., 1993. Editors, *Oxford Companion to the Bible*, Oxford University Press, New York, New York

Meyer, L. E., 2013. *As You Tithe So You Prosper: A Series of Four Lessons in Tithing*, Literary Licensing, LLC (e-book) and Unity School of Christianity, Kansas City, Missouri, 1937 (soft cover)

Mickelsen, A. Berkeley, 1963. *Interpreting the Bible*, Eerdmans, Grand Rapids, Michigan

Milgrom, Jacob, 1976. *Cult and Conscience: The Asham and the Priestly Doctrine of Repentance*, E. J. Brill, Leiden, Netherlands

Milgrom, Jacob, 2000. *The Anchor Bible: Leviticus 17-22*, Doubleday, New York, New York

Milgrom, Jacob, 2001. *The Anchor Bible: Leviticus 23-27*, Doubleday, New York, New York

Millard, A. R. and Wiseman, D. J., 1983. Editors, *Essays on the Patriarchal Narratives*, Second Edition, Intervarsity, Leicester, England

Milton, Terry S., 1975. *Biblical Hermeneutics*, Second Edition, Zondervan, Grand Rapids, Michigan

Mitchell, H. G., Smith, J. M. P. and Brewer, J. A., 1912. *The International Critical Commentary on the Holy Scriptures of the Old and New Testaments: Haggai, Zechariah, Malachi and Jonah*, T & T Clark, Edinburgh, Scotland

Moffatt, James, 1924. *The International Critical Commentary: Epistle to the Hebrews*, T & T Clark, Edinburgh, Scotland

Montgomery, James A., 1934. *Arabia and the Bible*, University of Pennsylvania Press, Philadelphia, Pennsylvania

Morris, Robert, 2004. *The Blessed Life: The Simple Secret of Achieving Guaranteed Financial Results*, Regal Books, Ventura, California

Murdoch, Brian, 2003. *The Medieval Popular Bible: Expansions of Genesis in the Middle Ages*, D. S. Brewer, Cambridge, United Kingdom

Murdock, Mike, 1997. *31 Reasons People Do Not Receive Their Financial Harvest*, The Wisdom Center, Denton, Texas

Murdock, Mike, 1997a. *Secrets of the Journey: Leadership Secrets for Excellence & Increase*, Wisdom International, Dallas, Texas

Myers, Jacob M., 1965. *The Anchor Bible: 2 Chronicles*, Doubleday, Garden City, New York

Neusner, Jacob, 2002. *The Tosefta Translated from the Hebrew with a New Introduction*, Hendrickson Publishers, Peabody, Massachusetts

Neyrey, Jerome H., 1991. Editor, *The Social World of Luke-Acts: Models for Interpretation*, Hendrickson, Peabody, Massachusetts

North, Gary, 1987. *The Dominion Covenant: Genesis: An Economic Commentary on the Bible*, Volume 1, Institute for Christian Economics, Tyler, Texas

North, Gary, 1994. *Tithing and the Church*, Institute for Christian Economics, Tyler, Texas

Noth, Martin, 1962. *Exodus: A Commentary*, The Westminster Press, Philadelphia, Pennsylvania

Oakman, Douglas E., 1986. *Jesus and the Economic Questions of his Day: Studies in the Bible and Early Christianity*, Volume 8, The Edwin Mellen Press, Lewiston-Queenston, Ontario, Canada

Oakman, Douglas E., 2002. "Money in the Moral Universe of the New Testament," *The Social Setting of Jesus and the Gospels*, Editors, W. Stegemann, B. J. Malina and B. Theissen, Fortress Press, Minneapolis, Minnesota

Oaks, D. H., 1994. "Tithing," *Ensign*, May, www.lds.org/portal/site/LDSOrg/menuitem

Ortberg, J., Pederson, L. and Poling, J., 2000. *Giving: Unlocking the Heart of Good Stewardship*, Willow Creek Association, Zondervan, Grand Rapids, Michigan

Osborne, Grant R., 1991. *The Hermeneutical Spiral: A Comprehensive Introduction to Biblical Interpretation*, InterVarsity Press, Downers Grove, Illinois

Otto, Rudolf, 1946. *The Idea of the Holy*, Oxford University Press, Oxford, United Kingdom

Oxford University Press, 1971. *Compact Edition of the Oxford English Dictionary*, Glasgow, Scotland

Pagolu, Augustine, 1998. *The Religion of the Patriarchs*, Sheffield Academic Press, Ltd., Sheffield, England

Parsley, Rod, 1992. *Repairers of the Breach*, Results Publishing, World Harvest Church, Columbus, Ohio

Peake, A. S. and Grieve, A. J., 1920. *Peake's Commentary on the Bible*, T.C. & E.C. Jack, Ltd., London, United Kingdom

Pearson, Anthony, 1730. *The Great Case of Tithes Truly Stated, Clearly Opened, and Fully Resolved*, published by Samuel Fuller, *The Globe*, Dublin, Ireland, (microfilm, Goldsmiths- Kress Library of Economic Literature, University of Rochester, Rochester, New York)

Pick, Clive, 1998. *Open Heaven: The Transformation*, Crossroads Christian Communications, Inc., Visualeyes Communications, Burlington, Ontario, Canada

Pick, Clive, 2005. *Living Under an Open Heaven: Lessons on Tithes and Offerings*, East Hill Church, Pathways Resource Center, Gresham, Oregon, May 18-20 (CD set)

Pink, A. W. (no publication date provided). *Tithing*, Reiner Publications, Swengel, Pennsylvania

Ponder, Catherine, 1976. *The Millionaires of Genesis: Their Prosperity Secrets for You!* Devorss & Company, Camarillo, California

Powell, Marvin A., 1987. Editor, *Labor in the Ancient Near East*, American Oriental Society, New Haven, Connecticut

Pritchard, James B., 1969. Editor, *Ancient Near Eastern Texts Relating to the Old Testament* (Third Edition with Supplement), Princeton University Press, Princeton, New Jersey

Ramm, Bernard, 1970. *Protestant Biblical Interpretation: A Textbook of Hermeneutics*, Baker Book House, Grand Rapids, Michigan

Richardson, Alan, 1947. *Christian Apologetics*, Harper & Brothers, New York, New York

Richardson, Alan, 1962. Editor, *A Theological Word Book of the Bible*, Macmillan, London, United Kingdom

Riché, Pierre and Lobrochon, Guy, 1984. *Le Moyen Age et la Bible*, Éditions Beauchesne, Paris, France

Ritchie, Bill, http://www.crossroadschurch.net/

Roberts, Oral, 1975. *Seed-Faith Commentary on the Holy Bible*, Pinoak Publications, Tulsa, Oklahoma

Robertson, A.T., 1932. *Word Pictures in the New Testament*, Broadman Press, Nashville, Tennessee

Roth, Andrew G., 2008. *Aramaic English New Testament*, Fourth Edition, Mari, Netzari Press, LLC, Sedro Woolley, Washington

Rushdoony, Rousas J. and Powell, Edward A., 1979. *Tithing and Dominion*, Ross House Books, Vallecito, California

Sapp, Roger, (no publication date provided). *Take the Tithing Test: How Much Do You Really Know About Tithing?* All Nations Publications, Springtown, Texas

Sarna, Nahum M.,1989. *The JPS Torah Commentary: Genesis*, Jewish Publication Society, Philadelphia, Pennsylvania

Sasson, J. M., 1995. Editor, *Civilizations of the Ancient Near East*, Charles Scribner's Sons and Simon and Schuster, New York, New York

Schaff, Philip, (no publication date provided). *History of the Christian Church*, Associated Publishers and Authors, Wilmington, Delaware

Scheidler, Bill with Iverson, Dick and Conner, Kevin J., 1976. *Principles of Church Life*, City Bible Publishing, Portland, Oregon

Scheidler, Bill, 2002. *The Local Church Today*, City Bible Publishing, Portland, Oregon

Scheidler, Bill, 2005. *Growing Strong Churches: 19 Keys to a Healthy, Growing Church*, City Bible Publishing, Portland, Oregon

Schiffman, Lawrence H., 2008. *The Courtyards of the House of the Lord: Studies on the Temple Scroll*, Editor, F. G. Martinez, Koninklijke Brill, NV, Leiden, The Netherlands

Schüssler, Fiorenza, E., 1988. "The Ethics of Interpretation: De-Centering Biblical Scholarship," *Journal of Biblical Literature*, 107:3-17

Seymore, Bob, 1996. "Principles of First Fruits," City Christian Publishing, City Bible Church, Portland, Oregon, cassette tape #126-10-112

Siculus, Diodorus, *The Library of History*

Siebert, Phyllis and Lachman, Ann, 2005. *Education in Paradise: Learning for Profitable Employment Among the Old Order Amish of Lancaster County, Pennsylvania, USA*; Dissertation presented to Drs. Jochen Kaltschmid and Ulrich Baumann, Heidelberg, Germany

Silver, Morris, 1992. *Taking Ancient Mythology Economically*, E. J. Brill, New York, New York, 1992

Silver, Morris, 1995. *Economic Structures of Antiquity; Contributions in Economics and Economic History*, Number 159; Series Advisor, George Schwab; Greenwood Press, Westport, Connecticut and London, United Kingdom

Sinclair, Upton, 1994. *I, Candidate for Governor: And How I Got Licked* (1935), University of California Press reprint

Skilton, John, 1974. Editor, *The Law and the Prophets: Old Testament Studies Prepared in Honor of Oswald Thompson Allis*, Presbyterian and Reformed Publishing, Nutley, New Jersey

Skolnik, F. and Berenbaum, M., 2008. Editors, *Encyclopedia Judaica*, Second Edition, Macmillan Library Reference, New York, New York

Smith, J. Z., 1995. Editor, *HarperCollins Dictionary of Religion*, HarperSanFrancisco (HarperOne), San Francisco, California

Smith, W. Robertson, 1894. *The Religion of the Semites*, Adam and Charles Black, London, United Kingdom

Smith, Wendell, 2005. *Prosperity with a Purpose*, The City Church, Kirkland, Washington

Snell, Jay, 1995. *How to Claim the Abrahamic Covenant*, Trinity Broadcasting Network Edition of *How to Amass Abrahamic Wealth for Yourself and Your Family*, Jay Snell Evangelistic Association (Livingston, Texas), Santa Ana, California

Snell, Jay, 1995a. *How to Amass Abrahamic Wealth for Yourself and Your Family*, Jay Snell Evangelistic Association, Livingston, Texas, 1995 (www.jaysnell.org.)

Stansell, Gary, "Gifts, Tributes, Offerings," 2002. in *The Social Setting of Jesus and the Gospels*, Editors, W. Stegemann, B. Malina, G. Theissen, 2002., Fortress Press, Minneapolis, Minnesota

Stegemann, E. W. and Stegemann, W., 1995. *The Jesus Movement: A Social History of its First Century*, Translator, O. C. Dean, Jr., Fortress Press, Minneapolis, Minnesota

Stegemann, W., Malina, B. J. and Theissen, G., 2002. Editors, *The Social Setting of Jesus and the Gospels*, Fortress Press, Minneapolis, Minnesota

Strack, Hermann L. and Billerbeck, Paul, 1922. *Kommentar zum Neuen Testament aus Talmud und Midrasch*, C. H. Beck'sche Verlagsbuchhandlung, Oskar Beck, Munchen, Germany

Strong, Mark (no publication date provided). *The Lamp Series Step Two: Membership: Discovering Christian Community Responsibilities and Covenant*, Life Change Christian Center, Portland, Oregon

Stuart, Douglas K., 2009. *Old Testament Exegesis: A Handbook for Students and Pastors*, Westminster John Knox Press, Louisville, Kentucky

Swainston, Howard D., 1992. "Tithing," *Encyclopedia of Mormonism*, Editor, D. H. Ludlow, Macmillan, New York, New York

Sykes, J. B., 1982. Editor, *The Concise Oxford Dictionary of Current English*, 7th edition, The Clarendon Press, Oxford, United Kingdom, 1982, www.wikipedia.org: Ipse Dixit/bare assertion fallacy

Tarragon, Jean-Michel de, "Witchcraft, Magic, and Divination in Canaan and Ancient Israel," 1995., *Civilizations of the Ancient Near East*, Editor, J. M. Sasson, Charles Scribner's Sons and Simon and Schuster Macmillan, New York, New York, Volume 3

Tenney, M. C., 1975. Editor, *Zondervan Pictorial Encyclopedia of the Bible*, Zondervan, Grand Rapids, Michigan

Tenney, M.C., 2009. Editor, *Zondervan Encyclopedia of the Bible* (revised), Zondervan, Grand Rapids, Michigan

Thiessen, Henry C., 1949. *Introductory Lectures in Systematic Theology*, Eerdmans, Grand Rapids, Michigan

Thomas, Robert L., 1998. Editor, *New American Standard Exhaustive Concordance of the Bible*, Lockman Foundation Publications, Inc., La Habra, California

Thompson, Leroy, 1999. *Money Cometh! to the Body of Christ*, Harrison House, Tulsa, Oklahoma

Thompson, Leroy, 2003. *You're Not Broke You Have a Seed*, Ever Increasing Word Ministries, Darrow, Louisiana

Thrall, Margaret E., 1994. *International Critical Commentary: The Second Epistle to the Corinthians*, Volume 1, Editors, J.A. Emerton, C.E.B. Cranfield, G.N. Stanton, T & T Clark, Edinburgh, Scotland

Tigay, Jeffrey, H., 2007. "The Priestly Reminder Stones and Ancient Near Eastern Votive Practices," *Shay: Studies in the Bible, Its Exegesis and Language Presented to Sara Japhet*, Editors, M. Bar Asher, D. Rom-Shiloni, E. Tov and N. Wazana, Mosad Bialik, Jerusalem

Tomaschoff, Avner, 1994. Editor. The Mishnah, volume 1, issue 3, part 2, Tractate Zevahim, Pinhas Kehati, Chapter 10, Mishnah 3, Maor Wallach Press, Feldheim.com Publishers, 1994

Toorn, K. van der, 1989. "Female Prostitution in Payment of Vows in Ancient Israel," *Journal of Biblical Literature*, 108: 193-205

VanGemeren, W., 1996. Editor, *New International Dictionary of Old Testament Theology and Exegesis*, Zondervan, Grand Rapids, Michigan

Vaughan, Curtis, 1967. Editor, *New Testament from 26 Translations*, Zondervan, Grand Rapids, Michigan

Verhoef, Peter A., 1974. "Tithing: A Hermeneutical Consideration," *The Law and the Prophets: Old Testament Studies Prepared in Honor of Oswald Thompson Allis*, Editor, John Skilton, Presbyterian and Reformed Publishing, Nutley, New Jersey, 115-127

Verhoef, Peter A., 1987. *The Books of Haggai and Malachi: The New International Commentary on the Old Testament*, Eerdmans Publishing Co., Grand Rapids, Michigan

Viola, Frank and Barna, George, 2008. *Pagan Christianity? Exploring the Roots of our Church Practices*, Barna Books, imprint of Tyndale House Publishers, Inc., Carol Stream, Illinois

Vischer, L., 1966. *Tithing in the Early Church*, Translator, R. C. Shulz, Fortress Press, Philadelphia, Pennsylvania

Walker, Williston, 1970. *A History of the Christian Church*, Third Edition, Charles Scribner's Sons, New York, New York

Warren, Rick; www.saddleback.com/giving/opportunities/tithe/

Waterworth, J., 1848. Editor, *Council of Trent: The Canons and Decrees of the Sacred and Oecumenical Council of Trent*, Dolman Publishers, London, England; www.history.hanover.edu/texts/trent/trentall.html

Westermann, Claus, 1995. *Genesis 12-36: A Continental Commentary*, Translator, John J. Scullion, Fortress Press, Minneapolis, Minnesota

Weston, Charles, G., 1990. *The Seven Covenants*, Weston Bible Ministries, Apostolic Missions Foundation, Jefferson, Oregon, 1990

Whigham, Steve, 2004. *Throw Open the Floodgates: One Man's Surprising Discovery of God's Original Intent for the Tithe*, iUniverse, Inc., Lincoln, Nebraska

White, Jerry, 1983. *The Church & The Parachurch: An Uneasy Marriage*, Multnomah Press, Portland, Oregon

Whitehead, Bert, 2004. *Spirit of the Tithe: How God's Five Purposes for the Tithe Will Transform Your Life, Your Church and Your Community*, Infinity Publishing, Haverford, Pennsylvania

Wiener, Philip P., 1968. Editor, *Dictionary of the History of Ideas*, Charles Scribner's Sons, New York, New York

Wigram, George V. and Winter, Ralph D., 1978. *Word Study Concordance*, Tyndale House Publishers, Inc., Wheaton, Illinois

Wilson, J. Christy, Jr., 1989. *Today's Tentmakers: Self-support an Alternative Model for Worldwide Witness*, Tyndale House, Wheaton, Illinois

Wilson, W., 1900. *Wilson's Old Testament Word Studies*, Macdonald Publishing Co., McLean, Virginia

Wise, M., Abegg, M. and Cook, E., 1996. *The Dead Sea Scrolls: A New Translation*, Harper Collins, San Francisco, California

Young, Ray, 2005., Pick, Clive, 2005. *Living Under an Open Heaven: Lessons on Tithes and Offerings*, East Hill Church Pathways Resource Center, Gresham, Oregon, May 18-20 (CD set)

Young, Robert, 1964. *Young's Analytical Concordance*, Eerdmans, Grand Rapids, Michigan

Young, Robert, 2013. *Young's Literal Translation of the Holy Bible*, Delmarva Publications, Inc., Harrington, Delaware

Zodhiates, Spiros, 1992. *The Complete Word Study Dictionary New Testament*, AMG Publishers, Chattanooga, Tennessee

Zondervan, 1973. *Analytical Greek Lexicon*, Grand Rapids, Michigan

ANNOTATED LIST OF CITED SOURCES

(alphabetical order by last name)

YOHANAN AHARONI: Israeli Archeologist; Historical Geographer; Associate Professor of Archaeology, The Hebrew University; Chairman, Department of Near East Studies and The Institute of Archaeology, Tel-Aviv University, Tel Aviv, Israel; Co-author: *The Macmillan Bible Atlas* (Macmillan, 1968); *The Land of the Bible: A Historical Geography* (Westminster Press, 1979); *Mount Carmel as Border* (1969); *Arad Inscriptions* (Israel Exploration Society, 1981); *Investigations at Lachish* (Gateway Publishers, 1975) (d. 1976)

OSWALD T. ALLIS: American Presbyterian Theologian; Author: *Prophecy and the Church* (Wipf & Stock reprint, 2001); *The Five Books of Moses* (Wipf & Stock reprint, 2001); *God Spake by Moses* (Presbyterian and Reformed, 1951); *The Unity of Isaiah* (Wipf & Stock reprint, 2000); (d. 1973)

BERNHARD W. ANDERSON: Pastor; Archaeologist; Professor Emeritus of Old Testament Theology, Princeton Theological Seminary; Adjunct Professor of Old Testament Theology, Boston University School of Theology (during retirement); Translator: *A History of Pentateuchal Traditions* by Martin Noth (Pearson Education, Ltd., 1972); President, The Society of Biblical Literature (1980); President, The American Theological Society (1985); Recipient of the Julian Morgenstern Award (Society of Biblical Literature); Author: *Understanding the Old Testament* (Prentice Hall, 2006); *Out of the Depths: The Psalms Speak for Us Today* (Westminster John Knox Press, 2000); *Creation in the Old Testament* (Fortress Press, 1984); *From Creation to New Creation* (Wipf & Stock,

2005); *Contours of Old Testament Theology* (Fortress Press, 1999); *The Unfolding Drama of the Bible* (Fortress Press, 1988); (d. 2007)

GERVAIS ANGEL: Dean of Studies, Trinity College; Author: *A Positive Approach to the Gospels* (Theological Students Fellowship); *Delusion or Dynamite? Reflections on a Quarter-Century of Charismatic Renewal* (Marc, 1989)

MICHAEL C. ASTOUR: Professor of Yiddish and Russian Literature (Brandeis University) and Classical cultures and the Ancient Near East (Southern Illinois University); Author: *Hellenosemitica* (Brill, 1967); *Hittite History and Absolute Chronology of the Bronze Age* (P. Astrom, 1989); *841 B.C.: The First Assyrian Invasion of Israel* (American Oriental Society, 1971); *Semitic Elements in the Kumarbi Myth* (University of Chicago, 1968); *An Outline of the History of Ebla, Part 1* (Eisenbrauns); See also: *Crossing Boundaries and Linking Horizons: Studies in Honor of Michael C. Astour*, edited, G. D. Young, etc. (CDL Press, 1997). (d. 2004)

HAROLD W. ATTRIDGE: Sterling Professor of Divinity, Yale Divinity School; Author: *Hermeneia Commentary: Hebrews* (Fortress Press, 1989); *Essays on John and Hebrews* (Baker, 2012); *Hermeneia Commentary: John* (forthcoming); Co-editor: *The HarperCollins Study Bible* (Society of Biblical Literature, 2006); Editor: *Nag Hammadi Codex I* (E.J. Brill, 1985); *The Religion and Science Debate: Why Does It Continue?* (Yale University, 2009); Co-author: *The Phoenician History* (Catholic Biblical Association of America, 1981)

DAVID E. AUNE: The Walter Professor of New Testament and Christian Origins, University of Notre Dame; Author: *Jesus, Gospel Tradition and Paul in the Context of Jewish and Greco-Roman Antiquity* (WUNT: 303, Mohr Siebeck); *The Cultic Setting of Realized Eschatology in Early Christianity* (Brill, 1972); *Jesus and the Synoptic Gospels* (Theological Students Fellowship, 1980); *Prophecy in Early Christianity and the Ancient Mediterranean World* (Eerdmans, 1983); *The New Testament in Its Literary Environment* (Westminster Press, 1987); *Word Biblical Commentary: Volume 1: Revelation 1-5; Volume 2: Revelation 6-19; Volume 3: Revelation 17-22* (Word Books, 1997, 1998, 1998)

OTTO JUSTICE BAAB: Theologian; Professor of Old Testament Interpretation, Garrett-Evangelical Theological Seminary; Author: *Prophetic Preaching: A New Approach* (Abingdon, 1958); *Theology of the Old Testament: The Faith Behind the Facts of Hebrew Life and Writings* (1949; Literary Licensing reprint, 2012) (d. 1958)

WARREN BAKER: Former Assistant Professor, Hebrew and Old Testament studies, Faith Theological Seminary; General Editor: *The Complete Word Study Old Testament* (AMG Publishers, 1994); Co-author: *The Complete Word Study Dictionary Old Testament* (AMG Publishers, 2003)

GEORGE BARNA: Founder, The Barna Group; Visiting teacher, Biola and Pepperdine universities; conference speaker; researcher; Author: *Revolution* (Tyndale, 2005); *The Frog in the Kettle* (Gospel Light Publications, 1990); *Growing True Disciples* (WaterBrook Press, 2001); *The Power of Vision* (Regal, 2003); *Marketing the Church* (NavPress, 1988)

JAMES BARR: Oriel Professor of Interpretation of Scripture, Oxford University; Philologist; Author: *The Semantics of Biblical Language* (Wipf & Stock, 2004); *Holy Scripture: Canon, Authority, Criticism* (Clarendon Press, 1983); *The Concept of Biblical Theology: An Old Testament Perspective* (Augsburg Fortress, 1999); *Fundamentalism* (SCM Press, 1981); *Escaping from Fundamentalism* (SCM Press, 1984) (d. 2006)

GEORGE AUGUSTIN BARROIS: Professor Emeritus, History and Theology of the Medieval Church, Princeton Theological Seminary; Author: *Road From Rome* (Agora Publishing, 1948); *The Face of Christ in the Old Testament* (St. Vladimir's Seminary Press, 1974); *Scripture Readings in Orthodox Worship* (St. Vladimir's Seminary Press, 1977); *Jesus Christ and the Temple* (St. Vladimir's Press, 1980); Translator: *The Fathers Speak* (St. Vladimir's Seminary Press, 1986); Contributor: *The Interpreter's Dictionary of the Bible* (Abingdon, 1962)

JOHN R. BARTLETT: Former Associate Professor of Biblical Studies, Trinity College; Principal of the Church of Ireland Theological College;

Author: *Jews in the Hellenistic World Volume 1, Part 1: Josephus, Aristeas, the Sibylline Oracles, Eupolemus* (University of Cambridge, 1985); *First Maccabees* (Bloomsbury, 1998); *Archaeology and Biblical Interpretation* (Taylor & Francis, 2002)

FRANCIS (FRANK) W. BEARE: Professor of New Testament Studies, Trinity College, Toronto (1946 – 1968); Author: *St. Paul and His Letters* (1962); *The Gospel According to Matthew* (1981); Contributor: "Sayings of the Risen Jesus in the Gospel Tradition...," *Christian History and Interpretation: Studies Presented to John Knox* (1967); "Ephesians" in *The Interpreter's Bible* (Abingdon, 1957); various articles in *The Interpreters' Dictionary of the Bible* (Abingdon, 1962). He served as President of the Society of Biblical Literature (1969) as well as the Canadian Society of Biblical Studies (1941-42), which has an annual book prize named after him. (d. 1985)

ASTRID BILLES BECK: Retired Program Associate, Studies in Religion, University of Michigan; Managing Editor, *The Anchor Bible Dictionary* (Doubleday, 1992); Co-editor, *Eerdmans Dictionary of the Bible* (Eerdmans, 2000); Production Manager, *The Leningrad Codex: A Facsimile Edition* (Eerdmans, 1998)

DON C. BENJAMIN: Associate Professor, Biblical and Ancient Near Eastern Studies, Department of Religious Studies, Arizona State University; Lecturer of Religious Studies, Rice University, Houston, Texas; Author: *The Old Testament Story* (Fortress, 2003); *Stones and Stories: An Introduction to Archaeology and the Bible* (Fortress, 2010); Co-author: *Old Testament Parallels: Laws and Stories from the Ancient Near East* (Paulist Press, 2006); *Social World of Ancient Israel 1250-587 BCE* (Hendrickson, 1993)

JOHN WILSON BETLYON: Lecturer in Jewish Studies, Religious Studies, Classics and Ancient Mediterranean Studies; Numismatic Archaeologist/Expert, The Pennsylvania State University; Authors, *The Pre-Alexandrine Coinage and Mints of Syria-Phoenicia* (Harvard University, 1978); *The Coinage and Mints of Phoenicia* (Scholar Press,

1982); Co-author: *The Roman Frontier in Central Jordan: Volume 2* (Dumbarton Oaks Research Library and Collection, 2006); *A New Chronology for the Pre-alexandrine Coinage of Sidon* (American Numismatic Society, 1976); Contributor: "Coinage," *The Anchor Bible Dictionary* (Doubleday, 1992); "Money," *HarperCollins Bible Dictionary* (Harper, 1996); "Money" and "Shekel," *Harpers Bible Dictionary* (Harper & Row, 1982)

JULIUS AUGUST BEWER: Professor of Old Testament History and Theology, Union Theological Seminary; Lecturer, Teachers College, Columbia University, New York, New York; Author: *The Bible and Its Story* (multiple volumes); *Harper's Annotated Bible: The Gospel of John* (Harper, 1956); *The Literature of the Old Testament in its Historical Development* (Columbia University Press, 1922); *The Book of Daniel in the King James Version* (Harper, 1955); *Harper's Annotated Bible: The Book of the Twelve Prophets* (Harper, 1954); *The Book of Ezekiel: Volume 2* (Harper, 1954); *The Book of Isaiah* (Harper, 1950); Co-author: *ICC: A Critical and Exegetical Commentary on Micah, Zephaniah, Nahum, Habakkuk, Obadiah and Joel* (Charles Scribner's Sons, 1911); *The Book of Jeremiah* (Harper, 1952); *ICC: A Critical and Exegetical Commentary on Haggai, Zechariah, Malachi and Jonah* (Charles Scribner's Sons, 1912) (d. 1953)

PAUL BILLERBECK: Lutheran Minister; Judaism Scholar; Co-author: *Commentary on the New Testament from the Talmud and Midrash* (4 volumes; C. H. Beck, 1922,1924,1926) (d. 1932)

PHYLLIS A. BIRD: Associate Professor of Old Testament Interpretation, Garrett-Evangelical Theological Seminary; Author: *The Bible as the Church's Book* (Westminster Press, 1982); *Feminism and the Bible: a Critical and Constructive Encounter* (Canadian Mennonite Bible College, 1994); *Missing Persons and Mistaken Identities: Women and Gender in Ancient Israel* (Augsburg Fortress, 1997)

EDWARD BLEIBERG: Curator of Egyptian, Classical, and Ancient Middle Eastern Art at the Brooklyn Museum; Former Professor of

Egyptian hieroglyphs and Director of the Institute of Egyptian Art and Archaeology, University of Memphis, Memphis, Tennessee; Author: *Soulful Creatures: Animal Mummies in Ancient Egypt* (G. Giles Ltd., 2013); *Ancient Egypt: 2615-332, BCE.* (Gale Research International, Ltd., 2002); *Jewish Life in Ancient Egypt: A Family Archive from the Nile Valley* (Brooklyn Museum of Art, 2002)

JOSEPH BLENKINSOPP: Old Testament Scholar, John A. O'Brien Professor Emeritus of Biblical Studies in the Department of Theology, University of Notre Dame; Author: *Anchor Bible: Isaiah 1-39* (Doubleday, 2000); *Anchor Bible: Isaiah 40-55* (Doubleday, 2002); *Anchor Bible: Isaiah 56-66* (Doubleday, 2003); *The Pentateuch: An Introduction to the First Five Books of the Bible* (Doubleday, 1992); *The History of Prophecy in Israel* (Westminster/John Knox, 1983); *Ezra-Nehemiah: A Commentary* (Westminster, 1988)

ELIZABETH BLOCH-SMITH: Professor of Biblical and Ancient Near Eastern Archaeology, St. Joseph University; Author: *Judahite Burial Practices and Beliefs about the Dead* (JSOT Press, 1992)

MYLES M. BOURKE: Pastor, Corpus Christi Roman Catholic Church, New York, New York; Adjunct Professor, Fordham University; Author: *The Book of Job* (Paulist Press, 1962); "Rudolf Bultmann's Demythologizing of the New Testament" (Catholic Theological Society of America); *A Study of the Metaphor of the Olive Tree in Romans 11* (Catholic University of America, 1947); *The Passion, Death and Resurrection of Christ* (Paulist Press, 1963) (d. 2004)

COLIN BROWN: Lecturer, Trinity College, Bristol; Editor and Contributor: *The New International Dictionary of New Testament Theology* (Zondervan, 1967); Author: *Karl Barth and the Christian Message* (Wipf and Stock, 1998); *Christianity and Western Thought Volume I* (InterVarsity, 1990); *Miracles and the Critical Mind* (Eerdmans, 1984); Co-author: *Exploring the Christian Faith* (Thomas Nelson, 1996)

HAROLD BRODSKY: Associate Professor Emeritus, Department of Geographical Sciences, University of Maryland; Editor: *Land and*

ANNOTATED LIST OF CITED SOURCES | 315

Community: Geography in Jewish Studies (Capital Decisions, Ltd., 1998); Author: Mapping Geographic Information (Kendall Hunt Publishing Co., 2008)

FREDERICK FYVIE BRUCE: Rylands Professor of Biblical Criticism and Exegesis, University of Manchester; Author: *Are the New Testament Documents Reliable?* (InterVarsity, 1943); *The Books and the Parchments* (Pickering and Inglis, 1950); *The Book of Acts* (Eerdmans, 1954); *New Testament History* (Oliphants, 1969); *Epistle to the Hebrews* (Eerdmans, 1990), *The Tyndale New Testament Commentaries: The Letter of Paul to the Romans* (InterVarsity, 1985); *The Gospel of John* (Eerdmans, 1994) (d. 1990)

WALTER BURKERT: German Classicist; International Historian of Greek Religion; Professor Emeritus of Classics, University of Zurich; Author: *Ancient Mystery Cults* (Harvard University Press, 1987); *Greek Religion: Archaic and Classical* (Wiley Publishers, 2013); *Creation of the Sacred: Tracks of Biology in Early Religions* (Harvard University Press, 1998); *Structure and History in Greek Mythology and Ritual* (University of California Press, 1979); *Homo Necans: the Anthropology of Ancient Greek Sacrificial Ritual and Myth* (University of California Press, 1983)

ANTONY F. CAMPBELL: Professor of Old Testament, Jesuit Theological College, United Faculty of Theology, Parkville, Melbourne, Victoria; Author: *A Study Companion to Old Testament Literature* (Liturgical Press, 1992); *God First Loved Us: The Challenge of Accepting Unconditional Love* (Paulist Press, 2000); Co-author: *Unfolding the Deuteronomistic History: Origins, Upgrades, Present Text* (Fortress, 2000); *Sources of the Pentateuch: Text, Introduction, Annotations* (Fortress, 1993)

D. A. CARSON: Research Professor of New Testament, Trinity Evangelical Divinity School; Author: *Exegetical Fallacies* (Baker Academic, 1996); *The Intolerance of Tolerance* (Eerdmans, 2012); *New Testament Commentary Survey* (Baker Academic, 2013); *How Long, O Lord? Reflections on Suffering and Evil* (Baker Academic, 2006); *The King James Version Debate: A Plea for Realism* (Baker, 1978); *Telling the Truth:*

Evangelizing Postmoderns (Zondervan, 2009); *Christ and Culture Revisited* (Eerdmans, 2008)

EUGENE E. CARPENTER: Professor of Hebrew, Old Testament and Biblical Theology; Scholar-in-residence, Bethel College; Editor: *Asbury Bible Commentary* (Zondervan, 1992); *A Biblical Itinerary...Essays in Honor of George W. Coats* (Bloomsbury, 1997); Co-author: *The Complete Word Study Dictionary Old Testament* (AMG Publishers, 2003); *Holman Treasury of Key Bible Words* (Broadman & Holman, 2000) (d. 2012)

TONY W. CARTLEDGE: Former Pastor; Editor: *Baptists Today*; Professor, Old Testament, Campbell University Divinity School; Author: *Sessions with Genesis: The Story Begins* (Smyth & Helwys Publishing, 2012); "Vows in the Hebrew Bible and the Ancient Near East" *(Journal for the Study of the Old Testament,* 1992); *1 & 2 Samuel* (Smyth & Helwys, 2001)

BREVARD S. CHILDS: Yale Sterling Professor of Old Testament, Yale Divinity School (1958-1999); Author: *Struggle To Understand Isaiah As Christian Scripture (2004); Biblical Theology: A Proposal (2002); The Old Testament Library: Isaiah* (2001) and *Exodus* (2004); *The New Testament as Canon* (1994); *Biblical Theology of the Old and New Testaments (1993); Old Testament Theology in a Canonical Context (1989); Biblical Theology of the Old and New Testaments (1993); Myth and Reality in the Old Testament (1983); Introduction to the Old Testament as Scripture (1979); Biblical Theology in Crisis (1970); Memory and Tradition in Israel (1962); Isaiah and the Assyrian Crisis (1965)* (d. 2007)

RICHARD J. CLIFFORD: Professor of Old Testament, Weston School of Theology; Author: *The Old Testament Library: Proverbs* (Westminster John Knox, 1999); *Fair Spoken and Persuading: An Interpretation of Second Isaiah* (Academic Renewal Press, 2002)

RAYMOND F. COLLINS: Professor-in-Ordinary of New Testament Studies, Catholic University of Leuven; Retired Professor of New Testament, Catholic University of America; Author: *Introduction to the*

New Testament (Galilee Trade, 1987); *Preaching the Epistles* (Paulist Press, 1995); *Sexual Ethics and The New Testament: Behavior and Belief* (Herder & Herder, 2000); *1 & 2 Timothy and Titus: A Commentary* (Westminster John Knox Press, 2002); *First Corinthians* (Liturgical Press, 2007); *Divorce in the New Testament* (Michael Glazier Books, 1992); *These Things Have Been Written: Studies on the Fourth Gospel* (Eerdmans, 1991)

MICHAEL DAVID COOGAN: Professor of Religious Studies, Stonehill College; Co-editor/Translator: *Stories from Ancient Canaan* (2012); Author: *The Old Testament: A Historical and Literary Introduction to the Hebrew Scriptures* (2011); *God and Sex: What the Bible Really Says* (2010); *World Religions* (2003); *The Illustrated Guide to World Religions* (2003); "Joshua," *New Jerome Biblical Commentary* (1990); *West Semitic Personal Names in the Murasu Documents* (1976); Co-contributor: *NRSV: The New Oxford Annotated Bible* (2010); Editor: *The Oxford History of the Biblical World* (1998)

LEONARD J. COPPES: Pastor, Calvary Orthodox Presbyterian Church; Doctor of Theology; Old Testament Hebrew Scholar; Contributor: *Theological Wordbook of the Old Testament* (2003); Author: *The Baptism Debate* (Providence Presbyterian Church Press, 2002); *Are Five Points Enough? The Ten Points of Calvinism* (Reformation Educational Foundation, 1980); *The Covenant of Grace* (1994); *Dispensational Theology: A Presentation, Comparison and Evaluation of Old and New Dispensationalism* (1994); *Old Testament Biblical Theology* (Providence Presbyterian Press, 2004)

ROBIN C. COVER: Former Professor of Old Testament, Dallas Theological Seminary; Co-Chair, the Computer Assisted Research Group of the Society of Biblical Literature (1989); Contributor: *The Oxford Guide to Ideas and Issues of the Bible* (2001); *The Oxford Companion to the Bible* (1993); Co-Contributor: "Textual Criticism" in *Text Encoding Initiative: Background and Context*, edited by Nancy Ide and Jean Veronis (1995)

FRANK MOORE CROSS: Hancock Professor of Hebrew and Oriental Languages, Harvard University; Expert, Dead Sea Scrolls; Author: *Canaanite Myth and Hebrew Epic* (President and Fellows of Harvard College, 1973); *The Ancient Library of Qumran* (Sheffield Academic Press, Ltd., 1995); *From Epic to Canon* (John Hopkins University Press, 1998); Co-author: *Studies in Ancient Yahwistic Poetry* (Society of Biblical Literature, 1975) (d. 2012)

JOHAN HARM CROON: Greek Classicist; Author: *The Herdsman of the Dead: Studies on Some Cults, Myths and Legends of the Ancient Greek Colonization-Area* (Academic Thesis, 1952); Contributor: *The Oxford Classical Dictionary* (Oxford, 1970)

MITCHELL DAHOOD: Professor, Pontifical Biblical Institute; Hebrew, Ugaritic and Eblaite specialist; Author: *The Anchor Bible: Psalms 1-50* (Doubleday, 1966); *The Anchor Bible: Psalms 51-100* (Doubleday, 1968); *The Anchor Bible: Psalms 101-150* (Doubleday, 1970); *Ugaritic-Hebrew Philology* (Biblical Institute Press, 1989); *Proverbs and Northwest Semitic Philology* (Pontifical Biblical Institute, 1963); *Canaanite-Phoenician Influence in Qoheleth* (John Hopkins University, 1952); *Ugaritic Studies and the Bible* (Pontifical Gregorian University, 1962) (d. 1982)

EDWARD RUSSELL DALGLISH: Macon Professor Emeritus of Religion, Baylor University; Author: *Psalm Fifty-One in the Light of Ancient Near Eastern Patternism* (E. J. Brill, 1962); *The Great Deliverance: Studies in the Book of Exodus* (Broadman, 1977); Contributor: *The Interpreter's Dictionary of the Bible* (Abingdon, 1962) and *Wycliffe Bible Dictionary* (Hendrickson, 1998) (d. 2001)

FREDERICK WILLIAM DANKER: Classicist and Greek Lexicographer; Professor Emeritus of New Testament, Christ Seminary–Seminex, Lutheran School of Theology; Reviser: *A Greek-English Lexicon of the New Testament and Other Early Christian Literature* by Bauer, Arndt and Gingrich (University of Chicago Press, 2000); Author: *The Concise Greek-English Lexicon of the New Testament* (University of Chicago Press, 2009); *Multipurpose Tools for Bible Study: Revised Edition* (Fortress, 2003) (d. 2012)

GWYNNE HENTON DAVIES: Minister; Professor (Hebrew, Syriac and Old Testament), Bristol Baptist College and Durham University; Principal, Regent's Park College (Oxford); President, The Society for Old Testament Study and The Baptist Union of Great Britain; Author: *Exodus: Introduction and Commentary* (London, 1967); *The Broadman Bible Commentary: Genesis* (Nashville, 1969); *The Approach to the Old Testament* (Carey Kingsgate Press, 1953); Contributor: *The Interpreter's Dictionary of the Bible* (Abingdon, 1962) (d. 1998)

WILLIAM DAVID DAVIES: Congregational Minister, Theologian, Bible Scholar; Professor of Religion, Duke University Divinity School (1950-1955) and George Washington Ivey Professor of Advanced Studies and Research in Christian Origins (1966-1981); Author: *Paul and Rabbinic Judaism* (1948); *The Setting of the Sermon on the Mount* (1964); *Christian Origins and Judaism* (1962); *The Gospel and the Land* (1974); Co-author with Dale C. Allison: *International Critical Commentaries, Matthew 1-7* (2004); *Matthew 8-18* (2000); *Matthew 19-28* (2004); Co-editor: *The Cambridge History of Judaism*, volumes 1-3 (d. 2001)

JOHN DAY: Old Testament Scholar; Dean of Degrees, Faculty of Theology, Lady Margaret Hall, University of Oxford (2004-2013); Author: *God's Conflict with the Dragon and the Sea* (1985); *Yahweh and the Gods and Goddesses of Canaan* (2000); Editor: *In Search of Pre-Exilic Israel* (2004)

ROLAND GUERIN DE VAUX: Director, Ecole Biblique, Jerusalem/Jordan; Editor: *Revue Biblique*; Field Archaeologist; Biblical scripts and languages expert; Former guest Professor, Harvard Divinity School; Author: *The Cambridge Ancient History: Palestine in the Early Bronze Age, Volume 1* (Cambridge University Press, 1966); *Ancient Israel: Volume 1: Social Institutions* (McGraw-Hill, 1965); *Ancient Israel: Volume 2: Religious Institutions* (McGraw-Hill, 1965) (d. 1971)

BRUCE A. DEMAREST: Associate Professor, Conservative Baptist Theological Seminary; Co-author: *Integrative Theology* (Zondervan, 2010); Editor: *Four Views on Christian Spirituality* (Zondervan, 2012); *Seasons of the Soul: Stages of*

Spiritual Development (InterVarsity, 2009); *Jesus Christ, the God-man* (Victor Books, 1978); *The Cross and Salvation: The Doctrine of Salvation* (Crossway Books, 2006); *Who is Jesus?* (Wipf and Stock, 1984)

ALEXANDER A. DI LELLA: Retired Professor of Theology and Religious Studies, Catholic University of America; Author: *Daniel: A Book for Troubling Times* (New City Press of the Focolare, 1997); Co-author: *The Anchor Bible Volume 39: The Wisdom of Ben Sira* (Doubleday, 1987); *The Anchor Bible: The Book of Daniel* (Doubleday, 1978)

RICHARD J. DILLON: Professor Emeritus of Theology and New Testament; Retired Chair, Theology Department, Fordham University; taught at St. Joseph's Seminary and the Pontifical Biblical Institute; Former Editor, *The Catholic Biblical Quarterly*; President, Catholic Biblical Association of America; Author: *The Hymns of Saint Luke: Lyricism and Narrative Strategy in Luke 1-2* (Catholic Biblical Association of America, 2013); *From Eye-Witnesses to Ministers of the Word: Tradition and Composition in Luke 24* (Biblical Institute Press, 1978)

JAMES D. G. DUNN: Emeritus Lightfoot Professor of Divinity, University of Durham (retired, 2003); Author: *Christology in the Making* (Eerdmans, 1996); *The New International Greek Testament Commentary: The Epistles to the Colossians and to Philemon* (Eerdmans, 1996); *Jesus and the Spirit* (Eerdmans, 1975); *Did the First Christians Worship Jesus?* (Westminster John Knox Press, 2010); *Christianity in the Making: Volume 1: Jesus Remembered* (Eerdmans, 2003); *New Testament Theology: An Introduction* (Abingdon, 2009); *The Theology of Paul the Apostle* (Eerdmans, 1998); *Jesus, Paul, and the Gospels* (Eerdmans, 2011); *The Evidence for Jesus* (The Westminster Press, 1985); *Beginning from Jerusalem* (Eerdmans, 2009)

WALTHER EICHRODT: German Old Testament Scholar; Protestant Theologian; Professor, the University of Basel; Author: *The Sources of Genesis* (1916); *The Hope of Eternal Peace in Ancient Israel* (1920); *Man in the Old Testament* (1946); *Theology of the Old Testament* (1933-35, 4th ed. 1957); *Ezekiel: A Commentary* (The Westminster Press; SCM, Press, Ltd., 1970) (d. 1978)

SAMSON EITREM: Professor Emeritus, Classical Philology, University of Oslo; Author: *The Greek Magical Papyri in the British Museum* (Commissioned by J. Dybwad, 1923); *Notes on Some Greek Literary Papyri* (Dybwad, 1906); Contributor: *The Oxford Classical Dictionary* (Oxford University Press, 1970); "Dreams and Divination in Magical Ritual" in *Magika Hiera: Ancient Greek Magic & Religion*, edited by C. A. Faraone (Oxford University Press, 1991) (d. 1966)

CARL D. EVANS: Retired Professor of Religious Studies, University of South Carolina; Co-editor: *Scripture in Context: Essays on the Comparative Method* (Pickwick, 1980); Author: *Encountering the Other: A Social History on Ethnic and Religious Diversity in Ancient Judah* (forthcoming)

JOHN S. FEINBERG: American Author, Theologian, and Chair, Department of Biblical and Systematic Theology, Trinity Evangelical Divinity School; Contributor: "Theodicy," "Evil: Problem of," "Pain," *Evangelical Dictionary of Theology* (Baker, 1984); Author: *No One Like Him: The Doctrine of God* (Crossway Books, 2001); *The Many Faces of Evil* (Crossway Books, 2004); *Where is God?* (Broadman & Holman, 2004); Editor: *Continuity and Discontinuity: Perspectives on the Relationship between the Old and New Testaments* (Crossways, 1988)

DAVID HACKETT FISCHER: Pulitzer Prize Winner in History; Earl Warren Professor of History, Brandeis University; Author: *Historians' Fallacies* (Harper/Torchbook, 1970); *Washington's Crossing* (Oxford University Press, 2004); *Paul Revere's Ride* (Oxford University Press, 1994)

JAMES W. FLANAGAN: Archbishop Paul J. Hallinan Professor of Catholic Studies, Case Western Reserve University; Author: *David's Social Agenda: A Hologram of Israel's Early Iron Age, The Social World of Biblical Antiquity Series, 7* (Dunelm Enterprises, 1988); See also: *'Imagining' Biblical Worlds: Studies in Spatial, Social and Historical Constructs in Honor of James W. Flanagan* (Bloomsbury, 2003)

JARL E. FOSSUM: Associate Professor of New Testament Studies, University of Michigan; Adjunct Professor of Gnostic and Related

Studies, C. G. Jung Institute, Zürich, Switzerland; Author: *The Name of God and the Angel of the Lord - Samaritan and Jewish Concepts of Intermediation and the Origin of Gnosticism* (Francesco Taini, 1985); *The Image of the Invisible God: Essays on the Influence of Jewish Mysticism on Early Christology* (Vandenhoeck and Ruprecht, 1995); Co-author: *Jesus and the Gospels* (Wadsworth/Thomson Learning, 2003)

NILI SACHER FOX: Professor of Bible and Director of School of Graduate Studies, Hebrew Union College - Jewish Institute of Religion; Contributor: *Encyclopedia Judaica* (Thomson Gale, 2007); "Numbers" in *The Jewish Study Bible* (Oxford University Press, 2004); Author: *Royal Functionaries and State Administration in Israel and Judah During the First Temple Period* (University of Pennsylvania, 1997); *In the Service of the King: Officialdom in Ancient Israel and Judah* (Monographs of the Hebrew Union College 232; Cincinnati: Hebrew Union College, 2000)

HENRI FRANKFORT: Research Professor in Oriental Archaeology, University of Chicago; Director, Warburg Institute; Professor, History of Pre-Classical Antiquity, University of London; Author: *Ancient Egyptian Religion: An Interpretation* (Dover Publications, 2012); *The Art and Architecture of the Ancient Orient* (Yale University Press, 1996); *Kingship and the Gods* (University of Chicago Press, 1948); *The Problem of Similarity in Ancient Near Eastern Religions* (Clarendon Press, 1951) (d. 1954)

TERENCE E. FRETHEIM: Professor of Old Testament, Luther Northwestern Theological Seminary; Author: *Interpretation: Exodus* (John Knox Press, 1991); *The Suffering of God* (Fortress, 1984); *The Pentateuch* (Abingdon, 1996); *God and World in the Old Testament* (Abingdon, 2005); *Creation Untamed: The Bible, God, and Natural Disasters* (Baker Academic, 2010); *Abraham: Trials of Family and Faith* (University of South Carolina Press, 2007); *Jeremiah* (Smith & Helwys Publishing, 2002); *First and Second Kings* (Westminster John Knox Press, 1999)

RICHARD ELLIOTT FRIEDMAN: Ann and Jay Davis Professor of Jewish Studies, University of California at San Diego; Author: *Who Wrote the Bible?* (Harper, 1987); *The Bible with Sources Revealed* (Harper, 2003);

The Hidden Book in the Bible (Harper, 1999); *Commentary on the Torah* (Harper, 2003); *The Hidden Face of God* (Harper, 1996); Co-author with Shawna Dolansky: *The Bible Now: Homosexuality; Abortion; Women; Death Penalty; Earth* (Oxford University Press, 2011)

RUSSELL E. FULLER: Professor of Biblical Studies, University of San Diego; Hebrew Bible and Dead Sea Scrolls expert; Co-editor: *Discoveries in the Judean Desert: Volume XV, Qumran Cave 4* (Clarendon Press, 1997)

THEODOR HERZL GASTER: Professor of Ancient Civilizations, Fairleigh Dickinson University; Professor of Religion, Center for Advanced Judaic Studies, University of Pennsylvania; Author: *Thespis: Ritual, Myth, and Drama in the Ancient Near East* (Gordian Press, 1975); *The Holy and the Profane* (W. Sloane Associates, 1955); *The Dead Sea Scriptures* (Anchor Books, 1964); *The Oldest Stories in the World* (Penguin Group, 1958); *The New Golden Bough* (New American Library, 1964); *Myth, Legend, and Custom in the Old Testament* (Duckworth, 1970) (d. 1992)

VICTOR ROLAND GOLD: Professor, Old Testament, Pacific Lutheran Theological Seminary; Co-founder, Graduate Theological Union, Berkeley; Contributor: *Oxford Annotated Bible* (Oxford University Press, 1994); *The Interpreter's Dictionary of the Bible* (Abingdon, 1962); *The International Standard Bible Encyclopedia* (Eerdmans, 1986, revised); Author: *Studies in the History and Culture of Edom* (John Hopkins University, 1951); *Creation and Eschatology in the Bible* (Pacific Coast Theological Society, 1960) (d. 2008)

CYRUS HERZL GORDON: Professor Emeritus of Near Eastern Studies; Ugaritic and Minoan expert, Brandeis University; Professor of Hebrew Studies, New York University; Director, Center for Ebla Research; Author: *Alalecta Orientalia: 38: Ugaritic Textbook* (Editrice Pontificio Istituto Biblico, Rome, Italy, 1998); Co-editor: *Eblaitica: Essays on the Ebla Archives and Eblaite Language* (Ebla, Volume 4; Eisenbrauns, 2002); Co-author: *The Bible and the Ancient Near East* (W. W. Norton & Company, 1997); *Genesis: World of Myths and Patriarchs* (New York University Press, 1996) (d. 2001)

NORMAN KAROL GOTTWALD: Professor Emeritus of Biblical Studies, New York Theological Seminary; Author: *The Politics of Ancient Israel* (Westminster John Knox Press, 2001); *The Hebrew Bible: A Brief Socio-Literary Introduction* (Fortress Press, 2009); *The Tribes of Yahweh: A Sociology of Religion of Liberated Israel 1250-1050, BCE.* (Hymns Ancient and Modern Limited, 2013)

HEINRICH GREEVAN: Ernst Moritz Arndt, University of Greifswald; Reviser: *Hermeneia: James: A Commentary on the Epistle of James* by Martin Dibelius (Fortress, 1976); Editor: *Studies in the Acts of the Apostles* (SCM Press, 1956); Contributor: *The Theological Dictionary of the New Testament* (Eerdmans, 1964)

ANN C. GUNTER: Professor, Art History, Northwestern University; Former Curator, Ancient Near Eastern Art, Arthur M. Sackler Gallery and Freer Gallery of Art, Smithsonian Institution; Author: *The Gordion Excavations: The Bronze Age* (University Museum, University of Pennsylvania, 1991); *Marble Sculpture* (Svenska Forskningsinstitutet, 1995); *Greek Art and the Orient* (Cambridge University Press, 2012)

HARVEY H. GUTHRIE, JR.: Professor of Old Testament, Former Dean, Episcopal Divinity School; Author: *God and History in the Old Testament* (1960); *Israel's Sacred Songs: a Study of Dominant Themes* (1966); *Theology as Thanksgiving: From Israel's Psalms to the Church's Eucharist* (1981)

HANS-CHRISTOPH HAHN: University of Göttingen; The Protestant Academy, Bad Boll, Germany; Author: "Theology, Spirituality and Apostolate of the Evangelical Congregation of the Brethren," *The United Brethren: Moravian Studies*, edited by Buijtenen, Dekker & Leeuwenberg, 1975, 287-314; Co-author: *Zinzendorf and the Moravian Brotherhood* (Hamburg, Wittig)

VICTOR P. HAMILTON: Professor of Religion; Chairman, Philosophy and Religion Department, Asbury University (retired); Author: *New International Commentary on the Old Testament: Genesis* (two volumes;

Eerdmans, 1990;1995); *Exodus: An Exegetical Commentary* (Baker, 2011); *Handbook on the Historical Books* (Baker, 2010); *Handbook on the Pentateuch* (Baker, 2005)

WALTER J. HARRELSON: Distinguished Professor of Old Testament; Dean, Chicago Divinity School (___ - 1960); Vanderbilt University Divinity School (1967–1975); Professor of Religion, Wake Forest University (1995); Chair, the Task Force on Academic Freedom of the American Society of Theological Schools; Contributor to Vanderbilt University Special Collections including Ethiopian Manuscript Microfilm Library; President, Society of Biblical Literature (1972); Chairman, Society for Religion in Higher Education; Recipient of Harvie Branscomb Distinguished Professor Award, Thomas Jefferson Award and Alexander Heard Distinguished Service Professor Award; Contributor: *New Revised Standard Version of the Bible* (1990); Co-editor: *The New Interpreter's Study Bible: New Revised Standard Version with the Apocrypha* (2003) (d. 2012)

R. LAIRD HARRIS: Professor of Old Testament and Theology, Faith Theological Seminary; Author: *Introductory Hebrew Grammar* (Eerdmans, 1950); *Exploring the Basics of the Bible* (Crossway, 2005); *Inspiration and Canonicity of the Bible* (Wipf and Stock, 2008); *You and Your Bible* (Evangelical Training Association, 1990); *Man - God's Eternal Creation* (Moody, 1971); Co-editor: *Theological Wordbook of the Old Testament* (Moody, 2003); Co-editor: *Zondervan Pictorial Encyclopedia of the Bible* (Zondervan, 1975); Contributor: *The Wycliffe Bible Commentary* (Moody, 1962); *The Expositor's Bible* (BiblioBazaar reprint, 2009?); Chair, *NIV Bible* translation committee (d. 2008)

R. K. HARRISON: Old Testament Scholar; Hellmuth Professor of Old Testament Studies, Huron College, University of Western Ontario and Wycliffe College, University of Toronto; Author: *Introduction to the Old Testament* (Eerdmans, 1969); *Jeremiah and Lamentations* (InterVarsity, 2009); *Old Testament Times* (Baker, 2005); *Biblical Hebrew* (Hodder & Stoughton, 1992); *Leviticus: An Introduction and Commentary* (InterVarsity, 2008); *Archaeology and the Old Testament* (English Universities Press, 1957) (d. 1993)

CHRISTINE ELIZABETH HAYES: Weis Professor of Religious Studies in Classical Judaica, Yale University; Author: *Between the Babylonian and Palestinian Talmuds* (Oxford University Press, 1997); *Gentile Impurities and Jewish Identities: Intermarriage and Conversion from the Bible to the Talmud* (Oxford University Press, 2002); *The Emergence of Judaism: Classical Traditions in Contemporary Perspective* (Fortress Press, 2011); "Introduction to the Hebrew Bible," Open Yale Courses, 2012 (oyc.yale.edu.)

JOSEPH P. HEALEY: Headmaster, University Liggett School; Former Dean and Professor of Religious Studies, Hobart and William Smith Colleges; Contributor: *The Anchor Bible Dictionary* (Doubleday, 1992)

COLETTE C. HEMINGWAY: Independent Scholar; Co-author: *Sculpture Review: Ancrea del Verrochio; Colors on Ancient Greek Terra-cotta Figurines; Maudit Modi;* Joseph Sheppard (National Sculpture Society, Volume 1, Number 2, Summer, 2001)

RONALD S. HENDEL: Assistant Professor, Southern Methodist University; Author: *The Book of Genesis: A Biography* (Princeton University Press, 2013); *The Text of Genesis 1-11* (Oxford University Press, 1998); *Mind, Myth, and Genesis 2-11* (Harvard University, 1981); Co-author: *The Most Magic Word: Essays on Babylonian and Biblical Literature* (Catholic Biblical Association of America, 2002)

GARY A. HERION: Associate Professor, Religious Studies, Hartwick College; Associate Editor/Contributor: *The Anchor Bible Dictionary*, (Doubleday, 1992); Co-author: *Jesus and the Gospels* (Hartwick Humanities in Management Institute, 1995); *King David* (Hartwick Humanities in Management Institute, 2001); Editor: *Ancient Israel's Faith and History: An Introduction to the Bible in Context* by George Mendenhall (Westminster John Knox Press, 2001); *The Social Organization of Tradition in Monarchic Judah* (University Microfilms, 1984)

MENACHEM HERMAN: Ben Gurion University of the Negev, Be'Er Sheva, Hadarom, Israel; Author: *Tithe as Gift: The Institution in the*

Pentateuch and in Light of Mauss's Prestation Theory (Mellen Research Press, 1991); Translator: *Instructions for Jewish Living* (Kolell Ahirah Shahchar, 1984)

R. LANSING HICKS: Professor of the Literature and Interpretation of the Old Testament, Berkeley Divinity School (Episcopal) at Yale; Author: "Delet and Megillah: A Fresh Approach to Jeremiah XXXVI," VT 33 (1983) 46-66; "Messiah, Second Moses, Son of Man," ATR, 33 (195 1), 24-29. 7937; Contributor: *The Interpreter's Dictionary of the Bible* (Abingdon, 1962); *The New Oxford Annotated Bible* (Oxford University Press, 2010); "Capital Punishment, Gun Control" in *Preaching as a Prophetic Calling: Sermons that Work XII* (Morehouse Publishing, 2004); "The Door of Love" in *Love and Death in the Ancient Near East: Essays in Honor of Marvin Pope*, edited by J. H. Marks and R. M. Good (Guilford, Connecticut: Four Quarters, 1987) 153; Editor: "Essays in Honor of Fleming James" (*Anglican Theological Review*, vol. 34, no. 4, 1952)

SAMUEL HENRY HOOKE: Professor Emeritus of Old Testament Studies, London University; Author: *Christianity in the Making* (Methuen & Company, 1926); *What is the Bible?* (1948); *The Kingdom of God in the Experience of Jesus* (Darton, Longman & Todd, 1967); *The Resurrection of Christ as History and Experience* (Darton, Longman & Todd, 1967); *Alpha and Omega* (J. Nisbet, 1961); *Myth, Ritual and Kingship* (Clarendon Press, 1958); Co-author: *Myth and Ritual* (London, 1933); Translator: *Jesus* by Charles Guignebert (University Books, 1956); *The Parables of Jesus* by Joachim Jeremias (London, 1954) (d. 1968)

WALDEMAR JANZEN: Professor of Old Testament and German, Canadian Mennonite Bible College; Author: *The Mourning Cry* (Walter de Gruyter & Co., Berlin, Germany, 1972); *Old Testament Ethics: A Paradigmatic Approach* (Westminster John Knox Press, 1994); *Believers' Church Bible Commentary: Exodus* (Herald Press, 2000)

ROBERT J. KARRIS: Head researcher at the Franciscan Institute, St. Bonaventure University; Author: *Luke: Artist and Theologian: Luke's Passion Account as Literature*; *Invitation to Acts: A Commentary on the Acts of the Apostles...*; *What are they Saying About Luke and Acts?*

YOSHITAKA KOBAYASHI: Chairman, Old Testament Department, Asia Adventist Theological Seminary; Author: *Graphemic Analysis of Old Babylonian Letters from South Babylonia* (University Microfilms, 1982)

CRAIG R. KOESTER: Vice President of Academic Affairs, Professor and Asher O. and Carrie Nasby Chair of New Testament, Luther Seminary; Author: *The Anchor Yale Bible: Revelation* (Yale University Press, 2014); *The Word of Life: A Theology of John's Gospel* (Eerdmans, 2008); *Symbolism in the Fourth Gospel* (Fortress Press, 2003); *Revelation and the End of All Things* (Eerdmans, 2001); *The Anchor Yale Bible: Hebrews* (Yale University Press, 2001); *The Dwelling of God* (Catholic Biblical Association of America, 1989)

JOHN R. KOHLENBERGER, III: Biblical languages expert; taught at Multnomah Biblical Seminary and Western Seminary (Portland, Oregon); Author: *The Interlinear NIV Hebrew-English Old Testament* (Zondervan, 1987); *Read Through the Bible in a Year* (Moody, 2008); *The New American Bible: Revised Edition Concise Concordance* (Oxford, 2012)

VERNON H. KOOY: Professor of Hellenistic Greek and New Testament Exegesis, New Brunswick Theological Seminary; Contributor: *The Interpreter's Dictionary of the Bible*: "First-born;" "Heel, Lifted;" "Hospitality;" "Integrity;" "Symbol, Symbolism" (d. 2002)

JOHN A. LARSEN: Clinical Director, Midwest Christian Counseling Center, Kansas City, Missouri (retired); Private Therapist, Kansas City, Missouri; Author: *When a Member of the Family Needs Counseling* (Abbey Press, 1979)

SOPHIE LAWS: Lecturer, Regent's University, London from 1985; Academic Dean of RACL and WGS, (2005-2009); Program Director for Humanities and Study Abroad; Contributor: "James, Epistle of," *The Anchor Bible Dictionary* (Doubleday, 1992)

JOEL M. LEMON: Associate Professor, Old Testament; Recipient of Lilly Theological Research grant, Candler School of Theology, Emory

University; Elder, United Methodist Church; Author: *Yahweh's Winged Form in the Psalms: Exploring Congruent Iconography and Texts* (Academic Press Fribourg, 2010); Co-editor: *Method Matters, Essays on the Interpretation of the Hebrew Bible in Honor of David L. Petersen* (Society of Biblical Literature, 2009)

JON DOUGLAS LEVENSON: American Old Testament Scholar; Albert A. List Professor of Jewish Studies, Harvard Divinity School, Cambridge, Massachusetts; Author: *Inheriting Abraham: the Legacy of the Patriarch in Judaism, Christianity & Islam* (Princeton University Press, 2012); *Esther: A Commentary* (Westminster John Knox Press, 1997); *Sinai & Zion: An Entry into the Jewish Bible* (Harper & Row, 1985); *Resurrection of the Beloved Son: The Transformation of Child Sacrifice in Judaism and Christianity* (Yale University, 1993)

EDWARD LIPINSKI: Semitic Scholar and philologist; Author: *Semitic Languages: Outline of a Comparative Grammar* (Leuven, 2001); *The Aramaeans: Their Ancient History, Culture, Religion* (Leuven, 2002); *On the Skirts of Canaan in the Iron Age. Historical and Topographical Researches* (Leuven, 2006); *Resheph: A Syro-Canaanite Deity* (Peeters, 2009)

JOHN ARNOTT MACCULLOCH: Rector of St. Columba's, Portree, Isle of Skye; Canon of the Cathedral of the Holy Spirit, Cumbrae; Author: *Comparative Theology* (Methuen & Co., 1902); *Religion: Its Origin and Forms* (Dent, 1904); *The Childhood of Fiction* (E. P. Dutton, 1905); *The Religion of the Ancient Celts* (T. & T. Clark, 1911); *The Harrowing of Hell* (AMS Press, 1930) (d. 1950)

EUGENE H. MALY: Professor of Scripture, The Athenaeum of Ohio/Mount St. Mary's Seminary of the West; Author: *The World of David and Solomon* (Prentice-Hall, 1966); *The Old Testament Reading Guide: The Second Book of Samuel* (Liturgical Press, 1970) (d. 1980)

CLAUDE F. MARIOTTINI: Associate Professor of Old Testament, Northern Baptist Theological Seminary; Author: *Rereading the Biblical*

Text: Searching for Meaning and Understanding (Wipf & Stock, 2013); Contributor: "Malachi: A Prophet for his Time," *The Jewish Bible Quarterly* (Dor Ledor, Volume 26, 1998); Contributor: *The Anchor Bible Dictionary* (Doubleday, 1992); *The Holman Bible Dictionary* (Holman, 1991)

W. HAROLD MARE: Professor of New Testament, Covenant Theological Seminary; Author: *The Archaeology of the Jerusalem Area* (Wipf and Stock Publishers, 1987); Co-author: *The Expositor's Bible Commentary: 1 & 2 Corinthians* (Zondervan, 1995); *Mastering New Testament Greek* (Wipf & Stock, 2001); *A Study of the Greek [bomos] in Classical Greek Literature* (University of Pennsylvania, 1961) (d. 2004)

JEAN-CLAUDE MARGUERON: Professor of Archaeology; Emeritus Director of Studies, Ecole Pratique des Hautes Etudes, Sorbonne, Paris; Author: *Mesopotamia* (World Publishing, 1965); *The Mesopotamians* (second edition, Paris, 2003); *Sanctuaries and Clergy* (Strasbourg, 2003); "Architectural Design in the Middle East," *I Will Speak the Riddles of Ancient Times*, (Eisenbrauns, 2006); *A Guide to Mari* (Work's Council, 1995)

JOHN H. MARKS: Professor Emeritus, Near Eastern Studies Department, Princeton University; Author, *Visions of One World* (Four Quarters Publishing, 1985); *Love and Death in the Ancient Near East* (Four Quarters, 1987); Co-author: *A Beginner's Handbook to Biblical Hebrew* (Abingdon, 1958); *Interpreter's Concise Commentary: The Pentateuch* (Abingdon, 1983); Contributor: *The Interpreter's One-Volume Commentary on the Bible* (Abingdon, 1971); Translator: Gerhard von Rad, *Genesis: A Commentary* (Westminster, 1972); *God at Work in Israel* (Abingdon, 1980); *From Genesis to Chronicles* (Westminster, 1958) (d. 2009)

VICTOR HAROLD MATTHEWS: Professor and Dean, Department of Religious Studies, Southwest Missouri State University; Author: *Old Testament Turning Points: The Narratives That Shaped a Nation* (Baker Academic, 2005); *Studying the Ancient Israelites: A Guide to Sources and*

Methods (Baker Academic, 2007); Co-author: *The Old Testament: Text and Context* (Baker Academic, 2012); *Social World of Ancient Israel 1250-587 BCE* (Hendrickson, 1993)

WILLIAM STEWART MCCULLOUGH: Founding father of the Canadian Society of Biblical Studies and its President, 1947-48; Editor: *The Seed of Wisdom* (1964); *Jewish and Madaean Incantation Bowls in the Ontario Museum* (University of Toronto Press, 1967); *Two Mandaean Incantation Bowls - Primary Source Edition* (BiblioBazaar reprint, 2013); *Palestine: The Arabs, the Jews and the Peel Report* (1938); *A Short History of Syriac Christianity to the Rise of Islam* (Scholars Press, 1982)

JOHN EDGAR MCFADYEN: Professor, Old Testament Language, Literature, and Theology, University of Glasgow and Knox College; Author: *Introduction to the Old Testament* (A. C. Armstrong & Son, 1907); *Old Testament Criticism and the Christian Church* (Hodder & Stoughton, 1903); *The Interpreter's Commentary of the New Testament Volume VI: The Epistles to the Corinthians and Galatians* (A.S. Barnes & Co., 1909); *The Prayers of the Bible* (A. C. Armstrong & Son, 1909); *The Messages of the Prophetic and Priestly Historians; The Messages of the Psalmists* (Charles Scribner's Sons, 1904); *The Divine Pursuit* (Revell, 1901); *Thoughts for Silent Hours* (Revell, 1902) (d. 1933)

GEORGE EMERY MENDENHALL: Professor Emeritus of Biblical Studies, University of Michigan; Visiting Professor, Institute of Archaeology and Anthropology, Yarmouk University, Irbid, Jordan; Founder, the Biblical Colloquium; Author: *The Tenth Generation: The Origins of the Biblical Tradition* (Johns Hopkins, 1973); *Ancient Israel's Faith and History: An Introduction to the Bible in Context* (Westminster John Knox Press, 2001); *Our Misunderstood Bible* (BookSurge Publishing, 2006); See also: *The Quest for the Kingdom of God: Studies in Honor of George E. Mendenhall* (Eisenbrauns, 1983) (d. 2016)

ALLAN MENZIES: Professor of Divinity and Biblical Criticism, St. Mary's College, St. Andrew's University; Editor: *Ante-Nicene Fathers; Review of Theology and Philosophy*; Author: *Second Corinthians* (1912); Co-author:

A Study of Calvin and Other Papers (Macmillan, 1918); *National Religion: Sermons on the Ten Commandments* (Alexander Gardner, 1888); *The Critical Study of the New Testament: Inaugural Lecture* (Kessinger Publishing reprint, 2010) (d. 1916)

JACOB MILGROM: Conservative Jewish Rabbi, Professor Emeritus, Bible and Hebrew, University of California at Berkeley; Author: *The Anchor Bible: Leviticus 1-16* (Doubleday, 1991); *Leviticus 17-22* (Doubleday, 2000); *Leviticus 23-27* (Doubleday, 2001); *Cult and Conscience: The Asham and the Priestly Doctrine of Repentance* (E. J. Brill, 1976); *Studies in the Cultic Theology and Terminology* (E. J. Brill, 1983); *The Open Gate* (Sivan Press, 1961) (d. 2010)

ALAN RALPH MILLARD: Rankin Professor Emeritus of Hebrew and Ancient Semitic Languages; Honorary Senior Fellow, School of Archaeology, Classics and Egyptology (SACE), University of Liverpool; Co-editor/Contributor: *Essays on the Patriarchal Narratives* (InterVarsity, 1980); Author: *The Eponyms of the Assyrian Empire, 910-612, B.C.* (Neo-Assyrian Text Corpus Project, 1994); Co-editor: *Dictionary of the Ancient Near East* (Trustees of the British Museum, 2000)

MARTHA A. MORRISON: Adjunct Lecturer, Boston College; Research Associate, University Museum, Philadelphia; Co-author: *World Religions: Judaism* (Chelsea House of Infobase Publishing, 2009); Contributor: *Nuzi and the Hurrians Volume 4* (Eisenbrauns, 1993); Co-editor: *Nuzi and the Hurrians: In Honor of Ernest R. Lacheman* (Eisenbrauns, 1981)

JAMES MUILENBURG: Billings Professor of Old Testament Literature and Semitic Languages (Pacific School of Religion, 1936-1945); Davenport Professor of Hebrew and Cognate Languages (Union Theological Seminary, 1945-1963); Gray Professor of Hebrew Exegesis and Old Testament (San Francisco Theological Seminary, 1963-1972). Translator: The Revised Standard Version. See also The James Muilenburg Manuscript Collection (Princeton Theological Seminary). (d. 1974)

ROLAND E. MURPHY: George Washington Ivey Professor Emeritus of Biblical Studies, Duke University; Author: *The Tree of Life: An Exploration of Biblical Wisdom Literature* (Doubleday, 1990); *Word Biblical Commentary Volume 23: Ecclesiastes* (Thomas Nelson, 1992); *Responses to 101 Questions on the Biblical Torah: Reflections on the Pentateuch* (Better Yourself Books, 1997); Co-author: *Understanding the Bible Commentary Series: Proverbs, Ecclesiastes, Song of Songs* (Baker Books, 1999) (d. 2002)

MURRAY LEE NEWMAN: Professor of Old Testament, Protestant Episcopal Theological Seminary; *Genesis* (Forward Movement, 1999); *Exodus* (Forward Movement, 2000); *The People of the Covenant* (Abingdon, 1968); *The Sinai Covenant Traditions in the Cult of Israel* (University Microfilms, 1960)

JEROME H. NEYREY: Professor of New Testament Studies, Notre Dame University (retired); Author: *The Gospel of John* (2007); *The Resurrection Stories* (2007); *Render to God: New Testament Understandings of the Divine* (2004); *Honor and Shame in the Gospel of Matthew* (1998); *The Social World of Luke-Acts: Models for Interpretation* (1999); *The Anchor Bible Commentary: 2 Peter, Jude* (1994); *Paul, in Other Words: A Cultural Reading of His Letters* (1990); *Christ is Community: The Christologies of the New Testament* (1985)

SUSAN NIDITCH: Samuel Green Professor of Religion, Amherst College; Author: *The Old Testament Library: Judges* (Westminster John Knox Press, 2008); *A Prelude to Biblical Folklore: Underdogs and Tricksters* (Harper & Row, 2000); *Oral World and Written Word* (Westminster John Knox Press, 1996); *War in the Hebrew Bible* (Oxford University Press, 1993); *Ancient Israelite Religion* (Replica Books, 2000)

KJELD PYRDOL NIELSEN: Department of Food Science, University of Copenhagen; Author: *Incense in Ancient Israel* (Supplements to *Vetus Testamentum*, volume 38), Brill Academic Publishers (1997)

ROBERT MAXWELL OGILVIE: Scottish classical Scholar, University of St. Andrews; Author: *The Romans and their Gods in the Age of Augustus* (Chatto & Windus, 1969); *A Commentary on Livy, Books 1-5* (Clarendon Press, 1965); *Early Rome and the Etruscans* (Fontana, Collins, 1979); *Roman Literature and Society* (Penguin Books, 1980)

DENNIS T. OLSON: Charles T. Haley Professor of Old Testament Theology, Princeton Theological Seminary (Lutheran); Author: *Interpretation: Numbers* (Westminster John Knox Press, 1996); *Deuteronomy and the Death of Moses: A Theological Reading* (Fortress, 1994); *The Death of the Old and the Birth of the New* (Scholars Press, 1985); *Ethics for Living* (Augsburg, 1986); Co-author: *Created Anew* (Augsburg, 1987)

AUGUSTINE PAGOLU: Lecturer in Hebrew, Old Testament and Hermeneutics, Biblical Graduate School of Theology, Singapore; Author: *Patriarchal Religion as Portrayed in Genesis 12-50* (Oxford Center for Mission Studies and Open University, 1995); *The Religion of the Patriarchs* (Bloomsbury, 1998)

ANTHONY PEARSON: English Quaker, Secretary to Sir Arthur Hesilrig, member of House of Commons (1640-1659) and commander in First English Civil War (Parliamentarian side); Under-sheriff of Durham, England; Former Justice of the Peace in Westmorland; Author: *The Great Case of Tithes Truly Stated, Clearly Opened, and Fully Resolved*, Dublin, *The Globe,* published by Samuel Fuller, 1730 (microfilm Goldsmiths-Kress Library of Economic Literature, University of Rochester) (d. approx. 1670)

MELVIN K. H. PETERS: Professor of Religious Studies (Old Testament; Septuagint), Duke University; Author: "Septuagint," *The Anchor Bible Dictionary* (Doubleday, 1992); "Translating a Translation: Some Final Reflections on the Production of the New English Translation of Greek Deuteronomy," *Translation is Required: The Septuagint in Retrospect and Prospect* edited by Robert J. V. Hiebert; "Septuagint and Cognate Studies," (Society of Biblical Literature, 2008:365; 2010:248); "Deuteronomion, To The Reader," edited by Pietersma & Wright

(Oxford, 2007.141-173); Editor: "XIII Congress Of The International Organization For Septuagint And Cognate Studies" (Ljubljana, 2007)

PHEME PERKINS: Professor of New Testament, Boston College; Author: *Introduction to the Synoptic Gospels* (Eerdmans, 2007); *Reading the New Testament* (Paulist Press, 2012); *Gnosticism and the New Testament* (Augsburg Fortress, 1993); *Interpretation: First and Second Peter, James, and Jude* (John Knox Press, 1995); *Abingdon New Testament Commentaries: Ephesians* (Abingdon, 1997)

ROBERT HENRY PFEIFFER: Hancock Professor of Semitic Languages and Curator of the Semitic Museum, Harvard University; Author: *Miscellaneous Texts from Nuzi* (Harvard University Press, 1942); *Introduction to the Old Testament* (Harper, 1948); *History of New Testament Times with an Introduction to the Apocrypha* (Harper, 1949); *Religion in the Old Testament* (Harper, 1961) (d. 1958)

JOHN BERTRAM PHILLIPS: Bible Scholar, Writer, Minister (Anglican); Translator: *The New Testament in Modern English; The Newborn Christian: 114 Readings from J.B. Phillips (Macmillan, 1984); The Church Under the Cross* (Macmillan, 1956); *Table Laid Bare* (Sava Books, 1998); *The Price of Success* (H. Shaw, 2000); *Given* (Sava Books, 1998); *God Our Contemporary* (Literary Licensing, LLC, 2012); *New Testament Christianity* (Literary Licensing, LLC, 2012); *A Man Called Jesus* (Wipf & Stock, 2012) (d. 1982)

ARTHUR WALKINGTON PINK: Pastor, Evangelist, Calvinist Bible teacher; Author: *The Attributes of God* (Baker Books, 1975); *The Divine Inspiration of the Bible* (Bible Truth Depot, 1917); *Gleanings in Genesis* (Digireads.com, 2005); *An Exposition of Hebrews* (Start Publishing, LLC, 2012) (d. 1952)

JOHN F. PRIEST: Professor of Religion and Director of Graduate Humanities, Florida State University; Author: "The Messiah and the Meal in 1QSa," *Journal of Biblical Literature*, 82 (1963) 95-100; "Mebaqqer, Paqid, and the Messiah," *Journal of Biblical Literature*, 81 (1962): 55-61;

"Opkia in the Iliad and Consideration of a Recent Theory," *Journal of Near Eastern Studies* (1964): 48-56; "The Covenant of Brothers," *Journal of Biblical Literature*, 84 (1965): 400-406; Contributor: "Moses, Testament of," *The Anchor Bible Dictionary* (Volume 4, 920-922, Doubleday, 1962) and "Ecclesiastes," "Etiology," "Messianic Banquet," *The Interpreter's Dictionary of the Bible, Supplementary Volume*, (Abingdon, 1976)

OTTO PROCKSCH: Old Testament Scholar; Author: *Genesis: Commentary on the Old Testament, Volume 1* (Leipzig: Deichertsche, 1913); *The Minor Prophets According to the Exodus* (Stuttgart: Calwer, 1916); *Theology of the Old Testament* (Gutersloh, 1950); *First Isaiah* (Leipzig: Deichert, 1930) (d. 1947)

WILLIAM MITCHELL RAMSAY: Archaeologist; Asia Minor expert; Professor of Classical Art and Architecture, Oxford University; New Testament Scholar and Teaching Fellow at Exeter and Lincoln colleges (Oxford); Author: *St. Paul the Traveler and the Roman Citizen* (Hodder and Stoughton, 1897); *Historical Commentary on First Corinthians* (Kregel, 1996); *Pauline and Other Studies in Early Christian History* (A. D. Armstrong & Son, 1906); *The Education of Christ* (G.P. Putnam's Sons, 1902); *Luke the Physician and Other Studies in the History of Religion* (Lodder & Stoughton, 1908) (d. 1939)

WILLIAM L. REED: Professor of Old Testament, The College of the Bible; Co-editor: *Translating & Understanding the Old Testament* (Abingdon, 1970); Contributor: *The Interpreter's Dictionary of the Bible* (Abingdon, 1962)

GARY A. RENDSBURG: Professor of Near Eastern Studies, Cornell University; Co-author: *The Bible and the Ancient Near East* (W. W. Norton & Company, New York, New York, 1997)

ERNEST JOHN REVELL: Professor Emeritus, Near and Middle Eastern Civilizations, University of Toronto; Author: *Hebrew Texts with Palestinian Vocalization* (Toronto, 1970); *Biblical Texts with Palestinian Pointing and their Accents: Issue 4 of Masoretic Studies* (Scholars Press,

1977); Co-author: *The Designation of the Individual: Expressive Usage in Biblical Narrative* (1996); Translator/Editor: *Introduction to the Tiberian Masorah* by Israel Yeivin (1980); Editor: Proceedings of the Twelfth International Congress of the International Organization for Masoretic Studies (1995); Contributor: "Masoretes," *The Anchor Bible Dictionary* (Doubleday, 1992)

CYRIL CHARLES RICHARDSON: Washburn Professor of Church History, Union Theological Seminary; Author: *The Church in Ignatius of Antioch* (University of Chicago Press, 1937); *Zwingli and Cranmer on the Eucharist* (Seabury-Western Theological Seminary, 1949); *The Doctrine of the Trinity* (Abingdon, 1958); Editor: *Early Christian Fathers* (Westminster, 1955) (d. 1976)

MARTIN ROSE: Professor Emeritus of Theology, University of Neuchâtel (retired); Author: "The Exclusiveness of Yahweh: Theology of the Deuteronomic School and the Popular Piety in the Late Monarchic Period" (1975); "The Deuteronomist and the Jahwist: On the Points of Contact in Both Literatures" (ATANT 67; Zurich: Theologischer Verlag, 1981); *Understanding the Hermeneutics of the Old Testament* (Geneve, Labor et Fides, 2003)

NAHUM M. SARNA: Professor Emeritus, Brandeis University; Author: *Understanding Genesis* (Schocken Publishing House, 1970); *The JPS Torah Commentary: Genesis* (The Jewish Publication Society, 1994); *Exploring Exodus* (Random House, 1996); *Studies in Biblical Interpretation* (Jewish Publication Society, 2000); *On the Book of Psalms* (Schocken Publishing House, 1995); Co-author: *From Ancient Israel to Modern Judaism* (BiblioBazaar, 2009) (d. 2005)

DONALD G. SCHLEY: Assistant Professor of Bible and Religion, College of Charleston; Author: "Shiloh: A Biblical City in Tradition and History," *Journal for the Study of the Old Testament: Supplement Series 63* (Sheffield Academic Press, 1989); Translator: *The Ancient Orient: An Introduction to the Study of the Ancient Near East* by Wolfram von Soden (Eerdmans, 1994)

PHILIP C. SCHMITZ: Professor of the History of Religions and Historical Methodology; Academic Service-Learning Fellow, Eastern Michigan University; Specialist in Phoenician language and history; Assistant Editor: *The Anchor Bible Dictionary* (Doubleday, 1992); currently researching a *Dictionary of Ancient Phoenician Civilization*. See www.emich.edu.

JOHANNES SCHNEIDER: Professor of New Testament, Humboldt University of Berlin; Author: *Church and World in the New Testament* (Mercer University Press, 1983); *Baptism and Church in the New Testament* (Carey Kingsgate Press, 1957); Contributor: *Theological Dictionary of the New Testament* (Eerdmans, 1964) (d. 1970)

J. N. SCHOFIELD: Lecturer in Hebrew and Old Testament, Cambridge University; President, The Society for Old Testament Study (1969); Author: *Introducing Old Testament Theology* (1964); "'All Israel' in the Deuteronomic Writers," *Essays and Studies Presented to Stanly Arthur Cook* (Editor, D. W. Thomas; London, 1950)

BARUCH J. SCHWARTZ: Associate Professor of Bible, Hebrew University; Author: "The Visit of Jethro: A Case of Chronological Displacement? The Source-critical Solution," in *Mishneh Todah: Studies in Deuteronomy and its Cultural Environment in Honor of Jeffrey H. Tigay*, editors, N. S. Fox, D. A. Glatt-Gilad and M. J. Williams, Winona Lake, Indiana (Eisenbrauns, 2009); "The Ultimate Aim of Israel's Restoration in Ezekiel," in *Birkat Shalom: Studies in the Bible, Ancient Near Eastern Literature and Post-biblical Judaism*, editors, Ch. Cohen, et al., Winona Lake, Indiana (Eisenbrauns, 2008); "The Flood Narratives in the Torah and the Question of Where History Begins," in *Shai le-Sara Japhet: Studies in the Bible, its Exegesis and its Language*, editors, M. Bar-Asher, et. al., Jerusalem: Bialik Institute (2007)

JOHN J. SCULLION: Professor of Old Testament Exegesis, United Faculty of Theology, Melbourne; Author: *Faith in the Risen Jesus* (A.C.T.S. Publications, 1979); *Studies in Isaiah chapters 56-66* (Institut Catholique, Paris, France, 1960); *Amos, Hosea, Micah* (M. Glazier, 1981); Co-author:

The Word in the Bible (Australian Council of Churches, 1968); Co-editor/Contributor: *Original Sin* (Dove Communications, 1970); Contributor: *The Anchor Bible Dictionary* (Doubleday, 1992) (d. 1989)

JOHN SKINNER: Professor of Old Testament Exegesis, Westminster College, Cambridge; Author: *A Critical and Exegetical Commentary on Genesis (1910); The Book of the Prophet Isaiah* (1902) (d. 1925)

W. ROBERTSON SMITH: Minister; Orientalist; Old Testament Scholar; Professor of Arabic, University of Cambridge; Author: *The Old Testament in the Jewish Church* (Adam & Charles Black, 1881); *The Prophets of Israel* (Adam & Charles Black, 1895); *The Religion of the Semites* (Adam and Charles Black, 1894); Editor-in-chief, *Encyclopedia Britannica* (1881-1888); Contributor: *Encyclopedia Biblica*; *Encyclopedia Britannica* ("Bible," "Sacrifice," etc.) (d. 1894)

FRANK ANTHONY SPINA: Professor of Old Testament and Biblical Theology, Seattle Pacific University; Episcopal Priest; Author: *The Faith of the Outsider: Exclusion and Inclusion in the Biblical Story* (Eerdmans, 2005); "The Concept of Social Rage in Israel and the Ancient Near East," (doctoral dissertation); "Multiplying Divisions: A Figural Reading of the Story of the Levite's Concubine (Judges 19-21)," Winifred Weter Faculty Award lecture, 2008; Contributor: "I and 2 Kings," *The Wesley Study Bible* (Abingdon, 2009)

GUSTAV STÄHLIN: German Lutheran Theologian; Professor, Leipzig and Gurukul Theological Seminary; Lecturer: University of Madras, India; Professor, New Testament, universities of Erlangen and Mainz; Contributor: *The Theological Dictionary of the New Testament* (Eerdmans, 1962); Author: *The Acts of the Apostles* (Cambridge University Press, 1962); *Fellowship with the Bible* (Evangelical Lutheran Churches of India, 1939); Co-author: *Sin* (Adam & Charles Black, 1951); *Wrath* (Adam & Charles Black, 1964) (d. 1985)

GEORGE STOB: Doctor of Theology, Princeton Theological Seminary; Peace and Civil Rights Advocate; Minister of the Christian Reformed

Church, Washington, D. C.; Founding Member: *Reformed Journal;* Author: *The Christian Reformed Church and Her Schools* (Princeton Theological Seminary, 1955); *Handbook of Bible History: Book II – Old Testament* (Eerdmans, 1956); *That I May Know* (CRC Publications, 1982) (d. 2002)

HERMANN LEBERECHT STRACK: German Protestant Theologian; Orientalist; Assistant Professor, Old Testament Exegesis and Semitic Languages, University of Berlin; Talmudic and Rabbinic Scholar; Author: *Introduction to the Talmud and Midrash* (Atheneum, 1976); Co-author: *Commentary on the New Testament from the Talmud and Midrash* (C.H. Beck, 1922; 1924; 1926; 4 volumes) (d. 1922)

DOUGLAS K. STUART: Professor of Old Testament and Chair, Division of Biblical Studies; Gordon-Conwell Theological Seminary; Linguist; Pastor; Author: *Old Testament Exegesis: A Handbook for Students and Pastors* (Westminster John Knox Press, 2009); Co-author with G. Fee: *How to Read the Bible Book by Book,* (Zondervan, 2002); *How to Read the Bible for All It's Worth* (Zondervan, 2003)

LAWRENCE E. TOOMBS: Professor Emeritus of Old Testament, Religion and Culture, Wilfrid Laurier University; Field Archaeologist; Author: *The Threshold of Christianity: Between the Testaments* (Westminster, 1960); *Tell el-Hesi: Modern Military Trenching and Muslim Cemetery in Field I, Strata I-II* (Wilfrid Laurier University Press, 1985); *Moses* (Graded Press, 1979); *Nation Making: Exodus, Numbers, Joshua, Judges* (Lutterworth Press, 1962); *A Year with the Bible* (United Church of Canada, 1953); *The Old Testament in Christian Preaching* (Westminster Press, 1961); Co-author: *The Tell el-Hesi Field Manual, Volume 1* (Eisenbrauns, 1993) (d. 2007)

KAREL VAN DER TOORN: Professor of Ancient Religions, universities of Utrecht, Leiden and Amsterdam; Chairman of the Board, University of Amsterdam; Author: *Scribal Culture and the Making of the Hebrew Bible* (President and Fellows of Harvard College, 2007); *Family Religion in Babylonia, Syria & Israel* (E. J. Brill, 1996); Co-editor: *Dictionary of Deities* and Demons in the Bible (Brill, 1999); *Mesopotamian Magic* (STYX Publications, 1999)

HERMAN TE VELDE: Chair, Egyptology, University of Groningen (retired); Author: *Seth, God of Confusion* (Leiden, E.J. Brill, 1967); "Mut," *The Oxford Encyclopedia of Ancient Egypt* (Oxford University Press, 2001); "Towards a Minimal Definition of the Goddess Mut," JEOL 26 (1979-1980): 4-5; "The History of the Study of Ancient Egyptian Religion and Its Future," *Egyptology at the Dawn of the Twenty-First Century: Volume 2* (American University in Cairo Press, 2003); "Some Egyptian Deities and their Piggishness," *The Intellectual Heritage of Egypt* (Budapest: Eotvos Lorand University, 1992)

PIETER ADRIAAN VERHOEF: Professor Emeritus of Old Testament, Stellenbosch University, South Africa; Author: *The Books of Haggai and Malachi* in *The New International Commentary on the Old Testament* (Eerdmans, 1987) (d. 2013)

FRANK VIOLA: Christian Blogger; Speaker; Author: *Who is Your Covering?* (Seedsowers, 2002); *Reimagining Church* (David C. Cook, 2008); *Revise Us Again* (David C. Cook, 2010); *God's Favorite Place on Earth* (David C. Cook, 2013); *Jesus Now* (David C. Cook, 2014); Co-author: *Pagan Christianity* (Tyndale, 2010)

STANLEY D. WALTERS: Professor of Old Testament Languages and Literatures, Knox College, University of Toronto; Author: *Early Old Babylonian Letters and Documents from Larsa* (Yale University, 1962); *Water for Larsa: An Old Babylonian Archive Dealing with Irrigation* (Yale University Press, 1970); *Go Figure: Figuration in Biblical Interpretation* (Pickwick Publications, 2008); Contributor: *The Anchor Bible Dictionary* (Doubleday, 1992)

MOSHE WEINFELD: Professor Emeritus of Bible, Hebrew University; Author: *Deuteronomy and the Deuteronomic School* (Oxford University Press, 1972); *Normative and Sectarian Judaism in the Second Temple Period* (Bloomsbury Academic, 2005); *The Place of the Law in the Religion of*

Ancient Israel (Brill, 2004); *The Anchor Bible: Deuteronomy 1-11* (Doubleday, 1991); *Getting at the Roots of Wellhausen's Understanding of the Law of Israel* (Institute for Advanced Studies, The Hebrew University, 1979); *Social Justice in Ancient Israel and in the Ancient Near East* (Augsburg Fortress, 1995); Co-editor: *Studies in Historical Geography & Biblical Historiography* (Brill, 2000); Contributor: "The Decalogue: Its Significance, Uniqueness, and Place in Israel's Tradition," in *Religion and Law* (1990, Eisenbrauns) (d. 2009)

GORDON J. WENHAM: Former Professor of Old Testament, University of Gloucestershire; Lecturer: Trinity College Bristol; Author: *Word Biblical Commentary: Genesis 16-50* (Word, 1994); *The Book of Leviticus* (Eerdmans, 1979); *Psalms as Torah* (Baker Academic, 2012); *Story as Torah* (Baker, 2004); *Exploring the Old Testament: A Guide to the Pentateuch* (InterVarsity Press, 2003)

CLAUS WESTERMANN: Professor Emeritus of Old Testament, University of Heidelberg; Author: *Continental Commentary: Genesis 1-11* (Fortress Press, 1984); *Genesis 12-36* (Fortress Press, 1995); *Genesis 37-50* (Augsburg Publishing House, 1986) (d. 2000)

JOHN WILLIAM WEVERS: Linguist; Septuagint Scholar; Professor Emeritus of Near Eastern Studies, University of Toronto; Author: *Text History of the Greek: Leviticus - Issue 153* (Vandenhoeck & Ruprecht, 1986); *Text History of the Greek: Exodus* (Vandenhoeck & Ruprecht, 1990); *Notes on the Greek Text of Genesis* (Scholars Press, 1993); *Text History of the Greek: Numbers - Issue 125* (Vandenhoeck & Ruprecht, 1982); *Notes on the Greek Text of Deuteronomy* (Society of Biblical Literature, 1995); *Notes on the Greek Text of Leviticus* (Scholars Press, 1997); *Studies in the Text Histories of Deuteronomy and Ezekiel* (Vandenhoeck & Ruprecht, 2003) (d. 2010)

JAMES ALLEN WHARTON: Minister; Professor of Old Testament, Austin Presbyterian Theological Seminary; Professor of Homiletics, Perkins School of Theology, Southern Methodist University; Author: *Job* (Westminster John Knox Press, 1999); *Easter: Aids for Interpreting the*

Lessons of the Church Year (Fortress Press, 1987); *Smitten of God: A Theological Investigation of the Enemies of Yahweh in the Old Testament* (Austin Presbyterian Theological Seminary, 1960) (d. 2012)

FRANS A. M. WIGGERMANN: Expert in Ancient Near Eastern iconography, demonology and Semitic languages; Field Archaeologist at Tell Sabi Abyad, Syria (Late Bronze Age Project) and "The *Dunnu* [fortified estate] and Empire in Texts;" Professor Emeritus in Assyriology, Free University (VU), Amsterdam (retired); Contributor: *Ancient Near Eastern Seals from the Kist Collection* by Joost Kist (Brill, 2003); *Mesopotamian Protective Spirits: The Ritual Texts* (Groningen, Netherlands: Styx, 1992); Co-author: *Magic in History: A Theoretical Perspective and Its Application to Ancient Mesopotamia* (Groningen, 1999)

JOHN CHRISTIAN WILSON: Minister; Ancient Language Specialist; Professor, Religious Studies, Elon University; Author: "Tithe," *The Anchor Bible Dictionary* (Doubleday, 1992); "What Does a Tithe Mean? Ten Percent of What?" (*Invitation to Belief*, volume 4, Nashville, Tennessee, 6-10); *Jesus and the Pleasures* (Fortress, 2003); *Five Problems in the Interpretation of the Shepherd of Hermas* (Mellen Biblical Press, 1995)

DAVID P. WRIGHT: Professor of Bible and the Ancient Near East, Brandeis University; Chief Editor: *Pomegranates and Golden Bells: Studies in Biblical, Jewish and Near Eastern Ritual, Law, and Literature in Honor of Jacob Milgrom* (Eisenbrauns, 1995); Author: *Inventing God's Law: How the Covenant Code of the Bible Used and Revised the Laws of Hammurabi* (Oxford University Press, 2009); *The Disposal of Impurity: Elimination Rites in the Bible and in Hittite and Mesopotamian Literature* (Scholars Press, 1987); *Ritual in Narrative: The Dynamics of Feasting, Mourning, and Retaliation Rites in the Ugaritic Tale of Aqhat* (Eisenbrauns, 2001)

GALE A. YEE: Nancy W. King Professor of Biblical Studies, Episcopal Divinity School; Editor: Texts @ Contexts Series (Fortress Press); *Judges and Method: New Approaches in Biblical Studies* (Augsburg Fortress, 1995); Co-editor: *Fortress Bible Commentary* project; Author: *Open Your*

Hand to the Poor: The Creation of Poverty in Ancient Israel (forthcoming); *Poor Banished Children of Eve: Woman as Evil in the Hebrew Bible* (Augsburg Fortress, 2003); *Composition and Tradition in the Book of Hosea* (Scholars Press, 1987); *Jewish Feasts and the Gospel of John* (Michael Glazier, Inc., 1989)

WALTHER THEODOR ZIMMERLI: Professor of Old Testament, University of Göttingen; Author: *The Law and the Prophets* (1965); *Hermeneia: Ezekiel*, 2 volumes (Fortress Press, 1979/1983); *I Am Yahweh* (John Knox Press, 1982); *The Old Testament and the World* (SPCK, 1971); *The Fiery Throne: The Prophets and Old Testament Theology* (Fortress, 2003) (d. 1983)

ABOUT THE AUTHOR

David G. Mackin is the founder and presenter of Journey to Truth Christian Ministries, LLC. With degrees in Bible and Religion, he has functioned as a teacher, editor and ghost-writer. For nearly a decade, he taught college classes on a variety of biblical, ministerial and religious subjects and used his research skills to assist in the development of a biblical worldview curriculum. David's passion is to free Christians from religious tradition by helping them understand Scripture in context.

TO CONTACT THE AUTHOR
david@jttcm.com

TO ORDER MORE COPIES OF THIS BOOK
amazon.com

FOR PUBLICATION DATES OF *THE TITHING SERIES*
jttcm.com/books

www.ingramcontent.com/pod-product-compliance
Lightning Source LLC
Chambersburg PA
CBHW050614300426
44112CB00012B/1494